GRAPHIC PRACTICES AND LITERACIES
IN THE HISTORY OF ENGLISH

UTRECHT STUDIES IN MEDIEVAL LITERACY

61

UTRECHT STUDIES IN MEDIEVAL LITERACY

General Editor

Marco Mostert (Universiteit Utrecht)

Editorial Board

Gerd Althoff (Westfälische-Wilhelms-Universität Münster)
Pierre Chastang (Université Versalles St-Quentin-en-Yvelines
Erik Kwakkel (University of British Columbia)
Mayke de Jong (Universiteit Utrecht)
Rosamond McKitterick (University of Cambridge)
Arpád Orbán (Universiteit Utrecht)
Francesco Stella (Università degli Studi di Siena)
Richard H. Rouse (UCLA)

GRAPHIC PRACTICES AND LITERACIES IN THE HISTORY OF ENGLISH

edited by

Matti Peikola, Jukka Tyrkkö, and Mari-Liisa Varila

BREPOLS

British Library Cataloguing in Publication Data

A catalogue record for this book is available from the British Library

© 2025 – Brepols Publishers n.v., Turnhout, Belgium

All rights reserved. No part of this publication may be reproduced, stored in a retrieval system, or transmitted, in any form or by any means, electronic, mechanical, photocopying, recording, or otherwise, without the prior permission of the publisher.

D/2025/0095/113

ISBN 978-2-503-60045-1

e-ISBN 978-2-503-60046-8

DOI: 10.1484/M.USML-EB.5.129562

ISSN 2034-9416

e-ISNN 2294-8317

Printed in the EU on acid-free paper

Table of Contents

Abbreviations — vii
Acknowledgements — ix
List of Illustrations — xi

Graphic Practices in Early English Texts
    MATTI PEIKOLA, JUKKA TYRKKÖ, and MARI-LIISA VARILA — 1

Part I

Conventionalising Strategies of Verbal and Visual information
    COLETTE MOORE — 25
The Pragmatics of Late Medieval English Accounts: A Case Study
    KJETIL V. THENGS — 47
Plague on the Page: *Mise-en-page* and Visual Highlighting in the *John of Burgundy Plague Tract* from the Fourteenth to the Seventeenth Century
    ALPO HONKAPOHJA — 65
The Pragmatics of Punctuation in Early English Medical Recipe Books
    JAVIER CALLE-MARTÍN and JESÚS ROMERO-BARRANCO — 105
Visual Pragmatics and Late Modern English Letters
    INGRID TIEKEN-BOON VAN OSTADE — 127

Part II

The *A* to *Z* of Middle English Indexing? The Tables
of John Trevisa's *Polychronicon*
    WENDY SCASE   153
A Visual and Linguistic Interpretation of the *Pater Noster* Table
  of the Vernon Manuscript
    OLGA TIMOFEEVA   181
Visual Chronologies in Early Modern English Historiography
    AINO LIIRA, MATTI PEIKOLA, and MARJO KAARTINEN   201
Visual Representation of Information in Medical Texts, 1500-1700
    MARI-LIISA VARILA, CARLA SUHR, and JUKKA TYRKKÖ   227
Verbal and Visual Instruction in Early Dance Manuals:
  The Curious Case of John Playford's Tables
    HANNA SALMI   259
Graphic Elements in Early Printed Grammar Books
    JANNE SKAFFARI and JUKKA TYRKKÖ   281

Afterword
    JEREMY J. SMITH   309

Bibliography   311
Index   341
Notes on Contributors   353

Abbreviations

CME — *Corpus of Middle English Prose and Verse* (University of Michigan) <https://quod.lib.umich.edu/c/cme/>.

DMLBS — *Dictionary of Medieval Latin from British Sources*, ed. R.K. ASHDOWNE, D.R. HOWLETT, and R.E. LATHAM (Oxford, 2018).

ECCO — *Eighteenth Century Collections Online* (Gale).

EEBO — *Early English Books Online* (ProQuest).

EETS O.S. — *Early English Text Society, Original Series*.

EMEMT — *Early Modern English Medical Texts*, compiled by I. TAAVITSAINEN, P. PAHTA, T. HILTUNEN, M. MÄKINEN, V. MARTTILA, M. RATIA, C. SUHR, and J. TYRKKÖ (Amsterdam, 2010), CD-ROM.

ESTC — *English Short Title Catalogue* (The British Library).

LALME — A. MCINTOSH, M.L. SAMUELS, and M. BENSKIN, with the assistance of M. LAING and K. WILLIAMSON, *A Linguistic Atlas of Late Mediaeval English*, 4 vols. (Aberdeen, 1986).

MED — *Middle English Dictionary*, ed. R.E. LEWIS *et al.* (Ann Arbor, MI, 1952-2001). Online edition in *Middle English Compendium*, ed. F. MCSPARRAN *et al.* (Ann Arbor, MI, 2000-2018). <https://quod.lib.umich.edu/m/middle-english-dictionary/ dictionary>.

MELD — *A Corpus of Middle English Local Documents – MELD version 2017.1*, comp. M. STENROOS, K.V. THENGS, and G. BERGSTRØM (University of Stavanger) <http://www.uis.no/meld>.

ODNB — *Oxford Dictionary of National Biography* (Oxford University Press) <http://www.oxforddnb.com>.

OED — *Oxford English Dictionary* online (Oxford University Press) <https://www.oed.com>.

STC — POLLARD, A.W., and G.R. REDGRAVE, *A Short-Title Catalogue of Books Printed in England, Scotland, and Ireland, and of English*

	Books Printed Abroad 1475-1640, 2nd edn comp. W.A. JACKSON, F.S. FERGUSON, and K.F. PANTZER, 3 vols. (London, 1976-1991).
USTC	*Universal Short Title Catalogue* (University of St. Andrews) <https://www.ustc.ac.uk/>.
WING	WING, D.G., *Short-Title Catalogue of Books Printed in England, Scotland and Ireland, Wales, and British America and of English Books Printed in Other Countries, 1641-1700*, 2nd edn, revised and enlarged by J.J. MORRISON and C.W. NELSON, with the assistance of M. SECCOMBE, 4 vols. (New York, 1972-1998).

Acknowledgements

Matti PEIKOLA, Jukka TYRKKÖ, and Mari-Liisa VARILA

This book grew out of the 2021 workshop 'Graphic literacy in the history of English' we organised in the 21st International Conference on English Historical Linguistics in Leiden. In addition to chapters developed from papers given in the workshop, the volume also contains other invited contributions by experts in the field. We wish to thank all the contributors for their invaluable collaboration and their commitment. The research project Early Modern Graphic Literacies (EMODGRAL), funded by the Research Council of Finland (340005) and the University of Turku, has supported the making of the book both intellectually and financially. We are grateful to the project members and our key collaborators for all their work towards the publication of this volume and for insightful discussions along the way. We also wish to thank Anna Runsio for her important assistance in copyediting. Last but not least, our sincere thanks go to the anonymous reviewer for their helpful comments and to Marco Mostert for his professional and erudite work as the General Editor of the series.

List of Illustrations

[Colette MOORE]
Fig. 1	MS San Marino, Huntington Library, HM 129, f. 114r.	29
Fig. 2	Einar Haugen's model for standardisation.	33
Fig. 3	Processes of conventionalisation.	34
Fig. 4	Origin of the Ampersand (reproduced by permission of the Tschichold family).	36
Fig. 5	Alphabet with ampersand in N. WEBSTER, *The American Spelling Book, Containing the Rudiments of the English Language, for the Use of Schools in the United States* (Middletown, CT, 1831), p. 15.	38
Fig. 6	First page treatment over time (after SMITH, *The Title Page*, p. 50).	43

[Kjetil V. THENGS]
Fig. 1	Example of traditional layout, MS Oxford, Oxfordshire History Centre, PAR211/4/F1/2/100 (St. Michael at the North Gate, 1520).	53
Fig. 2	Example of prose style layout, MS Oxford, Oxfordshire History Centre, PAR211/4/F1/2/78 (St. Michael at the North Gate, 1501).	55
Fig. 3	List of examined London churchwardens' accounts at London Metropolitan Archives.	59
Fig. 4	2-shaped pragmatic marker indicating that a numeral follows. MS Oxford, Oxfordshire History Centre, PAR211/4/F1/1/70.	61

[Alpo HONKAPOHJA]
Fig. 1	A small skull drawn in the margin, presumably by Robert Thornton. MS Lincoln, Cathedral 91, f. 300v. Photo courtesy of Lincoln Cathedral.	76
Fig. 2	The Bubo-Man, MS London, British Library, Egerton 1624, f. 216v. Photo courtesy of the British Library.	77
Fig. 3	Development of some *mise-en-page* features.	81

Fig. 4	Marginal comments. MS London, British Library, Sloane 2507, f. 10v. Photo courtesy of the British Library.	88
Fig. 5	The list of contents in MS London, British Library, Sloane 1588, f. 54.	89
Fig. 6	Subject index in MS London, British Library, Sloane 207, ff. 3v-4r.	90
Table 1	The corpus.	71
Table 2	Apothecaries' weights in recipes.	85
Table 3	Visual highlighting of recipes.	85

[Javier CALLE-MARTÍN and Jesús ROMERO-BARRANCO]

Fig. 1	Recipe for the headache, fifteenth century. MS Glasgow University Library, Hunter 328, f. 2v. With permission of University of Glasgow Archives and Special Collections.	115
Fig. 2	Recipe for headache, sixteenth century. MS Glasgow University Library, Ferguson 7, f. 16r. With permission of University of Glasgow Archives and Special Collections.	115
Fig. 3	Recipe for headache, seventeenth century. MS Glasgow University Library, Hunter 64, f. 14r. With permission of University of Glasgow Archives and Special Collections.	116
Fig. 4	MS Glasgow University Library, Hunter 328, f. 2v. With permission of University of Glasgow Archives and Special Collections.	117
Fig. 5	MS Glasgow University Library, Hunter 64, f. 14r. With permission of University of Glasgow Archives and Special Collections.	117
Fig. 6	Distribution of visual elements in the titles of recipes (%).	117
Table 1	Scribal choices with the absence of punctuation marks (%).	118
Table 2	Distribution of punctuation marks in the corpus (%).	120
Table 3	Distribution of punctuation marks after the title section (%).	121
Table 4	Distribution of punctuation marks after the ingredients section (%).	122
Table 5	Distribution of punctuation marks after the preparation section (%).	123
Table 6	Distribution of punctuation marks after the application section (%).	123
Table 7	Most frequent punctuation symbols after rhetorical moves over time.	125

[Ingrid TIEKEN-BOON VAN OSTADE]

Table 1	Abbreviation stops, ampersands, and end-of-line hyphenation in the different sets of letters analysed, normalised to 1000 words.	144

[Wendy SCASE]

Fig. 1	Oxford, Magdalen College, MS Lat. 147, f. 235r, the opening of a table to the Latin *Polychronicon* with the heading "*Tabula communis de chronicis supradictis*". Reproduced with the permission of the President and Fellows of Magdalen College, Oxford.	162

List of Illustrations   xiii

Fig. 2   Oxford, Magdalen College, MS Lat. 147, f. 242v, the opening of a table to the Latin *Polychronicon* with the heading "*Tabula specialis [de eodem* [sic] *chronicis*". Reproduced with the permission of the President and Fellows of Magdalen College.   163

[Olga TIMOFEEVA]
Fig. 1   The *Pater Noster* table in the Vernon MS (MS Oxford, Bodleian Library, Eng. poet. a. 1, f. 231v, *c.* 1390). © Bodleian Libraries, University of Oxford.   183
Fig. 2   Transcription of the *Pater Noster* table (expansions of abbreviations given in italics; underlined text is written in red ink in the original).   184
Fig. 3   Lancelot playing chess. From the British Library Collection: MS London, British Library, Add. 10293, f. 302r, early fourteenth century.   187
Fig. 4   The Exchequer of Ireland at work. *Facsimiles of Irish Manuscripts*, vol. 3, plate XXXVII, early fifteenth century. Accessed on Virtual Record Treasury of Ireland <https://virtualtreasury.ie/item/VRTI-FAX-2>.   191
Fig. 5   The *Pater Noster* table, detail, *Castitas / Chastite & Cleannesse*, MS Oxford, Bodleian Library, Eng. poet. a. 1, f. 231v, *c.* 1390. © Bodleian Libraries, University of Oxford.   192

[Aino LIIRA, Matti PEIKOLA, and Marjo KAARTINEN]
Fig. 1   Schematic illustration of marginal annotations.   209
Fig. 2   Schematic illustration of a list and table.   211
Fig. 3   Schematic illustration of an account-type list.   212
Fig. 4   Schematic illustration of a table with horizontal and vertical rulings.   213
Fig. 5   Schematic illustration of a table without rules.   214
Fig. 6   Schematic illustration of a vertically ruled table.   214
Fig. 7   Schematic illustration of a 'mileage-type' table.   215
Fig. 8   Schematic illustration of a tree diagram.   216

[Mari-Liisa VARILA, Carla SUHR, and Jukka TYRKKÖ]
Fig. 1   Overall diachronic trend of graphic devices; markers represent texts in EMEMT.   237
Fig. 2   A fold-out flowchart explaining humours attached to Thomas Brugis, *Marrow of Physick* (1640). STC 3931. Image: Wellcome Collection / Public Domain Mark.   242
Fig. 3   Example of plant illustrations from the 1636 edition; the same illustrations appear on the same page in the 1633 edition discussed above. *The herball, or general historie of plantes / Gathered by John Gerarde [...] Very much enlarged and amended by Thomas Johnston.*

	STC 11752, p. 927. Image: Wellcome Collection / Public Domain Mark.	247
Fig. 4	Image of a skeleton with tie marks to the Latin names of the bones. William Bullein, *Bulwarke of defence against all sickness [...]* (1562). STC 4033, no folio number. Image: Wellcome Collection / Public Domain Mark.	254
Table 1	The numbers and ratios of texts with graphic devices in each text category.	238
Table 2	The numbers of texts with different types of graphic devices in each text category. D = Diagram, Da = Diagram (arithmetic), Db = Diagram (brace), Tc = Table (calendar), Ts = Table (small), Tm = Table (medium), Tl = Table (large), G = General image, Gt = General image with text.	239

[Hanna SALMI]

Fig. 1	A transcription of the first dance, conserving key aspects of the layout and visual elements (Playford 1651, first edition). Font sizes, column widths, and so on are rough approximations, and white space at the bottom of the page has not been reproduced. The musical notation is reproduced using Elam Rotem's specialist font EMS Serenissima; ties were left out, however, since they are not integrated in the font and are not relevant for the argumentation in this chapter.	271
Table 1	The editions considered for this chapter. The third edition is only partially available through the Library of Dance, and the eleventh not at all. For this reason, they are not included in the current analysis. The number of dances follows the publisher's numbering in the book.	267
Table 2	The development of the table format between 1651 and 1703. The column labelled 'Average line notation' shows the length of the musical notation in lines; the column 'Average no. of cells' shows the average number of cells in the table.	274

[Janne SKAFFARI and Jukka TYRKKÖ]

Fig. 1	Variation in the arrangement of the indicative, imperative, potential, and infinitive moods (Wharton, p. 47) under the general heading 'A Verb Neuter with his Moods, Tenses, and Persons'. From the British Library collection. Image published with permission of ProQuest. Further reproduction is prohibited without permission.	292
Fig. 2	Irregular verbs in two main columns, with base form and "imperfect tens" linked with the vertically printed "is formed" (Wharton, p. 49). "Of a Verb", the phrase at the top, is a running head, not part of the graphic device. From the British Library collection. Image published	

List of Illustrations XV

	with permission of ProQuest. Further reproduction is prohibited without permission.	293
Fig. 3	Auxiliaries and tenses (Aickin, Part II, pp. 12-13). From the Lambeth Palace Library collection. Image published with permission of ProQuest. Further reproduction is prohibited without permission.	294
Fig. 4	The first conjugation of verbs in Aickin's Part II, between pp. 14-15. From the Lambeth Palace Library collection. Image published with permission of ProQuest. Further reproduction is prohibited without permission.	296
Fig. 5	Symbolic alphabet in Aickin, Part I, between pp. 16-17. From the Lambeth Palace Library collection. Image published with permission of ProQuest. Further reproduction is prohibited without permission.	297
Fig. 6a	Butler (p. 41) on reflexive and demonstrative pronouns. From the Huntington Library collection. Image published with permission of ProQuest. Further reproduction is prohibited without permission.	299
Fig. 6b	Wharton (p. 41) on reflexive and demonstrative pronouns. From the British Library collection. Image published with permission of ProQuest. Further reproduction is prohibited without permission.	299
Table 1	The six grammars in chronological order, with tabular or diagram-type devices per word class. √ devices used; – devices not used; an empty cell signifies a topic not covered in a section of its own.	303

Graphic Practices in Early English Texts[*]

MATTI PEIKOLA, JUKKA TYRKKÖ, and MARI-LIISA VARILA

The 2000s have witnessed a marked and increased interest in historical studies addressing visual aspects of written communication. A shared characteristic of much of this research is cross-disciplinarity. On the one hand, there has been cross-fertilisation of approaches and methods from historical fields of study such as art history, palaeography, history of science and philology. On the other hand, insights from primarily non-historically oriented fields have been brought in to enrich analyses of multimodal historical data sets. Such primarily non-historical disciplines include, for example, social semiotics, educational psychology, knowledge and information visualisation and graphic design.[1] In linguistics and literary studies, cross-disciplinary en-

---

[*] Research for this chapter has been supported by the Research Council of Finland, grant number 340005.

[1] For historical applications using theoretical and methodological insights from some of these and related fields, see e.g. F.T. MARCHESE, "Tables and early information visualization", in: *Knowledge Visualization Currents: From Text to Art to Culture*, ed. F.T. MARCHESE and E. BANISSI (London, 2013), pp. 35-61; G. ARMSTRONG, "Coding continental: Information design in sixteenth-century English vernacular manuals and translations", *Renaissance Studies* 29 (2015), pp. 78-102; P. ANESA and I. FORNASINI, "The modernity of Middle English manuscripts: A multimodal investigation", *Elephant & Castle* 17 (2017), pp. 5-41; C. MOORE, "Paratext, in-

Graphic Practices and Literacies in the History of English, ed. Matti PEIKOLA, Jukka TYRKKÖ, and Mari-Liisa VARILA, *Utrecht Studies in Medieval Literacy*, 61 (Turnhout: Brepols, 2025), pp. 1-21.

BREPOLS ❧ PUBLISHERS   DOI 10.1484/M.USML-EB.5.143819

deavours that combine the study of the verbal with the visual have resulted in novel approaches, concepts and methods such as 'visual pragmatics', 'visual rhetoric', 'visual grammar' and 'visual prosody', with applications to historical materials.[2] Moreover, advances in digital humanities have marked a major contribution to the research on historical multimodal communication, with regard to both methods of analysis and the availability of curated primary data from the past.[3]

The developments outlined above may be associated with the so-called material, digital and multimodal 'turns' in the humanities and social sciences.[4] In various ways, these paradigmatic shifts focus our attention on the interpretative importance of documents and artefacts in which written communication is preserved and transmitted, as well as the major contextual role played by different technologies of preservation / transmission and their affordances. In comparison to research focusing on linguistic meaning only, including non-textual modalities and multiple semiotic resources in analyses allows for a more com-

---

formation studies, and Middle English manuscripts", in: *The Dynamics of Text and Framing Phenomena: Historical Approaches to Paratext and Metadiscourse in English*, ed. M. PEIKOLA and B. BÖS (Amsterdam, 2020), pp. 289-307.

[2] See e.g. T.W. MACHAN, "The visual pragmatics of code-switching in late Middle English literature", in: *Code-Switching in Early English*, ed. H. SCHENDL and L. WRIGHT (Berlin, 2011), pp. 303-333; K. ACHESON, *Visual Rhetoric and Early Modern English Literature* (Farnham, 2013); A. MEURMAN-SOLIN, "Visual prosody in manuscript letters in the study of syntax and discourse", in: *Principles and Practices for the Digital Editing and Annotation of Diachronic Data*, ed. A. MEURMAN-SOLIN and J. TYRKKÖ (Helsinki, 2013), n.p., available at <https://varieng.helsinki.fi/series/volumes/14/meurman-solin_a/>.

[3] See e.g. J. TYRKKÖ, "Quantifying contrasts: A method of computational analysis of visual features on the early printed pages", in: *Verbal and Visual Communication in Early English Texts*, ed. M. PEIKOLA, A. MÄKILÄHDE, H. SALMI, M.-L. VARILA, and J. SKAFFARI (Turnhout, 2017), pp. 95-122; G. PROOT, "The transformation of the typical page in the handpress era in the Southern Netherlands, 1473-c. 1800", in: *Impagination – Layout and Materiality of Writing and Publication: Interdisciplinary Approaches from East and West*, ed. K. CHANG, A. GRAFTON, and G.W. MOST (Berlin, 2021), pp. 237-272.

[4] For the 'material turn', see e.g. D. DELIYANNIS, H. DEY, and P. SQUATRITI, "Introduction: Things, matter and meaning in Late Antiquity and the Early Middle Ages", in: *Fifty Early Medieval Things: Materials of Culture in Late Antiquity and the Early Middle Ages*, ed. D. DELIYANNIS, H. DEY, and P. SQUATRITI (Ithaca, NY, 2019), pp. 1-32, esp. at pp. 6-8; for the 'digital turn', e.g. B. NICHOLSON, "The digital turn: Exploring the methodological possibilities of digital newspaper archives", *Media History* 19 (2013), pp. 59-73, esp. at pp. 61-64.; for the 'multimodal turn', e.g. J. BATEMAN, J. WILDFEUER, and T. HIIPPALA, *Multimodality: Foundations, Research and Analysis. A Problem-Oriented Introduction* (Berlin, 2017), p. 15. A 'visual digital turn' has recently been identified by M. WEVERS and T. SMITS, "The visual digital turn: Using neural networks to study historical images", *Digital Scholarship in the Humanities* 35 (2020), pp. 194-207.

prehensive and nuanced understanding of historical written communication. All this can be viewed as a welcome antidote to what Michelle P. Brown, Ildar H. Garipzanov and Benjamin C. Tilghman describe as "a broader logocentricism that has characterized much of European thought and scholarship" and "generally ignored the visual nature of writing".[5]

Graphic Features of Communication

The understanding of visuality and materiality as inherent qualities of written communication also lies at the foundation of the present volume. By focusing on 'graphic' practices and literacies in our title, we wish to evoke the polysemy of this adjective in English.[6] To begin with, 'graphic' reminds us about those processes of drawing, engraving, impressing, and so on, that constitute the physical execution and reproduction of writing across different material media. It also highlights how writing systems are essentially based on visual symbols (graphs) with their socially agreed upon and historically changing shapes and significations.[7] In English studies with a historical orientation, graphic features of writing in this sense have especially caught the attention of palaeographers and historical linguists focusing primarily on the medieval period.[8]

In terms of its value and legacy, the work of M.B. Parkes on English scribal practice cannot be overestimated, including both aspects of handwriting and design of layout, as well as the development of punctuation as a graphic communicative system.[9] The overall research approach favoured by Parkes tends to

---

[5] M.P. BROWN, I.H. GARIPZANOV, and B.C. TILGHMAN, "Introduction: The role of graphic devices in understanding the early decorated book", in: *Graphic Devices and the Early Decorated Book*, ed. Michelle P. BROWN, I.H. GARIPZANOV, and B.C. TILGHMAN (Woodbridge, 2017), pp. 1-11, at p. 2. See also J.F. HAMBURGER, *Script as Image* (Paris, 2014), at p. 2.

[6] OED Online, Oxford University Press, August 2022, s.v. *graphic*, adj. and n.

[7] In a major recent study, W. SCASE, *Visible English: Graphic Culture, Scribal Practice, and Identity, c. 700-c. 1550* (Turnhout, 2022) argues for the importance of graphic aspects of writing for identity formation in medieval communities (see especially pp. 14-21).

[8] SCASE, *Visible English*, footnote 68, at pp. 23-24, provides a useful summary of recent cross-disciplinary research on the visuality of writing in pre-modern (predominantly English) contexts.

[9] See e.g. M.B. PARKES, *Their Hands Before Our Eyes: A Closer Look at Scribes. The Lyell Lectures Delivered at the University of Oxford 1999* (Aldershot, 2008); M.B. PARKES, "The influence of the concepts of *ordinatio* and *compilatio* on the development of the book", in: *Medieval Learning and Literature: Essays Presented to Richard William Hunt*, ed. J.J.G. ALEXANDER and M.T. GIBSON (Oxford, 1976), pp. 115-141; M.B. PARKES, *Pause and Effect: An*

be inductive, proceeding from individual features to the reconstruction of more general practices, which has made it appealing to philologists and textual scholars focusing on graphic features of the language of material texts. Parkes's work has played a major role in leading to a tradition of studies of the *mise-en-page* in manuscript scholarship.[10] Another major research tradition with a foundational contribution to the study of graphic features in English studies is that represented by Scottish historical linguists, originally formed around Angus McIntosh and M.L. Samuels. Their fundamental insight was to introduce into English historical linguistics the premise that "[t]he written language can be studied in its own right" independently of the spoken language, and to apply concepts and ideas from research on writing systems to the study of linguistic variation.[11]

In English linguistics today, the legacy of these research traditions may be seen especially in how the domain of historical pragmatics has developed in recent years. As Jeremy J. Smith observes,

> the domain has become more capacious and qualitative in orientation, including as additional objects of enquiry features that have traditionally been seen as non-linguistic. Such features include what have been called 'textual traces' or 'graphic cues', e.g. punctuation, word division, capitalisation and script- / font-choice, and also broader codicological / bibliographical matters such as page / folio organisation, annotation and paratextual features generally.[12]

Introduction to the History of Punctuation in the West (Aldershot, 1992).

[10] For applications to medieval English manuscripts, see e.g. A. BUTTERFIELD, "'Mise-en page' in 'Troilus' manuscripts: Chaucer and French manuscript culture", *Huntington Library Quarterly* 58 (1995), pp. 49-80; A. NAFDE, "Hoccleve's hands: The mise-en-page of the autograph and non-autograph manuscripts", *Journal of the Early Book Society for the Study of Manuscripts and Printing History* 16 (2013), pp. 55-83, 314; M. PEIKOLA, "Guidelines for consumption: Scribal ruling patterns and designing the mise-en-page in later medieval England", in: *Manuscripts and Printed Books in Europe 1350-1550: Packaging, Presentation and Consumption*, ed. E. CAYLEY and S. POWELL (Liverpool, 2014), pp. 14-31. Also several chapters of the present volume contribute to this research tradition (see e.g. the chapters by A. HONKAPOHJA, C. MOORE, and K.J. THENGS).

[11] A. McINTOSH, M.L. SAMUELS, and M. BENSKIN, with the assistance of M. LAING and K. WILLIAMSON, *A Linguistic Atlas of Late Mediaeval English*, vol. 1 (Aberdeen, 1986), p. 5. An important early publication is A. McINTOSH, "The analysis of written Middle English", *Transactions of the Philological Society* 55 (1956), pp. 26-55.

[12] J.J. SMITH, *Transforming Early English: The Reinvention of Early English and Older Scots* (Cambridge, 2020), p. 11; see his footnote 1 (at pp. 11-12) for a summary of relevant scholarship.

Smith emphasises that these features – traditionally viewed as non-significant 'accidentals' by many textual scholars and linguists – should instead be understood as potentially "related intimately to the socio-cultural functions performed by the texts in which they appear".[13]

The present volume embraces the position advocated by Smith and views the graphic features listed by him as integral in the meaning-making potential of written communication as examined in historical pragmatics and pragmaphilology.[14] In a sense, this book continues from and expands the recent edited collection *Verbal and Visual Communication in Early English Texts*, whose editors also included two members of the present editorial team.[15] Building upon the foundation laid out in the 2013 article "Pragmatics on the page", the volume brought into focus the various ways in which visual and verbal elements interact in material texts in books, documents and other artefacts from the Old English to the Early Modern English period, especially with regard to the communicative functions of layout, script and typography.[16]

In addition to drawing attention to the inherent visuality of writing and 'pragmatics on the page', our titular choice of 'graphic' for this volume expands from this foundation by evoking the more specific denotation of the word "[p]ertaining to the use of diagrams, linear figures, or symbolic curves".[17] As well as focusing on historical uses, functions and social meanings of graphic features of writing in their material contexts, our contributors thus also examine multimodal graphic devices situated between text and image, such as diagrams,

---

[13] SMITH, *Transforming Early English*, p. 14. See also J. THAISEN and H. RUTKOWSKA, "Introduction", in: *Scribes, Printers, and the Accidentals of Their Texts*, ed. J. THAISEN and H. RUTKOWSKA (Frankfurt am Main, 2011), pp. 9-13.

[14] See also Smith's "Afterword" in the present volume. The term 'pragmaphilology' was introduced by A. JACOBS and A.H. JUCKER, "The historical perspective in pragmatics", in: *Historical Pragmatics: Pragmatic Developments in the History of English*, ed. A.H. JUCKER (Amsterdam, 1995), pp. 3-33, at p. 11, as a label for a substrand of historical pragmatics that "describes the contextual aspects of historical texts, including the addressers and addressees, their social and personal relationship, the physical and social setting of text production and text reception, and the goal(s) of the text"; see also I. TAAVITSAINEN and A.H. JUCKER, "Twenty years of historical pragmatics: Origins, developments and changing thought styles", *Journal of Historical Pragmatics* 16 (2015), pp. 1-24, at p. 16. SMITH, *Transforming Early English*, uses the term 'reimagined philology' for this kind of pragmatic research (e.g. at pp. 29 and 238).

[15] *Verbal and Visual Communication in Early English Texts*, ed. M. PEIKOLA, A. MÄKILÄHDE, H. SALMI, M.-L. VARILA, and J. SKAFFARI (Turnhout, 2017).

[16] R. CARROLL, M. PEIKOLA, H. SALMI, J. SKAFFARI, M.-L. VARILA, and R. HILTUNEN, "Pragmatics on the page: Visual text in late medieval English books", *European Journal of English Studies* 17 (2013), special issue *Visual Text*, ed. J. KENDALL, M. PORTELA, and G. WHITE, pp. 54-71.

[17] OED Online, s.v. *graphic*, adj. and n., 5a.

tables and lists. In this approach, the volume is closely connected with thematic concerns of the research project Early Modern Graphic Literacies with which the editors and several of the contributors are associated.[18]

Multimodal graphic devices are typically used to visualise and classify information in various ways, and they may also work towards the conceptualisation and construction of knowledge. Research into their historical development and functions has predominantly been conducted by historians of science, manuscript scholars, book historians, and classicists, with a marked focus on texts written in Latin and other classical languages of learning (Greek, Hebrew, Arabic).[19] In comparison, little research has been devoted to the ontology, use and circulation of these kinds of devices in medieval and early modern vernacular literary cultures, including their linguistic contextualisation and aspects of writer – reader interaction associated with them.

Although tabular and diagrammatic devices are found in texts written in or containing English already in the Old English period (as attested for example by the eleventh-century Byrthferth's *Enchiridion*), existing scholarship on their

---

[18] The project is funded by the Research Council of Finland and the University of Turku (2021-2025; Research Council of Finland funding decision 340005); for further information about the project, see <https://blogit.utu.fi/emodgral/project/>. The typology of graphic devices developed by the project is introduced in S. RUOKKEINEN, A. LIIRA, M.-L. VARILA, O. NORBLAD, and M. PEIKOLA, "Developing a classification model for graphic devices in early printed books", *Studia Neophilologica* 96.1 (2024), pp. 69-93.

[19] Major contributions include H.G. FUNKHOUSER, "Historical development of the graphical representation of statistical data", *Osiris* 3 (1937), pp. 269-404; J.E. MURDOCH, *Album of Science: Antiquity and the Middle Ages* (New York, 1984); *Books and the Sciences in History*, ed. M. FRASCA-SPADA and N. JARDINE (Cambridge, 2000); *The History of Mathematical Tables: From Sumer to Spreadsheets*, ed. M. CAMBELL-KELLY, M. CROARKEN, R. FLOOD, and E. ROBSON (Oxford, 2003); *The Power of Images in Early Modern Science*, ed. W. LEFÉVRE, J. RENN, and U. SCHOEPFLIN (Basel, 2003); *Transmitting Knowledge: Words, Images and Instruments in Early Modern Europe*, ed. S. KUSUKAWA and I. MACLEAN (Oxford, 2006); J. CHABÁS and B.R. GOLDSTEIN, *A Survey of European Astronomical Tables in the Late Middle Ages* (Leiden, 2012); K. HENTSCHEL, *Visual Cultures in Science and Technology: A Comparative History* (Oxford, 2014); I. GARIPZANOV, "The rise of graphicacy in Late Antiquity and the Early Middle Ages", *Viator* 46.2 (2015), pp. 1-21; M.R. CRAWFORD, *The Eusebian Canon Tables: Ordering Textual Knowledge in Late Antiquity* (Oxford, 2019); A.M. RIGGSBY, *Mosaics of Knowledge: Representing Information in the Roman World* (New York, 2019); J.F. HAMBURGER, *Diagramming Devotion: Berthold of Nuremberg's Transformation of Hrabanus Maurus's Poems in Praise of the Cross* (Chicago, IL, 2020); *The Visualization of Knowledge in Medieval and Early Modern Europe*, ed. M. KUPFER, A.S. COHEN, and J.H. CHAIES (Turnhout, 2020); A. EVEN-EZRA, *Lines of Thought: Branching Diagrams and the Medieval Mind* (Chicago, IL, 2021); M. FRIENDLY and H. WAINER, *A History of Data Visualization and Graphic Communication* (Cambridge, MA, 2021).

use before the eighteenth century remains sporadic.[20] While there is some research into graphic devices that occur in individual texts and textual traditions, systematic studies addressing the types of device in vernacular contexts more generally or surveying the use of devices across genres or domains are scarce.[21] The few pieces of scholarship that address the design and use of early English diagrammatic, tabular or list-like devices beyond specific textual traditions, genres or communities include Wendy Scase's study of late medieval tables of contents, Daniel Wakelin's survey of late medieval graphic materials in the Bodleian Library, Kathleen Acheson's book about visual rhetoric in Early Modern English literature, and a recent edited volume by Eva von Contzen and James Simpson about the use of lists in medieval and early modern literary texts.[22] As Acheson points out, graphic devices that "are neither iconographic nor narrative" have been largely overlooked in previous research in this field.[23] Her study provides illustrative examples of them from a variety of utilitarian,

---

[20] For the *Enchiridion*, see P.S. BAKER, "Byrthferth's *Enchiridion* and the computus in Oxford, St. John's College 17", *Anglo-Saxon England* 10 (1982), pp. 123-142.

[21] For graphic devices in manuscripts and texts written in or containing Middle English, e.g. A. HENRY, "'The Pater Noster in a table ypeynted' and some other presentations of doctrine in the Vernon manuscript", in: *Studies in the Vernon Manuscript*, ed. D. PEARSALL (Cambridge, 1990), pp. 89-113; L.E. VOIGTS, "The Golden Table of Pythagoras", in: *Popular and Practical Science of Medieval England*, ed. L.M. MATHESON (East Lansing, MI, 1994), pp. 123-139; N. PATTWELL, "Providing for the learned cleric: Schemas and diagrams in *Sacerdos Parochialis* in British Library MS Burney 356", *Journal of the Early Book Society for the Study of Manuscripts and Printing* 10 (2007), pp. 129-149; M. PEIKOLA, "Tables of lections in manuscripts of the Wycliffite Bible", in: *Form and Function in the Late Medieval Bible*, ed. E. POLEG and L. LIGHT (Leiden, 2013), pp. 351-378; M. PEIKOLA and M.-L. VARILA, "Multimodal and multilingual practices in late medieval English calendars", in: *Multilingualism from Manuscript to 3D: Intersections of Modalities from Medieval to Modern Times*, ed. M. WŁODARCZYK, J. TYRKKÖ, and E. ADAMCZYK (New York, 2023), pp. 93-118. Studies addressing the use of tabular and diagrammatic elements in Early Modern English materials include L.A. FERRELL, "Page *techne*: Interpreting diagrams in Early Modern English 'how-to' books", in: *Printed Images in Early Modern Britain: Essays in Interpretation*, ed. M. HUNTER (Farnham, 2010), pp. 113-126; K. HUNT, "Convenient characters: Numerical tables in William Godbid's printed books", *Journal of the Northern Renaissance* 6 (2014), n.p.; L. DASTON, "Super-vision: Weather watching and table reading in the early modern Royal Society and Académie Royale des Sciences", *Huntington Library Quarterly* 78 (2015), pp. 187-215.

[22] W. SCASE, "'Looke this calender and then proced': Tables of contents in medieval English manuscripts", in: *The Dynamics of the Medieval Manuscript: Text Collections from a European Perspective*, ed K. PRATT, B. BESAMUSCA, M. MEYER, and A. PUTTER (Göttingen, 2017), pp. 287-306; D. WAKELIN, *Designing English: Early Literature on the Page* (Oxford, 2018), especially at pp. 117-127; Acheson, *Visual Rhetoric*; *Enlistment: Lists in Medieval and Early Modern Literature*, ed. E. VON CONTZEN and J. SIMPSON (Columbus, OH, 2022).

[23] ACHESON, *Visual Rhetoric*, p. 1.

technical and religious genres, such as horticultural guides, military strategy handbooks and Bibles.[24] A key argument made by Acheson is that images of this kind "insinuated ways of thinking in their audiences, and that those ways of thinking could migrate [...] away from the images themselves and affect concepts and communication in other forms".[25] This is also one of the major premises underlying the present volume.

Graphic Literacies, Practices and Events

Another key premise of the present volume is that the successful use and comprehension of the kinds of graphic features and devices discussed in the previous section requires a variety of skills and competencies from readers and writers. Although the perception of graphic features of text ultimately depends on human sensory physiology, the ability to make sense of their meaning is culturally and socially conditioned and must essentially be acquired.[26] The competencies required from readers and designers of images and complex graphic devices and visualisations of data such as diagrams, tables and maps are often viewed under a distinct label like 'graphicacy', 'graphical literacy', 'visual literacy' or 'multimodal literacy'.[27]

---

[24] For visual features in historical English technical writing, see also E. TEBEAUX, *The Emergence of a Tradition: Technical Writing in the English Renaissance, 1475-1640* (London, 2017 [1997]); E. TEBEAUX, *The Flowering of a Tradition: Technical Writing in England, 1641-1700* (London, 2017 [2014]).

[25] Acheson, *Visual Rhetoric*, p. 2. In making this argument, Acheson aligns herself with W.J. ONG, "From allegory to diagram in the Renaissance mind: A study in the significance of the allegorical tableau", *The Journal of Aesthetics and Art Criticism* 17 (1959), pp. 423-440, and E.L. EISENSTEIN, *The Printing Press as an Agent of Change: Communications and Cultural Transformations in Early-Modern Europe*, 2 vols. (Cambridge, 1979).

[26] SCASE, *Visible English*, discusses a variety of contexts of instruction and pedagogical models of graphic competencies in medieval England.

[27] For these and other related labels, see e.g. J. ELKINS, "Introduction: The concept of visual literacy, and its limitations", in: *Visual Literacy*, ed. J. ELKINS (New York, 2009), pp. 1-9; X. DANOS and E.W.L. NORMAN, "The development of a new taxonomy for graphicacy", in: *The Design and Technology Association International Research Conference 2009*, ed. E. NORMAN and D. SPENDLOVE (Wellesbourne, 2009), pp. 69-84, at pp. 71-72; R. EMANUEL and S. CHALLONS-LIPTON, "Visual literacy and the digital native: Another look", *Journal of Visual Literacy* 32 (2013), pp. 7-26; F. SERAFINI, "Multimodal literacy: From theories to practices", *Language Arts* 92 (2015), pp. 412-423, at pp. 413-414; R. WALLER, "Graphic literacies for a digital age: The survival of layout", *The Information Society* 28 (2016), pp. 236-252, at pp. 247-248.

The adoption of such labels emphasises how the skills in question supplement or possibly differ from the more traditionally understood reading and writing literacies. Moreover, different types of graphic devices may require different competencies of reading.[28] In line with our discussion of the concept of 'graphic' in the previous section, our use of the label 'graphic literacies' in this volume is likewise broad – ranging from practices associated with the graphic articulation of language and text by means of script / typography, punctuation and layout to the use of multimodal devices of information visualisation and knowledge construction.[29] In different configurations on both micro and macro levels of linguistic and textual structure, the "four methods of visually highlighting an element on the page of a book", as formulated by Ruth Carroll *et al.*, may be viewed as the basic repertoire of the graphic resources with which these literacies operate, i.e. colour, size, style and position (space).[30]

There exists a considerable amount of empirical evidence about the operation of present-day graphic literacies in a variety of contexts and languages, as may be gleaned for example from research reported in journals such as *Visual Literacy*, *Visual Communication*, the *Journal of Literacy Research*, *Literacy Research and Instruction* and the *Journal of Adolescent and Adult Literacy*. For historical graphic literacies, however, the possibilities for research design are crucially different from those allowed by carefully regulated studies conducted with current data elicited in laboratories or through fieldwork. The major difference is obviously that in historical research we cannot directly elicit data from

---

[28] See e.g. P. WRIGHT, "Tables in text: The subskills needed for reading formatted information", in: *The Reader and the Text*, ed. L.J. CHAPMAN (London, 1981), pp. 60-69; H.C. PURCHASE, "Twelve years of diagrams research", *Journal of Visual Languages and Computing* 25 (2014), pp. 57-75, at p. 65; K. OOMS, P. DE MAEYER, L. DUPONT, N. VAN DER VEKEN, N. VAN DE WEGHE, and S. VERPLAETSE, "Education in cartography: What is the status of young people's map-reading skills?", *Cartography and Geographic Information Science* 43 (2016), pp. 134-153.

[29] These features essentially encompass both the "'intrinsic' and 'extrinsic' features of graphic language" discussed by M. TWYMAN, "Articulating graphic language: A historical perspective", in: *Toward a New Understanding of Literacy*, ed. M.E. WROLSTAD and D.F. FISHER (New York, 1986), pp. 188-251, at pp. 190-191 (quoted from p. 190).

[30] CARROLL *et al.*, "Pragmatics on the page", p. 57. See also M.-L. VARILA, H. SALMI, A. MÄKILÄHDE, J. SKAFFARI, and M. PEIKOLA, "Disciplinary decoding: Towards understanding the language of visual and material features", in: *Verbal and Visual Communication in Early English Texts* (Turnhout, 2017), ed. M. PEIKOLA, A. MÄKILÄHDE, H. SALMI, M.-L. VARILA, and J. SKAFFARI, pp. 1-20, especially at pp. 11-12. For empirical findings about the function of these factors in the process of reading, see e.g. S. LECKNER, "Presentation factors affecting reading behaviour in readers of newspaper media: An eye-tracking perspective", *Visual Communication* 11 (2012), pp. 163-184.

human research participants to understand how their graphic literacy skills and cognitive competencies operated. Yet we can attempt to reconstruct some of these skills and competencies more indirectly by examining those graphic practices that emerge from historical textual evidence.

By 'graphic practices' we mean text producers' and consumers' culturally, socially and situationally conditioned understanding of what different graphic features and devices conventionally communicate and how meaning is made with them in text. These practices also constitute at least some awareness of how graphic features and devices are transmitted and can be technologically (re)produced in the given context and medium.[31] Conceived in this way, graphic practices can be viewed as a concept comparable to 'literacy practices', understood by Jennifer Rowsell *et al.* as "cultural models" about using written language to make meaning that are "embedded in all aspects of the social situation".[32] It should be recognised, however, that graphics can and do exist without any accompanying 'written language', so graphic literacy practices extend beyond practices associated with conventional writing literacy, as was already emphasised above.

'Eliciting' historical graphic practices from texts requires us to pay close attention to the visual and spatial forms of graphic features and devices in their individual attestations, interpret their communicative functions in those contexts, and examine the overall patterns arising from the data. As David Barton and Mary Hamilton point out, "practices are not observable units of behaviour since they also involve values, attitudes, feelings and social relationships".[33] In the operationalisation of socially-based literacy research, the basic analytical units therefore correspond to 'literacy events', understood as "observable epi-

---

[31] See F. EGMOND and S. KUSUKAWA, "Circulation of images and graphic practices in Renaissance natural history: The example of Conrad Gessner", *Gesnerus* 73 (2016), pp. 29-72. The classic conceptualisation of 'practice' by S. SCRIBNER and M. COLE, *The Psychology of Literacy* (Cambridge, MA, 1981), p. 236, as being constituted of "three components: technology, knowledge, and skills" is still useful as basic model for understanding the complexity of the dimensions involved.

[32] J. ROWSELL, D. BLOOME, M.L. CASTANHEIRA, and C. LEUNG, "Introduction: Lost in our meditations about re-theorizing literacy practices across complex social and cultural contexts", in: *Re-Theorizing Literacy Practices: Complex Social and Cultural Contexts*, ed. D. BLOOME, M.L. CASTANHEIRA, C. LEUNG, and J. ROWSELL (New York, 2019), pp. 1-11, at p. 4.

[33] D. BARTON and M. HAMILTON, "Literacy practices", in: *Situated Literacies: Reading and Writing in Context*, ed. D. BARTON, M. HAMILTON, and R. IVANIČ (London, 2000), pp. 7-15, at p. 7.

sodes which arise from practices and are shaped by them".[34] In a similar way, we propose that individual situationally contextualised uses of graphic features and devices in texts may be understood as 'graphic events'. To understand historical graphic practices we should therefore essentially begin by examining individual graphic events. Reconstructing the culturally and socially conditioned communicative models (graphic practices) associated with the use of red colour in late medieval English manuscripts, for example, would ideally proceed from the examination of the attestations of 'red' (in its different forms and hues) in individual writers' (scribes', rubricators', illuminators') hands in individual manuscripts. This examination would involve the careful recording of both the linguistic context of the usage and of the parameters of the situational context with regard to text / work, genre, domain, addressee / primary audience, date and provenance of the book, and the material features of the writing support (etc.). As the next step, observing correlations and patterns between individual events that involve the use of red (in dialogue with previous scholarship) would then enable the identification of communicative functions associated with the usage and eventually allow for the reconstruction of the cultural / social meanings and models associated with red in late medieval graphic literacies.[35]

In current literacy research conducted from the social perspective, events are essentially conceptualised as activities in which people interact with written text in various ways.[36] Graphic events observed in historical texts may similarly be viewed as actions that involve communicative participants (who may be more or less distant temporally). Most graphic features and devices we encounter in historical texts originated in and were transmitted by text producers such as scribes, printers, or engravers. Although the scope of 'literacy' traditionally includes both the activities of writing and reading, some researchers of present-

---

[34] BARTON and HAMILTON, "Literacy practices", p. 8. See also D. BARTON, *Literacy: An Introduction to the Ecology of Written Language*. 2nd edn (Malden, MA, 2007), pp. 35-36; D. SCHIPOR, *A Study of Multilingualism in the Late Medieval Material of the Hampshire Record Office*. PhD thesis, University of Stavanger (Stavanger, 2018), pp. 39-40.

[35] Cf. the method of analysis involving consecutive 'etic' and 'emic' stages advocated by CARROLL *et al.*, "Pragmatics on the page", at p. 56.

[36] M. HAMILTON, "Expanding the new literacy studies: Using photographs to explore literacy as social practice", in: *Situated Literacies: Reading and Writing in Context*, ed. D. BARTON, M. HAMILTON, and R. IVANIČ (London, 2000), pp. 16-34, e.g. at pp. 28 and 32.; see also BARTON and HAMILTON, "Literacy practices", p. 8; SCHIPOR, *A Study of Multilingualism*, p. 40.

day literacy prefer to distinguish creation and design from literacy proper.[37] Richard Emanuel and Siu Challons-Lipton, for example, delimit the concept of 'visual literacy' to "the ability to read, decode and interpret visual images", and identify 'visual creation / design' as a distinct component under the overall umbrella of 'visual proficiency'.[38] In their model, the components of visual literacy and visual creation / design are connected to each other via the component of 'visual thinking' that both of them require.[39] All three components are expressed through 'visual vocabulary', "which enables image readers and writers to express to others what they see".[40] This highlights the importance of verbal communication for visual proficiency.

In the present volume, graphic practices and events examined by the contributors involve both aspects of production (creation and design) and reception (reading and interpretation) of graphic features. The further back in time we extend our inquiry, however, the more difficult it generally becomes to find evidence that directly targets original reception. In more remote historical contexts, evidence about graphic literacy practices must, by necessity, often be extrapolated from the use of graphic features observed in primary sources like books and other material forms of text. The output of text producers (creators and designers of graphic features) – which in various ways reflects their cultural models, audience expectations and technological competencies – thus becomes a major source for reconstructing graphic literacies of the past. In this volume, too, producers' decisions are viewed as an integral component of historical literacy events and practices. The producers whose work is examined by contributors include especially scribes and printers, but authors, editors and translators also feature in several chapters. This approach is in line with other recent research into the visual communication of early English texts in which graphic decisions made by producers and designers play an important role. Daniel Wakelin, for example, is specifically interested in practical decisions

---

[37] Historically, too, despite their close connection and interaction, a distinction can be made between reading and writing literacies, of which the former has traditionally been the major focus of literacy scholarship; see e.g. T. FAIRMAN, "Strike-throughs: What textual alterations can tell us about writers and their scripts, 1795-1835", in: *Studies in Late Modern English Correspondence: Methodology and Data*, ed. M. DOSSENA and I. TIEKEN-BOON VAN OSTADE (Bern, 2008), pp. 193-212; U. HOWARD, *Literacy and the Practice of Writing in the 19th Century: A Strange Blossoming of Spirit* (Leicester, 2012), at pp. 1, 189-191.

[38] EMANUEL and CHALLONS-LIPTON, "Visual literacy and the digital native", p. 9.

[39] EMANUEL and CHALLONS-LIPTON, "Visual literacy and the digital native", p. 9. See also M.D. AVGERINOU and R. PETTERSSON, "Toward a cohesive theory of visual literacy", *Journal of Visual Literacy* 30.2. (2011), pp. 1-19.

[40] EMANUEL and CHALLONS-LIPTON, "Visual literacy and the digital native", p. 9.

made by text producers with regard to aspects of graphic design.[41] By illustrating the sometimes considerable challenges involved in the successful design and execution of spatial and multimodal features on the page, Wakelin reminds us about the material and technological constraints that necessarily shape graphic literacy practices.[42] Similarly, Wendy Scase approaches medieval English community-based graphic practices especially through the output of scribes.[43] Katherine Acheson's study examines the use and design of graphic devices in a variety of Early Modern English text genres; her research also features a reception-related dimension by examining how major literary authors of the period were influenced by this graphic culture in their rhetoric.[44]

It may be surmised that for successful communication to take place, the expected consumers (intended audiences, implied readers, projected users) of a text would often have had at least some familiarity with the practices reflected in the producers' design and execution of that text's graphic features. This cannot, however, be taken for granted without a closer scrutiny of the communicative situation and the context of textual production – a major research theme that runs through all contributions in this volume. Sometimes text producers also had to create new solutions of graphic design that might (or might not) evolve into socially shared conventions and practices. The development of linguistic and graphic conventions is theorised further by Colette Moore in this volume. The emergence of and variations in these conventions are addressed by several contributors. Javier Calle-Martín and Jesús Romero-Barranco, for example, present evidence for a widely attested emerging punctuation practice in medical recipes. This trajectory may be contrasted with that examined by Kjetil V. Thengs – an innovation in the *mise-en-page* of late medieval churchwardens' accounts that does not seem to have caught on more lastingly.

One important factor that may historically have led to innovations in graphic practices has to do with the language(s) of the communicative situation. The graphic events examined in this volume are in most cases embedded in English-language or multilingual communicative situations that involve the use of English. The focus on primarily vernacular contexts highlights the possible language-specific nature of graphic practices and reminds us that they may not always be readily 'transferable' from one language to another. Primarily discussing the Middle English period, Daniel Wakelin argues that "the lower sta-

---

[41] WAKELIN, *Designing English*, p. 5.
[42] WAKELIN, *Designing English*, pp. 121-127.
[43] SCASE, *Visible English*.
[44] ACHESON, *Visual Rhetoric*.

tus of English and less organized systems for copying it" could mean that producers did not necessarily have an existing set of graphic conventions of format and layout to draw on, but books "often had to be designed anew".[45] Wendy Scase, while emphasising the major importance of "the pedagogy of Latin grammar" as the foundation for literacy in medieval English, also shows "that the encoding and decoding of English texts were not regarded or experienced as straightforward" by those equipped with this Latin base.[46] Even in the Early Modern English period, we cannot take it for granted that the social meanings associated with the graphic features of Latin source texts would be carried over unchanged in translated or otherwise adapted material, in a different linguistic context and by members of different language communities.[47] In this volume, too, the texts examined by the contributors are often translations or adaptations from Latin, or modelled after some established Latin genre, which makes the question about language-related transmission constraints relevant. This applies for example to the English 'special' tables that appear alongside Latin tables in many manuscripts of the Middle English *Polychronicon*, examined by Wendy Scase. Overall, the general influence of Latin traditions on graphic practices in English is highlighted in several contributions. Janne Skaffari and Jukka Tyrkkö, for example, observe how producers of seventeenth-century English grammars were in various ways guided by Latin models in their graphic choices. The diagrammatic *Pater Noster* table discussed by Olga Timofeeva is in itself a multilingual device in Latin and English; as Timofeeva argues, the English elements are no mere glosses of Latin, but they also carry independent linguistic and visual meanings.

The chosen medium, material support and techniques of origination and multiplication might also have required new graphic solutions from producers in the course of textual transmission.[48] A case in point are the conspicuously different technological affordances of manuscript and print production with regard to the execution of graphic features and devices, for example concerning

---

[45] WAKELIN, *Designing English*, p. 8.

[46] SCASE, *Visible English*, pp. 352-353.

[47] Consider e.g. the varying communicative meanings associated with certain scripts and typefaces in different languages in the early modern period discussed by S. KAISLANIEMI, "Code-switching, script-switching, and typeface-switching in Early Modern English manuscript letters and printed tracts", in: *Verbal and Visual Communication in Early English Texts*, ed. M. PEIKOLA, A. MÄKILÄHDE, H. SALMI, M.-L. VARILA, and J. SKAFFARI (Turnhout, 2017), pp.165-200.

[48] For the useful distinction between the 'origination' and 'multiplication' stages in book production, see M. TWYMAN, *The British Library Guide to Printing: History and Techniques* (London, 1998), pp. 8-15.

the use of colour, size of text, the shaping and positioning of lines and rules, as well as the overall feasibility of integrating textual and visual features on the page.[49] The sources of graphic materials also extended beyond manuscript and print, as some printers provided the readers with paper parts and assembly instructions for devices such as dials, quadrants and clocks in order to provide a cheaper alternative for metal instruments.[50] In this volume, Ingrid Tieken-Boon van Ostade usefully compares graphic practices between handwritten and printed letters; she also highlights the influence of transmission by paying attention to differences between drafts and fair copies.

An important source of text-internal evidence that may contribute to the contextual interpretation of a graphic event and the practices reflected by it is the metacommunication of text producers (cf. the 'visual vocabulary' in Emanuel and Challons-Lipton's model of visual proficiency discussed above).[51] Complex graphic devices such as tables and diagrams, in particular, may be furnished with captions or associated with some other primarily linguistically presented information about them.[52] Such metacomments can be mainly instructive, intended for reader support, but they may also have a more argumentative function, for example in order to persuade readers about the benefits of an emerging graphic practice.[53] Metacomments may also offer insights into the

---

[49] See e.g. B. MAK, *How the Page Matters* (Toronto, 2011); G. DE YOUNG, "Mathematical diagrams from manuscript to print: Examples from the Arabic Euclidean transmission", *Synthese* 186 (2012), pp. 21-54.

[50] C. GRIFFIN, *Instructional Writing in English, 1350-1650: Materiality and Meaning* (Abingdon, 2019), pp. 129-131.

[51] For a rich variety of the possible uses of historical metacommunication in historical pragmatics, see *Investigations into the Meta-Communicative Lexicon of English: A Contribution to Historical Pragmatics*, ed. U. BUSSE and A HÜBLER (Amsterdam, 2012). EMANUEL and CHALLONS-LIPTON, "Visual literacy and the digital native", p. 9.

[52] In multimedia learning, captions and other linguistic metacomments that support the reader's comprehension of the text may be viewed as instances of 'cueing'; see T. VAN GOG, "The signaling (or cueing) principle in multimedia learning", in: *The Cambridge Handbook of Multimedia Learning*, 3rd edn, ed. R.E. MAYER and L. FIORELLA (Cambridge, 2021), pp. 221-230.

[53] See e.g. J. BERNARD, "Using extended captions to improve learning from instructional illustrations", *British Journal of Educational Technology* 21 (1990), pp. 215-225. Types of book producers' metacomments in a historical context are discussed e.g. by M.V. DOMÍNGUEZ-RODRÍGUEZ and A. RODRÍGUEZ-ÁLVAREZ, "'The reader is desired to observe ...': Metacomments in the prefaces to English school grammars of the eighteenth century", *Journal of Historical Pragmatics* 16.1 (2015), pp. 86-108. For metacomments associated with Middle English graphic devices, see M. PEIKOLA and M.-L. VARILA, "Presenting manuscript tables and diagrams to the Middle English reader", *Journal of Historical Pragmatics*, published online ahead of print 27 August 2024.

cognitive operation of graphic devices, as envisaged by text producers.[54] Their presence (or absence) may provide evidence as to whether a certain graphic practice is expected to be understood by text producers' anticipated audiences, or whether readers are felt to require some guidance in their acquisition of the practice. As Elizabeth Rowley-Jolivet observes, the historical absence of explanatory metacomments on graphic devices may also suggest a type of discourse tradition or genre, such as the published surgical lecture, in which certain kinds of graphic element were understood to form an "integral part" of the narrative, "as shown by their integration into both the spatial layout of the page and the syntax of the sentence".[55] In the present volume, too, contributors highlight text producers' metacomments (or their absence) as potential evidence of the anticipated audiences' graphic practices and literacy competencies. In addition to captions for graphic devices, also paratexts like title pages and prefaces are tapped into for such information. Text categories examined from this perspective include for example works of historiography (Liira, Peikola and Kaartinen), medical books (Varila, Suhr and Tyrkkö) and dance manuals (Salmi).

Literacy events that consist of annotations and other material traces left on the page by book users may for their part offer unique evidence about actual (vs. implied) readers' graphic practices.[56] In a Bodleian Library copy of Leonard Digges's *A prognostication euerlasting of right good effect* (1564), for example, a roughly contemporary reader (as may be judged by their handwriting) added two data columns to a lunar table and supplemented the printed user

---

[54] See e.g. the chapter by A. LIIRA, M. PEIKOLA and M. KAARTINEN in this volume. For the 'communicative work' associated with captions in Present-Day English academic journal articles, see J. SMITH, "A content analysis of figure captions in academic journals from four disciplines", *IEEE Transactions on Professional Communication* 63.4 (2020), pp. 341-360.

[55] E. ROWLEY-JOLIVET, "The emergence of text-graphics conventions in a medical research journal: *The Lancet* 1823-2015", *ASp [Online]* 73 (2018), paragraph 40. DOI: <https://doi.org/10.4000/asp.5107>.

[56] The rich potential of such material for the understanding of medieval and early modern English literacies has been demonstrated e.g. by E. DUFFY, *Marking the Hours: English People and Their Prayers, 1240-1570* (New Haven, CT, 2006) and W.H. SHERMAN, *Used Books: Marking Readers in Renaissance England* (Philadelphia, PA, 2008). A useful typology of readers' annotations is provided by C.J. GRINDLEY, "Reading Piers Plowman C-text annotations: Notes towards the classification of printed and written marginalia in texts from the British Isles 1300-1641", in: *The Medieval Professional Reader at Work: Evidence from Manuscripts of Chaucer, Langland, Kempe and Gower*, ed. K. KERBY-FULTON and M. HILMO (Victoria, BC, 2001), pp. 73-141. See also A. LIIRA, *Paratextuality in Manuscript and Print: Verbal and Visual Presentation of the Middle English* Polychronicon (Turku, 2020), pp. 210-238, available at <https://urn.fi/URN:ISBN:978-951-29-8058-1>.

instructions pertaining to a table for finding the golden number.[57] The meticulous and systematic nature of these and several other annotations made by this reader suggests that they were made by someone who was very well versed in the subject matter.[58] In general, interpreting this kind of evidence is often complicated by the absence of unambiguous information about the date of the graphic event and the identity of the annotator. Despite such limitations, however, evidence from annotations may provide a valuable additional dimension to the understanding of graphic practices in their historical contexts. Among the contributions to this volume, Alpo Honkapohja pays attention to early modern marginal annotations in manuscript copies of John of Burgundy's widely disseminated plague tract.

The discussion above demonstrates that 'graphic practices' and 'graphic literacies' are complex concepts, and approaching them in historical materials requires contextually sensitive readings of primary materials. The present volume examines graphic literacy events such as punctuation and choice of script / font and practices associated with these areas. However, the contributions also expand this focus and take a broader stance towards graphic literacies by including in our scope practices associated with tables, diagrams and other structurally and spatially complex graphic devices.

The Present Volume

The chapters of this volume investigate the forms and functions of graphic elements in a variety of genres, text types and domains from the late medieval period until the late eighteenth century. The contributors address multimodal relationships between textual and graphic elements and pay attention to the linguistic contextualisation of the elements for vernacular audiences. Technological and other medium-related constraints and affordances concerning the use of the graphic features are also addressed in the volume through contributions focusing on handwritten and printed texts.

The volume is divided into two main sections. The contributions in Part I focus on variation and change in graphic practices and conventions related to supra-textual features such as layout, rubrication and punctuation. Colette

---

[57] L. DIGGES, *A Prognostication Euerlasting of Right Good Effect* (London, 1564: STC 435.41), E2r, F1r; accessed via EEBO.

[58] The annotator might be the "John Stibbynge" who wrote his name on the title page; no further information is available to us about him.

Moore's chapter opens Part I with a theoretical discussion of patterns in the historical spread of graphic conventions of textual organisation. Informed by research into other processes of language change such as standardisation and grammaticalisation, Moore develops a model for the development of writing conventions in English. The model posits that the starting point for conventionalisation of writing practices is the variation of forms of textual features ("from punctuation and word order to ink colour and headings") and the proliferation of functions.[59] When a specific form starts to fulfil a specific function more frequently (repetition) and across registers and text types (elaboration), it becomes conventionalised and specialised, potentially even obligatory for performing this function. Moore's model offers a new frame for understanding the graphic features of writing, one that is grounded in research on analogous processes of language change.

Kjetil V. Thengs discusses the pragmatic functions of late medieval English churchwardens' accounts, with a focus on accounts from the church of St. Michael at the North Gate in Oxford. Spanning the century from the 1420s to the 1520s, the accounts in this collection interestingly display different layouts, including some accounts that have been formatted as prose, in contrast to the usual list-like style of presentation. Thengs comes to the conclusion that the unconventional layout of these documents did not in the end decisively affect the pragmatic function of the account as a text type. His analysis suggests, however, that the prose format may have been more cumbersome for the reader, which may explain why it was not conventionalised as a more widespread graphic practice.

Alpo Honkapohja traces the *mise-en-page* and strategies of visual highlighting in the John of Burgundy plague tract from the fourteenth to the seventeenth century. This diachronic examination of one of the most widely disseminated medical texts of medieval England and Scotland investigates both Middle English and Latin versions of the tract. The quantitative and qualitative survey of thirty-one copies of the tract shows, for instance, that there was a gradual shift from marking metatextual divisions with rubrics to indicating them with white space. Furthermore, Honkapohja's analysis suggests that although scribes and rubricators relatively rarely highlighted the medical recipes in the tract, marginal annotation shows signs of readers interacting with and using these recipes.

Javier Calle Martín and Jesús Romero Barranco examine the pragmatics of punctuation in early English recipe books. They investigate 150 medical recipes

---

[59] Quoted from C. MOORE, this volume, p. 33.

from the fifteenth, sixteenth and seventeenth centuries to present a typology of punctuation symbols used for marking rhetorical moves in the recipes and to examine the synchronic and diachronic variation present in the manuscript data. The authors suggest that the Early Modern English period was a turning point in scribal practices, as the use of the paragraph mark and a different ink to mark rhetorical moves gradually gave way to spacing and capitalisation. Although the general direction of change seems to be towards a less heavily punctuated system, the authors show that this pattern varies depending on the section of the recipe examined (e.g. title or ingredients).

In the final chapter of Part I, Ingrid Tieken-Boon van Ostade explores the visual pragmatics of eighteenth-century letter-writing with reference to the correspondence between the grammarian Roberth Lowth and his rival William Warburton. The study focuses on three select features of graphic practice in punctuation and abbreviation: the so-called abbreviation stop (e.g. *Sepr.* for September), the ampersand, and hyphenation at line breaks. Findings about the use of these features in handwritten letters by Lowth and Warburton are usefully compared with contemporaneous printed versions of some of the letters. The author examines the sociopragmatic significance of the graphic forms, including what they can tell us about letter-writing practices of the period and what insight they might provide about the different personalities of Lowth and Warburton as letter-writers.

The second part of the book (Chapters 7-12) focuses on practices related to specific graphic devices like diagrams and tables. Wendy Scase investigates the use of alphabetical tabulation as a form of visual and intellectual organisation of information in the manuscripts of John Trevisa's Middle English translation of the *Polychronicon*. She pays attention to the presence of both Latin and English tables in several of the *Polychronicon* manuscripts, arguing that they represent two distinct subtypes of the medieval alphabetical table: the *tabula communis* and the *tabula specialis*. According to Scase, the latter subtype, written in English, was designed for a projected vernacular audience whose needs differed somewhat from those of the projected Latinate audience of the *tabulae communes*.

Olga Timofeeva addresses visual and linguistic features of the Latin and English *Pater Noster* table in the late-fourteenth-century Vernon Manuscript (Bodleian Library MS. Eng. poet. a. 1). Timofeeva first discusses the diagrammatic form of the table, paying attention to its visual similarities with the chess board and the medieval exchequer table, and shows how these forms may have provided contemporary frames for interpreting the religious meaning of the table. In the second part of the analysis, Timofeeva focuses on the Middle English coordinated word pairs (binomials) that are used in the table for vices, virtues and gifts of the Holy Spirit. She finds the lexical composition of the binomials innovative, and concludes that the linguistic variation shown by the binomials aligns well with the visual design of the table that highlights mutability in various ways.

Aino Liira, Matti Peikola, and Marjo Kaartinen discuss how time was represented visually in sixteenth- and seventeenth-century English works addressing chronology, and how these graphic practices were communicated to the reader. The authors examine the forms of visualisation used in these printed books, including their structuring principles and dating systems. Of the forty-nine titles examined, half are found to contain some visualisation of time in the form of tables, lists, marginal annotations or tree-diagrams. The study also pays attention to how authors and other book producers referred to the chronological visualisations, including the terminology used to describe their use and benefits. Producers' metacomments often emphasise how graphic devices allow the reader to take in synchronised chronological data visually. Their audiences' varying levels of graphic literacy are also noted in these comments.

Mari-Liisa Varila, Carla Suhr, and Jukka Tyrkkö examine variation in the use of images, tables, and diagrams across printed medical books in English, published between 1500 and 1700. Using the Early Modern English Medical Texts (EMEMT) corpus as a starting point for data selection, the authors conduct a quantitative and qualitative survey of graphic devices in different kinds of medical books ranging from learned treatises to popular manuals. Overall, the results suggest that tables and diagrams were not common in sixteenth- and seventeenth-century English medical books. Even images were relatively scarce, and often generic rather than specific in terms of information content. The use of graphic devices was also found to vary considerably depending on the type and audience of the text; for example, braces are typically used in recipes, while images appear in herbals and anatomical and surgical texts.

Hanna Salmi examines the verbal and visual practices of describing movement in early English dance manuals, especially John Playford's seventeenth-century work *The English Dancing Master*. Salmi investigates the tabular format introduced by Playford to connect dance figures to movement and traces the developments in the presentation of this table throughout successive editions of Playford's manual from the 1650s to the beginning of the eighteenth century. Although Playford's tabular format appears innovative and practical, it gradually disappears from the manual. Salmi argues that there may have been several reasons for this: firstly, the labour-intensive process of printing the table; secondly, the potential primacy of presenting music notation over providing dance notation; and, finally, the constant need to add new, beginner-friendly dances to the manual that were simple enough to describe verbally.

The final chapter of Part II, by Janne Skaffari and Jukka Tyrkkö, focuses on graphic elements in seventeenth-century English grammar books. More specifically, the authors examine the purpose and use of graphic features in the grammars by Jeremiah Warton (1654) and Joseph Aickin (1693), compared with other contemporary grammars of English. Their findings indicate that a wide range of graphic elements were used in these books for the pedagogical purposes of listing, grouping and otherwise arranging grammatical information, including lists, tables and diagrams. While the authors discern some variation between the titles examined, they also observe that some topics were particularly prone to attract visual treatment in all grammars, word classification being a case in point. Earlier Latin grammars provided models for these graphic practices.

The afterword by Jeremy J. Smith situates the present book in the wider paradigmatic context of recent scholarly developments in linguistic pragmatics. Smith underlines the need for interdisciplinary and collaborative work in historical pragmatics to break down boundaries between disciplines such as book history, textual criticism and historical linguistics. For him, the approach taken in this volume represents a "reimagining of traditional philology" – a characterisation with which the editors are glad to concur.[60]

---

[60] Quoted from J.J. SMITH, this volume, p. 309.

Part I

Conventionalising Strategies of Verbal and Visual Information

COLETTE MOORE

Introduction

Graphical practices in English texts have taken shape over several centuries of written usage, and it is important to consider the processes through which they develop. Features of layout, design and paratext are critical for conveying meaning in text, and these develop through processes parallel to those of other forms of language change. In what follows, I propose a model for approaching the development of textual organising features.

This examination builds upon the scholarly conversation in historical graphical studies. Examining the ways that aspects of language work together with aspects of visual organisation has progressed in recent years through conversations around what was called by Carroll *et al.* "Pragmatics on the page" and by Tim Machan "Visual pragmatics".[1] This conversation has examined the ways that information is

---

[1] R. CARROLL, M. PEIKOLA, H. SALMI, M.-L. VARILA, J. SKAFFARI, and R. HILTUNEN, "Pragmatics on the page: Visual text in late medieval English books", *European Journal of English Studies* 17.1 (2013), pp. 54-71; T.W. MACHAN, "The visual pragmatics of code-switching in Late Middle English literature", in: *Code-Switching in Early English*, ed. H. SCHENDL and L. WRIGHT (Berlin, 2011), pp. 303-333.

Graphic Practices and Literacies in the History of English, ed. Matti PEIKOLA, Jukka TYRKKÖ, and Mari-Liisa VARILA, *Utrecht Studies in Medieval Literacy*, 61 (Turnhout: Brepols, 2025), pp. 25-45.

visually transmitted in manuscripts and print text (well summarised in Varila *et al.*, and exemplified in Jeremy Smith's recent set of case studies).[2]

The examination also contributes to recent scholarship in Middle English studies that examines early processes of linguistic standardisation. Middle English studies has had some important conversations about standardisation in recent years (in Laura Wright's 2020 collection on multilingualism, Anita Auer's research group on standardisation, the work of Terttu Nevalainen and others on supralocalisation, Joanna Kopaczyk's work on standardisation in legal language, Merja Stenroos and her group working on standardisation in the local documents corpus, Ursula Schaefer's collection on standardisation, and standardisation contributions to handbooks by Joan Beal and Schaefer and others).[3] The discourse on standardisation in Middle English has focused on various elements of language: earliest, in the tradition of M.L. Samuels, focusing on orthography and morphosyntax, more recently expanding to bigger pieces of discourse (e.g. Kopaczyk's work on lexical bundles).[4] The attention has fallen centrally on linguistic features, though, and I would like to extend this conversation to include graphical features of the language on the written page. While I do not mean to imply that standardisation only affects written

---

[2] M.-L. VARILA. H. SALMI, A. MÄKILÄHDE, J. SKAFFARI, and M. PEIKOLA, "Disciplinary decoding: Towrads understanding the language of visual and material features", in: *Verbal and Visula Communication in Early English Texts*, ed. M. PEIKOLA, A. MÄKILÄHDE, H. SALMI, M.-L. VARILA, and J. SKAFFARI (Turnhout, 2017), pp. 1-20; J.J. SMITH, *Transforming Early English: The Reinvention of Early English and Older Scots* (Cambridge, 2020).

[3] *The Multilingual Origins of Standard English*, ed. L. WRIGHT (Berlin, 2020); T. NEVELAINEN, "Processes of supralocalisation and the rise of Standard English in the Early Modern Period", in: *Generative Theory and Corpus Studies*, ed. R. BERMÚDEZ-OTERO, D. Denison, R.M. HOGG, and C. MCCULLY (Berlin, 2000), pp. 329-371J. KOPACZYK, "Textual standardization of legal Scots *vis a vis* Latin", in: *The Multilingual Origins of Standard English*, ed. L. WRIGHT (Berlin, 2020), pp. 487-514; M. STENROOS, "Regional variation and supralocalization in Late Medieval English: Comparing administrative and literary texts", in: *Records of Real People: Linguistic Variation in Middle English Local Documents*, ed. M. STENROOS and K.V. THENGS (Amsterdam, 2020), pp. 95-128; U. SCHAEFER, *The Beginnings of Standardization: Language and Culture in Fourteenth-Century England* (Berlin, 2006); U. SCHAEFER, "Middle English: Standardization": in: *English Historical Linguistics*, ed. A. BERGS and L.J. BRINTON, 2 vols. (Berlin, 2012), 1, pp. 519-533; J. BEAL, "Standardization", in: *The Cambridge Handbook of English Historical Linguistics*, ed. M. KYTÖ and P. PAHTA (Cambridge, 2016), pp. 301-317.

[4] M.L. SAMUELS, "Some applications of Middle English dialectology", *English Studies* 44 (1963), pp. 91-94; J. KOPACZYK, *The Legal Language of Scottish Burghs: Standardisation and Lexical Bundles 1380-1560* (Oxford, 2013). See also L. WRIGHT, "A critical look at previous accounts of the standardisation of English", in: *The Multilingual Origins of Standard English*, ed. L. WRIGHT (Berlin, 2020), pp. 17-38, at p. 25.

language, comparative work suggests that written language is fundamentally linked to standardising practice. So considering language standardisation together with conventions of written practice seems important.

It has been suggested that our modern ways of reading and the graphic practices that make them possible took shape in the medieval period.[5] Jane Roberts and Pamela Robinson point out that most of the conventionalising features of written books developed during the Middle Ages: lists of contents, illustration, pagination, punctuation, and indexes. They note that even the font in which contemporary books are printed is derived from Caroline minuscule, a script that emerged in Francia in the late eighth and ninth centuries and spread through Western Europe.[6] These early conventions develop to organise the codex, and the graphic practices of the late Middle Ages continued to expand rapidly because of an increasing culture of literacy and an accompanying increase in the functionality of written texts. Later practices developed using these as the cornerstones, and shared similar paths to becoming conventions. This discussion will therefore draw from transhistorical examples, since Middle English writing primarily provides evidence for the proto-stages of writing conventionalisation. These dynamics are not a single thread in written language, moreover; they are processes which continue to present new practices of written conventions as our written media and genres develop and change.

It is important, therefore, to think about processes in the development and spread of conventions of written organisation on the page. This work considers analogues from theories of standardisation, grammaticalisation, and constructionalisation to examine processes through which marks and variations on the page become conventions and the ways that these conventions work together with syntactic and discursive practices to organise information: in local ways in a single text or a single section of a text, or supralocally, across manuscripts and books, across textual communities, or across national and linguistic traditions.

The discussion will first exemplify the connections between linguistic and graphical organisation, then it will clarify foundational assumptions and pro-

---

[5] See, for example, Paul Saenger's claim that "by the year 1400, virtually every attribute of the page that was later to characterize the privately and silently read printed volumes of the fifteenth and sixteenth century had been created" (P. SAENGER, "Orality and visible language", in: *The Oxford Handbook of Latin Palaeography*, ed. F.T. COULSON and R.G. BABCOCK (Oxford, 2020), pp. 693-704, available at <https://doi-org.offcampus.lib.washington.edu/10.1093/oxfordhb/9780195336948.013.112> [accessed 16 Jan 2023].

[6] J. ROBERTSON and P. ROBINSON, *The History of the Book in the West* (London, 2010), p. XI.

vide a brief description of analogous models for discussing organising practice in grammaticalisation, constructionalisation, and standardisation, before presenting the model for conventionalisation processes with some examples. The penultimate section offers a case study of the development of title pages to illustrate the model, and the final section presents some summarising and concluding remarks.

Graphical and Linguistic Organisation

To illustrate the ways that linguistic and graphical strategies work together in the *mise-en-page*, we might look at the organising devices on the manuscript page in Figure 1 from MS San Marino, Huntington Library, HM 129 from the Northern Homily Cycle.

Some features of organisation strike us visually: the pointing finger or *manicula*,[7] the paraph marks, the *nota* in the margin, the red braces. Other features can be found in the words and the grammar of the language. Textual organisation, therefore, can be found in morphosyntactic, lexical, and graphical structures, and these often share the information load.

Consider, for example, the ways that tyhe line-endings are indicated in Figure 1. They are organised metrically through rhyme, which creates the structure of the verse line. This structure, however, is also part of the grammatical form, and it is highlighted visually by the red braces (also calles brackets or tie lines[8]). In this case, textual structure is created by signalling through graphical and metrical means, and one kind of signalling is heightened by signals through another form.

Another representative aspect of textual structure can be found in the beginnings of lines. These verse lines often begin with the word *and*; of the lines on this page, 16 of the 44 lines begin with *and*. The conjunction serves here, we assume. paratactically, to link one line to the next grammatically and logically, but it also creates a visual repetition on the page, which is highlighted by the red ink that touches the letters which begin each line. The words and design work together.

---

[7] M.P. BROWN, *Understanding Illuminated Manuscripts: A Guide to Technical Terms*, rev. E.C. TEVIOTDALE and N.K. TURNER (Los Angeles, CA, 2018 [1994]), p. 66.

[8] D. SAWYER, *Reading English Verse in Manuscript: c. 1350-c. 1500* (Oxford, 2020), p. 123.

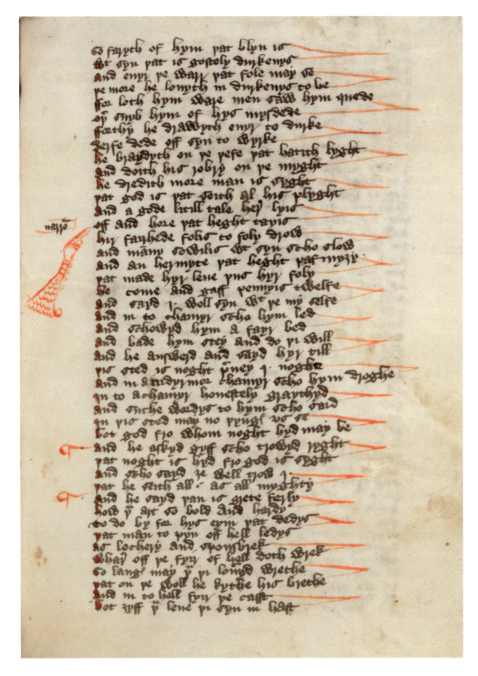

Fig. 1   MS San Marino, Huntington Library, HM 129, f. 114r.

Words themselves can also constitute paratextual organisation as well, through headings and the like. On this page, a marginal *nota*, nominally a lexical feature, is situated in a marked location on the page outside of the block of text. It is also marked as metadiscourse by being in Latin: "*narrō*", abbreviating '*narratio*'. And it is framed in red ink, drawing visual attention to it. Using the *nota* together with the *manicula*, the page calls attention to the section break, to the onset of the saint's life, the tale of St. Thais. The words of the tale do this too: "*And a gode litill tale her lyis / off and hore þat heght tayis*" ("And a good little tale here lies, of a whore that was called Thais"). The organisational structures – words, grammar, graphical elements, layout – work together and influence one another. Sabina Nedelius, in her recent study of ME punctuation, for example, noted a relatively high usage of punctuation in ME manuscripts, except in one manuscript, a collection of culinary recipes in MS London, British Library, Arundel 334. As she points out, the recipes are part of a genre with a highly formalised layout which may have served pragmatic ends similar to punctuation in structuring the information.[9] One possible reason for the sparse punctuation, therefore, may have been that it was not needed in the same way in that manuscript. We see how – on the manuscript page – the layout, the ounctuation, and the words all share the work of information organisation.

How does the writing system, therefore, develop strategies of organisation which become shared practice and winnow down variation for conventionalisation / standardisation of these strategies? Surely this is a process which includes linguistic aspects of standardisation in conjunction with graphical aspects of conventionalisation.

---

[9] S. NEDELIUS, "Changed perspectives: On modernised punctuation in Middle English texts", unpublished doctoral dissertation (University of Oslo, 2021), p. 207. For a discussion of the ways the abbreviations and punctuation are linked to shifts in the construction of texts, see also A, HONKAPOHJA and A. LIIRA, "Abbreviations and standardisation in the *Polychronicon*: Latin to English and manuscript to print", in: *The Multilingual Origins of Standard English*, ed. L. WRIGHT (Berlin, 2020), pp. 269-316.

Conventions Are Subject to Collective Change

The proposed framework rests upon two axiomatic assumptions about the functions and informational force of graphical conventions.

First axiom: features of design and discourse are ordered and have the potential of being regularised.

Textual features include both linguistic and visual elements, and these provide structure to individual texts and can also be subject to intertextual norms: shared practices across texts. Sometimes such regularisation is a factor of production norms or the conventions of a community of textual practice, and the conventions can be precise enough to use for identification. Consider shifts in ruling practice in the thirteenth century, for example. From a point in the early thirteenth century, scribes started writing the first line of the text on a page below the top ruled line rather than above it.[10] This transformation was relatively quick – between the 1220s and the 1240s – and pervasive enough that it has been used as a dating criterion for manuscripts.[11] This collective decision-making about layout practice presumably comes through the dynamics of communities of scribal practice.

Second axiom: regularised features of design and discourse can take on textual functionality and can become information-bearing conventions in the writing system.

Once a verbal or visual feature becomes regularisable, it takes on the potential of information load for the system of written English. The convention can serve a structural, organisational function, and the collection of these features works together in the pragmatics of a written language. The most common example of this would be the development of punctuation conventions, but other kinds of visual or paratextual markers are relevant here, too: indenting paragraphs, boldface headings, etc.

---

[10] N.R. KER, "From 'above top line' to 'below top line': A change in scribal practice", in: *Books, Collectors, and Libraries: Studies in Medieval Heritage,* ed. A.G. WATSON (London, 1985), pp. 71-74; D. WAKELIN, *Designing English: Early Literature on the Page* (Oxford, 2018), p. 56.

[11] E. KWAKKEL, "Cultural residue in medieval manuscripts", in: *The Medieval Manuscript Book,* ed. M. JOHNSTON and M. VAN DUSSEN (Cambridge, 2015), pp. 60-76, at p. 65.

These tenets undergird the model on the processes of the development of graphical conventions.

Background: Analogous Processes

The organisation of written language happens through a collection of strategies that develops over time by adapting existing pieces for collectively-determined functions. This process resembles other processes of language change, particularly in the ways that organising norms and conventions evolve through collective practice.

One analogous model, the theory of grammaticalisation, describes how lexical items take on grammatical and organising functions in a language.[12] A frequently cited example of grammaticalisation, for example, is the way that content words progress along a cline of grammaticality to become affixes:[13]

content item > grammatical word > clitic > inflectional affix

In this way, the word *full* became the inflectional affix *-ful* (help*ful*) as it grammaticalised over time. The process of grammaticalisation has been examined both historically and synchronically, and it describes a range of phenomena concerned with how a lexical item can take on grammatical properties. Some of the characteristic aspects of grammaticalisation are relevant for the development and diffusion of language norms more broadly. In particular, in the parameters that Christian Lehmann sets for grammaticalisation, one of them, 'obligatorification', describes the systematic constraint of choice in which the grammaticalised item becomes largely obligatory.[14] In this way, the grammaticalisation process models a change to the system as speakers become constrained to adopt it.

More recently, constructionalisation has been suggested as a broader process that would include grammaticalisation. A construction, in this framework, does not have to be a word, it could be a word, phrase, or pattern of usage that takes on semantic content: a pairing of form and meaning.[15] Grammatical

---

[12] The term comes originally from A. MEILLET, "L'évolution des formes grammaticales", *Scientia* (Rivista di Scienza) 12.26 (1912), pp. 130-148; see also *Approaches to Grammaticalization*, ed. E. TRAUGOTT and B. HEINE (Amsterdam, 1991).
[13] P. HOPPER and E. TRAUGOTT, *Grammaticalization* (Cambridge, 1993), p. 7.
[14] C. LEHMANN, *Thoughts on Grammaticalization*, 3rd edn (Berlin, 2015), pp. 148-49.
[15] P. KAY and C. FILLMORE, "Grammatical constructions and linguistic generalisations: The

constructionalisation, therefore, includes particular items like the affixes described above, but could also include abstract schemas like information structure constructions.

Grammaticalisation and constructionalisation, while they certainly involve social actions, are both described language-internally. Standardisation, however, is a process that has been theorised in both a linguistic and social way. Einar Haugen's 1966 model for standardisation is still cited in this regard.

	Form	Function
Society	selection	acceptance
Language	codification	elaboration

Fig. 2   Einar Haugen's model for standardisation.

Haugen delineated different stages in the process of language standardisation: selection (the identification of a norm), codification (the stabilisation of the norm selected), acceptance (the process by which institutions and social groups implement the norm), and elaboration (the process by which the norms are disseminated across different genres and functions).[16] Conventions of layout for the written language share aspects of this development, so I am proposing a modified version of this schema for the development of writing conventions that borrows some of the features for linguistic processes of grammaticalisation and constructionalisation.

Conventionalisation

The gist of the process of the development of graphical conventions may be summed up as follows: writers of English use a wide range of strategies to organise their words, from punctuation and word order to ink colour and headings. The functionality of these structural, design and paratextual features are

---

what's X doing Y? construction", *Language* 75.1 (1999), pp. 1-33; W. CROFT, *Radical Construction Grammar: Syntactic Theory in Typological Perspective* (Oxford, 2001); E. TRAUGOTT and G. TROUSDALE, *Constructionalization and Constructional Changes* (Oxford, 2013), p. 1.

[16] E. HAUGEN, "Dialect, language, nation", in: *The Ecology of Language: Essays by Einar Haugen*, ed. A.S. DIL, (Stanford, CA, 1972 [1966]), pp. 237-254, at pp. 251-252.

worked out in individual manuscripts and printed books and then spread through networks of manuscript and printed book production and dissemination. Over time, the strategies are refined: becoming specialised for a particular function and dominant in usage, eventually passing a tipping point of conventionalisation in which their use would be an expected norm of written English.

Figure 3 sketches out features that are potentially part of the development of writing conventions. These features do not all seem necessary, however, and the process is clearly not a unidirectional journey towards ever-increasing organisation in texts. In the same way that grammaticalisation produces layers of usage rather than a unidirectional path for development, conventionalisation can create shared usages in some genres, in some writing communities, at some times. Moreover, conventionalisation is continual, since media and registers for written English continue to change and generate new constraints and pragmatic pressures for organising written text.

feature	preconvention	development of convention
form	variation	⇒ repetition & elaboration
function	proliferation	⇒ specialisation & obligatorification

Fig. 3. Processes of conventionalisation.

In this model, the preliminary textual state before conventionalisation begins is one of variation of textual features and proliferation in functions performed by those features. If a feature begins to conventionalise, it occurs more frequently in that function, 'repetition', and across different registers and text types, 'elaboration'. It also begins to be functionally 'specialised', to be used just for that purpose, and usages of it can sometimes become 'obligatory' to the given function. The following section will discuss each of these processes.

Variation and Proliferation

Prior to conventionalising, marks are used in polyfunctional ways and functions are achieved through different marks. I regard this state of variation in form and proliferation of functionality to be necessary for later conventionalisation, since possibilities multiply first before they can be winnowed down. Louise Sylvester noted a similar process for lexical standardisation, in which increased variation in words lays the ground for semantic differentiations of register, and potential lexical standardisation.[17]

Consider, for example, the proliferation of functions for particular graphical marks: paraph marks, midline dots, virgules – these can indicate rhetorical pauses, or they can indicate grammatical or metrical structure, emphasis, numbers.[18] I have elsewhere discussed how the use of red ink in ME manuscripts is polyfunctional, and how the overlapping functions for rubrication lead to a shift in designation: the red ink sometimes marks authoritative quotations and sometimes it simply marks represented speech and sometimes different scribes of the same text employ the red ink in varying pragmatic ways.[19]

Another example might be found in the ways that footnotes were not designated by a standard system for centuries. Manuscripts and printed books often used footnote symbols in seemingly haphazard ways, sometimes even within the same page, employing a variety of letters, asterisks, daggers, the diesis (double dagger), double lines, three dots, and other marks.[20] The proliferation of these marks creates a range of graphical choices. When the strategies become conventions, it is often because these features are repeated in texts and start to specialise for particular purposes.

Repetition

Psychologists talk about 'habituation', a decline in the tendency to respond to stimuli that have become familiar because repeated. This concept seems to

---

[17] L. SYLVESTER, "The role of multilingualism in the emergence of a technical register in the Middle English period", in: *The Multilingual Origins of Standard English*, ed. L. WRIGHT (Berlin, 2020), pp. 365-379.

[18] A. HONKAPOHJA, "Functions of punctuation in six Latin and English versions of the plague treatise of John of Burgundy", in: *Punctuation in Context – Past and Present Perspectives*, ed. M. KYTÖ and C. CLARIDGE, (Bern, 2019), pp. 151-178, at p. 171.

[19] C. MOORE, "Visual pragmatics: Speech presentation and Middle English manuscripts", in: *The Cambridge Handbook of English Historical Linguistics*, ed. M. KYTÖ and P. PAHTA (Cambridge, 2016), pp. 481-496, at pp. 492-495; and C. MOORE, "Discourse variation, *mise-en-page*, and textual organisation in Middle English saints' lives", in: *Verbal and Visual Communication in Early English Texts*, ed. M. PEIKOLA, A. MÄKILÄHDE, H. SALMI, M.-L. VARILA, and J. SKAFFARI (Turnhout, 2017), pp. 23-40, at pp. 25-28.

[20] K. HOUSTON, *Shady Characters: The Secret Life of Punctuation, Symbols, & Other Typographical Marks* (New York, 2013) p. 111, and available at <http://shadycharacters.co.uk/2011/06/the-ampersand-part-2-of-2/>; E. KWAKKEL, "medievalbooks", available at <https://medievalbooks.nl/2014/12/19/the-medieval-origins-of-the-modern-footnote/>.

apply to linguistic forms of stimuli as well.[21] For structural content, familiarity would lead to faster processing, owing to the lessening novelty for the design feature; this would then make the content more effective as a backgrounded structural marker.

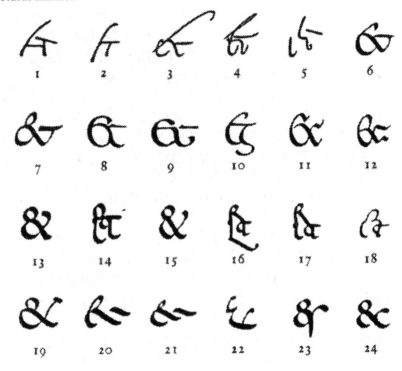

Fig. 4. Origin of the Ampersand (reproduced by permission from the Tschichold family).

Repetition has often been spoken of as a factor in grammaticalisation: that the reiteration of the usage makes possible its development as a structural feature.[22] For grammaticalization, this repetition is addressed as spoken process, and the increased frequency of the utterance acts as a major factor in phonetic

---

[21] J. HAIMAN, "Ritualization and the development of language", in: *Perspectives on Grammaticalization,* ed. W. PAGLIUCA (Amsterdam, 1994), pp. 3-28, at p. 7.

[22] HAIMAN, "Ritualization and the development of language"; J. BYBEE, "Mechanisms of change in grammaticization", in: *The Handbook of Historical Linguistics*, ed. B.D. JOSEPH and R.D. JANDA (Oxford, 2003), pp. 602-603.

reduction, the way that, for example, *going to* reduces to *gonna* in the grammaticalised form.[23] Analogically, it seems also true that the repeated use of a convention in writing entails that there is increased frequency in visual processing for readers, either locally in a particular text or more broadly across multiple texts, and that this increased frequency leads to expedited processing of the usage in that particular function.

Sometimes this kind of repetition might be accompanied by visual simplification as a character is written rapidly and repeatedly (analogous to the phonological reduction involved in grammaticalisation). I have discussed this in past work with reference to the usage of the speech verb *quod* as a formulaic marker of quoted speech in ME manuscripts before the advent of inverted commas or any punctuation dedicated to marking quotation. In quotative clauses, *quod* is often abbreviated (*qd* or *q̣*) and sometimes touched with red ink on the page. As such, it can sometimes look and function visually more like a punctuation mark than a word.[24] As the lexeme develops a heightened function of textual organisation, therefore, repetition and visual simplification permit it to serve as a graphical convention.

Another example of visual simplification can be seen in the development of the ampersand. The ampersand is derived from a ligature of the Latin word *et*, so it is also a word that developed into a symbol – in the liminal space between lexicon and design. Jan Tschichold charted the development of the ampersand (Fig. 4).

Some of these forms in Figure 4 are still fairly discernible as the ligature, and others have evolved to look more like a single character. #1 is Pompeiian graffiti, #8 is insular majuscule from the Book of Kells, and #13 is from an eighth-century Merovingian manuscript, already pretty similar to our modern versions.[25] We can see that the written word *et* was transformed by repetition and routinisation into a grapheme, and used as a writing convention across linguistic and national boundaries. Keith Houston (cf. Fig. 5) describes how the alphabet in the nineteenth century was even regarded as having the character at the end.[26]

The name *ampersand*, in fact, is thought to come from the recitation of the end of the alphabet: "x, y, z, and, *per se*, and" (meaning 'and, by itself, and'),

---

[23] J. BYBEE, "From usage to grammar: The mind's response to repetition", *Language* 82.4 (2006), pp. 711-733, at p. 720.

[24] C. MOORE, "Talking about talk: *quethen, quoth, quote*", in: *The Pragmatics of Quoting Now and Then*, ed. J. ARENDHOLZ, W. BUBLITZ, and M. KIRNER (Berlin, 2015), pp. 255-270, at p. 260; also C. MOORE, *Quoting Speech in Early English* (Cambridge, 2011), p. 27.

[25] TSCHICHOLD, *Formenwandlungen der &-Zeichen*; HOUSTON, *Shady Characters*, p. 68.

[26] HOUSTON, *Shady Characters*, p. 68.

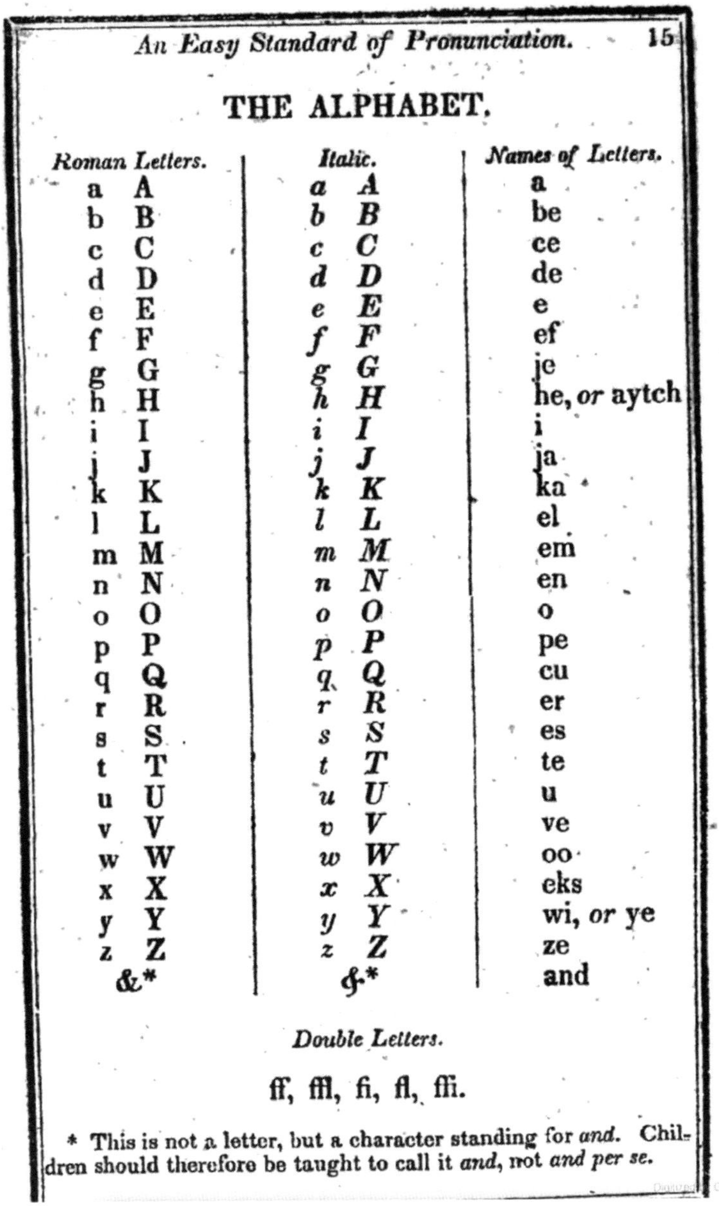

> *An Easy Standard of Pronunciation.* 15
>
> ## THE ALPHABET.
>
> | Roman Letters. | Italic. | Names of Letters. |
> |---|---|---|
> | a A | *a A* | a |
> | b B | *b B* | be |
> | c C | *c C* | ce |
> | d D | *d D* | de |
> | e E | *e E* | e |
> | f F | *f F* | ef |
> | g G | *g G* | je |
> | h H | *h H* | he, *or* aytch |
> | i I | *i I* | i |
> | j J | *j J* | ja |
> | k K | *k K* | ka |
> | l L | *l L* | el |
> | m M | *m M* | em |
> | n N | *n N* | en |
> | o O | *o O* | o |
> | p P | *p P* | pe |
> | q Q | *q Q* | cu |
> | r R | *r R* | er |
> | s S | *s S* | es |
> | t T | *t T* | te |
> | u U | *u U* | u |
> | v V | *v V* | ve |
> | w W | *w W* | oo |
> | x X | *x X* | eks |
> | y Y | *y Y* | wi, *or* ye |
> | z Z | *z Z* | ze |
> | &* | *&** | and |
>
> *Double Letters.*
>
> ff, ffl, fi, fl, ffi.
>
> * This is not a letter, but a character standing for *and*. Children should therefore be taught to call it *and*, not *and per se*.

Fig. 5   Alphabet with ampersand in N. WEBSTER, *The American Spelling Book, Containing the Rudiments of the English Language, for the Use of Schools in the United States* (Middletown, CT, 1831), p. 15.

which transforms through rapid speech into *ampersand*. The representation of *et* and its christening as an *ampersand* show how a functional and backgrounded word can become 'graphemised', with clear parallels to the ways that a functional word can become an affix. Processes of encoding information in design, therefore, are similar in some ways to encoding information in morphosyntax. Just as the process of grammaticalisation or constructionalisation describes how a lexical item can be routinised into an affix, so the process of conventionalisation describes how a lexical item might be routinised into a graphical symbol.

Interestingly, an earlier symbol for *and*, the sign , used in early English manuscripts, is also derived from the written form of Latin *et*; it is the shorthand Tironian note, similar to the one for the letter *T*, an abbreviated way to write *et*. Both symbols appear in the alphabet recorded in Byrhtferth's Latin and Old English *Manual* in 1011.[27] The Tironian is a variant, another graphemised version of *et*; it spread through early medieval texts and then was replaced by the *&*.

We see that the use of *and*, the act of appending things and linking them together, is a highly functional organising notion for texts. *And* is a lexical item, but also, through abbreviation and graphical repetition, *&* is a graphical convention that has been considered either a mark of punctuation or an alphabetic character. The separation between lexical features and graphical ones is sometimes a porous boundary, as the representations of *et* indicate.

Elaboration

Haugen describes standardisation as involving elaboration, the spread of forms across a wider range of genres and functions. Similarly, for a feature of textual organisation to be acknowledged as a widespread convention, one tendency is that its use spreads across various text types and registers. Some conventions are used in genre-specific ways – the rhyme braces in Figure 1, for example, are typically used in verse to connect rhyming words (there are some similar braces and tie lines in other genres, but these braces are broadly connected to the genre of verse). But others extend across a broad range of texts, like the paraph marks or the *punctus elevatus*.

Some conventions are not extended by elaboration and remain restricted to particular text types; they illustrate how this process is not always a predictable next step. In previous work, I discussed the use of the word *videlicet* and its

---

[27] *Byrhtferth's Manual (A.D. 1011)*, ed. S.J. CRAWFORD (Oxford, 1929: EETS O.S. 177).

abbreviations *viz*, *vizt*, and *vid* as markers of direct speech in defamation depositions.[28] This use of *videlicet* is common to flag the onset of quoted speech in the depositions, but the usage did not spread more widely as a marker of quoted speech. Its use as a quotative marker in defamation depositions, therefore, emerged from a particular set of pragmatic constraints (the need to indicate textual transitions to the purported defamatory words of the defendant) and this genre was not influential enough for elaboration of the usage. When elaboration occurs through the generic diffusion of usage, it contributes to the prevalence of a convention and to an increasing expectedness in its appearance.

Specialisation and Obligatorification

Marks that advance further in conventionalisation might also undergo specialisation or obligatorification.

'Specialisation' entails stripping off other competing functions, particularly those which will conflict. Marks are sometimes selected as conventions because they do not have other strong competing functional attachments, of course, though sometimes competing functional roles only become apparent after the fact. Consider a recent example: when Ray Tomlinson selected the @ sign for addresses in the ARPANET (the predecessor to the internet), he chose it because it is an available keystroke, but one that was underused. There were incompatible uses for the @ sign, though, such as its use in Multics (the predecessor to UNIX) as an indicator to "erase all preceding characters on this line".[29] Eventually, the conflict was resolved by modifying Multics. Thus the @ sign became dedicated primarily for email addresses (and, later, Twitter handles and addressing practices in other digital media) and its other functions were modified or disappeared: this is what is meant by specialisation.

Specialisation is not requisite for the connection of design with function, however, and many design features go on serving multiple functions. Often, though, one function becomes the primary one and others that do not conflict take on less frequent usages. The single baseline dot or period, for example, is primarily the syntactic full stop which ends a sentence, but it can also serve to mark abbreviations (e.g. *Mr.*) and has recently taken on another function as

---

[28] C. MOORE, "The use of *videlicet* in Early Modern slander depositions: A case of genre-specific grammaticalization", *Journal of Historical Pragmatics* 7.2 (2006), pp. 245-263; MOORE, *Quoting Speech in Early English*, pp. 61-68.

[29] HOUSTON, *Shady Characters*, p. 84.

rhetorical punctuation in particular informal registers like text messages, marking pauses and emphasis (e.g. *so. much. homework.*) In the case of the baseline dot, we see that specialisation is not always a one-way street, and competing functionality can emerge later for written conventions.

The flip side of a feature of construction becoming specialised for a particular function is when a particular function begins to be indicated primarily or completely by the given feature or construction. When this happens, it reinforces the one-to-one relationship that characterises a dedicated convention. We see this in, for example, the way that inverted commas in the eighteenth century became essentially obligatory as quotation marks for marking direct speech in English. Prior to this, in the sixteenth and seventeenth centuries, the primary punctuation mark for quoted speech was the use of parentheses around quotative clauses in sentences, e.g. *(quod he)*. The convention of using parentheses for quotative clauses became quite widespread (occurring in EEBO books about 40% of the time with quotative clauses using *quoth* or *say*),[30] but the parentheses retained other functions and did not specialise for marking quoted speech. This may be one of the reasons why the quotative parentheses ultimately gave way to the inverted commas; these more effectively specialised for quoting direct speech.

In the Middle English period, not many discourse organising conventions were specialised or obligatory yet.[31] Discourse conventionalisation in medieval texts is characterised more by the earlier processes and less by the two developments mentioned above, since the practices of written usage had not become fixed to the point where those later steps could occur. Late Middle English was a time for variation and proliferation of writing conventions, where many possible strategies emerged and each manuscript was a system of its own. In the wake of Jeremy Smith, scholars of standardisation recognise a distinction between 'fixed' standards and processes of 'focusing'.[32] While fixed standards are not pervasive for language and layout in Middle English manuscripts, we do see focusing taking place within communities of practice or textual genres. This kind of localised winnowing occurs in different ways in written English – see,

---

[30] C. MOORE, "The path not taken: Parentheses and written direct speech in early printed books", in: *Punctuation in Context – Past and Present Perspectives*, ed. M. KYTÖ and C. CLARIDGE, (Bern, 2019), pp. 85-101, at p. 94.

[31] See also A. HONKAPOHJA, "Functions of punctuation in six Latin and English versions of the plague treatise of John of Burgundy", in: *Punctuation in Context – Past and Present Perspectives*, ed. M. KYTÖ and C. CLARIDGE, (Bern, 2019), pp. 151-178, at p. 160.

[32] J.J. SMITH, *An Historical Study of English: Function, Form, and Change* (London, 1996), p. 66.

for example, Matti Peikola's examination of patterns of ruling on the manuscript page that shows shared practice developing in Wycliffite texts, presumably because these texts were produced by a community of practice.[33] The variation is a critical part of the model, though: an important step before norm formation can happen.

Sometimes variation is perceived as the opposite of standardisation, and in some ways it can be. But this model posits that the variation and proliferation that occurs is a critical part of standardising processes: narrowing cannot happen until choice is possible and multiple options are available. The graphical variation in ME shows the overgrowth of strategies before the pruning of focusing processes and the increased structural efficiency created through specialisation and obligatorification.

Case Study: Title Pages

One shift in book information design in Early Modern print practices is the adoption of the title page: one of the most definitive paratextual features in the modern book, containing different kinds of information about publisher, author, and genre.[34] The spread of the title page presents an illustrative look at conventionalisation.

Before the advent of print, handwritten manuscripts were more often bespoke in production, so an opening incipit was enough to signal the identity of the text.[35] The medium of print made possible the production of many copies at once: changing the ways that books were distributed, and creating the need to store and protect the volumes. Early books printed after the development of the printing press were not typically created and stored with bindings; they would be bound when delivered to the customer. Being unbound made them cheaper to store and ship, and meant that booksellers could bind books at the point of sale. Thus it became useful to have a covering sheet that signalled the identity of the book from the outside, and protected the leaves of the volume with text on them. This sheet quickly became a space for providing information and

---

[33] M. PEIKOLA, "Guidelines for consumption: Scribal ruling patterns and designing the mise-en-page in later medieval England", in: *Manuscripts and Printed Books in Europe 1350-1550: Packaging, Presentation and Consumption,* ed. E. CAYLEY and S. POWELL (Liverpool, 2013), pp. 14-31.

[34] G. GENETTE, *Paratexts: Thresholds of Interpretation*, trans. J. LEWIN (Cambridge, 1997), pp. 32-33.

[35] M.M. SMITH, *The Title Page, Its Early Development, 1460-1510* (London, 2000), p. 27.

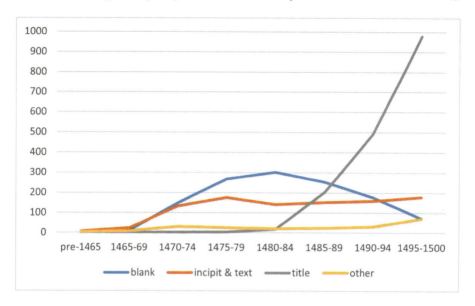

Fig. 6   First page treatment over time (after SMITH, *The Title Page*, p. 50).

marketing of the book.[36] The development of the title page, then, stemmed from practical and material shifts in the distribution of written texts.

The early years of printing present a reset moment of sorts for writing conventions, in which a new medium for information has emerged and the constellation of writing practice negotiates which kinds of information will be represented. At first, several possibilities for the covering page of the print book emerged. Margaret Smith surveys incunables (books printed before 1501) and examines the negotiation of increasing information on the title page. She finds four primary first pages: 1) incipit + text: 23.3%; 2) blank: 29.4%; 3) title: 40.7%; 4) other (prefaces, tables, text with no incipit): 6.6%.[37] Once title pages began to have more than a simple label, they began to load information onto the page more expansively. Smith looked at printers' marks, authors' names, quali-

---

[36] G. COLE, "The historical development of the title page", *The Journal of Library History (1966-1972)* 6.4 (1971), pp. 303-316, at p. 305; R.W. MCCONCHIE, "Some reflections on early modern printed title pages", in: *Principles and Practices for the Digital Editing and Annotation of Diachronic Data,* ed. A. MEURMAN-SOLIN and J. TYRKKÖ (Helsinki, 2013: *Studies in Variation, Contacts and Change in English* 14), available at <https://varieng.helsinki.fi/series/volumes/14/mcconchie/>.

[37] SMITH, *The Title Page,* p. 49.

fications, dates, decoration including woodcuts, layout, stance markers and descriptors (famous, most excellent, illustrious, venerable).

At first, several strategies rise together for the first page: a direct onset with an incipit and text; a blank page; a page with title information; and a combination of information. Smith notes that, given the nature of the titles, the title could almost be regarded as an incipit, just separated from the onset of the text itself.[38] The line on the graph that jumps dramatically beginning in 1480 is the tally for 'title': it rises more slowly than the others in the first two decades on the x-axis, but then quickly becomes the predominant strategy for the first page.[39]

In the stark rise of the title line on this graph (Figure 6), we might see the shape of the S-curve, which has been used to model diffusion in linguistic change.[40] The shape of the line describing this rise of the title page has the characteristic S-curve trajectory: flatter at the start, then rising steeply. Presumably, extending the data chronologically would show the line flattening out again at the tail end of the S-curve, after the title page has become the dominant practice. The similarity of the diffusion of written conventions to the diffusion of linguistic features indicates that we are right to find analogues in the process of writing conventions to the other kinds of linguistic norm development.

The model that I propose in Figure 3 describes what happens in the development of title page conventions. The title page is innovated after the onset of print books, and then there is a period in which information proliferates on the title page, with variation in what is presented and which functions the information serves. Eventually, the information depicted begins to conventionalise. Certain choices get 'repeated' across title pages, and 'elaborated' across different genres of book production. Functionally, particular constructions and usages begin to 'specialise' and certain practices become more 'obligatory' to their functions.

We even see auxiliary specialisation in paratextual lexical development. Mari-Liisa Varila and Matti Peikola did a study of the pre-1550 title pages in EEBO and looked at the specialising use of modifiers. Modifiers of time more

---

[38] SMITH, *The Title Page*, p. 62.
[39] The first title opage in an English text is credited to *A Passing Gode Lityll Boke Necessarye [and] Behouefull a[g]enst the Pestilence* (London, 1485: STC 4591).
[40] D. DENISON, "Log(ist)ic and simplistic S-curves", in: *Motives for Language Change*, ed. R. HICKEY (Cambridge, 2003), pp. 54-70, at p. 54; T. NEVALAINEN, *Descriptive Adequacy of the S-curve Model in Diachronic Studies of Language Change* (Helsinki, 2015: *Studies in Variation, Contact, and Change in English* 16), available at <https://varieng.helsinki.fi/series/volumes/16/nevalainen/>.

often get attached to verbs (83%) and modifiers of quality more often get attached to nouns (54%).[41] We see, as the paratextual genre of the title page becomes more established, that generic norms for the use of language emerge: not just the presence of the title page but even practices in titling become subject to norming conventions. This suggests that stylistic tropes and expectations for genre-specific practices might also become more predictable as writing conventions develop.

The conventions of organising information in book production stem from a multilingual and multinational constellation of practice. The spreading of conventions through the European book market results from the circulation of books and the mimicry of innovations across geographic and linguistic boundaries.

Conclusion

Conventions of the written page provide substantial textual and linguistic information. The conventions develop as a product of pragmatic pressures both internal and external to the writing system. As features of the page get repeated and elaborated, they become load-bearing features of the information structure, and sometimes become specialised and obligatory in their roles. This is not a process that happens once, but it is continually being renegotiated, particularly in the development of new written genres and in new media of communication. The Middle English period is an essential one for this development in written English, and it is the variation and proliferation of late medieval written practice that makes possible the narrowing that occurs in the development of shared writing conventions. Different possibilities emerge and coexist, and then sometimes one emerges as the dominant choice and rises through repetition and elaboration. We see this diffusion in the S-curve of the rise of the title page in Figure 6. Having a model for standardisation / conventionalisation / norm development that is capacious enough for graphical and layout features offers an important perspective on the connectedness of features in texts.

---

[41] M.-L. VARILA and M. PEIKOLA, "Promotional conventions on English title-pages up to 1550: Modifiers of time, scope, and quality", in: *Norms and Conventions in the History of English*, ed. B. BÖS and C. CLARIDGE (Amsterdam, 2019), pp. 73-97, at p. 90.

The Pragmatics of Late Medieval English Accounts: A Case Study

KJETIL V. THENGS

Introduction

This is a case study of a set of late medieval English churchwardens' accounts from the parish church of St. Michael at the North Gate in Oxford. It draws on insights from the Pragmatics on the Page project at the University of Turku,[1] with particular emphasis on graphic practices and what Tim William Machan terms 'visual pragmatics'.[2]

Churchwardens' accounts are complete records made annually or semi-annually of income and expenses connected to the daily running and upkeep of

---

[1] R. CARROLL, M. PEIKOLA, H. SALMI, J. SKAFFARI, M.-L. VARILA, and R. HILTUNEN, "Pragmatics on the page: Visual text in late medieval English books", *European Journal of English Studies* 17 (2013), special issue *Visual Text*, ed. J. KENDALL, M. PORTELA, and G. WHITE, pp. 54-71.

[2] T.W. MACHAN, "The visual pragmatics of code-switching in late Middle English literature", in: *Code-Switching in Early English*, ed. H. SCHENDL and L. WRIGHT (Berlin and Boston, MA, 2011), pp. 303-333.

a church or a chapel, and as such also of the parish,[3] and are among the earliest administrative documents systematically written in English; the present collection from St. Michael's contains English texts from 1424 onwards. Comparable collections from other places, such as London, Cornwall and Dorset show a similar date pattern when it comes to choice of language.

Because of their explicit connections to a given location, these accounts are very much local records, drawn up by local, mainly secular people.[4] While such accounts may be somewhat limited for research purposes in terms of lexicon and syntax, their local connection provides an abundance of variation when it comes to orthography and morphology, and also, as this study shows, their visual appearance. Variation in visual layout, as is the case for linguistic variation, could be tied to social and geographical factors but also to material considerations, such as format, medium and the availability of various inks and pigments.

The study is concerned with the communicative aspects of churchwardens' accounts in terms of their visual appearance; it assesses the pragmatic functions of medieval accounts and their use of pragmatic markers, and attempts to answer the following question: what happens to the pragmatic function when the visual aspect of an otherwise easily recognisable text type deviates from its traditional form?

Background

This case study draws inspiration from the Pragmatics on the Page project, conducted at the University of Turku until 2017. The methodology devised by the project team employs pragmatic theory together with materialist philology to take textual communication beyond the linguistic utterance.[5] It considers all aspects of the page, including text, paratext, images, figures, script, ink, format, material, layout and manuscript context, showing how everything on the page contributes to the overall textual communication. In the present study, the main focus is on what Machan calls 'visual pragmatics', that is, how graphic practices influence the way in which a text communicates with its audience.[6] In

---

[3] B. KÜMIN, "Late medieval churchwardens' accounts and parish government: Looking beyond London and Bristol", *The English Historical Review* 119 (2004), 87-99.
[4] B. CUSACK, *Everyday English 1500-1700: A Reader* (Edinburgh, 1998), p. 43.
[5] CARROLL *et al.*, "Pragmatics on the page".
[6] MACHAN, "The visual pragmatics".

Machan's study, he explicitly excludes, among other text types, legal texts and business accounts;[7] however, his idea of how visual pragmatics influence certain scribal strategies could also be applied to the material included in the present study.

Accounts

From a present-day perspective, most people have an idea or an expectation about what an account is and what it looks like. However, this idea might not necessarily be the same for everyone. The OED defines a financial account as "a statement of financial expenditure and receipts relating to a particular period or purpose, with calculation of the balance; a detailed statement of money due".[8] This definition refers to the function of accounts; however, accounts come in many forms and sizes, they range from simple lists of items with a value for each item to large corporate spreadsheet accounts with multiple columns, and they can be hand-written or, more commonly nowadays, digitised. Still, no matter how simple or complex the layout is, or what medium is used, the basic function remains the same: accounts serve as a means of communicating to e.g. individuals, families, institutions or government bodies, both present and future, an official record of tangible transactions that have taken place, with a balance of credits and debts. Accounts are essentially non-personal, as they do not usually state an explicit addressee, and their pragmatic function thus differs from that of other, more personal documentary text types, such as letters, awards, grants and petitions.

Medieval accounts are not all that different from modern-day accounts, neither concerning their function nor their visual appearance, and can in general be recognised at a glance by a present-day reader. Like present-day accounts, medieval ones also come in various forms and sizes, they list items and sums relating to income and expenses in separate sections with sub-totals added in-between, and have a total balance calculated at the end.

More specifically, based on extensive archival research and text collection for the Corpus of Middle English Local Documents (MELD) at the University of Stavanger, Norway, medieval accounts usually consist of one or more rolled-up sheets of parchment or paper; often they are also found in the form of booklets

---

[7] MACHAN, "The visual pragmatics", p. 306.
[8] OED Online <https://www.oed.com/dictionary/account_n?tab=meaning_and_use> (sense II) [accessed 29.09.2023].

or codices.⁹ Like most documentary texts, accounts tend to follow a set template. However, while other types of documents contain more or less running prose from start to finish, accounts in general, and churchwardens' accounts in particular, mainly consist of lists of items and sums. They start with a heading containing the name of the place for which the account is made, the relevant financial year, and the names of the people responsible for the accounts that year. The heading is followed by detailed lists of receipts and expenses in separate sections, often with marginal headings indicating the different sections, with intermediate and total sums added in-between. Sometimes there are also sections on rentals and debts or allowances.[10]

English churchwardens' accounts survive in abundance, especially from the Early Modern period onwards, and they are generally found all over the country. Until the early fifteenth century, accounts across England were almost without exception written in Latin. Accounts written in English tend to appear from the second half of the fifteenth century, with some examples from as early as the 1420s. While matrix language might have played a role in the scribes' choice of visual layout, all the texts included in the present study are part of the MELD corpus, and thus by definition are all written wholly or partly in English.[11] Choice of language is therefore not included as a factor of this study.[12]

---

[9] M. STENROOS, K.V. THENGS, and G. BERGSTRØM (compilers), *A Corpus of Middle English Local Documents – MELD version 2017.1*. <http://www.uis.no/meld>.

[10] See e.g. J.C. COX, *Churchwardens' Accounts from the Fourteenth Century to the Close of the Seventeenth Century* (London, 1913), pp. 32-33, for a description of the format and contents of the accounts relating to St. Botolph without Aldersgate in Westminster.

[11] See the MELD Manual 2017.1 on the website for the *Middle English Scribal Texts programme* (MEST), hosted by the University of Stavanger, for a description of the sampling, transcription conventions and presentation of the MELD corpus. <https://www.uis.no/en/meld-corpus-files>.

[12] For a wider discussion of language choice in legal documents, see M. STENROOS, and K.V. THENGS, "Local documents as source material for the study of late medieval English", in: *Records of Real People. Linguistic Variation in Middle English Local Documents*, ed. M. STENROOS, and K.V. THENGS (Amsterdam, 2020), pp. 3-21, at pp. 11-15; M. STENROOS, G. BERGSTRØM, and K.V. THENGS, "The categorization of Middle English documents. Interactions of function, form and language", in *Records of Real People. Linguistic Variation in Middle English Local Documents*, ed. M. STENROOS, and K.V. THENGS (Amsterdam, 2020), pp. 37-67, at pp. 56-62.

Churchwardens

Churchwardens were generally elected from among local craftsmen, artisans and farmers, for a term of one year, and there were usually two wardens in each parish. However, the practice varied from parish to parish; some parishes had only one warden with several lower officials, and in other parishes the wardens were elected for two years, sometimes overlapping for better continuity.[13] Until 1571, they were lay persons elected by the whole body of the parishioners. It was not a popular duty, but one it was difficult to get out of once chosen.[14] The churchwardens were responsible for the daily running of the church, and for keeping accounts of the church funds and expenditure – the so-called churchwardens' accounts, audited each year for the common parish assembly, where, depending on the practice of the parish, the new wardens were elected and presented with the previous year's accounts.[15]

Sometimes the wardens wrote their own accounts, but as being able to write was not a requirement for the position, they could also be written by the parish clerk or another clerk hired for the occasion, in case the wardens were illiterate.[16] The function of the parish clerk was primarily to assist the parson in his pastoral duties, as well as overseeing the upkeep of the church and its belongings and making sure that all the duties of the church were fulfilled.[17]

It is difficult to ascertain who the scribes involved in producing the present material were; however, many of the texts in the material specifically list how much was spent on parchment and the writing of the accounts, and one states that they paid a certain sum to "a clerk" for the accounting, which might suggest that scribes were hired to do the work. From the sixteenth century onwards it became increasingly common to list entries for expenses relating to the writing of the accounts.[18] Parish clerks were usually appointed for life, in principle by the head of the religious institution (the rector, vicar, abbot or patron, depending on the institution), though in practice by the parishioners.[19] Given the

---

[13] Cox, *Churchwardens' Accounts*, pp. 4-5.
[14] A.T. Hart, *The Man in the Pew, 1558-1660* (London, 1966), pp. 60-61.
[15] Borthwick Institute for Archives, University of York. <https://www.york.ac.uk/media/borthwick/documents/5Churchwardenabt.pdf>. [Accessed 24.05.2023]
[16] Cusack, *Everyday English*, p. 43.
[17] D. McKay, "The duties of the medieval parish clerk", *The Innes Review* 19 (1968), pp. 32-39, at p. 32.
[18] Cusack, *Everyday English*, p. 43.
[19] J. Christie, *Some Account of Parish Clerks, More Especially of the Ancient Fraternity (Bretherne and Sisterne) of S. Nicholas, Now Known as the Worshipful Company of Parish Clerks* (London, 1893), p. 18.

large number of scribes involved here (twenty-five in all, see "Material" below), it seems unlikely that the parish clerk was responsible for all the texts.

Historical Context

By any standards, present-day Oxford is not a large city, and in the fifteenth century its boundaries did not go far beyond the walls of what is now the city centre. Nevertheless, there were no fewer than fourteen parishes in and around the city, twelve of which were within the city walls, and most of them were tied to one or more of the Colleges of the University.

St. Michael at the North Gate was a relatively small parish at the start of the fifteenth century but was then joined with the parishes of St. Mildred and All Saints. Richard Fleming, Bishop of Lincoln, founded Lincoln College in the extended parish of St. Michael at the North Gate in 1427. Lincoln College was very much concerned with tradition, and strongly opposed the changes to the Church brought on by Henry VII. St. Michael's was the Collegiate Church of Lincoln College.[20]

Material

In all, twenty-seven accounts are included from the church of St. Michael's, all written wholly or partly in English. They cover a whole century from 1424 to 1525. The accounts are held by the Oxfordshire History Centre in Oxford, and form part of a larger collection of accounts. All accounts are written in various shades of dark ink on parchment, and are in the form of single rolls (now kept flat in two large modern book volumes, reference codes PAR211/4/F1/1 and PAR211/4/F1/2). Most have writing on one side only, while others also contain writing on the dorse. They vary in size from 12×18 cm to 24×60 cm.

Transcriptions of all twenty-seven texts form part of the Corpus of Middle English Local Documents (MELD), a digital text corpus compiled from original manuscripts by the Middle English Scribal Texts programme team (MEST) at the University of Stavanger, Norway, including texts from the period 1399-1525. The first instalment of the MELD corpus, covering the eastern counties, is

---

[20] *British History Online* <https://www.british-history.ac.uk/vch/oxon/vol3/pp163-173>. [Accessed 29.09.2023]

The Pragmatics of Late Medieval English Accounts

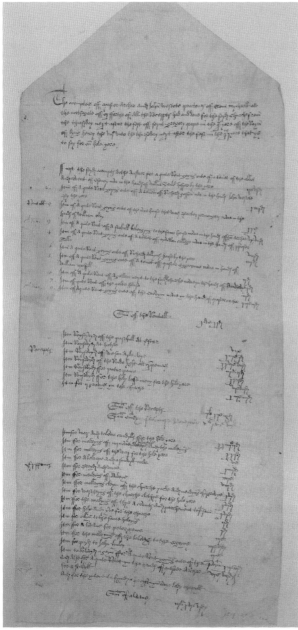

Fig. 1 Example of traditional layout, MS Oxford, Oxfordshire History Centre, PAR211/4/F1/2/100 (St. Michael at the North Gate, 1520).

freely available on the University of Stavanger website.[21] All texts included in this present study have been examined from manuscript facsimiles in the image archive of the MEST programme. Around twenty-five different scribes seem to have been involved in the making of the St. Michael accounts over the century from 1424-1525. However, several scribes are responsible for more than one text each, and care has therefore been taken to include at least one text from each scribe, in order to get a representative sample for the study. The chronological run of texts is reasonably complete, but with a gap of twenty-two years from 1457 to 1479, when all the texts were written in Latin, and therefore are not included in MELD.

Figure 1 presents what appears to be a typical example of a late medieval English account. It follows what one might consider the usual template, with a heading followed by lists of receipts and payments, with subheadings in the left margin, sums along the right margin, and subtotals between the different sections. All accounts from the Oxford parish church of St. Peter in the East, dating from 1483-1525, follow this same layout, as do all accounts from another Oxford church, St. Peter le Bailey, dated between 1477-1499. Based on the present research, this is the layout most commonly found in English accounts throughout at least the southern part of the country during the fifteenth and early sixteenth centuries. However, even though most English accounts follow this template, there are differences to be found.

Several accounts, here exemplified by an account from St. Michael at the North Gate, dated 1501, show a very different layout from the typical template (Figure 2; transcribed in Example 1).[22] The order of the sections is the same, starting with a heading, followed by rentals, receipts, expenses and allowances, with a note from the auditors, in a different hand and usually in Latin, at the bottom (excluded in the transcription); however, the entire account is written out like prose, with the sums being part of the bulk of the text.

---

[21] <https://www.uis.no/en/meld-corpus-files>.

[22] The MELD corpus is available in four versions meant for different uses. The 'Base' version preserves the team's own coding and commentary, and gives the fullest information about the text as it appears in the manuscript. The 'Concordance' version provides text files that are especially designed for use with a concordancer or other corpus software. The 'Readable' version is similar to a traditional edition, and is meant for easier reading and browsing. Finally, the 'Diplomatic' version is similar to the Readable one, but reproduces abbreviations and symbols iconically (see STENROOS et al., *A Corpus of Middle English Local Documents*). The present transcriptions are in the 'Readable' format. For a full explanation of the transcription conventions used in the examples, see the MELD Manual 2017.1, downloadable on the project website: <https://www.uis.no/en/meld-corpus-files>. Note that the lineation is not reproduced in Example 1.

The Pragmatics of Late Medieval English Accounts

Fig. 2 Example of prose style layout, MS Oxford, Oxfordshire History Centre, PAR211/4/F1/2/78 (St. Michael at the North Gate, 1501).

Example 1:

The compte of wlam Plumpton' And of Thoms Nyhtyngale proocturs of our lady Chapell in þe Chirche of Sent
Mychaell wt-in the north ȝat of oxford made on the xij day in marche ˄ by-fore the fest of [...] þt was in þe ȝer' of þe
Reynyng kyng herr' þe vijthe vnto þe xj da [sic] of marche in xvjth yer'
receyuud
in þe box of the last acompt xx s' Jtmm of xiij s' iiij d for for [sic] þe croune in the handes of mr Thoms Danvers

Rentall

Jtm' for laurens x s' in the handes of lyncoln College Jtm' of xxti d for John Carr' bedyll in þe hondes of lyncolln

College Jtm' of vj s' vijj [sic] d for þe grete houce in Bedford lane Jtm' of ij s' for the litil houce nex it in þe seid lan

Jtm' of iiij s' for the myddyl houce A-boue Jtm' of iiij s' for þe hyde houce Jtm' for ij s' for A Croft in stocwell

Sma – iij li iij s' viij d

Recetes

Jtm' the same ʒelde A-Compt ofe iiij s' receyuud of A-rerage in the handes of Crofton' sma – iiij s'

Jtm' for the by-quest of stephan' tyler – ij s'

Sma – vjs' [Latin: Sma totl [...]] – iij li viij ix s' viijd

Iowans

Jtm' þe same acomptans Aske Alowans of iiij s' x d for wax spendyd in this ʒer' Jtm for menyng

A aube & A amys & for wasshyng iij d Jtm' for sett' on the parers on ij Aubʒ & ij Amys j d Jtm' for mennyng

the second best vestment ij d Jtm' payd for syngyng bred xij d Jtm' for syngyng wyne iij s' xj d

Jtm' for maky wrytyng of the visitacion massus of þe uysitacion' & the transfiguration' wt þe stuf – xiiij d

Jtm' for j lib talow cardull j d Jtm' for ij d to Assheley at his cecond Acomptes

Sma – xj s' viij d

Jtm' same Acomptans Aske to be alowede of xix d for the ij howce be-neth for the foydans of x wekes

Jtm' of vj d for þe hy houce aboue for the foydans of vj wekes

Jtm' for bordes to mende the dores the flores & the wallus iiij bordes viij d & for naylus iij d

Jtm' for A lode Erthe iiij d Jtm' þey Aske alowans of xiij s' iiij d for the Crovne Jtm' of

x s' for laurens hall Jtm' of xx d for Caire bedyll And of ij s' for stocwewel [sic] strette

Jtm' for mennyng the Chalys ad [sic] for gyldyng v s' iij d

Sma – xxx s' vij d [Latin: Sma totl] – xlvij s' iij d

(MS Oxford, Oxfordshire History Centre, PAR211/4/F1/2/78; MELD code D2282)

At first glance this looks nothing like one would expect an account to look like, at least from a modern-day perspective. However, the fact that the accounts were accepted by the auditors in their note signifies that this was an acceptable way of accounting at the time. There is overall much variation when it comes to the visual appearance of the accounts in the collection from St. Michael's in Oxford. The early rolls up until 1478 follow the regular template with lists and sums on the right; the same is also the case from 1502 onwards. In the period in between, however, from 1479 to 1501, we find several rolls, in seven different hands, with this alternative prose-style layout.

In addition, during the same period there are also several rolls by at least seven different scribes with sums on the left, as in Example 2, and two with a mix of sums on the right and left, in two different hands. It is interesting to note that none of the St. Michael accounts from this period follow the regular layout with sums on the right that we find in the collection of the adjacent parishes of St. Peter in the East, situated less than 800 metres to the east of St. Michael's, and St. Peter le Bailey, situated approximately 300 metres south-west of St. Michael's.

Example 2:

fyrst they axe A-lowans of **ij s' iij d** for A-mennyng of A chalys ~~~
Jtm' of **iij s'** fore on vn' of syluer that was put to þᵉ chalys ~~~
Jtm' of **ij s' ix d** payd fore newe wex bogtht a-genys the fest of Ester ~~~
Jtm' of **j d ob** for makyng' of a li tapyr [...] be-fore *our* lady in *our* lady chapell ~~~
Jtm' of **ij d** payd for makyng' of iiij li of beters ~~~
Jtm' of **j** [...] payd for makyng' of ij li of syngyng candyls ~~~
Jtm' of **iiij s' iiij d ob** for x li of newe wex boght A-genys þᵉ fest of *cristes*masse
~~~

(MS Oxford, Oxfordshire History Centre, PAR211/4/F1/1/57. MELD code 2261)

Accounts from London, Cornwall and Dorset

In preparation for this study, accounts from Cornwall, Dorset and London, as well as accounts from two other Oxford parishes, St. Peter in the East and St. Peter le Bailey, were examined in addition to the material from St. Michael at the North gate. London in particular is incredibly rich in medieval churchwardens' accounts. Despite the fact that most of the City of London's churches were either wholly or partly destroyed in the Great Fire of 1666, fifteenth and early sixteenth century account books survive from many of the London parishes. To get an overview of the material I did a preliminary survey of the records of sixteen London parish churches (see Figure 3), most of which are huge codices with hundreds of folios, though some accounts, in particular from St. Botolph without Aldersgate, are in the form of rolls. They were examined as thoroughly as possible in terms of their visual layout, and the overall impression is that there is much variation when it comes to their visual appearance.

The early London accounts until around 1470 mainly follow the regular template with lists and sums on the right; the same is also the case from 1510 onwards. Ten of the London codices contain only accounts with the conventional layout. Allhallows London Wall has one account in what I choose to call a 'mixed layout', that is, parts of the account consist of lists of items and sums, while other parts consist of prose sections with sums included in the running text. St. Dunstan in the East has four such mixed accounts, while the two books from St. Mary at Hill show a more or less consistent use of mixed accounts from 1478-1524. It is sometimes difficult to judge whether the layout should be considered mixed or regular; this requires careful reading of each entry to see if sums listed in the body of the text should be added together or whether they serve another purpose. This is extremely time-consuming and has not been possible to carry out in any systematic way for the present study, so the division into regular-, mixed- and prose-style layout is based here purely on visual appearance.

The Cornwall material includes a wide variety of accounts from around 1440-1525, most of which are either related to private estates or town administration, and only one set of accounts, dated 1480, relates to a religious house. However, none of these accounts deviate from the usual form: they all appear in the form of delimited lists with sums on the right.

The Dorset account material consists of churchwardens' accounts relating to Wimborne Minster, dated from 1472 onwards, and is thus directly comparable to the Oxford material. The earliest of these accounts, written in a mix of Latin and English, shows a very similar layout to the prose accounts from St. Michael's (Figure 3). There is overall much variation in the layout in the Dorset material, including one account with sums on the left, but after 1519 all accounts follow what here is referred to as the regular layout.

St. Mary at Hill	1422-1525
St. Peter Westcheap	1441-1450
Allhallows London Wall	1455-1525
St. Michael Cornhill	1455-1475
St. Andrew Hubbard	1456-1524
St. Botolph without Aldersgate	1466-1487
St. Martin Orgar	1471-1473
St. Stephen Walbrook	1474-1523
St. Stephen Coleman Street	1486-1507
Allhallows Staining	1492-1525
St. Dunstan in the East	1494-1509
St. Margaret Pattens	1506-1525
St. Martin Outwich	1509-1525
St. Michael-le-Querne	1514-1525
St. Dunstan in the West	1517-1525
St. Mary Magdalen Milk Street	1518-1525

Fig. 3 List of examined London churchwardens' accounts at London Metropolitan Archives.

Pragmatic Markers

Pragmatic markers are often referred to as being discourse markers.[23] However, Karin Aijmer and Anne-Marie Simon-Vandenbergen argue that there is a distinction between the two, in that discourse markers are primarily defined as 'discourse-marking', while pragmatic markers refer more specifically to their pragmatic function.[24] Such functions include a wide variety of options, and while there seems to be little consensus on a common definition of pragmatic markers as such, the term may serve as an umbrella category of markers that

---

[23] For example D. SCHIFFRIN, *Discourse Markers* (Cambridge, 1987); A.H. JUCKER and Y. ZIV ed., *Discourse Markers. Description and Theory* (Amsterdam, 1998).

[24] K. AIJMER and A.-M. SIMON-VANDERBERGEN, "Pragmatic markers", in: *Discursive Pragmatics*, ed. J. ZIENKOWSKI, J.-O. ÖSTMAN, and J. VERSCHUEREN (Amsterdam, 2011), pp. 223-247, at pp. 226-227.

signal various transitions and are used contextually to create coherence in spoken or written discourse, often filling an indexical function.[25]

In a study of bibliographic codes as pragmatic markers, Justyna Rogos-Hebda applies the term to medieval manuscripts, and states:

> It is first and foremost through visual elements that manuscripts communicate their contents to the reader. Therefore, ultimately, every visual aspect of a medieval manuscript page serves as a pragmatic marker in the sense that it supports the interaction between the text and its reader, as well as organises and monitors 'manuscript discourse'.[26]

This is very much in line with the methodology devised for the Pragmatics on the Page project,[27] and although the present study does not take all visual elements on the manuscript page into consideration, the term is here still employed in the sense that every visual feature that enhances communication between the text and its reader might be considered a pragmatic marker.

In addition to the immediate visual layout that has been described so far, the scribes who produced the churchwardens' accounts have different ways of marking the various components that are included in an account. A common trait for the accounts included in this study is the heading being clearly marked with either a larger initial or a slightly larger script for the first word. Another common feature is formed by the different sections of the account being marked with subheadings, though not always in the same place on the page. Most often the subheading is in the left margin, but it may also occur above the section or in the right margin. It may be written in Latin or, more commonly, in English. The scribes of these accounts only use the 'text ink', so there is no rubrication present, nor are there any other items in a different colour or hue. None of these features are exclusive to accounts, but there are other features that clearly set them apart from other text types. Perhaps the most obvious feature is the presence of multiple sets of numerals that make up the sums, usually listed for each individual item on the right-hand side, as explained above.

---

[25] K. AIJMER, "The interface between grammar and discourse: 'The Fact is That.'", in: *Connectives as Discourse Landmarks*, ed. A. CELLE and R. HUART (Amsterdam, 2007), pp 31-46, at p. 37.

[26] J. ROGOS-HEBDA, "The visual text: Bibliographic codes as pragmatic markers on a manuscript page", *Studia Anglica Posnaniensia* 51 (2016), pp. 37-44, at pp. 39-40.

[27] CARROLL et al., "Pragmatics on the page".

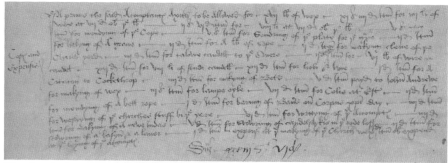

Fig. 4   2-shaped pragmatic marker indicating that a numeral follows. MS Oxford, Oxfordshire History Centre, PAR211/4/F1/1/70.

When looking more closely at how sums are marked, one can see that there are several options for a scribe. In a regular layout, the item may be connected with the corresponding sum on the page in various ways. Numerals are often preceded by what at first glance may look like simple lines, which may or may not be joined at the end, depending on the length of the description of the item. However, there is a common denominator for all the different line shapes. A closer look at the beginning of the lines reveals that they all start with what looks like the numeral 2, with an elongated tail of varying length (Fig. 4).

This 2-shaped symbol was something the present author discovered while working on his PhD thesis, and is commonly used before numerals in all kinds of text-types. No mention of this has been found in any of the palaeographical manuals consulted for this study;[28] the closest item would be the *virgula plana* (horizontal virgule) described by Malcolm B. Parkes, at least from a visual point of view, though according to Parkes the *virgula plana* signified a final pause and was not commonly used in the late medieval period.[29] In the transcriptions for the MELD corpus, for lack of a better term, this symbol is marked with <spn> (symbol preceding a numeral). Scribes use both the 'regular' 2-shape as well as an inverted version of the same.

New entries in an account are also usually marked. The most common marker is the word 'Item', either written out in full or in various abbreviated forms. Other common markers of a new item include 'And', 'Et', and 'Also'. More specific markers are also used, depending on the context, such as 'Re-

---

[28] A. CAPPELLI, *Lexicon abbrevaturarum: Dizionario di abbreviature latine ed italiane*, 6th edn (Milan, 1990 [1929]); M.B. PARKES, *Pause and Effect: An Introduction to the History of Punctuation in the West* (Aldershot, 1992); *The Oxford Handbook of Latin Palaeography*, ed. F.T. COULSON and R.G. BABCOCK (New York and Oxford, 2020).
[29] PARKES, *Pause and Effect*, pp. 46, 307.

ceived', 'Paid', and 'Allocated', in various orthographic forms. A scribe may stick to one marker throughout an entire account, or he may vary his usage. For instance, one scribe uses 'Item' for the receipts of rent, and 'And' for the expenses, before again reverting to 'Item' for the next new entry. However, the basic function of these words is the same, as they all mark the beginning of a new entry. One particular scribe uses a double virgule to delimit two entries on the same line. This seems to be an idiosyncratic feature, as this has not been found in any of the other accounts examined for this study. This same scribe does not generally precede numerals with the 2-shaped marker, except before the final sums.

The prose account from St. Michael's in Example 1, written on a single sheet of parchment, follows the conventional layout in terms of headings and the order of the different sections. The subheadings are in Latin and English, and there are intermediate total sums following each section. The less conventional aspect is how the scribe has chosen to organise the different entries within each section, in that he deviates from the typical list of items, and instead writes everything out as running prose. However, what at first glance seems somewhat chaotic turns out to be perfectly orderly. The scribe uses the 2-shaped marker before each numeral as a visual aid to set it off from the text – the marker may not be equally 2-shaped in all instances; however, it is still recognisable as a pre-numeral marker. Additionally, each new entry starts with the common marker 'Item', here in the slightly abbreviated form 'Jtm', with an upward-curling otiose stroke connected to the final 'm', and with the long 'J' as the initial, which also sets it apart both functionally and visually from the preceding entry. The combined use of these markers, which are commonly used with the same function in all kinds of accounts and as such come across as salient markers, makes it easy for a trained eye to make out the different entries and their corresponding sums, and thus the layout of the separate sections may be considered less important.

It is interesting to note that the prose-style layout seems to appear first around the same time as several syntactic changes of formulaic phrases in other types of documentary texts, that is, during the first part of the reign of Edward IV. A study of opening and closing formulae in fifteenth- and early sixteenth-century Northwest Midland texts classified as conveyances showed a clear development during the same period towards what Matti Rissanen calls "compactness of expression", where the initial witnessing clause exhibited a change from 'this x *bears witness* that' to 'this x *witnesses* that', and the final witnessing clause showed a change from 'in witness *of the which thing*' to 'in witness *whereof*.[30] However, while the syntactic changes of opening and closing formulae endured for centuries, the prose-style layout of accounts seems to have been a rather short-lived affair, limited to certain scriptoria, during the reigns of Edward IV, Richard III and Henry VII, that is, from around 1470 to 1500. This indicates that perhaps it was, in the end, perceived as more cumbersome to read than the regular list-style layout. The scribes responsible for this innovation may have had good reasons for doing so, such as saving space on the page; another explanation might be that they were less familiar with the design of accounts and were more accustomed to writing prose texts; a third option might be that the style was inherited from Latin exemplars. However, for now this remains speculation. The second half of the fifteenth century seems in general to have been a period of experimentation, not only in terms of syntax and visual aspects, but also in terms of choice of language. One should note that different categories of legal documents develop differently over time due to their pragmatic functions and what Parkes refers to as pragmatic literacy, that is "the literacy of one who has to read or write in the course of transacting any kind of business".[31]

Some of the London accounts show elements of the prose-style layout well into the reign of Henry VIII. However, in the London accounts the prose-style layout seems to be used only for a summary or memorandum of expenses, the original lists of which are contained in separate accounts. Moreover, the London accounts are different from the ones in Oxford and Dorset in that they are contained in codices; they appear to be audited summaries meant as a starting point for the following year's account rather than full records of every receipt and payment.

Conclusion

A tentative answer to the initial question regarding what happens to the pragmatic function when the visual aspect of an otherwise easily recognisable text type deviates from its traditional form would be: not much. The overall layout of a page may function as a more macro-level pragmatic marker in itself;

---

[30] K.V. THENGS, "Compactness of expression in Middle English legal documents", *Filologia Germanica – Germanic Philology* 7 (2015), pp. 163-181; M. RISSANEN, "Language of law and the development of Standard English", in: *Writing in Nonstandard English*, ed. I. TAAVITSAINEN, G. MELCHERS, and P. PAHTA (Amsterdam, 1999), pp. 189-203, at pp. 191-192.
[31] M.B. PARKES, "The literacy of the laity", in: *The Mediaeval World*, ed. D. DAICHES and A. THORLBY (London, 1973), pp. 555-577, at p. 555.

however, while the macro-level differences in the layout certainly influence the way the text is visually perceived at first glance, the present study shows that the function of various micro-level visual markers remains the same regardless of the overall visual layout, and as such the macro-level visual variation does not compromise the overall function of the text. One might, at least from a present-day perspective, consider the prose-style layout less intuitive, but the fact is that someone at some point thought this was a better way of conveying the information needed than the other way. This could be a purely pragmatic choice, on at least two levels; first of all, the prose-style requires less physical space on the page compared to the regular, list-style layout, and may thus have been perceived as a more economic way of preserving the records. Secondly, it falls in line with Parkes' statement about pragmatic literacy above, in that accounts mainly were produced for a specific function, namely that of record-keeping, and that the users of the texts thus would be less reliant on form as they would in any case be able to recognise the relevant features by way of salient micro-level pragmatic markers related to record-keeping. Based on medieval text-copying practices, where scribes often copy or translate verbatim from an exemplar, it is also not unlikely that the prose-style might have been the result of mimicking the layout of a Latin exemplar, or, as stated above, a result of following the layout that the scribe was most familiar with from other text production, both of which would also be pragmatic choices on the part of the scribe. Clearly, more work needs to be done in order to get a full picture of who used which style of layout, and why, and work is in progress for a more comprehensive study of late medieval churchwardens' accounts from around the country, as well as a full-scale study of the visual pragmatics of the London accounts.[32]

---

[32] These studies are carried out by the present author in connection with the LiTra project (*Linguistic Traces: low-frequency forms as evidence of language and population history*) at the University of Stavanger, funded by an ERC Advanced Grant awarded to professor Merja Stenroos for the period 2025-2029.

Plague on the Page: *Mise-en-page* and Visual Highlighting in the *John of Burgundy Plague Tract* from the Fourteenth to the Seventeenth Century

ALPO HONKAPOHJA

Introduction

The plague tract attributed to John of Burgundy survives in over one hundred manuscripts, including several versions in Latin, English, French, Dutch and Hebrew. In particular, John's work became the most widely circulated text dealing with the bubonic plague in medieval England and Scotland.[1] The earliest known copies of this popular text localisable to England date from the fourteenth century, while the latest ones were copied in the late sixteenth or early seventeenth century. Such a long and wide circulation provides

---

[1] See A. HONKAPOHJA and L. JONES, "From *Practica Phisicalia* to *Mandeville's Travels*: Untangling the misattributed identities and writings of John of Burgundy", *Notes and Queries* 67.1 (2020), pp. 18-27; L. JONES, "Itineraries and transformations: John of Burgundy's plague treatise", *Bulletin of the History of Medicine* 95.3 (2021), pp. 277-314; and L. JONES, *Patterns of Plague: Changing Ideas about Plague in England and France, 1348-1750* (Montreal, 2022).

Graphic Practices and Literacies in the History of English, ed. Matti PEIKOLA, Jukka TYRKKÖ, and Mari-Liisa VARILA, *Utrecht Studies in Medieval Literacy*, 61 (Turnhout: Brepols, 2025), pp. 65-103.

excellent data for studying the development of graphic literacy over the two hundred years that saw the paper revolution and the introduction of printing.

John of Burgundy Plague Tract (henceforth *JoBT*) is a short work that focuses on the causes, identification, prevention and treatment of the bubonic plague. I refer to it with the term 'tract', following Jolliffe, who uses the term for shorter texts on a particular topic and reserves the term 'treatise' for "a long and ordered work like *The Cloud of Unknowing*".[2] Even though Jolliffe's focus is on theological tracts and treatises, this distinction works equally well for medical texts.

The focus of this study is on how the text on the page is presented and how it changed in a corpus consisting of dated and dateable copies of *JoBT*. There is much we can piece together from performing a close analysis of the manuscript page. As Carroll *et al.* put it, "[r]eaders experience books as physical objects which provide visual encounters as well as linguistic content".[3] Features such as changes in script, *mise-en-page*, and rubrication were used to direct the reader's attention, providing structure for organising information. Additionally, medieval readers interacted with the books by making their own notes in the margins and the writing area. This study primarily considers text-internal graphic practices of text producers, while also including annotations made by the user.

The textual content of *JoBT* can be divided into three text types: metatext (headings, incipits and explicits), the running text and recipes.[4] This study focuses on three levels of features:

mise-en-page (how metatext and running text are laid out),
recipes (how they are visually highlighted),
additional visual highlighting of textual content.

The features are studied by examining manuscripts or facsimile representations of copies of *JoBT*. The analysis creates descriptive statistics of a range of

[2] P.S. JOLLIFFE, *A Check-List of Middle English Writings of Spiritual Guidance* (Toronto, 1974), p. 23.

[3] R. CARROLL, M. PEIKOLA, H. SALMI, J. SKAFFARI, M-L. VARILA, and R. HILTUNEN, "Pragmatics on the page: Visual text in late medieval English books", *Visual Text*, special issue of European Journal of English Studies 17.1, ed. J. KENDALL, M. PORTELA, and G. WHITE (2013), pp. 54-71, at p. 55.

[4] A. HONKAPOHJA and J. SUOMELA, "'Lexical and function words or language and text type?' Abbreviation consistency in an aligned corpus of Latin and Middle English plague treatises", *Digital Scholarship in the Humanities* 37.3 (2022), pp. 765-787, available at <https://doi.org/10.1093/llc/fqab007>.

features in copies of *JoBT*, providing information on macro-level developments, such as the change from rubrication to the use of space and script-switching, as well as highlighting what people reading and annotating the tract considered noteworthy based on marginal comments, manicules and other visual means.

John of Burgundy's Tract

John of Burgundy (also known as John of Bordeaux, or 'bearded John', '*Jehan à la barba*', '*Johannes com barba*', '*Ioannes metten Barde*') is a name that rarely gets any kind of mention in general histories of medicine. Nonetheless, the person known by it wrote a plague tract, which became by far the most common text dealing with the causes, prevention, and treatment of the bubonic plague in medieval England and elsewhere in Northern Europe. The tract survives in over one hundred copies. According to the most up-to-date list by Jones, 137 copies in total have been identified (English Long: 14, English Short: 48, Latin Long: 31, Latin Short: 8, French Long: 1, Hebrew Long: 3, Hebrew Short: 2, Dutch Long: 1, Dutch Short: 1, Latin Epistolary: 23, Approbate: 2, Other: 3).[5] Such popularity makes the tract an excellent candidate for a study such as the present one, which aims to map developments over a long period.

Despite the popularity of the work, its author remains a shadowy figure. A medical practitioner known as John of Burgundy appears to have been active in Liège (in Burgundy, present-day Belgium) during the second plague pandemic in the 1360s (*pestis secunda, pestis puerorum*). Most of the biographical details for John come from the tract itself, although it is plausible that a 1386 reference to "*Mestre Johan ale Barbe*" in property records connected to the church of the Guillemites in Liège is to him.[6] Based on the information in the earliest copies, he wrote the tract in 1365.

---

[5] JONES, "Itineraries and transformations", pp. 308-314.

[6] *Mandeville's Travels, Translated from the French of Jean d'Outremeuse. Edited from* MS. *Cotton Titus C. xvi, in the British Museum*, 2 vols, ed. P. HAMELIUS (London, 1919: EETS O.S. 153, 154), 1, pp. 2-3. Interestingly, there is a long-running confusion with Sir John Mandeville, which can be traced back to the Paris, BNF fonds français, nouvelle acquisition MS 4516, which according to the colophon was presented to the king of France in 1371. The manuscript contains French translations of both *JoBT* and *Mandeville's Travels*, which makes them the earliest dated copies of both works. See HONKAPOHJA and JONES, "From *Practica Phisicalia* to *Mandeville's Travels*", for a fuller discussion.

JoBT is not particularly distinguished from other plague tracts of the fourteenth century in terms of its content. The organisation of the tract follows models that were well established by the second epidemic. The tract follows a tripartite structure of etiology, prophylaxis and remedial therapy, which is also found in medical tracts by the likes of Jacme D'Agramont, Gentile da Foligno, Ibn Khatimah, and Abraham Caslar after the first epidemic.[7] Like other treatises of the day, John of Burgundy attributes the cause of pestilence to corrupt air, and the original version places a major emphasis on astrology. This was the response of the medical establishment to a new, lethal disease that killed people without respect to the intricate system of opposites and humoral imbalances, which, according to the prevailing theory of the medicine of the day, caused sickness.

There were likely several reasons for the widespread distribution of *JoBT* in medieval England. One possible factor is that the tract provided "a short, practical set of rules and recipes" for combating the plague.[8] Its brevity and utility made it a valuable resource for those seeking to prevent or treat the disease. Additionally, it was evidently easy to adapt and revise the tract. Throughout its textual history, various versions of the tract were made, removing outdated content, organising the text into three or four chapters, and sometimes incorporating it into longer medical anthologies.

The original longer version of *JoBT* was reworked into three separate shorter versions, all of which have survived in multiple manuscript copies. The Short Version, which became the most popular Middle English plague tract, followed the same basic structure as the longer version but focused more on prevention and treatment while shortening the discussion of causes.[9] It was also divided into chapters more explicitly than the somewhat meandering Long Version. Additionally, a verse translation with an illustration of a 'Bubo-Man' not found in any of the prose versions survives in one manuscript (see below).

The tract also survives in an Epistolary Version, recognisable by its incipit "*dilectissime frater*" ("dear brother"), which appears to have originated as a letter and was copied in over twenty manuscripts. The Epistolary Version also considerably abbreviates the contents of the Long Version, summarising the advice for avoiding pestilence and collecting all the recipes at the end. Both the Short Version and the Epistolary Version remove John's personal introduction,

---

[7] JONES, "Itineraries and transformations", p. 282.

[8] L.M. MATHESON, "Medecin sans frontieres?: The European dissemination of John of Burgundy's plague treatise", *ANQ* 18 (2005), pp. 19-30, at p. 28; see also JONES, "Itineraries and transformations" and *Patterns of the Plague*.

[9] JONES, "Itineraries and transformations", p. 286.

which gives biographical details about the author, and the astrological discussion, which must have become outdated by the fifteenth century. The resulting tracts are concise, with the Short Version only about 3000-4000 words long and the Epistolary Version being even shorter at around 1000 words. Medical practitioners or scribes could easily copy either version into booklets or on blank flyleaves.

Despite the popularity of the English Short Version in the Middle Ages, it was never published as an early modern printed edition under the name John of Burgundy. Instead, a separate translation of the Latin Long Version by Friar John Moulton inherited the tract's popularity. Moulton shortened and rearranged the tract into three chapters and framed the plague as an act of God, stressing that it was first and foremost caused by rampant sin and corruption everywhere, including in the upper echelons of the Church – which must have suited the tastes of Reformation England. This derivative work, *The Myrour or Glasse of Helthe*, appeared in several editions and seems to have found a wide readership.[10] This notwithstanding, several post-1500 manuscript copies of the English Short Version also survive, with some dating from as late as the turn of the sixteenth and seventeenth centuries. The present study will not include Moulton's adaptation but will cover the post-1500 manuscript copies of the English Short Version.

The Corpus

I have looked at altogether 31 copies of the *JoBT*, which survive in 22 manuscripts (see Table 1). This discrepancy is caused by the fact that some manuscripts contain more than one copy of the tract. The fourteenth-century MS Durham, University Library, Cosin V.IV.1 contains both a copy of the Latin Long Version and an English Long Version, as does MS Cambridge, Trinity College R.14.52. Meanwhile, manuscripts that belong to the Voigts-Sloane Sibling Group contain a section on the plague, which comprises all three versions of the treatise: Latin Long, English Short and Latin Epistolary.[11] Survival

---

[10] See G.R. KEISER, "Two medieval plague treatises and their afterlife in early modern England", *Journal of the History of Medicine and Allied Sciences* 58.3 (2003), pp. 292-324 and JONES, "Itineraries and transformations" for more detail.

[11] L.E. VOIGTS, "The 'Sloane Group': Related scientific and medical manuscripts from the fifteenth century in the Sloane Collection", *The British Library Journal* 16.1 (1990), pp. 26-57; A. HONKAPOHJA, *Alchemy, Medicine, and Commercial Book Production: A Codicological and Linguistic Study of the Voigts-Sloane Manuscript Group* (Turnhout, 2017).

of different versions of the same tract in the same manuscript provides an opportunity to compare which graphic features are specific to the codex and which result from copying the conventions of the exemplar.

The corpus used in this study was selected based on the criteria of dating: the manuscripts must have been dated with a high level of certainty, either through external features such as exact dates given in colophons, or through internal or external manuscript features that provide a *terminus a quo* or *terminus ad quem*. I only rely on palaeographical dating for manuscripts which have been dated with precision, including the very detailed catalogue descriptions for Cosin V.IV.1 by A.I. Doyle or the Catalogue by McKitterick and Beadle for MS Cambridge, Magdalene College, Pepys 878.[12] Three of the manuscripts included in this study belong to the Voigts-Sloane Group, which was the subject of my PhD thesis and subsequent monograph.[13]

Ideally, an equal number of manuscripts from all periods would have survived, but unfortunately, this is not the case. As with many Middle English texts, the number of surviving copies is the highest towards the end of the Middle Ages. Many copies of the Middle English Short Version date from the late fifteenth century, particularly its third quarter. This pattern of survival has implications for my study, as mixed Anglicana and Secretary hands from this period are notoriously difficult to date.[14] Including manuscripts based on incorrect palaeographical dating could lead to unreliable results. Therefore, I have been selective about which manuscripts to include, excluding those that can only broadly be dated to the fifteenth century.

For the first two periods, I include manuscripts that have been dated to before 1400 or copied between 1400 and 1450. In order to have a sufficient number of manuscripts from the earlier periods, I also include copies of the Long Version, as there are not enough early copies of the English Short Version. For the period between 1450 and 1475, I have been more selective and aim to include a range of manuscripts that are reasonably different from each other, including Latin and English, and Long, Short and Epistolary Versions.

---

[12] A.I. DOYLE, *CATALOGUE of Durham University Library Cosin MS V.iv.1: medical recipes*, available at
<https://reed.dur.ac.uk/xtf/view?docId=ark/32150_s19s1616306.xml>; R. MCKITTERICK and R. BEADLE, *Catalogue of the Pepys Library at Magdalen College*, 7 vols. (Bury St. Edmunds, 1992), 5: Manuscripts, part 1: Medieval, p. 3.
[13] HONKAPOHJA, *Alchemy, Medicine, and Commercial Book Production*.
[14] M.B. PARKES, *English Cursive Book Hands 1250-1500* (Oxford, 1969), p. xxv.

Table 1 The corpus.

MS	Version	Date
Before 1400		
Durham University Library, Cosin V.IV.1	Latin Long (ff. 2r-4v)	"Written in the north-east of England at the turn of the 14th/15th century".[1]
ibid.	English Long (ff. 37r-39r)	*ibid.*
Oxford, Bodleian Library, Rawlinson A.429	English Short (ff. 85v-86r)	Tables for calculating Easter for 1374 to 1402 in the same codicological unit.
1400-1450		
Lincoln Cathedral, 91 (formerly A.5.2)	English Short (ff. 300v-302r)	Lincoln Thornton copied between 1430-40.[2]
Cambridge, Emmanuel College, 69	English Short (ff. 205r-206v)	Early fifteenth century.[3]
Cambridge, Magdalene College, Pepys 878	English Short (ff. 187r-192v)	First half of the fifteenth century.[4]
London, British Library, Add. 43405	Latin Short (7v-9r)	Memoranda belonging to the abbots of Muchelney Abbey in Somerset. *JoBT* is copied followed by a deed dating from the time of Abbot John Cherde (1433-1466) and copied by the same hand. Based on names mentioned in the deed, Schofield dates it to 1444.[5]
London, British Library, Sloane 965	English Short (132r-143r)	Dated to 1449 based on astrological tables (ff. 9r-10v).
1450-1475		
Boston, Collectanea medica, Boston Medical Library, Francis A. Countway Library of Medicine, Ballard 19	Latin Long (ff. 33v-43r)	Copied in 1468 by William Ebesham for John Paston II.[6]

ibid.	English Short (ff. 43r-49r)	*ibid.*
ibid.	Latin Epistolary (ff. 49v-54v)	*ibid.*
London, British Library, Sloane 2320	Latin Long (ff. 13v-16r)	Voigts-Sloane Group: 1450s.[7]
ibid.	English Short (ff.16r-17v)	*ibid.*
ibid.	Latin Epistolary (17v-18v)	*ibid.*
Cambridge, University Library, Ll.1.18	Latin Epistolary (ff. 74r-75v)	A household miscellany associated with a collegiate community at Southwell. Most dates are from the third quarter of the fifteenth century, including for *JoBT*.[8]
ibid.	English Fragment (f. 3r)	*ibid.*
New Haven, Yale Center for British Art, Paul Mellon Collection, John Porter Manuscript	English Short (ff. 71r-72r)	Owned by John Porter, an M.P. from Worcester (fl. 1445-1485). The catalogue dates it to *c.* 1450.[9] The first text in the compilation is *Tractatus de armis* (ff. 1r-36v), a treatise on heraldry in Latin, which was compiled in 1449. It is likely that the *JoBT* copy dates slightly after 1450 rather than before.
Cambridge, Trinity College, R.14.52	English Long (ff. 153v-156v)	A large MS copied by the prolific Hammond scribe. Mooney narrows down the date of its copying to 1458 and 1468.[10]
ibid.	English Short (ff. 156v-158r)	*ibid.*

Plague on the Page 73

1475-1500		
Cambridge, Gonville & Caius College, 336/725	Latin Long (ff. 149v-153r)	Voigts-Sloane Group, Gonville & Caius 336/725, which can be dated to the 1480s or 1490s for the 1475-1500 subperiod.
ibid.	English Short (ff. 148v-150v)	*ibid.*
ibid.	Latin Epistolary (ff. 156r-157v)	*ibid.*
Oxford, Bodleian Library, Wood D.8	English Short (ff. 247v-251v)	Copied by Thomas Ponteshyde, rector of Blisland in Cornwall, who copied the MS in 1484-85, according to colophons.[11]
London, British Library, Egerton 2572, "guildbook of barber-surgeons of York"	English Short (ff. 67r-69r)	BL Egerton MS 2572, the Guild Book of Barber-Surgeons of York, in which *JoBT* is part of the 'Medieval Core', which can be dated to 1486.[12]
1500-1550		
Cambridge, Fitzwilliam Museum, 261	English Short (ff. 23r-26v)	Based on heraldry, we can identify the MS as belonging to Lady Margaret Beaufort (d. 1509), the mother of Henry VII.[13]
Oxford, Bodleian Library, Rawlinson A.393	English Short (ff. 95r-96r)	Rawlinson A.393 belongs to the reign of Henry VIII. Keiser dates it to 1528-29.[14]
London, British Library, Sloane 776	English Short (ff. 267v-271r)	Commissioned by the London-based barber-surgeon Nicholas White from the scribe Nicholas Browne in 1532, according to a colophon.

Cambridge, Trinity College, O.8.29	English Short (ff. 29r-32r)	An early modern copy of *JoBT* is bound together with fifteenth-century astronomical tables with text in Latin and Dutch.
After 1550		
London, British Library, Sloane 2507	English Short (ff. 10r-11v)	A short surgical MS, which includes three texts: the short version of John of Burgundy tract (ff. 1-20), *Thesaurus Pauperum* by Peter of Spain (fl. 13th century) and the Antidotary of Lanfrank' surgery.
London, British Library, Lansdowne 285	English Short (ff. 214r-214v)	Copied by Sir William Dethick (1542-1612), a heraldic officer and a member of the Society of Antiquaries founded by William Camden and Sir Robert Bruce Cotton.
London, British Library, Sloane 1588	English Short (281r-282v)	A copy from the turn of the sixteenth and seventeenth centuries, owned and annotated by Sir Edmund King (*c.* 1630-1709).

Notes to Table 1:

[1] See DOYLE, *Durham Catalogue*.

[2] J.J. THOMPSON, "The compilre in action: Robert Thornton and the 'Thornton Romances' in Lincoln Cathedral MS 91", in: *Manuscripts and Readers in Fifteenth-Century England*, ed. D. PEARSALL (Woodbridge, 1983), pp. 113-124; J.J. THOMPSON, *Robert Thornton and the London Thornton Manuscript* (Woodbridge, 1987).

[3] L.E. VOIGTS and M.R. MCVAUGH, "A Latin technical phlebotomy and its Middle English translation", *Transactions of the American Philkosophical Society: Held at Philadelphia for Promoting Useful Knowledge* 74.2 (1984), pp. 1-69.

[4] MCKITTERICK and BEADLE, *Catalogue*.

[5] *Muchelney Memoranda*, ed. B. SCHOFIELD (Somerset, 1927), pp. XLII, 11.

[6] A.I. DOYLE, "The work of a late-fifteenth century English scribe, William Ebesham", *Bulletin of the John Eylands Library, Manchester* 39 (1956), pp. 298-325.

[7] See VOIGTS, "The 'Sloane Group'"; HONKAPOHJA, *Alchemy, Medicine, and Commercial Book Production*.

Notes to Table 1 continued:

[8] R. BEADLE, "Cambridge University Library, MS LL.1.18: A Southwell miscellany", in: *Pursuing Middle English Manuscripts and Their Texts: Essays in Honour of Ralph Hanna*, ed. S. HOROBIN and A. NAFDE (Turnhout, 2017), pp. 99-112, at pp. 100, 104.
[9] See <https://collections.britishart.yale.edu/catalog/orbis:9470413>.
[10] L.R. MOONEY, "The scribe", in: *Sex, Aging, & Death in a Medieval Medical Compendium: Trinity College Cambridge MS. 14.52, Its Texts, Language, and Scribe*, ed. M.T. TAVORMINA (Tempe, AZ, 2006), pp. 55-63.
[11] G.R. KEISER, "Practical books for the gentleman", in: *The Cambridge History of the Book in Britain*, ed. L. HELLINGA and J.B. TRAPP, 7 vols. (Cambridge, 1999), 3, pp. 470-494, at pp. 476-477.
[12] *The Guild Book of the Barbers and Surgeons of York (British Library, Egerton MS 2572): Study and Edition*, ed. R.D. WRAGG (York, 2021), p. 1.
[13] F. WORMALD and P.M. GILES, *A Descriptive Catalogue of the Additional Illuminated Manuscripts in the Fitzwilliam Museum*, 2 vols. (Cambridge, 1982), 1, p. 196.
[14] G.R. KEISER, "MS. Rawlinson A. 393: Another Findern manuscript", *Transactions of the Cambridge Bibliographical Society* 7.4 (1980), pp. 445-448, at p. 446.

Methodology

The aim of this study is to provide an overall description of the evolution of *mise-en-page* and visual highlighting in handwritten copies of *JoBT* from the late fourteenth century to the turn of the sixteenth and seventeenth century. To achieve this, I employed a combination of quantitative and qualitative research methods.

In a first step, I conducted a close examination of manuscript copies and facsimiles of all the manuscripts included in the study to create a database of features for analysis (see the following sections for a detailed breakdown and Appendices 1-4 for the full data set).[15] Given the varying numbers of texts across different periods, I normalised the data to allow for meaningful comparisons. Specifically, I added up the number of manuscripts manifesting a particular codicological feature and divided it by the total number of manuscripts in each period. This approach provides simple descriptive statistics that show the proportion of each feature present in texts from the same period, rather than raw numbers.

To supplement the quantitative analysis, I carried out a qualitative analysis in which I verified the results through close reading. Furthermore, I have con-

[15] I am grateful to the British Academy, which supplied a small grant. Grant number NK1819\190000.

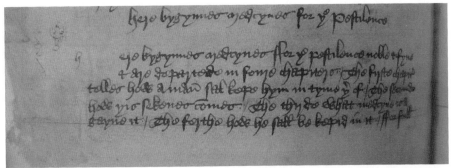

Fig. 1   A small skull drawn in the margin, presumably by Robert Thornton. MS Lincoln, Cathedral 91, f. 300v. Photo courtesy of Lincoln Cathedral.

textualised my findings in relation to other manuscripts and secondary literature.

The analysis and discussion takes place on three levels:

- *mise-en-page* (how the tract is laid out),
- visual highlighting of recipes, and
- additional visual highlighting of textual content.

While *JoBT* is plain-looking and utilitarian, I have also noted any relevant illustrations. Notably, the text does not feature any standard diagrams or illustrations that would be copied as a part of the text.

Illustrations in the JoBT

The *JoBT* did not feature a programme of illustrations which would have become standard for the Long, Short or Epistolary Versions of the work. While a few manuscripts contain illustrations, these are specific to those manuscripts and do not appear to have been copied into others. Only two manuscript copies feature figurative illustrations related to the plague: a skull in the margin of Lincoln 91 (see Figure 1), and a 'Bubo-Man' found in the apparently unique copy of the verse translation of the work (Figure 2). Later deluxe manuscripts of *JoBT* sometimes include decorations in the margins, but these do not seem related to the topic of the plague. For example, the owner of Fitzwilliam 261 can be identified as Lady Margaret Beaufort, based on the fact that "[t]he Beau-

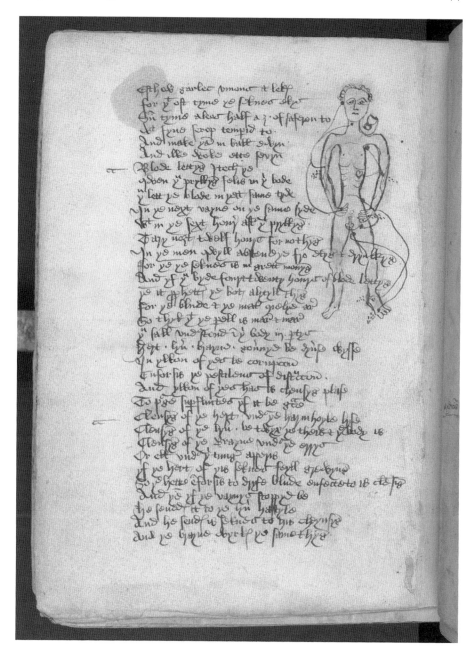

Fig. 2 The Bubo-Man. MS London, British Library, Egerton 1624, f. 216v. Photo Courtesy of the British Library.

fort badge, a portcullis, appears four times in the border together with the dragon gules and greyhound argent used as supporters by Henry VII".[16]

MS Lincoln 91, which is also known as the 'Lincoln Thornton', is a rather well-known manuscript, since we know it was copied by Robert Thornton, a Yorkshire gentleman who compiled a collection of romances and other literary texts for himself, *c.* 1330-140. The manuscript also contains a medical anthology as the final item, which was edited by Ogden as *Liber de diversis medicinis*.[17] This anthology also contains the Short English Version of *JoBT*, introduced with the heading "*here begynnes medycynes for y(e) pestilence*". Thornton left space for a coloured initial, but it was never added (this is different from the literary part of the manuscript). However, there is also a small skull, which may very well have been drawn by Thornton himself.

A much more interesting illustration is found in Egerton 1624, which contains a verse translation of *JoBT* copied in a Northern dialect. This manuscript contains a somewhat amateurish male figure copied into the margins of the tract, showing where to lance the buboes. As the *JoBT* explains, these would appear in the neck, armpits or groin – which we now know are the sites of lymph nodes. 'Bubo-men', which seem to have developed from Zodiac men and bloodletting men, are a feature of German medical tracts.[18] It is unclear whether the Northern poetic version of *JoBT* in Egerton 1624 had a connection to Germany. However, given that Northern England and Scotland were part of the Hansa trade network around the Baltic Sea and the North Sea, there is no specific reason why German influence could not have come via Northern ports. Nonetheless, if the bubo man represented innovation or the use of a German model, it did not become a part of the *JoBT* textual tradition as it remained a one-off curiosity.

Mise-en-page

According to Oxford Reference,

---

[16] WORMALD and GILES, *A Descriptive Catalogue*, p. 196.

[17] *Liber de Diversis Medicinis*, ed. M. OGDEN (London, 1938: EETS O.S. 207).

[18] L. JONES, "Bubo men? Repurposing medieval anatomic illustrations for plague therapy in the fifteenth and sixteenth centuries", in: *Death and Disease in the Medieval and Early Modern World: Perspectives from across the Mediterranean and Beyond*, ed. L. JONES and N. VARLIK (Cambridge, 2022), pp. 221-246.

Mise-en-page (the French expression means 'putting-on-the-page') is the physical arrangement of the text – e.g. features such as indentation, columns, spaces between paragraphs, etc. – but not the selection of words themselves".[19]

In order to study the evolution of *mise-en-page* in the *JoBT* manuscripts, I noted the following features for each manuscript:

- Is the main title on a separate line or part of the same text block as the running text?
- Is more than one colour ink used?
- Does the manuscript contain decorated capitals, including both historiated initials and simpler capitals supplied by the rubricator? I also noted if the scribe left a space for them, but the capital was not supplied.
- Are *litterae notabiliores* (defined as slightly larger minuscule letters, also highlighted by the rubricator) used?
- Are paraphs used? What colour are they?
- Is a different script used for metatext and the running text?
- Are marginal headings used to introduce chapters?
- Is underlining used for metatext?

In addition, while it is not strictly speaking a *mise-en-page* feature, I noted code-switching for metatext such as chapter headings.

Recipes

The second feature I focused on were the recipes, which are an easily identifiable text type characterised by their function of giving instructions and by "obligatory linguistic features and formulas".[20] Recipes can be recognised based on linguistic cues, as well as by specific visual features. They often begin with the Latin abbreviation ℞ (meaning 'recipe') and may include apothecaries' weights such as ʒ (for 'drachm'), β (for 'semis [half]'), or formulaic abbreviations like *an^a* (instructing to add the same amount of an ingredient as previously). I also noted whether any forms of visual highlighting were used to set

---

[19] *Oxford Reference*, available at <https://www.oxfordreference.com/view/10.1093/oi/authority.20110810105417351>.
[20] R. CARROLL, "The Middle English recipe as a text-type", *Neuphilologische Mitteilungen* 100 (1999), pp. 27-42, at p. 27.

them apart from the running text. In the data set, I noted three features for each recipe:

- Does the recipe begin with the ℞ abbreviation?
- Are precise measurements and apothecaries' weights used?
- How is the recipe visually separated from the running text?

Additional Visual Highlighting of Textual Content

The final feature I analysed was additional visual highlighting of content within the tract. This refers to various features that can draw attention to different elements of the text, such as marginal comments, Latin *notae* in the margins, manicules, underlining, script-switching, and other means used for visual highlighting. I excluded features that are part of the *mise-en-page*, focusing instead on additional means used to direct the reader's attention to the content of the text. I use the term 'visual highlighting' as an umbrella term, following Kaislaniemi, to refer to these features.[21] In addition, I paid attention to script-switching, defined by Kaislaniemi as "visual highlighting [...] achieved through changing the type of writing (the script or typeface)".[22]

- Are there marginal comments (considered separate from marginal headings)? What do they comment on?
- Are Latin *notae* used in the margins to call attention to parts of the text?
- Are manicules used to call attention to parts of the text?
- Is underlining used for highlighting other sections of the text than metatext or recipes?
- Is script-switching used to highlight words in the text?
- Are any other means used for visual highlighting?

As a part of highlighting, I will also note the appearance of reference devices in these manuscripts, such as indexes.

---

[21] S. KAISLANIEMI, "Code-switching, script-switching, and typeface-switching in Early Modern English manuscript letters and printed tracts", in: *Verbal and Visual Communication in Early English Texts*, ed. M. PEIKOLA, A. MÄKILÄHDE, H. SALMI, M.-L. VARILA, and J. SKAFFARI (Turnhout, 2017), pp. 165-200, at p. 173.

[22] KAISLANIEMI, "Code-switching, script-switching, and typeface-switching", p. 174.

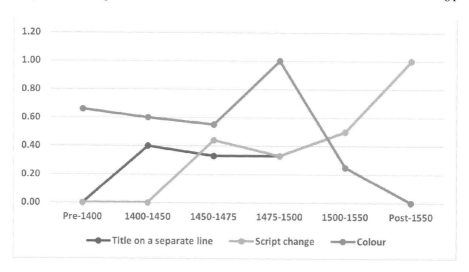

Fig. 3   Development of some *mise-en-page* features.

Results

For the following, please consult also the appendices at the end of this article.

Mise-en-page

Continuity and change are both evident in the *mise-en-page* of *JoBT* copies. Figure 3 illustrates features which display some of the biggest changes.

One feature that shows clear increase is the use of a separate line for metatext. Prior to 1400, no *JoBT* copy had the title on a separate line. However, by the final period, all texts had some space before and after headings. The change was not complete until the late sixteenth century. Between 1500 and 1550, only two out of four manuscripts had space before and after the metatext. It is worth noting that the two manuscripts representing older practices, Fitzwilliam 261 (copied for Margaret Beaufort, d. 1509) and Rawlinson A.393 (copied by an ageing scribe in an Anglicana script conservative for the 1520s), were both early in the period.

Similarly, with script-switching, Fitzwilliam 261 and Rawlinson A.393 stand out by not featuring script-switching to make metatextual divisions. Two other manuscripts from 1500 to 1550 used script-switching to mark divisions. After 1550, all manuscripts used more than one script. In the period from 1500 to 1550, only two out of four manuscripts used more than one script, but these are the same two, Fitzwilliam 261 and Rawlinson A.393, that exhibit continuity with medieval graphic practices.

While there is continuity and change in *mise-en-page* features of *JoBT* copies, there are some differences in the earlier period regarding the use of space between metatext and running text and script-switching. In fact, script-switching is not attested in a single manuscript before 1450, which suggests that this feature, deemed crucial for early modern correspondence and printing by Kaislaniemi, emerged only in the late medieval period.[23]

On the other hand, some graphic practices disappeared by the final period. One of the main ones is the use of colour, as manuscripts in the final period (post-1550) do not use coloured ink at all. They are also all copied on paper. The only manuscript to contain colour after 1500 is Fitzwilliam 261, which is a deluxe manuscript owned by a royal patron and may have a date prior to 1500.

The use of coloured ink reached its peak in the final quarter of the fifteenth century. This is the period when deluxe manuscripts became prevalent in the twenty-five years after the printing press. During this period, people who could afford to commission hand-copied books did so to showcase their wealth. Examples of deluxe manuscripts include Gonville & Caius 336/725 and Egerton 2572 (Barber-Surgeons MS). However, two other deluxe manuscripts, Sloane 965 and Fitzwilliam 261, may date slightly earlier or later by ten years. Sloane can be dated to 1449 based on astrological tables, and Fitzwilliam to pre-1509 (by Margaret Beaufort's death). The period of the most luxurious *JoBT* production was thus close to the second half of the fifteenth century and peaking in the last quarter.

The use of *litterae notabiliores* falls out of use with that of coloured ink. By the sixteenth century, they were not used at all. Similarly, the practice of underlining to mark textual divisions and metatext also decreased. Post-1500, it is only found in two of the earliest manuscripts, Fitzwilliam 261 and Rawlinson A.393.

Post-1500 manuscripts are generally more workmanlike, being copied in cursive Secretary hands on paper without rubrication or the careful professional

---

[23] KAISLANIEMI, "Code-switching, script-switching, and typeface-switching".

book hands of medieval manuscripts. However, some manuscripts from the period 1500 to 1550 continued to adhere to medieval practices. For instance, Sloane 776, which was copied by the professional scribe Nicholas Browne for the barber-surgeon Charles White in 1532, has unused spaces for decorated initials. Compared to the rest of the manuscript, *JoBT* is sparse. The manuscript also contains copies of John of Arderne's *Practica* and *Experimenta*, which White seems to have regarded as its main contents, as in his 1545 will he refers to it as his "John of Ardren". The copies of Arderne are "profusely illustrated in ink and colour wash".[24] Rawlinson A.393 also contains unused space for decorated initials. Since Fitzwilliam 261 has decorated capitals, this means that most of the manuscripts in the first half of the sixteenth century contain this feature. However, none of the copies dating after 1550 contain this feature.

The level of decoration and visual aids can vary between different versions of the same text in the same manuscript. For example, Cosin V.IV.1, which is possibly the earliest English *JoBT* MS surviving, contains both a Latin and English Long Version, which are copied by the same scribe.[25] However, in the English Long Version, the rubricator supplied simple red capitals, paraphs, and underlined metatextual passages in red, whereas the Latin copy is completely plain. This may suggest that the scribe copied decoration from the exemplar or that the decoration programme was not necessarily specific to the codex. Cambridge University Library (CUL) Ll 1.18 has marginal headings in the English Long Version, but not in the Latin version. It is, however, codicologically much more complex, comprising "the remains of fifteen gatherings (now bound as sixteen), of widely varying lengths", which "fall into several distinct groups of the kind commonly designated as booklets".[26]

There are also a few visual features in which the picture is a much more mixed one. These include marginal headings, which are not all that common throughout the period. We can find them in Emmanuel 69 (1400-1450), Sloane 2320, CUL Ll.1.18 and Trinity R.14.52 (1450-1475), which have them, as does Sloane 2507 (post-1550).

With code-switching, the version and translation seem to matter more than diachronic developments. Matheson identified as many as six different translations for the English Short Version.[27] Latin passages in Middle English texts

---

[24] P.M. JONES "John Arderne's afterlife in manuscript and print", in: *Genre in English Medical Writing, 1500-1820: Sociocultural Contexts of Production and Use*, ed. I. TAAVITSAINEN, T. HILTUNEN, J.J. SMITH, and C. SUHR (Cambridge, 2022), pp. 13-31, at p. 16.
[25] DOYLE, *Durham Catalogue*.
[26] BEADLE, "A Southwell miscellany", p. 100.
[27] MATHESON, "Medecin sans frontieres", p. 23.

can be found in several manuscripts from different periods, including Cosin V.IV.1 (pre-1400), Pepys 878 and Sloane 965 (1400-1450), Ballard 19, Sloane 2320, CUL Ll.1.18, Trinity R.14.52 (1450-1475), Gonville & Caius 336/725 (1475-1500), Fitzwilliam 261, Rawlinson A.393 and Trinity O.8.29 (1500-1550) as well as in all three post-1550 manuscripts. The use of Latin neither increases nor decreases over two centuries. Using code-switching in post-1500 copies occurs in manuscripts that are closely related textually.[28]

In summary, there is a shift towards using layout and script rather than rubrication to indicate textual divisions. This trend begins before the advent of printing, possibly related to the 'paper revolution' of the fifteenth century, although obtaining comprehensive statistics on paper usage is challenging. Studies suggest that paper became more widely available and affordable during this period, which may have led to the increased use of space to indicate textual divisions.

Recipes

The use of measurements in *JoBT* copies is largely determined by the version of the text. None of the recipes in Short Versions of the tract have precise measurements, but rather provide a list of ingredients. English and Latin Short Versions also do not contain the ℞ abbreviation, which is used to mark the beginning of a recipe. The two English Long Versions included in the data set contain exact measurements, but they also do not make use of the ℞. It seems that language and version determined the use of this abbreviation. Specifically, it is only found in the Latin copies of the tract.

In terms of marking the beginning of a recipe, one manuscript stands out as unique. The post-1550 Sloane 2507 uses *viz.* in front of the lists of ingredients, which seems to be an innovation, as it does not have a parallel in any of the other sixteen copies of the English Short Version. It is worth noting that Sloane 2507 is one of the sixteenth-century copies that were likely owned by a medical practitioner, so the use of *viz.* may have been a professional practice at the time.

---

[28] See A. HONKAPOHJA, "Tracing the Early Modern John of Burgundy", in: *Genre in English Medical Writing, 1500-1820: Sociocultural Contexts of Production and Use*, ed. I. TAAVITSAINEN, T. HILTUNEN, J.J. SMITH, and C. SUHR (Cambridge, 2022), pp. 68-88, Table 5.2.

Plague on the Page 85

Table 2 Apothecaries' weights in recipes

Version	Number of copies	℞	Apothecaries' weights
Latin Long	3	3	3
English Long	2	0 ('Take' in expanded English)	2
Latin Short	1	0	0
English Short	17	0	0
Latin Epistolary	4	3	3

Some manuscripts employ additional visual highlighting to differentiate recipes from the rest of the text. Underlining is the most common method, seen in Rawlinson A.429, Sloane 2320 and Fitzwilliam 261. In the Yale Porter manuscript, recipes are marked with small Latin *notae* in the margins. Sloane 2507 uses script-switching for ingredients. The English Long Version in Cosin V.IV.1 features decorated initials and coloured paraphs at the beginning of each recipe. Interestingly, the Latin copy in the same manuscript has no rubrication at all, providing a striking contrast.

However, in the vast majority of manuscripts (twenty-six in total), recipes are not given any special treatment by scribes or rubricators. In thirteen copies, recipes begin with paraphs, appearing as paragraphs on the same level as the main text. In another thirteen copies, they are not highlighted at all. Despite the lack of emphasis by the scribes and rubricators, recipes still appear to have been of interest to readers, as they were often highlighted by later annotators.

Table 3 Visual highlighting of recipes

Period	Recipes not highlighted	Recipes highlighted	Recipes highlighted by a later hand
pre-1400	Cosin V.IV.1 (Latin Long): nothing Cosin V.IV.1 (English Long): red paraphs only	Rawlinson A.429: red underlining and paraphs	
1400-1450	Lincoln 91: recipes have their own paragraphs Emmanuel 69: nothing		Sloane 965: even though recipes are not highlighted, a later hand has listed their ingredients in the mar-

	Pepys 878: nothing BL Add. 43405: nothing		gins (ff. 141r, 143r), also adding a small cross at the spot where the recipe begins; on f. 141r there is also a manicule pointing to the recipe.
1450-1475		$Sloane 2320: faint scribal underlining – a faint vertical line in margin close to a recipe (ff. 14v, 17v) Yale, Porter MS: small *notae* in margins	Ballard 19: (f. 39v), a non-scribal hand comments on a recipe. Sloane 2320: a manicule pointing to a recipe (f. 17v). Trinity R.14.52: extensive marginal comments, including on recipes (ff. 155r, 155v); a manicule pointing towards a recipe (f. 157v).
1475-1500	Gonville & Caius 336/725: only paraphs Wood D.8: red paraphs and underlinings, but the treatment of recipes does not differ from other paragraphs. Egerton 2572 'Guildbook of Barber-Surgeons of York': nothing		
1500-1550	Sloane 776: nothing Trinity O.8.29: nothing	Fitzwilliam 261: ingredients underlined in red	Rawlinson 393: marginal comments, including "*sepi(us) probatu(m) bo (num)*" ('often tried good') (f. 7v).

| post-1550 | Lansdowne 285: nothing | Sloane 2507: ingredients highlighted by script change (f. 11v) | |
| | Sloane 1588: nothing | | |

Additional Visual Highlighting of Recipes and Other Textual Content

Although recipes are often not visually distinguished from the running text in most manuscripts, they frequently receive marginal comments from later readers. For example, in Sloane 965, a later annotating hand listed ingredients in the margins and added a small cross or a manicule pointing to the recipes (ff. 141r, 143r). Similarly, in the Latin Version in Ballard 19, a non-scribal hand made a comment on a recipe, though it has been partly lost due to cropping. In Sloane 2320 (Latin Long), recipes receive visual highlighting through various means, such as manicules, marginal comments and faint scribal underlining. There are also faint vertical lines in the margins close to recipes to draw attention to them (ff. 14v, 17v).

Even though marginal comments are often associated with recipes, there are also other types of content that receive annotations. In Ballard 19, which was copied by William Ebesham, the rubricator (likely Ebesham himself) added a red manicule pointing towards the phrase "*et super omnia caveas coitum*" ("and above all avoid sexual intercourse"), which was considered dangerous during the plague, as it opened the pores of the body and allowed pestilential air to enter.[29] Rawlinson A.393, copied by Sir John Reed, an active annotator throughout the manuscript, includes a record of the actual treatment of the plague in its margin. Here, he summarises typical advice against the plague and finishes with the phrase "*sepius probatum bonum*" ("often tried good").[30] In Sloane 2507's utilitarian and workmanlike copy of *JoBT* (Figure 4), the annotator has listed the three main cleansing places of the body (heart, liver, and *harnes*, 'the brain') using Arabic numerals. He also added a manicule and the comment "*this is wrought by ivell ayer*". The marginal annotations make use of script-switching, using Italic instead of Secretary for the main text.

Some of the longer medical texts show signs of extensive use. For example Sloane 1588, which belonged to Sir Edmund King (d. 1709), contains records

---

[29] See HONKAPOHJA, *Alchemy, Medicine, and Commercial Book Production*.
[30] For a more detailed discussion, see HONKAPOHJA, "Tracing the Early Modern John of Burgundy", p. 77.

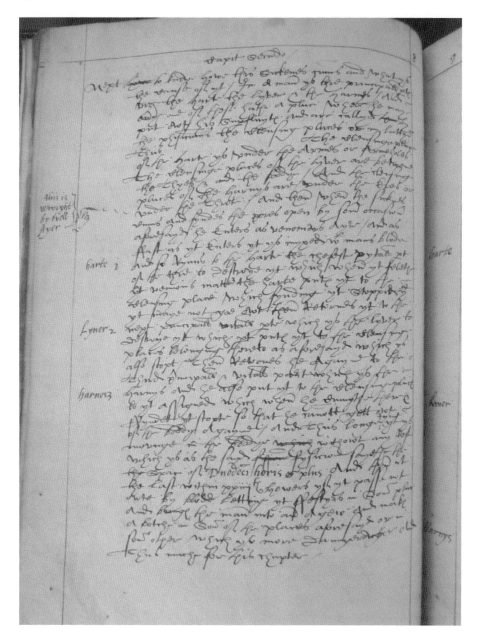

Fig. 4 Marginal comments. MS London, British Library, Sloane 2507, f. 10v. Photo courtesy of the British Library.

of his cures and annotations, although there is no evidence that he made use of or took an interest in *JoBT*. Gonville & Caius 336/725, a deluxe volume containing the Voigts-Sloane Sibling Set Text, contains numerous annotations throughout the volume, but they do not extend to the three *JoBT* copies in the book. In contrast, Trinity R.14.52, another actively annotated large codex, contains various comments on the two copies of *JoBT*. They were also copied in the fifteenth century into Trinity O.8.29.

Tables of Contents and Indices

In the final period, indices as reference devices become increasingly prevalent. Here it is useful to refer to the work of Scase, who distinguishes between codex-specific tables, which are specific to a particular codex, and non-codex-specific tables, which can be reproduced across manuscripts.[31] It is in the latter type of tables that we see developments in later copies of *JoBT*.

Tertia notha	Bastarde tertiane	233
Quartana	Ffeuer quartayne	235
Quotidiana	Quotidiane feuer	239
Hectica febris	Hectique feuer	242
Semitertiana	Semitise feuer	245
Pestilentia	**Plague or pestilence**	248

Fig. 5　The list of contents in MS London, British Library, Sloane 1588, f. 5r.

Two manuscripts from the post-1550 period that appear to have been used actively for medical purposes feature helpful indexes: Sloane 1588 (Figure 5), which belonged to Edmund King, and Sloane 2507 (Figure 6). Sloane 1588 includes an index of various topics with a Latin term on the left and an English

---

[31] W. SCASE, "'Looke this calender and then proced': Tables of contents in medieval English manuscripts", in: *The Dynamics of the Medieval Manuscript: Text Collections from a European Perspective*, ed. K. PRATT, B. BESAMUSCA, M. MEYER, and A. PUTTER. (Göttingen, 2017), pp. 287-306, at p. 291.

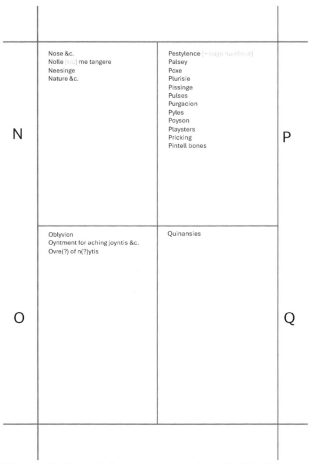

Fig. 6 Subject index in MS London, British Library, Sloane 2507, ff. 3v-4r.

paraphrase on the right with the corresponding page numbers. *JoBT* is listed under the reference term "*pestilentia: plague or pestilence*". It is only one of several texts and recipes related to the disease. In each section, there are blank pages following the texts, allowing for additional texts to be copied. This is an example of what Scase refers to as an open system, which was "devised to enable the work of compilation and access to information to continue".[32]

Similarly, Sloane 2507 (Figure 6) contains a subject index that is an open system and shows active engagement with the text. Someone organised it al-

---

[32] SCASE, "Looke this calender", p. 298.

phabetically, with space to add topics under each letter. Section *P* contains the headword *Pestylence* with page numbers that match the tract in the codex.

These examples illustrate the development of reference tools in copies of *JoBT* during the late sixteenth century. It is noteworthy that despite not appearing in print, the tract continued to be regarded as medically relevant rather than being considered as simply antiquarian.[33]

Conclusion

To conclude, *JoBT* is a noteworthy medical text that has survived in a whole range of manuscript contexts during a period of over two hundred years. Investigating this text demonstrates how a single tract evolved over time, reflecting significant changes and innovations that impacted how the text was laid out on the manuscript page. Interestingly, unlike some other medical texts such as John of Arderne's *Fistula in ano*, *JoBT* was not accompanied by a standard programme of illustrations. However, one manuscript, containing an apparently unique verse translation of the Latin Long Version, does exhibit innovation by incorporating a Bubo-man, but it did not get included in other prose versions of *JoBT*.

Perhaps the most significant development over time was a gradual shift from a medieval rubrication-based system to one in which metatextual divisions were indicated by space, a development that was complete by 1550. This shift was likely related to the paper revolution, which made writing supports more affordable. The printing press and the changes that occurred with the book industry may also have had an effect, as the traditional industry based around artisans copying and illuminating books gradually died out.

Another development that emerged over time was the increased use of script-switching, likely used to compensate for the loss of earlier practices such as coloured underlining or using differently coloured scripts. Switching between Roman and blackletter typefaces was also common in printed books, but in the present data, the practice appears after 1450, which does not support the notion that the practice would have been adopted from printed books.

JoBT reached its peak popularity during the period from 1450 to 1500, during which the Short English Version in particular can be found in multiple manuscript contexts. The tract also survives in as many as five deluxe copies made between 1449 and 1509. This phenomenon is indicative of the traditional

---

[33] See HONKAPOHJA, "Tracing the Early Modern John of Burgundy".

book industry's last surge, as luxurious manuscripts were still being produced after 1475. Wealthy individuals sought to flaunt their ability to purchase handmade books, resulting in lavish decoration and embellishments. By contrast, all three MSS post-dating 1550 are copied on paper in messy Elizabethan Secretary hands, which in two instances seem to belong to a medical practitioner and in one instance to an antiquarian.

Recipes are sometimes but not consistently highlighted to stand out from the text. Perhaps somewhat surprisingly, in most manuscripts they did not receive any kind of special emphasis from scribes or rubricators. Despite not receiving consistent highlighting, the recipes in *JoBT* were highly valued by their users, as is shown by the numerous marginal comments made by them. Furthermore, the final period of *JoBT*'s copying saw the development of good indices, which helped readers to locate texts or specific terms easily and testify to the continued relevance of the tract after 1550.

Although this survey has focused only on those copies of *JoBT* that could be dated with considerable confidence, it provides valuable descriptive statistics on important changes in *mise-en-page* that occurred over time. This is relevant for graphic literacy and will hopefully provide a foundation for further codicological work.

Appendix 1. Decoration

MS	Title on separate line	Coloured ink	Decorated capitals	Litterae notabiliores	Paraphs
Pre-1400					
Cosin V.IV.1 (Latin long, ff. 2r-4v)	No	No	No	No	No
ibid. (English long, ff. 37r-39r)	No	Red for paraphs, underlining and capitals	Yes	Yes	Red
Rawlinson A.429	No	Red for paraphs and underlining	No	Yes	Red

1400-1450					
Lincoln 91 (formerly A.5.2)	Yes: for the treatise	No	Space for caps not used	No	No
Emmanuel 69	No	Red			No
Magdalene Pepys 878	No	Red	Red	Yes (red highlighting strokes)	Red
BL Add. 43405	No	No	Space for caps not used	No	No
Sloane 965 (ff. 132r-143r)	No	5+ colours	Yes, with gold	No	Red and blue, sometimes gilded
1450-1475					
Ballard 19 (Latin long)	No	Red for paraphs and rubrics	Blue	No	Red
ibid. (English short)	No	Red for paraphs and rubrics	Blue	No	Red
ibid. (Latin epistolary)	No	Red for paraphs and rubrics	Blue	No	Red
Sloane 2320 (Latin long, ff. 13v-16r)	Yes	Red for paraphs and capitals	Red	No	Red
ibid. (English short, ff. 16r-17v)	Yes	Red for paraphs and capitals	Red	No	Red
ibid. (Latin epistolary, ff. 17v-18v)	Yes	Red for paraphs and capitals	Red	No	Red

CUL Ll.1.18 (Latin epistolary, ff. 74r-)	Yes	No	No	No	No
ibid. (English)	defective	No	No	No	No
Yale, John Porter MS.	No	No	No	No	No
Trinity R.14.52 (English long)	No?	Red for paraphs and rubrics	Yes	Yes	Red
ibid. (English short)	No?	Red for paraphs and rubrics	Yes	Yes	Red
1475-1500					
Gonville & Caius 336/725 (ff. 149v-153r)	No	5+ colours	Yes	Yes (decorad by yellow)	Red and blue
ibid. (ff. 153v-155v)	No	5+ colours	Yes (decorated by yellow)	Yes (decorad by yellow)	Red and blue
ibid. (ff. 156r-157v)	No	5+ colours	Yes	Yes (decorated by green)	Red and blue
Wood D.8	No	Red	No	Yes	Red
Egerton 2572, "guildbook of barber-surgeons of York" (ff. 67r-69r)	No	Multiple	Yes (but modest for this text)	Yes (red highlights)	No
1500-1550					
Fitzwilliam 261	No	Red	Yes	No	Illuminated
Rawlinson A.393	No	No	Space for caps not used	No	No
Sloane 776	Yes	No	Space for caps not used	No	No

Plague on the Page

Trinity O.8.29	Yes	No	No	No	No
Post-1550					
Sloane 2507	Yes	No	No	No	No
Lansdowne 285	Yes	No	No	No	No
Sloane 1588	Yes	No	No	No	No

Appendix 2. Highlighting

MS	Code switching	Script change	Marginal headings
Pre-1400			
Cosin V.IV.1 (Latin long, ff. 2r-4v)	No	No	No
ibid. (English long, ff. 37r-39r)	Yes ("item take")	No	No
Rawlinson A.429	No	No	No
1400-1450			
Lincoln 91 (formerly A.5.2)	No	No	No
Emmanuel 69	No	No	Yes
Magdalene Pepys 878	Yes[1]	No	No
BL Add. 43405	No	No	No
Sloane 965 (ff. 132r-143r)	Yes[2]	No	No
1450-1475			
Ballard 19 (Latin long)	No	No	No

ibid. (English short)	Yes (chapter headings in Latin)	No	No
ibid. (Latin epistolary)	No	No	No
Sloane 2320 (Latin long, ff. 13v-16r)	No	Yes (decorative script for metatext)	No
ibid. (English short, ff. 16r-17v)	Yes (text incipits and explicits in Latin)	Yes (decorative script for metatext)	Yes (for chapter one in Latin)
ibid. (Latin epistolary, ff. 17v-18v)	No	Yes (decorative script for metatext)	No
CUL Ll.1.18 (Latin epistolary, ff. 74r-)	No	Yes ("*dilectissime frater*")	No
ibid. (English)	Yes (marginals)	No	Yes
Yale, John Porter MS	No	No	No
Trinity R.14.52 (English long)	Yes	Yes	Yes
ibid. (English short)	Yes	No	Yes
1475-1500			
Gonville & Caius 336/725 (ff. 149v-153r)	No	No	No
ibid. (ff. 153v-155v)	Yes (chapter headings)	No	No
ibid. (ff. 156r-157v)	No	No	No

Wood D.8	No	Different script for marginal comments	English
Egerton 2572 "guildbook of barber-surgeons of York" (ff. 67r-69r)	No	Yes (decorative script for headings)	No
1500-1550			
Fitzwilliam 261	Yes	No	No
Rawlinson A.393	Yes	No	No
Sloane 776	No	Yes	No
Trinity O.8.29	Headings in Latin	Yes	No
Post-1550			
Sloane 2507	Headings in Latin, sexual terms in Latin, names of veins, ingredients in recipes	Yes (English in Secretary, Latin in italic)	Yes (cleansing places of the body listed in the margin with Arabic numerals)
Lansdowne 285	Only heading	Yes (English in Secretary, Latin heading in italic)	No
Sloane 1588	Only explicit in Latin. Indicated by script change	Yes (English in Secretary, Latin heading in italic)	No

[1] Occasional Latin phrases. In recipes Latin names provided for some ingredients with .i. flagging.

[2] Chapter headings, Cap. i. Taboo switching in Latin and rubricated, Latin technical names for medical terms, beginning .i. (f. 140).

Appendix 3. Recipes

MS	R+ abbreviation	Apothecaries' weights	How are recipes separated?
Pre-1400			
Cosin V.IV.1 (Latin long, ff. 2r-4v)	Yes	Yes	Nothing
ibid. (English long, ff. 37r-39r)	No ("Take" in English)	Yes	Its own paragraph beginning with coloured initial
Rawlinson A.429	No ("also it es gude")	No	Red underlining and paraph
1400-1450			
Lincoln 91 (formerly A.5.2)	No ("Take" in English)	No	own paragraphs
Emmanuel 69	No	No	Nothing
Magdalene Pepys 878	No	No	Nothing
BL Add. 43405	No ("Take" in English)	No	Nothing
Sloane 965 (ff. 132r-143r)	No	No	Nothing
1450-1475			
Ballard 19 (Latin long)	Yes	Yes	Paraphs (but Ebesham is pretty sparing in their use)
ibid. (English short)	No	No	Paraphs (but Ebesham is pretty sparing in their use)
ibid. (Latin epistolary)	No (spelled out)	Yes (but spelled out)	Paraphs (but Ebesham is pretty sparing in their use)
Sloane 2320 (Latin long, ff. 13v-16r)	Yes		Paraphs

Plague on the Page

Sloane 2320 (English short, ff. 16r-17v)	No	No	Paraphs
Sloane 2320 (Latin epistolary, ff. 17v-18v)	Yes	Yes (but always spelled out, except once)	Paraphs
CUL Ll.1.18 (Latin epistolary, ff. 74r-)	Yes	Yes	Nothing
ibid. (English)	No	No	Nothing
Yale, John Porter MS	No	No	Small nota in margins
Trinity R.14.52 (English long)	No	Yes (but spelled out)	Paraphs
ibid. (English short)	No	No	Paraphs
1475-1500			
Gonville & Caius 336/725 (ff. 149v-153r)	Yes	Yes	No special highlighting, but paraph in front of them as if they were paragraphs.
ibid. (ff. 153v-155v)	No	No	No special highlighting, but paraph in front of them as if they were paragraphs.
ibid. (ff. 156r-157v)	Yes	Yes (spelled out)	No special highlighting, but paraph in front of them as if they were paragraphs.
Wood D.8	No	No	Red paraphs and underlining like other paragraphs.

Egerton 2572 "guildbook of barber-surgeons of York" (ff. 67r-69r)	No	No	Nothing
1500-1550			
Fitzwilliam 261	No	No	Ingredients underlined in red
Rawlinson A.393	No ("Take" in English)	No	Nothing
Sloane 776	No	No	Nothing
Trinity O.8.29	No	No	Nothing
Post-1550			
Sloane 2507	"viz" instead of R+	No	Script change
Lansdowne 285	No	No	Nothing
Sloane 1588	No	No	Nothing

Appendix 4. Annotation by readers

MS	Manicules	Underlining	Notae (in which language?)	Marginal comments
Pre-1400				
Cosin V.IV.1 (Latin long, ff. 2r-4v)	No	No	Latin "*nota*", "*nota bene*"	One: "*imperialis*" introducing "*pulvis imperialis*"
ibid. (English long, ff. 37r-39r)	No	Yes (red), incipits	No	One: "pestilenc'"
Rawlinson A.429	No	Yes (red), first words after paraphs	In top margin before text (in red): "*nota omnia ista*"	No

Plague on the Page 101

1400-1450				
Lincoln 91 (formerly A.5.2)	No	No	Latin notae ("*nota bene*", "*nota optime*")	No
Emmanuel 69	No	Yes	No	No
Magdalene Pepys 878	No	Yes (chapter headings, code-switches and the first line of a new paragraph after the red paraph)	No	A recipe written in bottom margin after the treatise in final leaf.
BL Add. 43405	No	No	No	No
Sloane 965 (ff. 132r-143r)	Yes (in later hand, pointing to recipes)	No	No	Yes (a later hand has paraphrased recipes)
1450-1475				
Ballard 19 (Latin long)	No	Not systematically (one by hand making marginal comment)	No	Latin to mark recipes (in a later hand)
ibid. (English short)	No	No	No	No
ibid. (Latin epistolary)	Yes ("*super omnia caveas coitum*")	No	No	No

Sloane 2320 (Latin long, ff. 13v-16r)	No	Yes (weak and scribal)	No	No
ibid. (English short, ff. 16r-17v)	Yes (pointing to a recipe paraphrase, f. 17r)	Yes (weak and scribal)	No	Yes (in Latin)
ibid. (Latin epistolary, ff. 17v-18v)	No	Yes (weak and scribal)	Latin nota, indicating beginning of recipes	Yes (in Latin)
CUL MS Ll.1.18 (Latin epistolary, ff. 74r-)	No	Only explicit	Latin notae	No
ibid. (English)	No	Yes (black), ingredients	Latin	No
Yale, John Porter MS	No	Yes (black), heading and explicit	$Latin notae indicating recipes	No
Trinity R.14.52 (English long)	No	Yes (black), possibly by commentators	No?	Yes (in several hands, Latin and English)
ibid. (English short)	Yes	Yes (black), possibly by commentators	No?	Yes (in several hands, Latin and English)
1475-1500				
Gonville & Caius 336/725 (ff. 149v-153r)	No	No	No	No

ibid. (ff. 153v-155v)	No	No	No	No
ibid. (ff. 156r-157v)	No	No	No	No
Wood D.8	No	Yes (red), incipits and explicits, first words after par-aphs	No	English
Egerton 2572 "guildbook of barber-surgeons of York" (ff. 67r-69r)	No	No	No	No (only missing text added to margin by main scribe, f. 68r)
1500-1550				
Fitzwilliam 261	No	Yes (red), ingredients	Latin (illuminated)	No
Rawlinson A.393	No	Yes (black)	No	Yes (English)
Sloane 776	No	No	No	No
Trinity O.8.29	No	No	No	No
Post-1550				
Sloane 2507	Yes	No	Yes	Yes (English comments on content)
Lansdowne 285	No	No	No	No
Sloane 1588	No	No	No	No

The Pragmatics of Punctuation in Early English Medical Recipe Books[*]

JAVIER CALLE-MARTÍN and JESÚS ROMERO-BARRANCO

Introduction

A number of writers have come down to us due to their particular use of punctuation. William Faulkner, the American novelist, is well known for his decision to make the least use of punctuation marks to the extent that his novel *Absalom, Absalom* begins with a 122-word sentence that contains only one comma. His contemporary James Joyce is said to be another exponent of this concept of punctuation and, as shown in the following excerpt, commas appear nowhere in Joyce's own hand in the assumption that there is no need to punctuate to write properly, keeping punctuation marks to a minimum.[1]

---

[*] The present research has been funded by the Spanish Ministry of Science, Innovation and Universities (grant number PID2021-126496NB-100) and by the Andalusian Regional Government (grant numbers PY18-2782 and UMA18-FEDERJA-129). We are very grateful to the editors of the volume and to the reviewers, whose thoughtful comments have substantially improved the final version of the chapter. Figures 1-5 are reproduced by permission of University of Glasgow Library, Special Collections.

[1] See <https://www.openculture.com/2013/08/cormac-mccarthys-punctuation-rules.html>.

Graphic Practices and Literacies in the History of English, ed. Matti PEIKOLA, Jukka TYRKKÖ, and Mari-Liisa VARILA, *Utrecht Studies in Medieval Literacy*, 61 (Turnhout: Brepols, 2025), pp. 105-126.

BREPOLS PUBLISHERS   DOI 10.1484/M.USML-EB.5.143823

After all there's a lot in that vegetarian fine flavour of things from the earth garlic of course it stinks Italian organ grinders crisp of onions mushrooms truffles.[2]

Joyce's practice perfectly summarises the pragmatic side of punctuation, which is especially conceived by an author in light of the readers' different levels of literacy, thus contributing to meaning conveyance.[3] Pragmatics regards punctuation as part of an utterance that takes place in a specific discourse context and is, consequently, subject to variation depending on the target audience.[4] The pragmatics of punctuation, therefore, is concerned with the use and omission of punctuation symbols in particular contexts, trying to elucidate the circumstances motivating their use along with the functions of those marks in view of the genre and the target audience. Joyce in this case is perfectly aware that the prospective reader has a background solid enough to make the necessary pauses for the correct understanding of the utterance, which explains his decision to dispose of any punctuation symbols. When it comes to historical documents, and handwriting in particular, the medieval scribe also makes decisions as to when and where to punctuate for facilitating the readers' understanding of the utterance, especially in view of the fact that there was not a standard of punctuation such as we have it today.

In view of this, prior to the act of writing itself, the medieval scribe is committed to decide on the layout of the written artefact and, more importantly, on the level of compromise between the text and the audience. The first decision has to do with the dilemma between rhetorical or grammatical punctuation. While rhetorical punctuation aims to provide the text with the necessary rest points for a meaningful oral performance, grammatical punctuation signals the structural relationship between the sentence constituents in order to provide syntactic sense.[5] The issue is not straightforward and discerning the function of punctuation marks in a medieval text is often challenging. Lennard, for instance, argues that the syntactic and elocutionary functions have overlapping uses and that the crucial aspect is to decide whether the text was conceived to

---

[2] J. JOYCE, *Ulysses* (Minneapolis, MN, 2016), p. 160.

[3] A.H. JUCKER and P. PAHTA, "Communicating manuscripts: Authors, scribes, readers, listeners and communicating characters", in: *Communicating Early English Manuscripts*, ed. P. PAHTA and A.H. JUCKER (Cambridge, 2011), pp. 3-10, at p. 3.

[4] R. CARROLL, M. PEIKOLA, H. SALMI, M.-L. VARILA, J. SKAFFARI, and R. HILTUNEN, "Pragmatics on the page: Visual text in late medieval English books", *European Journal of English Studies* 17.1 (2013), pp. 54-71.

[5] J. CALLE-MARTÍN and A. MIRANDA-GARCÍA, "Aspects of scribal punctuation in the Old English *Apollonius of Tyre*", *Folia Linguistica Historica* 26.1-2 (2005), pp. 95-113.

be read silently or aloud.[6] Parkes, in turn, complains about the twofold function of punctuation, considering that it is just "the concern of the scribe or corrector to elucidate the text transmitted to him according to the needs of his own audience".[7] In view of this, medieval writers were surely searching for a regular system of punctuation to grant the correct understanding of the utterance and, consequently, "they switched from the rhetorical to the grammatical depending on their specific needs".[8]

A second decision has to do with the choice of punctuation marks, especially at a time when the repertoire of symbols was constrained and the ones in use had overlapping functions. Setting aside the paragraphus and the paragraph mark for the expression of macro-textual information, the period and the virgule – along with the perioslash (see 'The repertoire of punctuation symbols' below) or the double virgule – are the symbols in charge of the expression of the sentential and clausal requirements of the text, rhetorical needs included. The scribe is then compelled to decide when to use a mark of punctuation and, if that is the case, the mark that best expresses that specific need, considering that standardisation was still a *desiratum*.

These decisions become paramount across genres and text types, and more importantly in the so-called speech-related written genres such as speech-based genres (i.e. witness depositions with no direct speech presentation), speech-purposed genres (i.e. sermons and proclamations), and speech-like genres (i.e. personal correspondence, prose fiction with speech presentation, or plays),[9] where the illocutionary force is considered to play a relevant role. When it comes to writing-related genres, the picture is not free of controversy in view of the existence of texts written with a different inventory of symbols, from those that only use the paragraph mark (MS London, Wellcome Collection 409) or the period (MS London, Wellcome Collection 405) to those with a more sophisticated system of punctuation with the paragraph mark, the period, and the virgule (MS Glasgow University Library, Hunter 307, among others).[10] The

---

[6] J. LENNARD, "Punctuation: And – pragmatics", in: *Historical Pragmatics. Pragmatic Developments in the History of English*, ed. A.H. JUCKER (Amsterdam, 1995), pp. 65-98; L.C. HECTOR, *The Handwriting of English Documents* (London, 1958), p. 44.

[7] M.B. PARKES, "Punctuation, or pause and effect", in: *Medieval Eloquence. Studies in the Theory and Practice of Medieval Rhetoric*, ed. J.J. MURPHY (Berkeley, 1978), pp. 127-142, at p. 139.

[8] CALLE-MARTÍN and MIRANDA-GARCÍA, "Aspects of scribal punctuation", p. 96.

[9] J. CULPEPER and M. KYTÖ, *Early Modern English Dialogues. Spoken Interaction as Writing* (Cambridge, 2010), p. 18.

[10] Wellcome 409 and Wellcome 405 hold two late fourteenth-century remedy collections,

inventory of punctuation marks depends not only upon the genre but also upon the typology of the text.[11] Medical prose, for instance, is classified into theoretical treatises, surgical treatises, and recipe collections, the former considered to be the most academic register based on Graeco-Roman models, while the latter portray the language used by lay people with a longer history in the vernacular, mostly collections of recipes that families stored at home for their use. Surgical treatises, in turn, would fall between the abovementioned classes.[12] Variation is found when it comes to punctuation inasmuch as less formal texts are more heavily punctuated,[13] a fact that coincides with Smith's view that less heavily punctuated texts might have been intended for intensive reading by monastic readers trained in ruminative reading practices, and more heavily punctuated texts might have been intended for wider audiences.[14]

The present study focuses on the punctuation system of early English handwritten medical recipes. This text type is characterised by a fixed text structure with a series of rhetorical moves among which the following five are widely disseminated in both Late Middle and Early Modern English recipe collections: title, ingredients, preparation, application, and efficacy – among others.[15] Given

while Hunter 307 houses the English version of the treatise entitled *System of Physic*, also from the same century.

[11] While the concept of genre is used to describe the impact of the context of culture on language by exploring the staged, step-by-step structures that cultures institutionalise as ways of achieving goals, text types represent the linguistic realisations of genres, that is, they contain a series of linguistic features that may or may not belong to a common genre. D. BIBER, *Variation Across Speech and Writing* (Cambridge, 1988), p. 70; S. EGGINS, *An Introduction to Systemic Functional Linguistics* (London, 1994), p. 9; D. BIBER and S. CONRAD, *Register, Genre and Style* (Cambridge, 2009), p. 16.

[12] I. TAAVITSAINEN, "Changing conventions of writing: The dynamics of genres, text types, and text traditions", *European Journal of English Studies* 5.2 (2001), pp. 139-150, at p. 141.

[13] J. ROMERO-BARRANCO, "Punctuation in Early Modern English scientific writing: The case of two scientific text types in GUL, MS Hunter 135", *Studia Anglica Posnaniensia* 54.1 (2019), pp. 59-80.

[14] J.J. SMITH, "Punctuating Mirk's Festial: A Scottish text and its implications", in: *Preaching the Word in Manuscript and Print in Late Medieval England*, ed. M.W. DRIVER and V. O'MARA (Turnhout, 2013), pp. 161-192, at pp. 182-189; J.J. SMITH, "The afterlives of Nicholas Love", *Studia Neophilologica* 89.sup1 (2017), pp. 59-74, at p. 63; J.J. SMITH, "From 'secreit' script to public print: Punctuation, news management, and the condemnation of the Earl of Bothwell", *Huntington Library Quarterly* 80.2 (2017), pp. 223-238, at p. 237.

[15] T. HUNT, *Popular Medicine in Thirteenth-Century England: Introduction and Texts* (Cambridge, 1990), pp. 16-24; F. ALONSO-ALMEIDA, "'Gyf hyr þis medycyn': Analysing the Middle English recipe medical discourse", *Revista de lenguas para fines específicos* 5-6 (1998-99), pp. 48-81, at pp. 55-63; F. ALONSO-ALMEIDA and M. CABRERA-ABREU, "The formulation of promise in medieval English medical recipes: A relevance-theoretic approach", *Neophilologus* 86.1 (2002), pp. 137-154, at p. 138; M. MÄKINEN, "Efficacy phrases in Early Modern English

that members of all social classes had access to medical recipes, these can shed some new light on the pragmatics of punctuation and, more specifically, on the way in which punctuation marks the transition from one rhetorical move to the next. This is in line with Smith's argument that "shifts in punctuation practices correlate with changing patterns of literacy [and] socio-cultural developments [...] correlate quite closely with changes in the formal appearance of texts, including punctuation".[16] The study pursues the following objectives:

1) to assess the effect of visual elements on the organisation of the recipes;
2) to compare the punctuation systems in the recipes both synchronically and diachronically;
3) to create a typology of punctuation symbols that mark the beginning of a new rhetorical move in the periods; and
4) to ascertain whether rhetorical moves are signalled using the same punctuation symbol over time.

These objectives, specifically the first one, are concerned with the representation of visual elements on the page, a topic intrinsically connected with the subject of study of this book. In this vein, the term 'graphic practices' has been coined to denote the set of visual features that "affect the reception and interpretation of written texts in fundamental ways: for example, the use of italics, a different coloured ink or a different script type may signal code-switching".[17] In this chapter, the pragmatics of punctuation refer to punctuation as a recurrent visual aid helping amateur scribes to code their written artefacts in view of the idiosyncrasies of the prospective audience, securing a better understanding of utterances.

---

medical recipes', in: *Medical Writing in Early Modern English*, ed. I. TAAVITSAINEN and P. PAHTA (Cambridge, 2011), pp. 158-179, at p. 158; F. ALONSO-ALMEIDA, "Genre conventions in English recipes, 1600-1800", in: *Reading and Writing Recipe Books 1550-1800*, ed. M. DIMEO and S. PENNELL (Manchester, 2013), pp. 68-92, at p. 71; J. ROMERO-BARRANCO, "Early Modern English scientific text types: Edition and assessment of linguistic complexity of the texts in MS Hunter 135 (ff. 34r-121v)", unpublished doctoral thesis (Universidad de Málaga, 2017).

[16] SMITH, "The pragmatics of punctuation", p. 208; SMITH, "Punctuating Mirk's Festial"; SMITH, "The afterlives of Nicholas Love"; SMITH, "From 'secreit' script to public print".

[17] J. TYRKKÖ, "New methods of bringing image data into historical linguistics: A case study with medical writing 1500-1700", *Studia Neophilologica* 89.sup1 (2017), pp. 90-108, at p. 91.

Methodology

The source of evidence comes from *The Málaga Corpus of Early English Scientific Prose*, both from the Late Middle English and the Early Modern English components (1350-1500 and 1500-1700, respectively).[18] The former is a one-million-word corpus of late medieval science, mostly medical texts. Compiled on the basis of transcriptions of late Middle English handwritten texts, the corpus is lemmatised and annotated so that the user may search for the occurrence of particular items, both word- and lemma-based, context included. The latter, in its current version, houses one million words. It has been automatically annotated with the Constituent Likelihood Word-tagging System (CLAWS), developed by the UCREL team at the University of Lancaster.[19] The tagset includes more than 160 tags together with specific labels for the different marks of punctuation.

This corpus material is the result of a research project based at the University of Málaga in collaboration with the Universities of Murcia, Oviedo, Glasgow, Oslo, and Adam Mickiewicz University (Poznań). The aim of the project is twofold:

1) the preparation of semi-diplomatic editions to be freely offered online along with high-resolution images of the original manuscripts; and
2) the compilation of a normalised and POS-tagged corpus from this material.

The corpus holds transcribed handwritten material exemplifying the three branches of scientific writing, namely specialised treatises, surgical treatises, and recipe collections. The principles of semi-diplomatic transcription have been adopted for the whole set of treatises, meaning that the manuscripts have been transcribed according to the same principles, ensuring absolute comparability when it comes to orthographic elements like abbreviations, punctuation, and spelling, among others.[20]

The present study is based on a selection of 50 recipes from the fifteenth, sixteenth, and seventeenth centuries and, for uniformity, all of them are concerned with the cure and treatment of the head, the toothache, the plague, the

---

[18] <http://hunter.uma.es> – <http://modernmss.uma.es>.

[19] R. GARSIDE and N. SMITH, "A hybrid grammatical tagger: CLAWS 4", in: *The Computational Analysis of English*, ed. R. GARSIDE, G. LEECH, and G. SAMPSON (London, 1997), pp. 102-121.

[20] A.G. PETTI, *English Literary Hands from Chaucer to Dryden* (London, 1977), pp. 34-35; R. CLEMENS and T. GRAHAM, *Introduction to Manuscript Studies* (Ithaca, NY, 2007), pp. 75-81.

eyes, the ears, and the stomach, which are commonplace in every recipe collection of the period. These 150 recipes have been extracted from different volumes so as to account for any likely authorial variation, and thus gather together the scribes' standards of punctuation at the time.[21]

On methodological grounds, the recipes have been imported into an Excel spreadsheet in such a way that, apart from the century and the author – if known – it contains five different columns incorporating the five consistent moves in Late Middle and Early Modern English recipes: title, ingredients, preparation, application, and efficacy phrase. Each move is preceded by the corresponding mark of punctuation, so that the spreadsheet allows the sorting of the information according to, for instance, the century of composition or the particular stage of the recipe, thus facilitating the quantitative analysis of the phenomenon.

The Repertoire of Punctuation Symbols

The period 1450-1700 was crucial in the configuration of the English repertoire of punctuation symbols.[22] Apart from the paragraphus and the paragraph mark, which had been actively deployed throughout the Middle Ages for the expression of macro-textual requirements, the system progressively incorporated other symbols and devices for the expression of particular needs, which eventually contributed to the readers' understanding. As far as recipes are concerned, the different stages are mostly expressed in the following ways.

The absence of punctuation symbols is a recurrent practice in many of the recipes, especially in the Late Middle English period, often accompanied by the use of capitalisation. The use of capital letters in these environments is conceived to perform the role of an actual mark of punctuation, being a visual device for marking the beginning of a new stage in the recipe. If a mark of punctuation appears, the scribes are committed to the use of the paragraph mark, the period, the comma, the virgule, the perioslash, the colon, or the semicolon.

---

[21] The corpus provides general datings for the manuscripts which, for convenience, were converted into approximate pseudo-precise datings for the purposes of the visual data exploration. Thus, the sixteenth century has been interpreted as the middle of that century and represented as 1550.

[22] Instances of the different punctuation symbols by medieval and early modern scribes can be found in Figures 1-3.

The paragraph mark (¶) was widely used from the Middle Ages as a visual sign to mark "a significant pause in the flow of writing, when one idea or portion of narrative or argument has been completed, and some breathing space is needed, perhaps for thought on what has gone before, perhaps for anticipation of what is to come".[23] This explains the outstanding role of the paragraph mark in this text type as a grammatical symbol which signals the end of a unit and at the same time looks forward to a new structurally independent unit, becoming the proper rhetorical pause for the correct understanding of the utterance.[24]

The period (.) is the earliest mark of punctuation in English, introduced by the Romans from the Greek system. Its function as a major pause was already established in the fifteenth century, thus coexisting with its use as a medial pause until its eventual standardisation in the early seventeenth century.[25] The period thus stands out as the only mark of punctuation which could, in principle, be used for the expression of an array of functions, from marking the end of a sense unit to other sentential and clausal relations such as coordination, subordination, enumerations, parenthetical constructions, etc. When it comes to the structure of the recipe, it is precisely the potential for the expression of these relationships that confirms it as the ideal symbol to separate the moves of the recipe.

The virgule (/), or slash, begins to disseminate in English documents in the fourteenth century, gaining substantial ground among fifteenth-century scribes.[26] Even though this mark of punctuation was initially conceived to signal a short pause, it is often deployed to conclude a completed sentence.[27] The virgule then acts as another potential separator of the moves of a recipe, in many cases used in combination with the conjunction 'and'.[28] The comma (,),

---

[23] E. ZEEMAN, "Punctuation in an early manuscript of Love's *Mirror*", *Review of English Studies* 7.25 (1956), pp. 11-18, at p. 13.

[24] P.J. LUCAS, "Sense-units and the use of punctuation-markers in John Capgrave's *Chronicle*", *Archivum Linguisticum* 2 (1971), pp. 1-24, at p. 6; J. CALLE-MARTÍN and A. MIRANDA-GARCÍA, "Editing Middle English punctuation. The case of MS Egerton 2622 (ff. 136-152)", *International Journal of English Studies* 5.2 (2005), pp. 27-44, at pp. 32-33.

[25] J. CALLE-MARTÍN, "'His maiestie chargeth, that no person shall engrose any maner of corne': The standardization of punctuation in Early Modern English legal proclamations", in: *Punctuation in Context – Past and Present Perspectives,* ed. C. CLARIDGE and M. KYTÖ (Bern, 2019), pp. 179-200, at p. 188.

[26] CALLE-MARTÍN, "'His maiestie chargeth, that no person shall engrose any maner of corne'", p. 195.

[27] HECTOR, *The Handwriting of English Documents*, p. 47.

[28] SMITH, "The pragmatics of punctuation", p. 211.

introduced in English documents towards the sixteenth century and replacing the functions of the virgule,[29] is the shortest pause in the repertoire.[30]

The perioslash and the double virgule are characteristic of a more sophisticated system of punctuation.[31] The former consists of the use of a period together with a virgule, regardless of whether the virgule precedes the period (/.) or the other way round (./), and it is also commonplace for the virgule to be surrounded by two periods (./.).[32] The perioslash does not seem to have specific functions in handwritten documents, sharing the same functions as the virgule, the difference being basically of a visual nature.[33] The double virgule (//), in turn, is rather a metatextual mark of punctuation used to signify textual divisions, often for the expression of significant parts of the text.[34]

The colon (:) is used to indicate that "what follows the colon is an explication of what precedes it or a fulfilment of the expectation raised".[35] According to Calle-Martín and Miranda-García, different views are held with regard to the Elizabethan colon.[36] While Tannenbaum argues that the colon was used for commas, question marks, exclamation marks and periods, Petti states that it was

---

[29] J. CALLE-MARTÍN and A. MIRANDA-GARCÍA, "The punctuation system of Elizabethan legal documents: The case of G.U.L. MS Hunter 3 (S.1.3)", *Review of English Studies* 59.240 (2008), pp. 356-378.

[30] S.A. TANNENBAUM, *The Handwriting of the Renaissance* (New York, 1930), p. 140; PETTI, *English Literary Hands from Chaucer to Dryden*, p. 26; R. QUIRK, S. GREENBAUM, G. LEECH, and J. SVARTVIK, *A Comprehensive Grammar of the English Language* (London, 1985), p. 1615.

[31] These two symbols have been considered as a single mark of punctuation in view of their specific functions in Middle English handwritten material, since they often express functions which do not strictly correspond to those of the virgule (i.e. macro-textual functions, among others).

[32] P.G. ARAKELIAN, "Punctuation in a Late Middle English manuscript", *Neuphilologische Mitteilungen* 76.4 (1975), pp. 614-624, at p. 619.

[33] CALLE-MARTÍN and MIRANDA-GARCÍA, "The punctuation system of Elizabethan legal documents", p. 361.

[34] Interestingly enough, however, the double virgule is taken to have another role in other handwritten texts, where it has been found to occur "exclusively as a cue to the rubricator to insert a paraph sign or a *littera notabilior* at the beginning of the next section", quoted from A. HONKAPOHJA, "Functions of punctuation in six Latin and English versions of the plague treatise by John of Burgundy", in: *Punctuation in Context – Past and Present Perspectives,* ed. C. CLARIDGE and M. KYTÖ (Bern, 2019), pp. 151-178, at p. 165. The present study considers the double virgule as a mark of punctuation, irrespective of whether it originally marked where another metatextual device was bound to appear.

[35] QUIRK et al., *A Comprehensive Grammar of the English Language*, p. 1620.

[36] CALLE-MARTÍN and MIRANDA-GARCÍA, "The punctuation system of Elizabethan legal documents", pp. 372-373.

used in combination with the virgule to mark off the end of a paragraph, only acquiring its modern use at the end of the period.[37]

The semicolon (;) was originally attested in Venice in Bembo's 1494 edition of *De Aetna* and gained trans-European transmission by the second half of the sixteenth century. In England, Henry Denham in 1569 is said to be the first printer adopting the semicolon with propriety; afterwards, in the third quarter of the sixteenth century, the semicolon diffused with "a function between those of the other two marks", thus subsuming some of the functions of the virgule and the comma.[38]

Analysis

English medical recipes are characterised by a common structure featuring a series of rhetorical moves. The transition from one move to the next could be expressed in different ways and has no doubt evolved differently in view of the century of composition of the written artefact. In this fashion, the recipes in Figures 1, 2, and 3 (composed in the fifteenth, sixteenth and seventeenth centuries, respectively) are quite different because of two reasons: their use of visual elements and their marks of punctuation.

---

[37] TANNENBAUM, *The Handwriting of the Renaissance*, p. 142; PETTI, *English Literary Hands from Chaucer to Dryden*, p. 27.

[38] PARKES, "Punctuation, or pause and effect", p. 49; See also CALLE-MARTÍN and MIRANDA-GARCÍA, "The punctuation system of Elizabethan legal documents", p. 371.

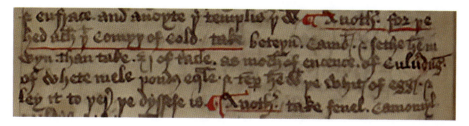

Fig. 1   Recipe for headache, fifteenth century. MS Glasgow, University Library, Hunter 328, f. 62v. With permission of the University of Glasgow Archives and Special Collections.

for þe hed ach þat Comyþ of Cold./ take beteyn. Camo*mille*. & sethe he*m* in wyn. than take. *ounce* j of t*r*iacle. as moch of encence. of Culu*er*dung of whete mele pond*us* equale. & te*m*pe*r* he*m* wit*h* þe whit*is* of eggis. & ley it to þere þe dyssese is.

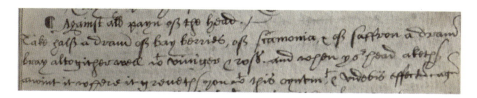

Fig. 2   Recipe for headache, sixteenth century. MS Glasgow University Library, Ferguson 7, f. 16r. With permission of University of Glasgow Archives and Special Collections.

Against all payn of the head./ Take half a dram of bay berries, of scammonia, & of saffron a dram bray altogither well w*ith* viniger & rose*s*. and when y*our* head aketh, anoint it where it greueth you w*ith* this oyntme*n*t, and videbis effectus magn*us*

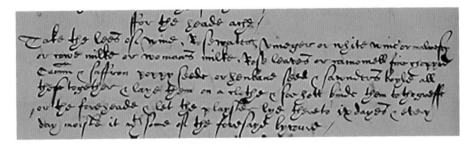

Fig. 3   Recipe for headache, seventeenth century. MS Glasgow University Library, Hunter 64, f. 14r. With permission of University of Glasgow Archives and Special Collections.

For the heade ache./ Take the lees of wine, Rosewater, vineger or white wine or malmesey or cowe milke or womans milke, Rose leaves or camomell fine chopped Cum*m*in & saffron poppy seede or henbane seed & sawnders boyle all these together & laye them on a clothe & soe hott binde them to the greffe or the foreheade & let the playster lye thereto ix dayes & every day moiste it w*ith* some of the foresayd lycoure./

Visual Elements

Figure 1 shows some visual elements helping the reader identify the different parts of the recipe, i.e. the title underlined with red ink along with the use of a paragraph mark indicating the end of the recipe. In Figures 2 and 3, the text is rendered in one colour, but the scribes resort to the use of spacing to mark off the beginning of a new recipe (the title stands alone on a separate line and the content of the recipe forms a paragraph; in Figure 2, a paragraph mark is also inserted). With these visual tools, the reader can easily identify the different recipes on the page (see also Figures 4 and 5).

To assess the use of visual elements in the titles of early English recipes, four different elements have been considered: the use of the paragraphus, the script (whether a different size or script is used), the ink colour, and the position of the title (either as part of the recipe or on a separate line). The data in Figure 6 suggests that there is a changing tendency in the periods under study. The use of the paragraph mark and ink colour decreases over time (29.4% and 42.7% in the fifteenth century and 5.3% and 7.9% in the seventeenth century, respect-

The Pragmatics of Punctuation in Early English Medical Recipe Books 117

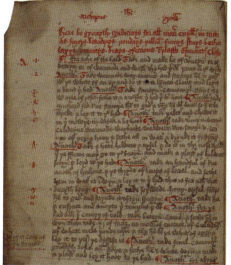

Fig. 4   MS Glasgow University Library, Hunter 328, f. 2v. With permission of University of Glasgow Archives and Special Collections.

Fig. 5   MS Glasgow University Library, Hunter 64, f. 14r. With permission of University of Glasgow Archives and Special Collections.

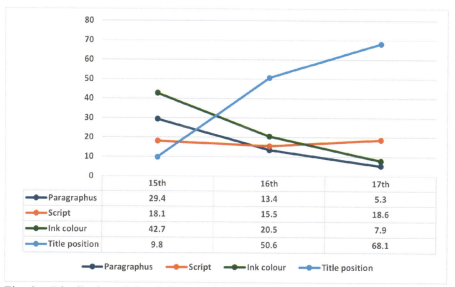

Fig. 6   Distribution of visual elements in the titles of recipes (%).

ively). These functions would later be expressed by the position of the title on a separate line (9.8% in the fifteenth century and 68.1% in the seventeenth century). The use of a different script remains somewhat stable throughout the period.

Spacing and Capitalisation

Spacing is taken to be another kind of visual element separating the different units of a text, no matter whether they are words, clauses or sentences. When it comes to the separation of longer units, medieval scribes often resorted to the strategy of inserting wider spaces in particular environments, and the moves of a recipe are a typical case. This strategy may be deployed in isolation

Table 1 Scribal choices with the absence of punctuation marks (%).

Title	15th	16th	17th
Capital	91	73	71
No Capital	9	27	29
Ampersand	0	0	0
Ingredients			
Capital	0	4	3
No capital	43	96	68
Ampersand	57	0	29
Preparation			
Capital	0	10	0
No capital	50	90	53
Ampersand	50	0	47
Application			
Capital	5	25	7
No capital	0	56	72
Ampersand	28	0	7
End	67	19	14

or in combination with other visual devices, such as the use of capital letters – either on the same line, or on a new one, or the ampersand. Table 1 presents the frequency of spacing in the four rhetorical moves over time, considering whether the separation is followed by the use of an ampersand or a capital letter or not.[39]

As shown, there seems to be a consistent practice in the use of spacing in combination with the particular moves of the recipe. As far as the title is concerned, spacing is overwhelmingly used in combination with capital letters regardless of the date of composition of the text, even though there is a slight decrease with the advent of the modern period – 73% and 71% in the sixteenth and seventeenth centuries, respectively – which coincides with the rise of minuscule letters – 27% and 29% in the sixteenth and seventeenth centuries.

The following two moves, the ingredients and the preparation section, present a different state of affairs, as capitalisation is found to have a negligible distribution in favour of minuscule letters and ampersands. Scribal practice, however, is observed to vary among medieval and Early Modern English scribes. The fifteenth century, on the one hand, presents a balanced distribution of both minuscule letters and ampersands, with a percentage of 43% and 57% in the ingredients section and 50% each in the preparation section. The sixteenth century, on the other hand, stands out as a transitional period with the progressive adoption of minuscule letters in combination with spacing.[40] The preference for minuscule letters over the ampersand is even more significant in the seventeenth century. The higher rate of the ampersand in the preparation section (47%) is explained in terms of the linguistic features of this section, consisting of a list of items in a series often connected with the coordinate conjunction 'and'.

Finally, the application section again witnesses the different attitudes of Middle English and Early Modern English scribes. While the former are more prone to the use of the ampersand, the latter seem to rule out the ampersand in favour of minuscule letters, with 56% and 72% in the sixteenth and seventeenth centuries, respectively. This different practice is also observed in the marking of the end of the recipe itself, inasmuch as medieval scribes are more consistent as to the use of a mark of punctuation in those environments (67%), while Early

---

[39] Even though it has been said that medical recipes typically contain five rhetorical moves (title, ingredients, preparation, application, and efficacy phrase), the last one has not been considered in the present analysis, given that it was not used in the recipes under study.

[40] The figures, however, may be misleading and the high rate of minuscule letters in comparison with the ampersand may be corpus-biased, possibly as a result of the higher number of recipes by the same hand.

Modern penmen feel that there is not as much of a need for a symbol there, with 19% and 14% in the sixteenth and seventeenth centuries, respectively.

All in all, the data confirm that there is a transition from a stricter to a less dependent system in these environments. Setting aside the title section, where the use of capitalisation is felt to be a prerequisite, the other rhetorical moves evolve to a looser system of punctuation. Spacing and capitalisation are taken to be two visual resources used for the same purposes, and therefore redundant for the marking of the very same thing. This obviously led to the progressive adoption of minuscule letters in these contexts, which outnumber the instances of capitalisation from the sixteenth century.

Punctuation

Table 2 Distribution of punctuation marks in the corpus (%).

Total	15th	16th	17th
Period	53	23	5
Perioslash	11	4	26
Virgule	1	0	1
Comma	0	22	11
Colon	0	1	0
Semicolon	0	1	1
No mark	35	49	56

When it comes to the use of punctuation marks, some differences arise across the recipes. Table 2 presents the occurrence of the different punctuation symbols used to mark the transition to a new rhetorical move in the three centuries under study.[41] The data tentatively allow us to gather the following four tendencies:

1) the period plunges down towards the end of the period (from 53% to 5% in the fifteenth and the seventeenth centuries, respectively);

---

[41] Even though the sources display a variety of punctuation marks for the expression of a number of uses and functions, this paper is exclusively concerned with those symbols to signal the boundaries of the rhetorical moves found in medical recipes.

2) the perioslash becomes the most frequent mark by the end of the period (26% in the seventeenth century);
3) the comma appears in the sixteenth century for the first time (22%) and is the second-most-used punctuation mark by the seventeenth century (11%); and
4) the virgule, the colon, and the semicolon are scarcely used. In addition to this, the rate of unpunctuated sections is 20 percentage points higher by the end of the period.

This picture varies, however, if one pays attention to the particular stages of the recipe. Different approaches have been made to the structure of recipes and their rhetorical moves in the literature. Alonso-Almeida and Cabrera-Abreu distinguished among title, ingredients, preparation, application (use and dosage)

Table 3 Distribution of punctuation marks after the title section (%).

Title	15th	16th	17th
Period	48	38	6
Perioslash	28	14	78
Virgule	2	0	2
Comma	0	2	0
Colon	0	2	0
Semicolon	0	0	0
No mark	22	44	14

and statement of efficacy.[42] Hunt listed six different components: rubric, indication, composition, preparation, application, and statement of efficacy.[43] In the present study, we have identified a total of four consistent rhetorical moves: title, ingredients, preparation and application. Table 3 reproduces the use of punctuation marks after the title section, from which it can be gathered that the period was already immersed in a process of specialisation in view of its decreasing role over time (from 48% of attestation in the fifteenth century to barely 6% of the instances in the seventeenth century). This specialisation is the direct cause of the spread of the perioslash in these environments (from 28% in

---
[42] ALONSO-ALMEIDA and CABRERA-ABREU, "The formulation of promise in medieval English medical recipes", p. 138.
[43] HUNT, *Popular Medicine in Thirteenth-Century England*, pp. 16-24.

the fifteenth century to 78% in the seventeenth century). The rest of the symbols are rarely witnessed after the title section, given that they perform other functions. Interestingly, the proportion of unmarked title sections also decreases slightly over time (22% in the fifteenth century and 14% in the seventeenth century).

Table 4 Distribution of punctuation marks after the ingredients section (%).

Ingredients	15th	16th	17th
Period	58	22	4
Perioslash	0	0	0
Virgule	0	0	0
Comma	0	34	18
Colon	0	0	0
Semicolon	0	0	2
No mark	42	44	76

Table 4 provides the occurrence of punctuation marks after the ingredients section, where it is again observed that the period plunges down from the fifteenth to the seventeenth century (from 58% to 4%, respectively). In addition to this, two issues stand out:

1) the comma spreads throughout the period (from 0% to 18% in the fifteenth and the seventeenth centuries, respectively); and
2) the proportion of unmarked instances is substantially higher, as the rate is almost doubled by the seventeenth century.

The same picture is witnessed after the preparation section, as shown in Table 5. The period, used in half of the recipes in the fifteenth century, is barely witnessed in the sixteenth and the seventeenth centuries (8% and 6%, respectively). Even though the comma is the most frequent punctuation symbol in the sixteenth and the seventeenth centuries (30% and 14%, respectively), the proportion of unpunctuated instances becomes higher throughout the period (from 40% in the fifteenth century to 80% in the seventeenth century).

The Pragmatics of Punctuation in Early English Medical Recipe Books 123

Table 5 Distribution of punctuation marks after the preparation section (%).

Preparation	15th	16th	17th
Period	54	8	6
Perioslash	6	0	0
Virgule	0	0	0
Comma	0	30	14
Colon	0	0	0
Semicolon	0	2	0
No mark	40	60	80

Table 6 presents the punctuation practice for the introduction of the last rhetorical move in English medical recipes – the application section, which is generally devoted to marking the end of the recipe itself. Two punctuation marks stand out here: the period and the perioslash. Traditionally deemed to have a macro-textual function for marking the end of sentences / paragraphs, the period was the preferred punctuation mark in the fifteenth century (44%), a role already subsumed by the perioslash in the seventeenth century with an incidence of 60%.

Table 6 Distribution of punctuation marks after the application section (%).

Application	15th	16th	17th
Period	44	26	8
Perioslash	22	10	60
Virgule	0	8	0
Comma	0	24	4
Colon	0	0	0
Semicolon	0	0	0
No mark	34	32	28

Concluding Remarks

The present chapter has evaluated the pragmatics of punctuation in early English medical recipes and, more specifically, the use of punctuation to introduce the different rhetorical moves of this particular text type. The study is based on a total of 150 medical recipes from the fifteenth, sixteenth, and seventeenth centuries taken from *The Málaga Corpus of Early English Scientific Prose*. This has allowed us to reach the following conclusions.

Apart from punctuation itself, visual elements have been studied as a side element contributing to the *mise-en-page* and the actual organisation of information on the page. Our analysis offers solid grounds to consider the Early Modern English period as the turning point towards a new scribal attitude. The use of the paragraph mark and a different ink plunged down towards the end of the medieval period, coinciding with the spread of spacing and capitalisation, deemed a more convenient form of textual organisation. The use of different scripts, however, both in terms of size and letterforms, remained a commonplace practice among both medieval and early modern scribes.

Capitalisation, in turn, has been assessed as a mark of punctuation proper in the assumption that it can perform the same function of a symbol, especially in those contexts where the mark itself is omitted. Capital letters, on the one hand, are found to decrease over time after the title section, becoming a sporadic option for the introduction of the other rhetorical moves. The ampersand, on the other hand, stands out as a recurrent practice to signal the beginning of the preparation section, the application section and, to a lesser extent, the efficacy phrase.

With regard to punctuation, the initial hypothesis was that, given that medical recipes were texts devoted to private and practical use, they would be heavily punctuated in view of the fact that they were written by non-practitioners for the use of laymen and physicians, who surely had more limited skills and expertise than other professional scribes. This hypothesis is only corroborated in the fifteenth century, where the proportion of punctuated rhetorical moves is higher than that of unpunctuated ones, as shown in Table 2. The situation turns out to be balanced in the sixteenth century, and it is in the seventeenth century when the absence of punctuation symbols in these environments becomes more frequent than punctuation itself. This fact may be explained in terms of the growing specialisation of Early Modern English amateur scribes, which progressively resulted in the adoption of shared norms of punctuation in these particular environments. The writers of recipe material were thought to belong

The Pragmatics of Punctuation in Early English Medical Recipe Books

to the same communities of practice where, through the repeated use of their punctuation habits, the understanding and socialisation of these conventions spread.[44] In this very case, it is likely that they reached a consensus on a lesser dependence on punctuation and spacing for marking the transitions. This contrasts with the practice of medieval writers, who resorted to the almost systematic use of the period as the only mark of punctuation then available to mark off the beginning of a new section or sense unit.[45] This transition is summarised in the following table.

Table 7 Most frequent punctuation symbols after rhetorical moves over time.

Symbols	15th century				16th century				17th century			
	Tit.	Ing.	Prep.	App.	Tit.	Ing.	Prep.	App.	Tit.	Ing.	Prep.	App.
Period	√	√	√	√								
Perioslash										√		√
Virgule												
Comma							√					
Colon												
Semicolon												
No mark					√	√		√		√	√	

The study offers data which, in our opinion, are in line with previous claims made by Smith,[46] who considered that pragmatics is intimately connected with punctuation to the extent that the latter varies in view of the text type and the target audience. In this case, the pragmatics of punctuation varies over time with a transition towards a less heavily punctuated system, in which the ampersand seems to have subsumed some of the uses of the punctus in the

---

[44] Mark Faulkner, personal communication; J. THAISEN, "Transparently hierarchical: Punctuation in the Townshend family recipe book", *International Journal of English Studies* 20.2 (2020), pp. 11-30, at p. 26.

[45] Importantly enough, there seems to be a process of specialisation of these symbols to the extent that the period progressively shares its functions with the other members of the repertoire. In this fashion, for instance, the macro-textual functions of the period are progressively subsumed by the perioslash, while at the same time the comma takes over many of the functions formerly performed by the period in the fifteenth century.

[46] SMITH, "The pragmatics of punctuation"; SMITH, "Punctuating Mirk's Festial"; SMITH, "The afterlives of Nicholas Love"; SMITH, "From 'secreit' script to public print".

Middle Ages. The relationship between pragmatics and punctuation is surely awaiting the curiosity of other scholars delving into the use and omission of punctuation marks in particular contexts and specific text types. For now, we can safely conclude that punctuation decreases after the title and the application section, and spreads after the ingredients and the preparation sections in the seventeenth century, an attitude that could be explained in terms of the writers' perception that there was a higher dependence on punctuation in those two stages, perhaps associated with the higher structural complexity of the stages at hand and, therefore, the particular requirements of the target audience.

Visual Pragmatics and Late Modern English Letters

INGRID TIEKEN-BOON VAN OSTADE

Introduction

Ms Oxford, Bodleian Library, Eng. lett. c. 572 contains two sets of letters that are part of the correspondence of the well-known eighteenth-century English grammarian Robert Lowth (1710-1787). His correspondence has never (yet) been published, but it has been collected for an analysis of his language in relation to the rules he formulated in his *Short Introduction to English Grammar* (London, 1762).[1] The first set consists of 65 letters that Lowth wrote to his wife while he was away in Ireland in 1755, and the second comprises the complete correspondence between Lowth and his literary – and ecclesiastical – rival, William Warburton (1698-1779). This second set, thirteen letters altogether, is of particular interest from the perspective of the present paper, since they also appeared in published form, not as a mod-

---

[1] For an overview of his attested letters, see I. TIEKEN-BOON VAN OSTADE, *The Bishop's Grammar. Robert Lowth and the Rise of Prescriptivism* (Oxford, 2011), pp. 295-297. Further letters that have come to light since then are listed in I. TIEKEN-BOON VAN OSTADE, *Nóg meer brieven van Lowth?!* (Leiden, 2021).

Graphic Practices and Literacies in the History of English, ed. Matti PEIKOLA, Jukka TYRKKÖ, and Mari-Liisa VARILA, *Utrecht Studies in Medieval Literacy*, 61 (Turnhout: Brepols, 2025), pp. 127-149.

ern edition but for the purpose of disclosing the dispute between the two men to the public. We therefore have the text in its visual outlook not only in manuscript form but also in its printed representation, on which others, in particular editors and typesetters who presumably used a printer's house style, left traces when adapting the text for publication.[2] Furthermore, the letters themselves were by men who each, as we will see, had their own private writing habits. How or where Lowth and Warburton acquired these habits will most likely be impossible to ascertain, and we will similarly be unable to trace the specific set of house style instructions that the editors or typesetters drew upon when preparing the letters for publication. For all that, my analysis, conducted along the lines of Mark Aronoff's reconstruction of the early sixteenth-century printer Wynkyn de Worde's spelling system,[3] will identify some of the printing instructions that resulted in the published text, alongside the authors' individual writing habits.

I will focus on three relatively marginal features: the abbreviation stop, as in Sep^r. 'September'; S^r. 'Sir', or y^t. 'that'; the ampersand (&); and hyphenation. The reason for doing so is that I previously noted Lowth's almost categorical use of the abbreviation stop following superscript letters: when transcribing his letters, the occurrence of a stop in words as in the above examples proved almost predictable.[4] Lowth's use of the ampersand, moreover, was attested with overwhelming frequency in his letters, and was part of his normal writing style irrespective of the formality of his letters. Hyphenation in his letters, used in breaking off words at the end of a line, invariably takes the form of a double colon, one at the end of a line and another at the beginning of the next one. According to Sue Walker, we see this practice today with young children when they are learning to spell and still misunderstand the function of the hyphen.[5] At the time, however, double hyphenation was common epistolary practice, and I have come across it also in letter writers other than Lowth and Warburton. I believe that this double marking of hyphenation served a visually

---

[2] Cf. C. SANCHEZ-STOCKHAMMER, "Present-day English hyphenation: Historical origin, functions and pragmatics", in: *Punctuation in Context – Past and Present Perspectives*, ed. C. CLARIDGE and M. KYTÖ (Bern, 2020), pp. 47-65, at p. 50. See also J. TYRKKÖ, "Printing houses as communities of practice: Orthography in early modern medical books", in: *Communities of Practice in the History of English*, ed. A.H. JUCKER and J. KOPACZYK (Amsterdam, 2013), pp. 151-176, at p. 152.

[3] M. ARONOFF, "The orthographic system of an early English printer: Wynkyn de Worde", *Folia Linguistica Historica* 8.1-2 (1989), pp. 65-97.

[4] Cf. TIEKEN-BOON VAN OSTADE, *The Bishop's Grammar*, pp. 199-200.

[5] S. WALKER, *Typography and Language in Everyday Life: Prescriptions and Practices* (Harlow, 2001), p. 57.

pragmatic function,[6] much like the repetition of quotation marks at the beginning of a line in contemporary publications (as in the correspondence concerned, both manuscript and in print); the practice indicates at a glance that the lines in question are part of an extended quotation. The hyphenation mark repeated at the beginning of a line similarly indicates that the text should be read as a continuation from the previous line, and that the first item of the line in question does not have independent word status. Printed practice, as we will see below, is different in this respect, and the feature was therefore typical of epistolary writing at the time. The use of the abbreviation stop and the ampersand reflects speed in writing but also a difference in the status of a letter, i.e. draft vs. fair copies, as well as different degrees of formality. Walker, for instance, notes that the more formal the letter, the more a writer will adhere to epistolary prescriptions;[7] as we will see below, in Late Modern English times such prescriptions comprise conventions such as the usage of abbreviations and contractions, which were considered unacceptable in formal letters.

While Lowth's usage of these features has been described in *The Bishop's Grammar*, Warburton's, which is different, has not, and it is of additional interest to see how printers' practice differed from private usage, Lowth's as well as Warburton's. "Letter writing", according to Walker, "provides a good source for studying the relationship between prescription and practice",[8] and this paper will show that this also applies to letters from the Late Modern English period. In contrast to the practice of the editors and typesetters of the letters, the private habits of the authors studied, like those of most letter writers at the time, reflect idiosyncratic practice, and Christina Sanchez-Stockhammer notes that such practice may even be used for authorship attribution.[9] As for autograph hyphenation practice, this is not followed in print. After all, the aim of the publication of the correspondence at the time was not to provide a diplomatic transcript of the text of the letters.[10]

---

[6] I have adopted the concept of "visual pragmatics" for this paper from Tim Machan (T.W. MACHAN, "The visual pragmatics of code-switching in late Middle English literature", in: *Code-Switching in Early English*, ed. H. SCHENDL and L. WRIGHT (Berlin, 2011), pp. 303-333). Though Machan deals with a different topic altogether (the visual designation of code-switching in Middle English texts), the term neatly fits what the current analysis is about. The two textual aspects may be regarded as part of the same phenomenon: presenting particular features of text for the reader's special visual attention.
[7] WALKER, *Typography and Language in Everyday Life*, p. 33.
[8] WALKER, *Typography and Language in Everyday Life*, p. 128.
[9] SANCHEZ-STOCKHAMMER, "Present-day English hyphenation", p. 63.
[10] That such differences are nevertheless important is argued by M.-L. VARILA, H. SALMI, A. MÄKILÄHDE, J. SKAFFARI, and M. PEIKOLA, "Disciplinary decoding: Towards understanding

In what follows, I will first briefly describe the nature of the dispute between Lowth and Warburton and the form their correspondence took. Next, I will discuss the three pragmatic features selected for analysis, the abbreviation stop, the ampersand, and hyphenation, as a basis for their analysis. Because letters may reflect certain social signals that are hidden in the text,[11] I will next discuss to what extent differences in usage between the two men may be interpreted as reflecting their different personalities. In doing so, this paper will fit into the newly emerging historical perspective of third-wave sociolinguistics which analyses the "construct[ion of] social meaning via linguistic variation".[12] Finally, I will argue by way of conclusion that greater visual attention should be paid to the usage of the type of features analysed here in producing diplomatic editions of Late Modern English letters, thus allowing readers to take account of the social implications that variation may convey, no matter how linguistically marginal such features may be.

The Lowth – Warburton Dispute

Brian Hepworth, in his biography of Lowth, describes the dispute between Lowth and Warburton as "the greatest literary battle of the century".[13] Ostensibly, the argument between the two men was about their different views relating to the Book of Job, but in reality, Hepworth argues, it was about ecclesiastical preferment. As clergymen, "both were heading for a bishopric", he explains, "but Warburton was fifty-seven; Lowth, forty-five".[14] Warburton became bishop of Gloucester in 1760, and Lowth's nomination followed six years later, first as bishop of St. Davids, in 1766, and later that same year of Oxford. His

---

the language of visual and material features", in: *Verbal and Visual Communication in Early English Texts*, ed. M. PEIKOLA, A. MÄKILÄHDE, H. SALMI, M.-L. VARILA, and J. SKAFFARI (Turnhout, 2017), pp. 1-20, at pp. 15-16.

[11] See VARILA *et al.*, "Disciplinary decoding", p. 4. See also P. PETRÉ, "Brains versus people in Early Modern English. Syntactic change as a socially embedded emergent phenomenon", plenary lecture at ICEHL-21, Leiden, 7-11 June 2021.

[12] J. BEAL, "Dialect and the construction of identity in the ego documents of Thomas Bewick", in: *Dialect Writing and the North of England*, ed. P. HONEYBONE and W. MAGUIRE (Edinburgh, 2020), pp. 51-74, at p. 52. Cf. P. ECKERT, "Three waves of variation study: The emergence of meaning in the study of variation", *Annual Review of Anthropology* 41 (2012), pp. 87-100; see also S. ADAMSON, "Where do we go from here? Prospects and problems for historicising third-wave sociolinguistics", paper presented at ICEHL-21, Leiden, 7-11 June 2021.

[13] B. HEPWORTH, *Robert Lowth* (Boston, MA, 1978), p. 104.

[14] HEPWORTH, *Robert Lowth*, p. 101.

major appointment as bishop of London was in 1777. Warburton died two years later: the controversy with Lowth is believed to have contributed to his "decline" according to the *Oxford Dictionary of National Biography*.[15] The affair generated a great deal of interest when it was made public upon the appearance in 1765 of Lowth's pamphlet *A Letter to the Right Reverend Author of The Divine Legation of Moses Demonstrated*, and even drew the attention of the king.[16] There was support from the public for both sides, and it is clear where the sympathies of the well-known bluestocking hostess Elizabeth Montagu (1718-1800) lay. In a study of Montagu's language, Anni Sairio cites a discussion of Lowth's public letter to Warburton when writing to her husband (bold type is used for emphasis throughout this paper):

> [...] we had a great deal of mirth about **Dr. Lowth's book** and I find his Grace [the Archbishop of York, at whose house the meeting took place] is as much pleased with it as you and I are. I hear Warburton like all bullies is frightened at a brisk attack, and the menace to attack the divine **legion** has made him shrink in his shell (1765).[17]

The word *legion* in this quotation, for which Sairio relies on a modern reproduction of the text, is at first sight puzzling, but most likely reflects her source's misrepresentation of the originally superscript characters in *leg^{ion}*. The form is short for 'Legation', and the reference is to Warburton's publication of the fourth edition of his *Divine Legation of Moses Demonstrated* in 1765, which revived his dispute with Lowth. Lowth retaliated by publishing the above-mentioned pamphlet ("Dr. Lowth's book") along with the letters he and Warburton had exchanged in 1756. This naturally incensed Warburton, who took up his pen once again to inform Lowth: "I do not know whether the Prudent will excuse me for venturing another Letter to you, after you had so grossly violated the most respected Laws of Society, in publishing my private letters to you, without my knowlege [sic] or consent" (21 November 1765).

In this revival of their former correspondence, further angry letters were exchanged by the two men, eventually leading to a sequel to the earlier pamphlet, called *The Second Part of a Literary Correspondence, between the Bishop of Gloucester and a Late Professor of Oxford* (1766). It is not immediately

---

[15] ODNB, s.v. "William Warburton".
[16] HEPWORTH, *Robert Lowth*, p. 105.
[17] A. SAIRIO, "Bluestocking letters and the influence of eighteenth-century grammars", in: *Studies in Late Modern English Correspondence: Methodology and Data*, ed. M. DOSSENA and I. TIEKEN-BOON VAN OSTADE (Bern, 2008), pp. 137-162, at pp. 141-142.

clear who published the document. The names of the author and the publisher are lacking in the copy in Eighteenth Century Collections Online (ECCO), but there happen to be several notes on the title page in an unidentified hand, which read: "Lowth, Bishop", "Not published", and "only 75 Copies of this part of the Appendix to **M^r. Towne**'s Remarks upon Dr Lowth's letter to Bp. Warburton were reprinted **by Dr Lowth**/ for distribution amongst his friends". John Towne (1711-1791) was a religious controversialist and one of Warburton's supporters against Lowth.[18] Towne published *Remarks on Dr. Lowth's Letter to the Bishop of Gloucester*, which was subtitled *With the Bishop's Appendix, and the Second Epistolary Correspondence between His Lordship and the Doctor Annexed* (London, 1766). A second edition came out that same year, and both editions were printed "without an imprimatur", as the title page indicates. This refers to the discussion in the correspondence (referred to above) as to whether it was ethical to publish the letters without obtaining permission from the writers involved. There is, however, one significant difference between the publication ascribed to Lowth and Towne's pamphlet in that the latter document includes an additional letter by Warburton, the final letter in the correspondence, dated 31 January 1766. It thus seems that Lowth had not waited for this letter, which ends with the words "I desire that this 8th Letter may be added, in the publication, to the ~~six~~ ^{seven} preceding", but went ahead and published the correspondence straight after he had informed Warburton in *his* last letter of only a week earlier: "I now ⁱⁿ My turn desire, that You would ~~give me leave~~ ^{consent} to ^{my} publish^{ing} Your part of ~~it~~ ^{the said Correspondence} together with my own" (Lowth to Warburton, 24 January 1766).[19] Warburton subsequently put all the letters at Towne's disposal, those he had received from Lowth and copies – it seems – of those he himself had sent to his opponent.

The letters concerned were thus written in two batches, the first in 1756, ending in a reconciliation between the two men, and the second in 1765-1766, when the dispute was resumed in full force. The first part of the correspondence had been initiated by Lowth, after learning about Warburton's objections to his ideas about the dating of the Book of Job from his friends and fellow Durham prebendaries Joseph Spence (1699-1768) and Thomas Chapman (1717-1760),[20] who had been sent to negotiate between the two men:

---

[18] ODNB, s.v. "John Towne".

[19] Quotations from the letters will be reproduced as closely to their originals as possible, thus including self-corrections like strikethroughs and insertions as well as abbreviated names and other words. The draft versions of the letters naturally contain considerably more of these.

[20] Lowth had been prebendary of Durham and rector of Sedgefield since 1755.

Our good Friends D^r. C. & M^r. S. have agreably to your desire communicated to me some particulars of y^e. conversation wch. you have lately had with them relating to me: f^m. wch. I collect that **you think you have reason to be offended with me** on acc^t. of some things wch. I have said in my Prelections on y^e. subject of the book of Job, wch. you look upon as aimed against you; & y^t. you expect y^t. I sh^d. explain myself on this head (9 September 1756).

The full title of Lowth's "Prelections", mentioned in the above passage, was *De Sacra Poesi Hebræorum Prælectiones* (1753), a second edition of which had been published in 1763. Because Lowth had not adapted his original views to those of Warburton in this edition, Warburton launched an attack on him in a new edition of the *Divine Legation of Moses* published in 1765, which led to the above-mentioned pamphlet by Lowth that same year. The appearance of the pamphlet caused Warburton to explode with rage because it included their private letters from 1756 in an Appendix. More letters were exchanged, some of them very long, others extremely short, like Lowth's very last letter of 24 January 1766.

Especially during the last phase of the correspondence, letters flew back and forth between the two men and were exchanged daily, delivered by hand, since Warburton lived in Prior Park, a country house near Bath, where Lowth was staying in December 1765. The above quotations show that Lowth's part of the correspondence has come down to us in the form of draft letters which he apparently kept as a record. This is evident from his use of initials rather than full names, as in the first letter quoted above (9 September 1756), as well as in the many self-corrections in his final letter mentioned at the end of the previous paragraph.[21] As fair copies, representing the form of the letters in which they were actually sent, Warburton's letters contain very few self-corrections. We thus have three different types of letters for analysis: draft versions, fair copies, and printed versions; the printed letters were, moreover, published by different publishers. The differences between these various forms of the letters will be reflected in the occurrence of the three features analysed, as shown in the section 'Private vs. Printed Practice'.

---

[21] These self-corrections represent various stages in the writing of this final letter, as I demonstrated in "Letters as a source for reconstructing social networks: The case of Robert Lowth", in: *Studies in Late Modern English Correspondence: Methodology and Data*, ed. M. DOSSENA and I. TIEKEN-BOON VAN OSTADE (Bern, 2008), pp. 51-76, at pp. 72-76.

Abbreviation Stops, Ampersands and Hyphenation Marks

Today, usage of the abbreviation stop, a term adapted from Nunberg, Briscoe and Huddleston's "abbreviation full stop",[22] is variable, not only between publishing houses but also between different varieties of English. The authors note that its "omission [...] is more common in BrE than in AmE", and that usage has decreased since the 1970s.[23] British English, they continue, distinguishes between abbreviations and contractions: abbreviations contain only the first part of a word, as in *Feb.* for 'February', while contractions end with one or more letters to indicate the closure of the word; in both, the stop is optional (*Feb / Feb., Mr / Mr.*).[24] In the historical development of punctuation, Claudia Claridge and Merja Kytö distinguish between its grammatical and rhetorical functions, and additionally mention a pragmatic function in providing guidance to the reader.[25] If usage of the abbreviation stop is variable, however, it has none of these functions, and might therefore be called superfluous – except for individuals who adopted the mark as part of their idiosyncratic writing style; as we will see below, Lowth is one of them, while Warburton is not.

The ampersand, according to Claridge and Kytö, is one of the few punctuation marks that is "verbalisable", i.e. as 'and'.[26] This is also true for the forward slash (/) for 'or', which will not be discussed here since I have not encountered it in Late Modern English letters. According to Walker, contracted forms are characteristic of what she calls the "graphic informality" of a text.[27] Contractions, either marked with abbreviation stops or not, are therefore part of the informal nature of a text, as is the occurrence of abbreviations. This is also true for the Late Modern English documents analysed here, as will be discussed below. The hyphen as a punctuation mark is important for linguists since it serves as "an indicator of word structure".[28] Here, however, I will be concerned

---

[22] G. NUNBERG, T. BRISCOE, and R. HUDDLESTON, "Punctuation", in: *The Cambridge Grammar of the English Language*, ed. R. HUDDLESTON and G.K. PULLUM (Cambridge, 2002), pp. 1723-1764, at p. 1731.

[23] NUNBERG, BRISCOE, and HUDDLESTON, "Punctuation", p. 1763.

[24] NUNBERG, BRISCOE, and HUDDLESTON, "Punctuation", pp. 1763-1764

[25] C. CLARIDGE and M. KYTÖ, "Introduction: Multiple functions and contexts of punctuation", in: *Punctuation in Context – Past and Present Perspectives*, ed. C. CLARIDGE and M. KYTÖ (Bern, 2020), pp. 9-20, at pp. 12-13.

[26] CLARIDGE and KYTÖ, "Introduction: Multiple functions and contexts of punctuation", p. 11.

[27] WALKER, *Typography and Language in Everyday Life*, p. 8.

[28] G. NUNBERG, *The Linguistics of Punctuation* (Menlo Park, CA, 1990), p. 68.

with hyphens as a visual element indicating a line break,[29] and especially with the form they take in the documents analysed.

According to Jeremy Smith, "[c]ertain rules for punctuation have been prescribed and codified since the eighteenth century in (e.g.) printers' manuals or schoolbooks".[30] Walker mentions John Smith's *The Printer's Grammar* (1755) and *Hart's Rules for Compositors and Readers Employed at the Clarendon Press, Oxford*,[31] first published in 1893 and still in use today as *New Hart's Rules* (2005);[32] she attributes some of the changing conventions over time to technological innovations like the typewriter. Accordingly, she notes, *Pitman's Manual* for typewriters (1893-1894) recommends avoiding superscript for M^r. and D^r. because "they take too long to type"; abbreviation stops, however, should be added to every abbreviation.[33] Late Modern English letter writers placed this stop underneath the final letter(s), which is hard if not impossible to reproduce in a modern edition when using a typewriter or a modern word processing program like Microsoft Word. Letter-writing manuals from the period might include rules for punctuation as well.[34] Grammars are not mentioned as sources of guidance on the use of these features in the literature I consulted for this paper, except for Nunberg, who briefly refers to Lowth's grammar (1762) in his book.[35] Checking his chapter on punctuation, however, showed that Lowth does not deal with any of the three punctuation marks discussed here. But other grammars of the period do.

One of them is *A Grammar of the English Tongue* (London, 1711), published anonymously and usually attributed to John Brightland, but written by Charles Gildon.[36] On page 152 of the grammar we find a list headed "Abbreviations of Words", which starts off with & and comprises *y* words, short forms for words like 'the' (y^e), 'that' (y^t) and 'them' (y^m), the spelling of which derives from medieval manuscript practice of writing the thorn,[37] as well as 'your' (y^r).

---

[29] Cf. VARILA et al., "Disciplinary decoding", p. 16.

[30] J.J. SMITH, "Textual form and textual function: Punctuation and the reception of early English texts", in: *Punctuation in Context – Past and Present Perspectives*, ed. C. CLARIDGE and M. KYTÖ (Bern, 2020), pp. 131-150, at p. 146.

[31] WALKER, *Typography and Language in Everyday Life*, p. 88.

[32] SMITH, "Textual form and textual function", p. 135.

[33] WALKER, *Typography and Language in Everyday Life*, p. 122.

[34] WALKER, *Typography and Language in Everyday Life*, p. 128.

[35] NUNBERG, *The Linguistics of Punctuation*, p. 86.

[36] A. BUSCHMANN-GÖBELS, "Bellum grammaticale (1712) – A battle of books and a battle for the market?", in: *Grammars, Grammarians and Grammar Writing in Eighteenth-Century England*, ed. I. TIEKEN-BOON VAN OSTADE (Berlin, 2008), pp. 81-100.

[37] In letters, the forms are graphic rather than spelling forms since their main purpose is to

Other forms in the list do have an abbreviation stop: titles like *St.* 'Saint', *Sr.* 'Sir', *Emp^r*. 'Emperor', *M^{ty}* 'Majesty', *Bp.* 'Bishop', *Mr.* 'Master', and *Mrs.* 'Mistress', some with and others without superscript; prepositions (*ab^t*. 'about' and *ag.* 'against') and nouns like *An*. 'Answer', *Qu.* 'Question', and *Acc^t*. 'Account'. As these examples show, the grammar does not distinguish between abbreviations and contractions, nor is there any consistency in the use of abbreviation stops (*Emp^r*. but *M^{ty}*) or superscript (*ab^t*. but *ag.*). No rules for hyphenation are given.

Another grammar that deals with abbreviations and contractions is John Carter's *Practical English Grammar* (Leeds, 1773).[38] These he defines on page 133 as forms in which "one or more *Letters* [...] are made to stand for the Whole", adding that "a *Period* [is] immediately put after such *Letter* or *Letters*". Carter provides a four-page list of words and their abbreviations, which includes *y* words and ends with the ampersand, explained as deriving – as indeed it does visually – from Latin *et* 'and'. The *y* words all end with superscript characters and abbreviation stops, as do the short forms for 'Company' and 'County' (both *C^o*.), and 'John' (*Jno*. [sic]). The use of the end-of-the-line hyphen is mentioned on page 36 of the grammar. Carpenter (London, 1796) likewise deals with contractions. Called *The Scholar's Spelling Assistant*, the book is not a grammar but a spelling book which provides lists of words divided into syllables.[39] It does not include *y* words, but does mention the ampersand in the list on pages 110-111. The list is a mixture of contractions (*R^t*. *Honble*. 'Right Honourable') and abbreviations (*Mo.* 'Month', *Nat.* 'Nathaniel'), but its inconsistencies (*Wk.* 'Week' but *W^t*. 'Weight') may be due to typesetting problems, since we also find *Edm$_d$*. and *Edw$_d$*. with sub- rather than superscript. The contraction *D^r*. stands for 'Debtor', not the more common 'Doctor'. All Carpenter's short forms end in an abbreviation stop, and letter writers consulting the book would have learnt that they would be allowed to use *S^r*. in opening formulas and *Ob^t. Servt*. in closures, though there only (see below). Carter lists these words without superscript.

---

speed up the writing. Jacob Thaisen, in his review of *Records of Real People: Linguistic Variation in Middle English Local Documents*, ed. M. STENROOS and K.V. THENGS (Amsterdam, 2020) in *English Language and Linguistics* 27.1 (2023), pp. 214-221, at p. 220, notes that this use of *y* belongs to "the interface between paleography and linguistics". *Y^r*. for 'your', however, is a proper contraction.

[38] J. CARTER, *A Practical English Grammar* (Leeds, 1773).
[39] T. CARPENTER, *The Scholar's Spelling Assistant* ([London], 1796).

Walker refers to the third edition of *The Complete* [or *Compleat*] *Letter Writer*, published in 1756.[40] Its first edition does not appear to have come down to us,[41] and the second, also from 1756, lists the hyphen in its overview of punctuation marks on pages 13-15, but does not deal with contractions or abbreviations. The third "improved" edition does: on page 54 there is a brief list of words headed "Explanation of common Abbreviations or Contractions of Words", adding: "A Point is always to be written after a Word thus abbreviated". This, it appears, does not apply to *y* words. The list includes the ampersand, and does not prescribe superscript for the use of short forms. As in the contemporaneous *The Printer's Grammar* by John Smith (London, 1755), also mentioned by Walker, no rules are found regarding the use of abbreviation stops, the ampersand or hyphenation for breaking off words.

Users looking for advice at the time, whether individuals or editors and typesetters, would thus have been unable to find any uniform or comprehensive directions for the use of the features analysed here. Recommendations, if present at all, were inconsistent, so this lack of clear guidance would not have done much to put an end to idiosyncratic usage on the part of individual letter writers. In any case, as comments in private letters show, the responsibility for correct spelling was generally expected to be that of the printers.[42] Stylesheets developed by a publisher would be a different matter, though even there we may not expect to encounter any universal rules.[43]

Private vs. Printed Practice

Walker cites the *Complete Letter Writer*'s advice that contractions should

---

[40] WALKER, *Typography and Language in Everyday Life*, p. 131.

[41] The first edition dates from 1755, according to L. FENS-DE ZEEUW, "The letter-writing manual in the eighteenth and nineteenth centuries: From polite to practical", in: *Studies in Late Modern English Correspondence: Methodology and Data*, ed. M. DOSSENA and I. TIEKEN-BOON VAN OSTADE (Bern, 2008), pp. 163-192, at p. 166. It is not included in ECCO, but the second and third editions, referred to next, are; both were published in London in 1756.

[42] I. TIEKEN-BOON VAN OSTADE, "Standardization of English spelling: The eighteenth-century printers' contribution", in: *Advances in English Historical Linguistics*, ed. J. FISIAK and M. KRYGIER (Berlin, 1998), pp. 457-470, at p. 458.

[43] Cf. WALKER, *Typography and Language in Everyday Life*, p. 86. Different spelling preferences across subsequent editions of, for instance, Samuel Johnson's *Dictionary of the English Language* (1st edn 1755), which thus reflect changing stylesheets over the years, are documented in N.E. OSSELTON, "Formal and informal spelling in the 18th century: Error, honour and related words", *English Studies* 44 (1963), pp. 267-275.

be avoided "as much as possible, unless it is for one's own private Use, and where it would be ridiculous to write them in Letters at length; as, &c. for and so forth, or [...] Mrs. for Mistress, &c.".[44] The manual continues by adding: "It argues [...] a **disrespect** and **slighting** to use Contractions to your Betters, and is often **puzzling** to others".[45] Similar advice is found in the works by Carter and Carpenter, discussed above. While Carpenter started his list on page 110 of *The Scholar's Spelling Assistant* by noting that "it is to be remembered [that], except in Addresses and Accompts, such Contractions in the Body of a Letter, are **improper**", Carter gives an explanation, clearly drawing on *The Complete Letter Writer* for this: "*Contractions*, except for private Use, should be as much as possible avoided. They argue **Disrespect** to Superiors, and are **puzzling** to others".[46] The occurrence of contractions in letters, but also of abbreviations and short forms like *wou'd* and *don't* as Carter wrote on page 140, was thus considered "disrespectful and too familiar". Elsewhere, I analysed whether their occurrence might be interpreted as an index of politeness, for which I drew on a number of formal and informal letters from my collected Lowth correspondence.[47] The analysis also included four of Lowth's letters to Warburton (out-letters), but no in-letters from Warburton. My findings showed that Lowth's draft letters contained many more contractions and abbreviations than the fair copies of letters, his own and those of his correspondents, but also that the letters by Edward Pearson, Lowth's secretary during his few months as bishop of St. David's in 1766, showed an exceptionally large number of short forms. This I attributed to the nature of their relationship: though certainly one of his "Betters", Lowth was very regularly in touch with Pearson, for whom letter writing formed a large part of his daily activities. My collection includes fifteen fairly lengthy letters by Pearson to Lowth, written in only two months; using contractions and abbreviations would have greatly speeded up the writing process.

Given the status of Lowth's letters to Warburton (drafts) and those of Warburton to Lowth (fair copies), we may therefore expect to find many contractions and abbreviations in Lowth's letters and only a minimum in Warburton's.

---

[44] WALKER, *Typography and Language in Everyday Life*, p. 54.
[45] WALKER, *Typography and Language in Everyday Life*, p. 131, citing (not always quite accurately) *The Complete Letter Writer*'s third edition of 1756 (available in ECCO).
[46] CARTER, *A Practical English Grammar*, p. 137.
[47] I. TIEKEN-BOON VAN OSTADE, "'Disrespectful and too familiar'? Abbreviations as an index of politeness in 18th-century letters", in: *Syntax, Style and Grammatical Norms: English from 1500-2000*, ed. C. DALTON-PUFFER, D. KASTOVSKY, N. RITT, and H. SCHENDL (Bern, 2006), pp. 229-247.

Visual Pragmatics and Late Modern English Letters 139

Since printed language represents a more formal medium than private letters, we may furthermore expect the printed letters to have fewer abbreviations and contractions. For any relationship between Lowth's and Warburton's practice and that of the works offering advice on the usage of abbreviations and contractions discussed in the preceding section, only *The Complete Letter Writer* would have been available to them. But whether educated men like them would ever have consulted a letter-writing manual is unlikely: Frances Austin argues that letter-writing manuals were intended for a very different class of people.[48] The patterns we will find are therefore expected to represent largely idiosyncratic usage. I expect to find the same for their usage of the ampersand and hyphenation practice.

Lowth's Practice

The seven out-letters in the Lowth – Warburton correspondence comprise 6606 words. Counting the number of stops in abbreviations and contractions, the letters produced 310 instances, not including the names of persons, as in Lowth's own signature (*R. L.*), those in the opening sentence of the first letter cited in section The Lowth – Warburton Dispute above (*C.* 'Chapman' and *S.* 'Spence'), and *Ss.* 'Solomon's Song', or the titles of books (*B. of Job*).[49] In only one case, i.e. y^e, a stop is lacking. Compared to 76 instances in which this form of the definite article does have an abbreviation stop this testifies to an extremely high degree of consistency on Lowth's part, which is all the more remarkable since we have to do with draft letters here. By contrast, the full form *the* was found 180 times in positions where $y^e(.)$ might have occurred, i.e. never in sentence-initial position or in directions.[50] The contraction is thus a minority form, but its high frequency is nevertheless visually conspicuous. Superscript is, moreover, found in practically all contractions, except for *Bp.* or *Bps.*, where it is not always clear whether the *p* appears in superscript or not, and in *Canon*

---

[48] F. AUSTIN, "Epistolary conventions in the Clift family correspondence", *English Studies* 54 (1973), pp. 9-22, 129-140.

[49] Shortened names and titles are of less interest in that their occurrence only illustrates incidental pragmatic practice which Lowth would not reproduce in his letters' fair copies. As discussed above, recommendations given by Carter and Carpenter only include some more common names, like *John*, *Nathanial* and *Edmund* or *Edward*.

[50] Since the form $y^e(.)$ is never encountered initially in either Lowth's own letters (nearly 100,000 words) or those of his correspondents (*c.* 34,000 words altogether), its occurrence was clearly positionally constrained.

of Ss. 'Canon of Scriptures'. Lowth's contractions include titles (*D^r.*, *L^d.*, *M^r.*, *Rev^d.* and *S^r.*); names of the months (*Sep^r.*, *Oc^r.* / *Oct^r.*, *Nov^r.* and *Dec^r.*; *Jan.* takes the form of an abbreviation); grammatical words like the definite article (*y^e.*), prepositions (*ag^t.*, *f^n.*, *wth.*), auxiliary verbs (*c^d.*, *sh^d.*, *w^d.*), pronouns (*w^{ch}.*, *y^m.*, *y^t.*, though *y^t.* also occurs as a conjunction), and some nouns commonly found in epistolary writing, such as *acc^t.* 'account' and *Servt.* 'Servant'. We also find abbreviations that are typical of a scholarly correspondence: *p.* 'page', *chap.* / *Ch.* / *cap.* 'chapter / caput' and *Ps.* 'Psalm'. Three unusual forms, *L^d.*, *W^{rs}.* and *F.*, reflect the draft status of the letters. The full forms, 'Learned Writers' and 'Future', as in 'Future State', can be retrieved from the immediate context, and shortening them would have increased the speed of writing. In the corresponding fair copies, these forms would have been expanded.

The letters contain 188 ampersands, ten of which are part of the common abbreviation *&c* 'etcetera' (and will be further excluded); the full form *and* occurs only six times. End-of-line hyphens were attested 106 times, in six Latin and three French words as well. They take the form of a double colon, one at the end of a line and one at the beginning of the next one; once, = is found at the end of a sheet (f. 141v), followed by : at the top of the next sheet (f. 142r). The reason for this is unclear. Sometimes words are broken off at what might be considered to reflect unexpected positions for someone as etymologically knowledgeable as Lowth: *cons-trued*, *loo-king*, *posse-ssing*, *pret-ends*, *res-trained*, *stric-tly* and *Subs-tance*. Clearly, breaking off words at their proper word boundaries was not a primary consideration in these relatively infrequent instances. Besides, the letters were drafts, and the fair copies might have looked different in this respect. For an overview of Lowth's usage of the three items analysed, see Table 1 in section The Printed Letters below.

Warburton's Practice

Though fair copies, Warburton's letters contain some self-corrections. Some of them have directions on the outside, others were hand-delivered. All of them were meant to be read by Lowth, as indeed they were, since he responded to them in minute detail (Warburton did so in his turn as well). In addition to the appearance of the features analysed in this paper, they are of visual interest since Warburton sometimes turned the page to a 90° angle. Linguistically, this means that he could produce longer lines and had less need to hyphenate words at the end. The letters comprise 4850 words.

Warburton used far fewer abbreviations and contractions than Lowth. Names (*P.P.* 'Prior Park', *Grosv^r Sq* 'Grosvenor Square') and titles of books (*D.L.* 'Divine Legation' or *B. of Virgil* 'Book of Virgil') were excluded from the count as well. Of the 26 instances found, only 11 have an abbreviation stop. The instances include names of the month (*Sept^r.*, *Oct^r.*, *Nov^r.*, *Dec^r.*, alongside *Dec^r*, *Jan^y*) and the title *D^r.*, though we also find *D^r*, which is once used as a contraction for 'Dear'. In addition there are *p.* (3), *Ed^n.* 'Edition' (2) and *P.S.* (1). *Servant* is mostly used in full (5 times), with one exception: *Servt* is found in the last angry letter to Lowth, along with *Grosv^r Sq.*, which occurs in full elsewhere. Here, Warburton clearly lost all patience with his correspondent, deliberately flaunting the handbook maxim, discussed above, that the use of abbreviations "argues disrespect" to one's "betters" or "Superiors". Lowth was of course not Warburton's superior in any way, but by refusing to put up even a minimal show of politeness, Warburton here shows himself at his most angry. Lowth had earlier allowed his anger with his opponent to show up linguistically as well. While during the first stage of the correspondence he had customarily used the intensifier *most* in his closing formulas ("Your **most** Obedient humble Servt."), he no longer used the word in the second part. His final letter to Warburton simply ends with "Your humble Servt.".[51] Contractions always end in a superscript letter, so if Warburton was inconsistent in his application of the abbreviation stop, he was at least consistent in his use of superscript. In contrast to Lowth's practice, Warburton did not use any *y* words.

Warburton's usage of the ampersand is likewise considerably rarer than Lowth's: I found only 46 instances compared to 47 of *and*. End-of-line hyphenation occurs 44 times (2 Latin words included). Warburton hyphenated by means of a double hyphen, one at the end of the line and the other at the beginning of the next. An overview of the instances found is presented in Table 1 in the next section.

The Printed Letters

According to the title page, Lowth's *Letter to the Right Reverend Author of The Divine Legation of Moses Demonstrated* (1765) was printed by "Clarendon

---

[51] Their lack of politeness is confirmed by a keyword analysis of the letters I presented in "Communicative competence and the language of eighteenth-century letters", in: *The Language of Public and Private Communication in a Historical Perspective*, ed. N. BROWNLEES, G. DEL LUNGO, and J. DENTON (Newcastle upon Tyne, 2010), pp. 24-45, at p. 39.

Printing-House", and published by Andrew Millar and James Dodsley, his regular publishers. The first part of the correspondence, five letters comprising 8712 words, is reproduced in the Appendix to the book. The second part was published twice in 1766, separately for private distribution by an unidentified publisher, and as part of the pamphlet by John Towne (see above), whose publishers were L. Davies and C. Reymers (see Table 1).

Comparing the letters reproduced in Lowth's pamphlet to their manuscript versions shows a number of editorial (or compositorial) changes that involve capitalisation – though without producing a consistent pattern – and spelling as well as a number of adaptations to what must have been the publisher's stylesheet. Verb forms ending in *'d* were expanded, and other epistolary spellings,[52] like Lowth's *satisfyed* and Warburton's *faithfull*, were modernised, as was Lowth's spelling of *immediatly*. As discussed in *The Bishop's Grammar*, he abandoned this form during the late 1760s, possibly under the influence of different spelling habits by his correspondents; the correction in the pamphlet suggests that exposure to printed texts may have influenced his changing spelling habits, too. Warburton's use of silent *-e* in words like *selfe* and *beliefe*, however, was mostly retained. His use of *it's* was twice corrected into *its*, and Lowth's use of *-ise* in *surpris'd* was changed into *-ize*. Punctuation was normalised throughout. Because Lowth's letters were draft versions, however, we cannot be exactly sure whether he himself made any changes to the text when producing fair copies. That a publisher's house style was used for the published document, no matter how haphazardly, is also evident from the fact that all underlining in the letters was changed into italics, and that italics were also occasionally used for Latin and French quotations. Also, Roman numerals were occasionally introduced to replace Arabic ones. If we turn to the three items analysed in this paper, we see that almost all short forms were expanded – only Warburton's two instances of *don't* and *won't* were left unchanged – and that all superscript has disappeared. Very few abbreviation stops remain: they are found only after *P.* or *p.* (9 instances), *pag.* (3), names of the months (*Sept.*, *Oct.* – 5 instances), *Ch.* (6), *P.S.* (2) and *B.* 'Book' (1). All abbreviated names were expanded.

The stylesheets used for the publication of the second part of the correspondence differ in a number of respects, though what both versions have in common with the first set of letters is a lack of consistency in capitalisation practice

---

[52] See N.E. OSSELTON, "Informal spelling systems in Early Modern English: 1500-1800", in: *English Historical Linguistics: Studies in Development*, ed. N.F. BLAKE and C. JONES (Sheffield, 1984), pp. 123-137.

(which differs from that of the manuscript letters) and the use of italics (not used in the manuscript letters). Another typically printed feature is the use of small capitals, attested in both pamphlets but more frequently in the Towne publication. In both, we find repeated quotation marks at the beginning of lines, as also used in the manuscript letters. Both later publications de-anonymised the letters by using the writers' full names, while the first batch of printed letters only provided initials. This inadvertently resulted in a form of Lowth's signature – ROB. LOWTH – which he never used himself.[53] In the Towne pamphlet the opening and closing formulas of the letters were omitted, leaving only the writers' signatures. Compared to the pamphlet whose publication was attributed to Lowth but for which we lack the name of a publisher or printer, the Towne text was more heavily edited, resulting in many changes in punctuation. Spelling, moreover, was often corrected. Whereas in the first text Warburton's spelling of *selfe* was allowed to stand, along with that of *knowlege* (see section 'The Lowth – Warburton Dispute'), in the Towne version all instances were modernised, including the change of *your selfe* into a single word (*knowlege*, however, was left uncorrected); short forms like *tho'* and *thro'* were – usually – expanded. Even the grammar was occasionally affected by editorial changes, as well as the paragraphing of the letters.

As for the features studied in this paper, all short forms were expanded in both versions, except for the names of the months, which became abbreviations rather than contractions because all superscripts were dropped. There is one exception only in the document attributed to Lowth, where we find Decr. 3^d in Warburton's last letter, with the abbreviation stop retained. Not including the headings introducing the letters (e.g. *LETTER I. / To The Reverend Dr W.*) or abbreviated names (like *P.P.* 'Prior Park') and book titles (*D.L.* 'Divine Legation'), as with the manuscript letters, I counted only eight and ten abbreviation stops, respectively – after normalisation to 1000 words, almost the same as the figure for the very first pamphlet (see Table 1). No ampersands were found (not counting their occurrence in *&c*, which has no expanded variant), and hyphenation occurred in 44 and 45 instances, respectively, thus slightly less frequently than in the first pamphlet. No unusual hyphenations were found.

Table 1, which presents the findings for the letters in their different versions (normalised to 1000 words), shows that abbreviation stops were very frequent in Lowth's (draft) letters (46.8), and that Warburton's usage is slightly lower than that of the printed letters (2.3 vs. 3.1/3.1/3.7 for the different printed pamphlets, respectively).

[53] TIEKEN-BOON VAN OSTADE, *The Bishop's Grammar*, p. 157.

Table 1 Abbreviation stops, ampersands and end-of-line hyphenation in the different sets of letters analysed, normalised to 1000 words.[54]

	abbreviation stops		ampersands		hyphenation	
	N	/1000	N	/1000	N	/1000
Lowth (draft letters) 6606 words	319	46.8	178	27	106	16.1
Warburton (fair copies) 4850 words	11	2.3	46	9.5	44	9.2
printed letters (Clarendon House) 8712 words	26	3.1	10	1.2	172	19.7
printed letters (unknown) 2560 words	8	3.1	0	0	44	17.2
printed letters (Davies & Reymers) 2712 words	10	3.7	0	0	45	16.6

While all instances of the ampersand were expanded in two of the printed versions of the letter, in the one printed by Clarendon House a number of instances were 'added' as well, resulting in 10 instances altogether – a little over one instance per 1000 words, lower than in Warburton's letters and much lower than in Lowth's. Application of the stylesheet rules by this publishing house was thus internally inconsistent. For Lowth, the ampersand was part of his general epistolary practice, for we find them in his formal letters as well.[55] Hyphenation in the printed documents is indicated by only a single hyphen at the end of the line. The figures do not differ much between the three sets of printed letters and Lowth's draft letters; the figure for Warburton's letters is much lower, which may partly be due to his longer lines (see above). In the early batch of the printed letters I have come across only a single unusual hy-

---

[54] The total number of words for the printed letters and their originals differs slightly because of minor changes to the printed text, including different hyphenation practices in the respective documents.

[55] TIEKEN-BOON VAN OSTADE, "Disrespectful and too Familiar?", p. 240.

phenation, i.e. *Chri-stiani*. In all other instances, hyphenation practice is morphologically or etymologically regular and much as we would find it today.

Visual Pragmatics and Authorial Personalities

One of the unfortunate aspects about doing research within historical sociolinguistics is that we do not have direct access to our informants. This is one of the reasons for calling the material analysed within this discipline 'bad data', a point first raised by William Labov in 1994 in his book *Principles of Linguistic Change*. There are nevertheless various ways in which sociohistorical linguists can draw on the available material in order, for instance, to learn about informants' personalities,[56] such as looking for occasional personal commentary from contemporaries or by closely analysing the informants' writing habits, as done in the present paper. For Lowth, we are fortunate enough to have some first-hand descriptions of the man. James Boswell (1740-1795), for instance, recorded in his diary on 11 April 1772 that he had "called [on Lowth] again this morning and found him at home in his house in Duke Street, Westminster. He seemed to be a **neat, judicious** little man in his conversation with me".[57] Another description of Lowth is found in the journal of H.J.A. Schultens (1749-1793), a young Dutch Arabist who studied in Oxford during the early 1770s and tried to obtain a Master's degree there, for which he invoked Lowth's assistance. Schultens visited Lowth several times and described him in a letter to his father as "*een alleraangenaamst, poliet en vriendelijk man*" ("a most pleasant, polite and friendly man"; 31 October 1772).[58] But Warburton, as he wrote in the letters analysed here, also met Lowth in person, and characterised him as follows:

> It would answer no end to tell you, what I thought of the Author of the Hebrew poetry, before I saw him. But this I may say, that I was never more surprised, when I did see him, than to find him of so **amiable** & **gentle** manners, of so **modest, sensible** & **disengaged** a deportment (17 September 1756).

---

[56] In his plenary lecture at ICEHL-21 (see note #11), Peter Petré drew attention to this much understudied topic, showing considerable potential in correlating what we can reconstruct of an author's personality with their language use.

[57] Cited in TIEKEN-BOON VAN OSTADE, *The Bishop's Grammar*, p. 137.

[58] For a digital edition of Schultens's letters to his father and of the diary he kept in Oxford, see <https://sites.google.com/site/haschultens/home>.

Lowth did not reciprocate with a description of his opponent, but Warburton characterised himself in the same letter as "[n]ot the most forbearing when I think my selfe ill treated". This tallies with my analysis of a batch of letters by Warburton in the possession of Leiden University Library, most of which are addressed to the Dutch Remonstrant minister, Cornelius Nozeman (1721-1786). The letters show that Warburton did not mince words when criticising the work of his colleagues: in the letters, we find words like *infamous, wicked, absurd, horrid, ridiculous, insolent,* and *paltry shred of dirty malice,* and he described Lowth in one of the letters as "very scurrelous" (4 December 1766).[59] Warburton himself was very much aware of his critical habits, for he wrote to Lowth on 2 December 1765: "I own I have exposed, or if you will, in your own language, abused (and I hope to the no small service of Religion & my Country) Writers of all ranks & Characters, Civil and Ecclesiastical, living & dead". In his letters to Lowth we find words like *disgust, insolent(ly), invidious,* and *scandalous,* which confirm Warburton's irascible personality. Elizabeth Montagu, moreover, in the letter quoted above, called Warburton a "bully". Lowth, however, could feel intense anger too, as becomes clear from his impetuousness in deciding to publish the second part of the correspondence without waiting for Warburton's reply, which found its way into the version published by Towne.

What light do the three features analysed here cast upon the men's characters? Though only Lowth's draft letters were available for analysis, we see that his usage of abbreviation stops is strikingly consistent. He only once missed one in his *y* words, for instance. What is more, his usage of superscript characters accompanying the stops is practically categorical. Only *Bp*(*s*). is exceptional in this respect. Using short forms was part of his epistolary practice, not only in his draft letters but also in the fair copies of letters to correspondents with whom he had a formal relationship.[60] At times he might even be said to be overdoing it, since contracting 'with' into wth. would barely have served a pragmatic function. All this, including his frequent use of the ampersand and his end-of-line hyphenation practice (double colons rather than single or double hyphens), gives the letters an idiosyncratic visual outlook. Though Boswell's use of *neat* in describing Lowth would have referred to the bishop's elegant

---

[59] Leiden University Library Manuscript MS SEM 45. See I. TIEKEN-BOON VAN OSTADE, "Late Modern English in a Dutch context", *English Language & Linguistics* 16.2 (2012), pp. 301-317, at pp. 307-308.

[60] TIEKEN-BOON VAN OSTADE, "Disrespectful and too Familiar?", p. 240.

appearance,[61] this description agrees well with Lowth's extreme consistency in spelling habits, even when drafting his letters.

Warburton's epistolary usage, as the figures in Table 1 show, was very similar to printed practice, as illustrated by the published letters. Superscript is rarely found in his letters either, and occasionally leads to ambiguous forms in isolation: *D^r*, with or without an abbreviation stop, stands for either 'Doctor' or 'Dear'. The difference in usage may have been determined by the state of the letters: Lowth's letters were drafts, while Warburton's were actually sent, and this might have made him aware of the need to engage in socially acceptable epistolary behaviour concerning the use of short forms in formal letters. Even in formal letters, though, as Carpenter wrote in 1796, it would have been acceptable to use abbreviated forms in the opening and closing formulas of letters. Warburton, however, chose to use full forms there, too, except for his final letter to Lowth of 31 January 1766. In dropping this last vestige of epistolary politeness in this distasteful exchange of letters, his irascible nature got the better of him.

Conclusion

"I have neither read nor seen, nor I believe ever shall, your printed Letter to me", Warburton informed Lowth on 21 November 1765. If he had seen the pamphlet, he would have noticed that, visually, the printed text of the letters was very different from that of their manuscript versions. Most noticeable are the absence of superscript characters and abbreviation stops to mark contractions, particularly in Lowth's letters; the use of single rather than double hyphens (Warburton) or colons (Lowth) at the end and beginning of lines; and the almost complete absence of the ampersand, though the latter feature illustrates different practices between different publishers. Analysing these features has also brought to light differences – but also inconsistencies – in the application of what appear to have been publishers' house styles. These house styles, in all three cases, involved the substitution of italics for manuscript underlining, different capitalisation and punctuation practices from that in the letters, the use of small capitals by two of them, and the expansion of the ampersand. Spelling changes modernised forms that were still typical of epistolary practice at the time, though the degree to which this was done varied between the publishers. If the changes made by Clarendon Printing-House, the printer of Lowth's pam-

---

[61] OED Online, *neat*, adj. 2a and b, available at <https://www.oed.com/>.

phlet, were quite inconsistent at times, some of their prescribed features agree with today's prescriptions in Oxford University Press's house style:[62] contractions, as instructions to authors specify today, do not end in a "full point" in British style.[63] Even the change of Lowth's *surpris'd* into *surprized* agrees with OUP's guidelines.[64] It would therefore be of interest to undertake an historical analysis of OUP's house style to see how it developed over the years. It is, finally, remarkable to see that Warburton's usage comes closest to printed practice. Lowth's usage of superscript and abbreviation stops is clearly idiosyncratic, whereas that of Warburton closely resembles that of the printed documents analysed. The acquisition of epistolary literacy largely took place in a family context at the time, as appears from Susan Whyman's book *The Pen and the People*, particularly among the middle classes.[65] Lowth's son Thomas Henry, for instance, was taught to spell by his mother,[66] but whether this was also true for Lowth himself we will probably never know. Warburton seems to have taken guidance from printed documents, as the similarity between his own practice and that of the printed pamphlets suggests.

This paper is a case study of a Late Modern English private correspondence that was also published, which has allowed for an analysis of "the interplay between prescription and practice" with respect to selected graphic features.[67] Considerable differences in preferred practice came to light, as between draft letters (Lowth's) and letters that were actually sent (Warburton's). Even at the time it was true that "[t]he more formal something is perceived to be by the writer, the more likely it is that she or he will follow prescriptions"[68] – prescriptions that Warburton appears to have found in published books. That, too, tells us something about his personality: he was willing to take the authority of printed texts as guidance for his formal, private writing. Lowth's idiosyncratic practice in this respect suggests an independent mind, but one which confirms him to be "neat" and precise. What this paper has also illustrated is the importance of reproducing Late Modern English letters as closely as possible to their originals, including idiosyncrasies like the use of superscript and abbreviation

[62] Clarendon Press today is an imprint of Oxford University Press.
[63] See the online overview of OUP's house style: <https://academic.oup.com/pages/authoring/books/preparing-your-manuscript/house-style>.
[64] Though not with the *New Oxford Spelling Dictionary: The Writer's and Editor's Guide to Spelling and Word Division*, ed. M. WAITE, 3rd edn. (Oxford, 2005).
[65] S.E. WHYMAN, *The Pen and the People. English Letter Writers 1660-1800* (Oxford, 2009).
[66] TIEKEN-BOON VAN OSTADE, *The Bishop's Grammar*, pp. 32-33.
[67] WALKER, *Typography and Language in Everyday Life*, p. 1.
[68] WALKER, *Typography and Language in Everyday Life*, p. 33.

stops. The failure to transcribe *leg^{ion}* 'legation' properly, discussed above, is a case in point. But the rendering of abbreviation stops in diplomatic editions of correspondences is equally important: one example of the failure to do so is the late Deirdre Le Faye's edition of Jane Austen's letters.[69] Jane Austen, as I have demonstrated in my detailed analysis of her letters, was quite as careful as Lowth in her use of abbreviation stops and superscript letters,[70] and this, too, provides an important detail about her personality that we might never have noticed otherwise.

---

[69] *Jane Austen's Letters*, 4th edn, ed. D. LE FAYE (Oxford, 2011). See my review of the book in *English Studies* 96.1 (2014), pp. 103-107.
[70] I. TIEKEN-BOON VAN OSTADE, *In Search of Jane Austen. The Language of the Letters* (Oxford, 2014), pp. 93-100.

Part II

The *A* to *Z* of Middle English Indexing? The Tables of John Trevisa's *Polychronicon*

WENDY SCASE

Originally composed in Latin in the mid-fourteenth century, the *Polychronicon* is an encyclopedia of world history and geography. A compilation of 'many chronicles', it is an extensive work in seven books, the first devoted to geography and the rest to history in broad chronological order. The work survives in three versions or recensions, each of which ends at a different date.[1] The author, Ranulph Higden, included with his work a Latin *tabula* ('table') as the rubrics refer to it.[2] In modern catalogues and other studies this addition is referred to as an 'index', but for the purposes of the present essay on an aspect of graphic practices and literacies I shall use Higden's medieval term '*tabula*' (or its English synonym 'table'). The term '*tabula*', denoting

---

[1] For the versions of the *Polychronicon* see J. TAYLOR, "The development of the *Polychronicon* continuation", *English Historical Review* 76.298 (1961), pp. 20-36.

[2] For the *tabulae* of the Latin *Polychronicon* see J. FREEMAN, "The manuscript dissemination and readership of the *Polychronicon* of Ranulph Higden, *c.* 1330-*c.* 1500", unpublished doctoral thesis (University of Cambridge, 2013), pp. 186-200. I am very grateful to Dr Freeman and the University of Cambridge for allowing me to consult this thesis. The Latin tables are unedited and no study has been made of their textual relations.

Graphic Practices and Literacies in the History of English, ed. Matti PEIKOLA, Jukka TYRKKÖ, and Mari-Liisa VARILA, *Utrecht Studies in Medieval Literacy*, 61 (Turnhout: Brepols, 2025), pp. 153-180.

surfaces that are prepared for receiving writing or for laying out objects, draws our attention to visual display, to layout and multi-directional modes of setting out and reading information, while 'index' (a term only denoting a finding aid from the late sixteenth century), meaning 'pointing finger', raises different expectations of the function of the finding-aid text and its relationships with the main text.[3] The term '*tabula*' connotes at-a-glance, visual organisation. Arranging headwords in an alphabetised list and displaying them in tabular form, Higden's *tabula* exploits both vertical and horizontal reading to enhance access to the content of his massive work, freeing the user to explore the text in a multiplicity of ways supported by a structure – alphabetical order – that is, at least on the surface, arbitrary rather than being driven by the organisation and agendas of the text.[4] Higden's table was widely copied with the *Polychronicon*, and on some occasions it was accompanied by other tables, including *tabulae speciales* or 'special tables' as I term them here. This tradition of tabulating large works should be seen as part of energetic tabulation of many works in late medieval English university and scholarly contexts.[5]

---

[3] In its principal senses, 'table' denotes a surface for writing on (a 'tablet') or for laying objects – chess pieces, food and dining implements – on, and a board marked out for special uses such as chess (see *Dictionary of Medieval Latin from British Sources* [DMLBS], ed. R.K. ASHDOWNE, D.R. HOWLETT, and R.E. LATHAM (Oxford, 2018), s.v. *tabula*; and MED, s.v. *table*, n. 1 and 2); in a transferred sense it denotes the arrangement itself; see MED, s.v. *table*, n. 5(a), "A columnar arrangement of written words, numbers, or symbols or some combination thereof which makes information on their relationships readily accessible" and DMLBS, s.v. *tabula*, 10(b): "(transf.) systematically arranged written presentation of numbers, words, or symbols, table, list". The earliest OED example of 'index' in English meaning a finding resource is dated 1580 and the earliest example of the term in Latin is dated 1578; see OED, s.v. *index*, n. 5(b). From Latin '*index*', the "finger used for pointing, or fore-finger" (DMLBS, s.v. *index*), the term perhaps suggests the function of index entry references to 'point to' locations in the main text. The DMLBS does not record any examples of '*index*' in the sense of a finding aid, suggesting that this is a post-medieval usage in Latin also. It would be interesting to investigate whether the late sixteenth-century use of '*index*' for a finding aid is related figuratively to the *maniculus* or image of a little hand with a pointing finger commonly used well before this date in the margins of manuscripts and printed books to make passages of special interest easy to find.

[4] As Lucy Freeman Sandler, writing of James le Palmer's alphabetical encyclopedia *Omne Bonum* (compiled before 1375), observes, "where units of information are organized in a non-prejudicial manner, as in alphabetical order, then the 'user' can combine and recombine them freely, in a spirit of inquiry that forecasts modern habits of thought" (L.F. SANDLER, *Omne Bonum: A Fourteenth-Century Encyclopedia of Universal Knowledge*, 2 vols. (London, 1996), 1, p. 35). Contrast C.F. BRIGGS, "Late medieval texts and *tabulae*: The case of Giles of Rome, *De regimine principum*", *Manuscripta* 37.3 (1993), pp. 253-275, "[t]o some extent the *tabulae* as access media would have influenced and pre-determined what their users might have looked for in the text" (at p. 266). I thank Matti Peikola for bringing Briggs's essay to my attention.

[5] On scholastic means of speeding up content discovery see, for example, BRIGGS, "Late

In this essay, I investigate the tradition of compiling *tabulae speciales* to shed light on problems raised by the English table in manuscripts of John Trevisa's Middle English *Polychronicon*. John Trevisa translated Ranulph Higden's *Polychronicon* from Latin into English around 1385-1387.[6] Trevisa's translation survives in fourteen manuscripts, in ten of which separate alphabetical *tabulae* in Latin and English, often rubricated as such, occur or are thought once to have occurred (some manuscripts are defective), while in three of the other four an English alphabetical *tabula* alone occurs.[7] The English *tabula* has been described as "the first official alphabetical index in English".[8] Despite its precocity it has drawn negative comment: "dysfunctional" is the term recently applied to it in Emily Steiner's important recent study. Steiner explains that it

medieval texts and *tabulae*"; M.B. PARKES, "The influence of the concepts of *ordinatio* and *compilatio* on the development of the book", repr. in: *Scribes, Scripts and Readers: Studies in the Communication, Presentation, and Dissemination of Medieval Texts* (London, 1991), pp. 55-74; R.H. ROUSE and M.A. ROUSE, "Concordances et index", in: *Mise en page et mise en texte du livre manuscrit*, ed. H.-J. MARTIN and J. VEZIN with J. MONFRIN (Paris, 1990), pp. 219-228; R.H. ROUSE and M.A. ROUSE, "*Statim invenire*: Schools, preachers, and new attitudes to the page", in: *Renaissance and Renewal in the Twelfth Century*, ed. R.L. BENSON and G. CONSTABLE with C.D. LANHAM (Oxford, 1982), pp. 191-219; SANDLER, *Omne Bonum*, esp. vol. 1, pp. 36-44; and *Taxonomies of Knowledge: Information and Order in Medieval Manuscripts*, ed. E. STEINER (Philadelphia, PA, 2015).

[6] For an edition of the Latin and Trevisa's translation see *Polychronicon Ranulphi Monachi Cestrensis with English Translations of John Trevisa and of an unknown Writer of the Fifteenth Century*, ed. C. BABINGTON (vols. 1-2) and J.R. LUMBY (vols. 3-9), 9 vols. (London, 1865-1886: *Rolls Series* 41). Hereafter cited as *Polychronicon*.

[7] For the *tabula* rubrics to the English table see A. LIIRA, *Paratextuality in Manuscript and Print: Verbal and Visual Presentation of the Middle English* Polychronicon. PhD thesis, University of Turku (Turku, 2020), available at <https://urn.fi/URN:ISBN:978-951-29-8058-1>, p. 138. Both the Latin and the English tables found in the Trevisa manuscripts are unedited. The following manuscripts of Trevisa's *Polychronicon* contain both Latin and English tables: MSS London, British Library, Addit. 24194; San Marino, Huntington Library HM 28561; Aberdeen University Library 21; Tokyo, Senshu University Library 1 (formerly Oslo / London, Schøyen Collection 194); London, British Library, Harley 1900; Cambridge, St. John's College 204 (H.1); Liverpool, Public Libraries f909 HIG; and Manchester, Chetham's Library 11379 (Mun.A.6.90). The following contain only the English table: MSS Glasgow University Library, Hunter 367; London, British Library, Stowe 65; and Princeton University Library, Taylor 6. The following have no table: MSS London, British Library, Cotton Tiberius D.vii; Princeton University Library, Garrett 151; and Cambridge, Corpus Christi College 354. See R. WALDRON, "The manuscripts of Trevisa's translation of the *Polychronicon*: Towards a new edition", *Modern Language Quarterly* 51.3 (1990), pp. 281-317, at pp. 286, 309-317.

[8] I do not know of an earlier Latin alphabetical table with an English text. Steiner describes Trevisa's English table as "one of the first alphabetical indexes in English" and "the first official alphabetical index in English" (E. STEINER, *John Trevisa's Information Age: Knowledge and the Pursuit of Literature, c. 1400* (Oxford, 2021), pp. 107, 108; cf. 109) but she does not consider whether there are earlier Latin tables for English texts.

conflates a table of contents and an index, many of its headwords are not proper nouns, its entries are given to sensationalism, and its original West Country spellings were a challenge to scribes from other dialect regions.[9] I argue that the English *tabula* belongs with the tradition of the *tabula specialis*, an alphabetical discovery tool arranged in tabular form and designed for a particular audience. The pairing of Latin and English *tabulae* in most of the Trevisa manuscripts reflects, I propose, the pairing of a *tabula specialis* with a *tabula communis* in some manuscripts of Higden's Latin text, '*specialis*' and '*communis*' being terms that I derive from headings in one example (see below). Comparing the English *tabula* with examples of Latin *tabulae speciales* and their pairings with *tabulae communes*, I propose that the English *tabula* is specially devised for a particular audience not served by the *tabula communis*. They were not served not just because the *tabula communis* was in Latin (it would, after all, have been relatively straightforward to translate the Latin table into English – the referencing had all been done, and only some relocation of headwords would have been necessary), but because its contents were a barrier to their participating in the literacy practices of user-driven free and rapid perusal and locating of content associated with the alphabetised table. To shed further light on ideas about this audience and their needs, I shall draw on Trevisa's *Dialogue between a Lord and a Clerk* and his *Epistola to Sir Thomas Berkeley*, short texts that discuss and defend the translation of the *Polychronicon* into English that travel with the translation in some of its manuscripts.[10] By creating a table for this projected audience, I argue, the compiler of the English text participates in the tradition of the *tabula specialis*.

The Problem of the Tables in Trevisa's Polychronicon

The Latin *tabula* in the manuscripts of Trevisa's *Polychronicon* is the kind of table associated with the intermediate and long versions of Higden's Latin text. Ninety-seven of the 135 manuscripts of the Latin *Polychronicon* have an alphabetical table that provides an alternative means of navigating the work, permitting readers to organise their finding and reading of the material in the-

---

[9] STEINER, *John Trevisa's Information Age*, pp. 117-124.

[10] Edited in R. WALDRON, "Trevisa's original prefaces on translation", in: *Medieval English Studies Presented to George Kane*, ed. E.D. KENNEDY, R. WALDRON, and J.S. WITTIG (Woodbridge, 1988), pp. 285-299. For Thomas Berkeley see R. HANNA, "Sir Thomas Berkeley and his patronage", *Speculum* 64.4 (1989), pp. 878-916.

matic rather than chronological ways and providing a quick means of discovering material in the text of interest to the reader.[11] The tables differ in different recensions of the text.[12] A major difference between the short version and the intermediate and long versions of the *Polychronicon* is that in the intermediate and long versions the seven books are subdivided into chapters. This structure made possible a system of location referencing that was text specific rather than codex specific.[13] In the categories of Richard Rouse and Mary Rouse, the Latin *tabula* would be an "index" that is "independent", that is to say useful regardless of the physical properties of the codex in which the main text travels.[14] In manuscripts of the so-called intermediate version that ends in 1340-1342, the *tabula* comprises alphabetical lists of headwords with references to the books and chapters in which the topics are to be found. This Latin *tabula* was useful for any text of the *Polychronicon* that was marked up with book and chapter divisions. It is this property of being useable in any codex, I suggest, that led to the description of the table as *"communis"* in one of the manuscripts I shall discuss. And the *communis* property of the Latin table indeed led to its prevalence in the manuscripts of the Latin *Polychronicon*. Its ubiquity derived, I surmise, not only because its mode of location referencing was independent of codex, but also because the textual layout fitted readily into a quire or quires that could easily be specially ruled with entry and reference columns (I discuss layout further below). Therefore it could easily be supplied even where a text did not originally include a *tabula*. James Freeman notes examples of manuscripts of the intermediate / long Latin text where a table occurs in different hands from those of the main text and in separate quires from those of the main text.[15] As a common table independent of codex it was, therefore, potentially

---

[11] FREEMAN, "The manuscript dissemination and readership of the *Polychronicon*", p. 186.

[12] FREEMAN, "The manuscript dissemination and readership of the *Polychronicon*", pp. 188-195.

[13] For these terms cf. my discussion of codex-specific and non-codex-specific tables of contents, W. SCASE, "'Looke this calender and then proced': Tables of contents in medieval English manuscripts", in: *The Dynamics of the Medieval Manuscript: Text Collections from a European Perspective*, ed. K. PRATT, B. BESAMUSCA, M. MEYER, and A. PUTTER (Göttingen, 2017), pp. 287-306. For six Latin *Polychronicon* manuscripts that contain tables that use folio numbers see FREEMAN, "The manuscript dissemination and readership of the *Polychronicon*", p. 188.

[14] ROUSE and ROUSE, "Concordances et index".

[15] A full study of the codicology and other traces of the tables' production is not possible here, but evidence such as differences in the hand of the table and the hand of the main text and its different placing in relation to the main text is deducible from the very useful manuscript descriptions provided by FREEMAN, "The manuscript dissemination and readership of the *Polychronicon*". Examples of apparent production of the table as an independent unit include: MS

transferable to Trevisa's Middle English translation of the text, since the translated text retains the book and chapter divisions and mark-up of the Latin. Its appearance in early manuscripts of the Trevisa translation shows that this additional potential for it to apply across languages was recognised and exploited. In the Trevisa codices as in those of the Latin text, the tables likewise appear in various configurations and guises that appear to reflect various production histories.[16]

Aberystwyth, Brogynton II.24, table on ff. ii r-xii r, seems to be in different hand from main text (FREEMAN, p. 215); MS Cambridge University Library Ii.2.24, table on ff. 5r-11v, in different hand from main text (FREEMAN, p. 221); MS Cambridge, Peterhouse 177, table on ff. 17r-36v, has signs of the replacement of an earlier table (FREEMAN, p. 234; cf. p. 195); MS Cambridge, St. John's College A.12, table on ff. 218-230r follows main text of *Polychronicon* rather than preceding it as is more usual and has emendations by the scribe (FREEMAN, p. 235); MS Cambridge, Trinity College R.5.25, table on ff. i r-x v, in a different quire, hand, and script, from main text (differences not noted by FREEMAN); MS Lincoln Cathedral Library 85, table on ff. 103v-105v follows main text and does not correspond to its referencing (FREEMAN, p. 247); MS London, British Library, Cotton Nero D.viii, table on ff. 333v-339v follows main text; table apparently in two hands (FREEMAN, p. 257); MS London, British Library, Egerton 871, table on ff. 318r-320v follows main text (FREEMAN, p. 257); MS London, British Library, Harley 3671, table on ff. 17r-24r in different hand from main text, in my opinion, and second table on ff. 1r-16v in a third hand, in my opinion (for these tables see further below); MS London, Inner Temple, Petyt 511.5, table on ff. 1r-9v in different hand from main text (FREEMAN, p. 277); MS London, Lambeth Palace 112, imperfect table on ff. 130r-132v in different hand from main text (FREEMAN, p. 280); MS Oxford, Bodleian Library, Lyell 21, table on ff. 223r-231r follows main text and additions (FREEMAN, p. 296); MS Oxford, Magdalen College, Lat. 147, tables on ff. 235r-242r and 242v-300v, both in hand of one of the volume's four scribes; the tables fall at the end of "production boundar[ies]" (R. HANNA, unpublished draft of entry for forthcoming new Magdalen manuscripts catalogue; I am most grateful to Anne Chesher of Magdalen College Library for supplying me with this draft); for these tables see further below.

[16] The Latin table in MS London, British Library, Addit. 24194 occurs with the English table on ff. 21r-35v, immediately before the main text; it is attributed to the hand of the main text scribe in L. MOONEY, S. HOROBIN, and E. STUBBS, *Late Medieval English Scribes, Version 1.0*, (2011), available at <http://www.medievalscribes.com>. For other table pairs placed together before the main text and attributed to one hand by *Late Medieval English Scribes* see: Senshu UL 1 (tables on ff. 1r-14v); Cambridge, St. John's 204 (H.1) (tables on ff. 19r-33v); Liverpool, Public Libraries, f909 HIG (tables on ff. 1r-13r); and Manchester, Chetham's MS 11379 (Mun.A.6.90) (tables on ff. 19r-34v). In Huntington HM 28561 the Latin and English tables (ff. 21r-40v) are separated from the main *Polychronicon* by Trevisa's *Dialogue* and *Epistola*; *Late Medieval English Scribes* identifies the hand of the tables as that of the main scribe (of four). In Aberdeen UL 21, the Latin and English tables (ff. 1r-11v [the English table is incomplete]) immediately precede the main text of the *Polychronicon*; *Late Medieval English Scribes* finds two hands in the main text but does not mention the hand of the tables. In BL, Harley 1900 the Latin and English tables (ff. 21r-41v) are separated from the main *Polychronicon* text by Trevisa's *Dialogue* and *Epistola*; *Late Medieval English Scribes* attributes the whole to one hand.

That the Latin *tabula* was readily available and easily transferable even to the translated *Polychronicon* raises the question of the purpose of the English *tabula*, especially where it occurs alongside the Latin table, as it does in most cases. Ronald Waldron suggests that the English table was made independently of the Latin, perhaps by Trevisa himself.[17] He proposes that the Latin table may have been added early – "rather superfluously" – in the textual transmission of the English *Polychronicon*.[18] Steiner suggests that later manuscript producers added the Latin *tabula* alongside the English one for reasons of its greater functionality: "it is simply more practical to use the Latin index than it is to use the English when trying to navigate Trevisa's translation of the *Polychronicon*".[19] Aino Liira proposes that the motivation for "retaining or reintroducing" the Latin *tabula* may have been that the two have different organising methods within sections – "alphabetical vs sequential" – or more likely that the contents are "complementary".[20] She proposes that the sequential method used in the English table may have been useful for readers who already knew the content; it served as a kind of memory aid "for a reader familiar with the text".[21] In the remainder of this essay I shall suggest that these questions about the origins and purpose of the English *tabula*, its relations with the Latin *tabula*, the reasons for the circulation of both *tabulae* together in several manuscripts, and the decision not simply to translate the Latin *tabula*, repay consideration in relation to a tradition of providing both a *tabula communis* and a *tabula specialis*. First, I shall introduce a tradition of double *tabulae*, and then consider how this tradition sheds light on the tables in the English *Polychronicon* manuscripts. The Latin *tabula*, I shall argue, belongs with the tradition of the *tabula communis* for the Latin *Polychronicon*, while the English *tabula* is a *tabula specialis*. I shall suggest that what makes the English table *specialis*, the motivation driving its composition, is that it inflects the visual model and literacy practices of the alphabetical Latin *tabula communis* in English for a particular audience. I

---

[17] WALDRON, "The manuscripts of Trevisa's translation", p. 284. One of his arguments in favour of this suggestion for authorship of the table is that "[s]ome of the entries [...] are stamped with Trevisa's typical engagement of interest in what he is translating [...] it testifies to an intimate acquaintance with the subject matter of the *Polychronicon* of a kind not likely to be picked up by a scribe in the process of copying the work" (R. WALDRON, "Dialect aspects of manuscripts of Trevisa's translation of the Polychronicon", in: *Regionalism in Late Medieval Manuscripts and Texts*, ed. F. RIDDY (Woodbridge, 1991), pp. 67-88, at pp. 76-77).
[18] WALDRON, "The manuscripts of Trevisa's translation", p. 284.
[19] STEINER, *John Trevisa's Information Age*, p. 122.
[20] LIIRA, *Paratextuality in Manuscript and Print*, p. 138. I discuss organising methods below.
[21] LIIRA, *Paratextuality in Manuscript and Print*, p. 139.

shall propose that, notwithstanding that the Latin *tabula* does not survive in all manuscripts, it is demonstrably a model for the English *tabula* visually and functionally, and that the English *tabula* was always meant to be seen in relation to it as a *tabula specialis* – whether it was bound with it or not – rather than as a replacement for it. That its compiler or compilers did not translate the Latin table demonstrates that its language is not the sole property that makes the English table special; to do so would not have fulfilled the rationale of the translation project set out by Trevisa. The English *tabula* engages the affordances of the alphabetised table to benefit the new, particular audience whose special needs the Lord and the Clerk discuss in Trevisa's *Dialogue* and on which further light is shed by his *Epistola*.

Double Tables and the Tabula Specialis

Examples of double *tabulae* for the *Polychronicon* occur in MS Oxford, Magdalen College, Lat. 147 and MS London, British Library, Harley 3671, both manuscripts of the intermediate / longer versions of the Latin text. Magdalen Lat. 147 dates to the mid-fifteenth century and is of Oxford provenance.[22] Harley 3671 dates to the turn of the fourteenth and fifteenth centuries and is associated with the library of Hospital of St. John the Baptist, Exeter, which was founded to educate twelve boarding scholars and a tutor.[23] Both manuscripts contain the usual *tabula*, and also contain, in addition, a fuller *tabula*. These fuller *tabulae* appear to be unrelated textually to one another.[24]

In Magdalen Lat. 147, the two *tabulae* to the *Polychronicon* occur on ff. 235r-242r and 242v-300v.[25] Both tables are in the same hand and have a running heading in the hand of the scribe. The first *tabula* is headed "*Tabula communis de chronicis supradictis*". This *tabula communis* is the Latin *tabula* found in many copies of the intermediate and longer versions of the

[22] HANNA, unpublished draft catalogue entry.
[23] See f. 25r for the hospital's inscription. For the hospital see I. MAXTED, "*Impressorie Arte*: The impact of printing in Exeter and Devon", in: *Print Cultures and Peripheries in Early Modern England*, ed. B.R. COSTAS (Brill, 2013), pp. 127-146, at p. 135.
[24] FREEMAN, "The manuscript dissemination and readership of the *Polychronicon*", p. 198.
[25] For the manuscript see H.O. COXE, *Catalogus Codicum MSS qui in Collegiis Aulisque Oxoniensibus Hodie Adservantur*, 2 vols. (Oxford, 1852), 2, p. 71; FREEMAN, "The manuscript dissemination and readership of the *Polychronicon*", p. 309; and HANNA, unpublished draft catalogue entry. These tables appear to be followed by extracts from the *Polychronicon* (ff. 303-316).

Polychronicon. The second *tabula* is headed "*Tabula specialis de eodem* [sic] *chronicis*".[26] The headers suggest that the two *tabulae* are conceived of in relation to one another and to the main *Polychronicon* ('*communis*' and '*specialis*' being antonyms applicable to a range of phenomena from a '*missa*' to a '*via*').[27] A relationship between the two is also suggested by similarities in layout. Both *tabulae* have the same two-column layout (see Fig. 1 and Fig. 2).

The *tabula communis* has a two-column text layout with each text column being subdivided into three data columns, one for the entry, one for the book number, and one for the chapter number or numbers. This layout reflects that found, for example, in the *tabula* in the intermediate version in MS San Marino, Huntington Library, HM 132, a manuscript that is thought to be in Higden's own hand. Here the headwords are laid out in two text columns. Each headword is distinguished by a red paraph mark. At the top of each headword column a majuscule letter provides a quick reference for identifying the part of the alphabetical sequence set out on the pages. The beginning of each new letter sequence is marked by an eye-catching enlarged red majuscule. The book and chapter references are set out in parallel data columns to the right of the headwords. In some instances, more than one reference is included under the same headword, though the ruling does not properly allow for this and the additional references are squeezed to the right of the book and chapter columns. For example, the entry about St. Chad, "*De Sancto Cedda episcopo*", bears the references book 5, chapters 17 and 18, the second chapter number spilling over the space in the column (f. 285v). Entries begin with "*De*" and each instance is painted red or blue to catch the eye.

In Magdalen Lat. 147 the *tabula specialis* reflects this tradition of layout. Like the common table in this manuscript, it has been ruled for two text columns each subdivided into three data columns. But there are some differences. The entries are signalled by alternating red and blue paraphs, and these are applied to subheadings also. For example, in the *A* sequence, "*Arthuri regis*" does not receive a paraph, but "*Guenevera uxo[r] eius*" and "*Baldewinus*" do

---

[26] I am most grateful to Leanne Grainger of Magdalen College Library for supplying images of the tables.

[27] DMLBS, s.v. *communis*, 9. Other medieval terms for a pair of tables are '*duae tabulae*' found in a fifteenth-century book catalogue from the York Augustinian friars ("*du[e] tabul[e] Egidii*", quoted by BRIGGS, "Late medieval texts and *tabulae*", p. 263) and '*tabula*' and '*contra-tabula*' ("*Explicit tabula super Egidium de regimine principum. Incipit contratabula super-eandem tabulam*"), quoted by BRIGGS, p. 270, n. 25, from MS Cambridge University Library, Ii.4.22, a late fourteenth- or early fifteenth-century manuscript of *De regimine principum* of Giles of Rome; according to BRIGGS, the *contratabula* here is a list of the headwords in the accompanying *tabula* (p. 258).

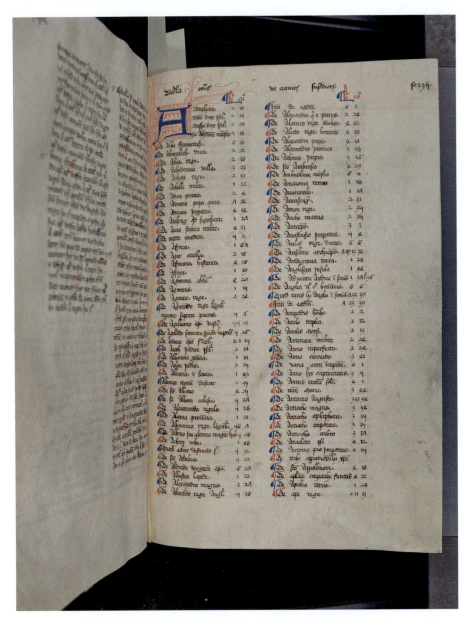

Fig. 1 Oxford, Magdalen College, MS Lat. 147, f. 235r, the opening of a table to the Latin *Polychronicon* with the heading "*Tabula communis de chronicis supradictis*". Reproduced with the permission of The President and Fellows of Magdalen College, Oxford.

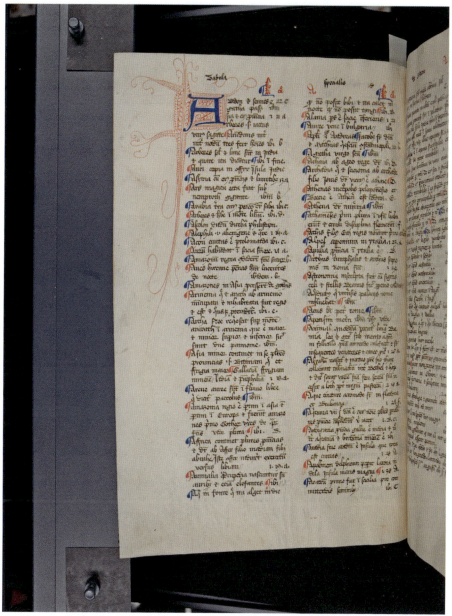

Fig. 2 Oxford, Magdalen College, MS Lat. 147, f. 242v, the opening of a table to the Latin *Polychronicon* with the heading "*Tabula specialis* [*de eodem* [*sic*] *chronicis*]". Reproduced with the permission of The President and Fellows of Magdalen College, Oxford.

(f. 246r). The *tabula* gives the visual impression of echoing the *tabula communis*, but actually the entries do not completely follow their model. Differing from the traditional model, in Magdalen Lat. 147 the writing in the entry column is frequently allowed to run into the location columns and on to the next line. This means that key words that could be headwords often do not fall at the beginning of lines. Sometimes, instead of a reference, "*ibidem*" is written, and the letters *a* to *d* are used to indicate location within a chapter.[28] The pattern of ruling with subdivided columns is abandoned by the end of the *tabula specialis* but nowhere is there much sign of using it. Location references are simply given on the last line of the entry after the text.

Turning to the structure of letter sections and entries in the Latin *tabula communis*, the *tabula* runs from "*Abraham*" to "*Zorobabel*". It is alphabetised to one letter. Entries are brief, usually just a proper noun and one or more qualifying words, for example,

De Edmundo rege, 6. 7
De Edmundo martire, 6. 16
Item de eodem, 5. 32
De Edmundo episcopo, 7. 34, 35
De Edwaldo frater eiusdem domini, 5. 32

(MS Cambridge, Trinity College R.5.24, f. iii v)[29]

It will be seen from the above example that the material is organised into sub-entries, for example, "*Edwald*" comes under "*Edmund*". But whereas a modern typesetter would indent '*Edwald*' under '*Edmund*', the common *tabula* is laid out in simple columns and the relationships between headwords and sub-entries are indicated grammatically: "*Edwald*, brother of the same lord", and above, under "*Edmund*, martyr", "*Item, de eodem*", "again, about the same".

The entries in the Magdalen Lat. 147 *tabula specialis* are longer than those of the *tabula communis*, and they are clustered around fewer headwords.

---

[28] The practice of using letters to indicate chapter position was first used in biblical concordances before being applied to other alphabetical reference works; see ROUSE and ROUSE, "Concordances et index", pp. 221-222.

[29] As the common table is unedited, it is necessary to quote from manuscript. I use the text of the Latin table in Trevisa *Polychronicon* manuscript Cambridge, Trinity R.5.25. I have chosen this manuscript because it contains a full text and is readily available online. I follow the foliation that is in small roman numerals in the top right of rectos. In this sequence the number vii appears to have been skipped. In all transcriptions I expand abbreviations silently and introduce modern capitalisation and punctuation.

Whereas the *tabula communis* is alphabetised to two letters, the *tabula specialis* is alphabetised to only the first letter. For example, the *Y* section includes "Ysaac", "Ymagines", "Ymago", "Ydolatria", "Ypocras", "Yemps", "Iubiter", and so on, ordering only under initial letter. Whereas the *tabula communis* headwords are usually proper nouns, those of the *tabula specialis* are often concepts, as the *Y* section attests. Sometimes gaps are left at the ends of letter sequences, for example after *Y* and *Z* (f. 300v). Examination of two entries in the *tabula specialis* suggests something of the particular interests and purposes of the compiler. The first example is an entry under the headword "*archiepiscopus*":

> ¶*Archiepiscopus Cantuarensis Robertus familiaris Sancti Edwardi Regis et Confessoris quondam monachus Gemmeticus post episcopus Londoniensis*, 6.24.a
> ¶*Iste Robertus tandem apud monasterium suum Gemmeticum obiit cui successit in sede Cantuarensis Stigandus qui quondam sedem Wyntonensis* [...]
>
> Magdalen Lat. 147, f. 244v

Here the *tabula* locates information about the appointment of Robert as archbishop of Canterbury, one-time monk of "*Gemmeticum*" (Jumièges). But the *Polychronicon* chapter to which it refers mainly deals with Earl Godwin and his rivalry with Edward I. The *tabula* entry brings together a reference from the beginning of the chapter about Robert's appointment to the see with a reference from later about his death.[30] This entry is one of many in the *A* section of the *tabula specialis* that are devoted to archbishops, others mentioned including Lanfranc of Canterbury, Aldred of York, Thomas of York, and Anselm of Canterbury (f. 245r). This headword would not be especially useful for anyone looking for names of particular archbishops or even a particular province, York or Canterbury. Nor is it particularly useful for locating notable accounts of archbishops in the *Polychronicon*. It does, however, serve the purpose of using the *Polychronicon* as a source of reference on archbishops, collating and referencing the information. It might be useful for someone teaching or learning about the archbishops of York and Canterbury who did not know much about them already. It would teach the names of the provinces, some of the names of the more famous archbishops, their dates, and show that several were members of religious orders when they were appointed.

The second example is an entry under the headword "*Anglia*":

---

[30] *Polychronicon*, 7, pp. 172, 180.

¶*Angliam vendicavit hereditarie* [claimed England by inheritance] *quidam scriptor Oxonie nomine Iohannes qui habuit mureligum sibi familiarem quamobrem de mendacio conuictus distractus et suspensus est*, 7.42, b.

Magdalen Lat. 147, f. 245v

This summarises a story in the *Polychronicon* about an event in 1318 when an Oxford scribe who had a cat as a familiar claimed he was the heir to England and was punished:

Quidem scriptor nomine Iohannes habens murilegum sibi familiarem asseruit publice apud Oxoniam circa festum Pentecostis se esse verum heredem Angliae, quamobrem apud Northamptoniam corem rege et proceribus de mendacio convictus, distractus et suspensus est.

Polychronicon, 7, p. 308.

The next entry is from the same chapter but concerns a completely different person:

¶*Andreas Harkley factus est comes de Carliell, ibidem*, d.
¶*Qui postea tanquam proditor capitur et suspenditur et decapitatur*

Magdalen Lat. 147, f. 245v

The *Polychronicon* chapter referenced begins the story with an account of how Andrew Harkley fought for Edward II, killing the earl of Hereford.[31] Later it tells how Harkley was made earl in 1323 at a parliament in York and subsequently was convicted.[32] It is hard to explain why these two events are selected from a chapter concerning the Scottish wars. Possibly it is because "*Andreas*" fits under *A*, but it seems more likely that the two events are linked logically in the compiler's mind by the theme of treason and justice in "*Anglia*". Such an interpretation would chime with a noticeable nationalistic focus in the *tabula*. In line with this nationalistic focus, headwords dominating the *B* section are "*bellum*" and "*Britannia*". Ff. 247v-248r of the *tabula specialis* have entries for battles at Haddon Hill, Crecy, and Evesham, Poitiers, and Rochelle. Battles are

---

[31] *Polychronicon*, 7, p. 312.
[32] *Polychronicon*, 7, p. 316.

sometimes specified as *"bellum nauale"* and the victories of the English are noted. For example:

¶*Bellum nauale inter anglicos et Flandrenses vicerunt Anglici*, 7. 48a
¶*Bellum nauale inter Anglos et Hispanos ante portum de Rochelle vbi Angli victi fuerunt et comes Pembrok captus est, ibidem*, b

Magdalen Lat. 147, f. 248r.

The *tabula specialis* compiles material under the headword *"bellum"* to teach the locations of famous battles won by the English and notable events at these battles such as, here, the capture of the Earl of Pembroke. The *tabula* is aimed at a user who does not already know the names and places of battles, but is imagined to need to know of famous historic victories of the English. Besides being focused on nationalistic matters, the *tabula* is also interested in other places and their customs. A recurrent headword in the *U* section is *"urbs"*. This entry compiles information about the founding of cities: Rome, York, Leicester, Corinth, and Palermo are among the cities mentioned (f. 299v), and the naming of the city of Rome after Romulus (f. 300r). Under *"uxores"* it is recorded that more than one wife is allowed to a man in India and other places (f. 299v).

To summarise, the *tabula specialis* in Magdalen Lat. 147 is an alphabetised structure for digesting material deemed to be of interest or importance to a particular audience. That audience is, by inference, male, clerical, nationalistic, curious about the world, but relatively uneducated and ill-informed compared with that anticipated for the *tabula communis*. The *tabula specialis* complements the *tabula communis* by providing access to the *Polychronicon* for those to whom the headwords of the usual *tabula* would not be known and for whom they would not be useful. It enables a relatively uneducated but perhaps aspirational, or would-be-clerical audience to benefit from the historical material in the *Polychronicon*. The *tabula specialis* in Magdalen Lat. 147 appears to be pedagogic, a step on the way to using the *tabula communis* and gaining access to the *Polychronicon* itself.

Our second example of double *tabulae* for the *Polychronicon*, in Harley 3671, does not use the headings *tabula communis* and *tabula specialis* but it clearly follows a similar model. Like Magdalen Lat. 147, Harley 3671 includes the usual Latin *tabula* (it runs from *"Abraham"* to *"Zorobabel"*, plus *"Zacarie"* and *"De Zebedeo"*, ff. 17r-24r) alongside an otherwise unwitnessed *tabula* (ff. 1r-16v) which, beginning on the headword *"Aaron"* and ending on the headword *"Lindeseia"* is now incomplete, the *tabula specialis* having perhaps lost two further quires before the usual *tabula communis* starts on what is now f. 17r.[33] The two tables are in different hands and their layout is different. Notably, while the *tabula communis* indicates headwords with tipping of "*De*" and the first letter of the headword in red, headwords in the *tabula specialis* are differentiated either with a paraph mark or simply with a majuscule. The paraphs and initials are in different brown ink and do not run the full length of the *tabula*. Perhaps they were supplied later by someone who gave up the effort. Perhaps the *tabula communis* was supplied to mitigate the loss of the quires from the *tabula specialis*, though that the *A-L* portion of the *tabula specialis* remains suggests that it is more likely that the two were perceived as complementary not duplicates, as in Magdalen Lat. 147.

Like the *tabula specialis* in Magdalen Lat. 147, that in Harley 3671 has many entries for certain headwords. It shares an interest in battles, particularly those relating to Britain or England. Entries with the headword "*bellum*" include "*Bellum primum inter Saxones*, 5. 7" (f. 4r). The chapter referenced relates how in the second year under the emperor Justinus, King Ethelberht of Kent gave battle to Ceaulinus, King of the West Saxons, and his brother at Willbandium, slaying two of his dukes, adding that this was the first battle among the Saxons.[34] The *tabula* entry picks out this last detail, omitting the names. Another entry simply records "there was a civil war" ("*Bellum civile fuit*", 3. 39', f. 4r) when the chapter referred to names the protagonists (two German brothers, both called Gracchus), and gives the reason for their aggression and what happened in considerable detail.[35] Another important headword is "*Anglia*". Key events in English history are included in the table: Anglia's being named, receiving the faith, being subjugated by the Romans, subjugating the Scots, being divided into three kingdoms, being excommunicated, longitude and latitude, and so on (f. 2r-v). This *tabula* shares the nationalistic and militaristic interests of that in Magdalen Lat. 147 and shares, too, the character of presenting information under keywords and not just under names. Compared with the Magdalen special *tabula*, however, it does include many proper nouns among its headwords, many of them figures of ancient history. But the provenance of the manuscript in a teaching institution suggests that its purpose too was primarily pedagogic.

Special *tabulae* are not always found physically bound with the common *tabula* or indeed with the *Polychronicon* text. An example of a free-floating

---

[33] FREEMAN, "The manuscript dissemination and readership of the *Polychronicon*", p. 264.
[34] *Polychronicon*, 6, p. 374.
[35] *Polychronicon*, 6, pp. 152-154.

special table, I would argue, is to be found in the work of the scribe John Benet. Benet, a priest who had died by 1474, was owner and copyist of most of MS Dublin, Trinity College 516 (E. 5. 10). The manuscript includes an alphabetical compilation made by Benet of extracts from the Latin *Polychronicon* together with some materials from other sources (ff. 49r-53v; 56r-75v). As I have argued in detail elsewhere, Benet seems to have modelled his work on the example of other *tabulae* to the *Polychronicon* and it is possible that he thought of his work as a table made for specific readers.[36] He furnishes his entries with careful book and chapter references, following the referencing method of the common table, and sometimes adds in a sidenote "*lege loco*", an instruction to look at the relevant entry in the *Polychronicon* text itself. He too leaves gaps at the ends of letter sections.

I have been proposing that Harley 3671 and Magdalen Lat. 147 belong with a tradition of double tables for the *Polychronicon*. In this tradition the *tabula communis* or 'usual Latin table' is supplemented by a *tabula specialis* produced for a particular audience. Its contents are targeted at the needs and interests of that audience and its purpose is pedagogic. The alphabetical structure provides a framework within which the *Polychronicon* material thought most relevant to the audience may be compiled and organised by keywords. This tradition may even inform tables such as John Benet's where no *tabula communis* (or even *Polychronicon* text) is found in the same codex as the special table. Our analysis of the special tables in the Latin manuscripts has shown that they share some characteristic differences from the common table. Location references are given in the form of book and chapter, as in the common table. But letter sections are alphabetised to one letter, not two. The alphabetised structure is harnessed to gather and organise material under important keywords: headwords are often keywords rather than proper nouns. Some headwords are opportunities for gathering material from across the work and they use the text as a source for an agenda appropriate for a particular audience. Because they are opportunities for structuring material under topics imputed to be key, entries are often long, running over many lines. Scribes have made efforts to maintain the visual model of the common table but these differences of content necessitate some variations from it. These differences from the common table indicate the compil-

---

[36] W. SCASE, "John Benet, scribe and compiler, and Dublin, Trinity College, MS 516", in: *Scribal Cultures in Late Medieval England: Essays in Honour of Linne R. Mooney*, ed. M. CONNOLLY, H. JAMES-MADDOCKS, and † D. PEARSALL (Woodbridge, 2022), pp. 241-258. Benet selects material that would have been of local interest to himself and his readers in the English east Midlands, in particular to the residents of Dunstable Priory, in whose gift lay the vicarage of Harlington that he held from 1443 to 1471.

ers' expectations of their audience and their understanding of the purpose of the table. From the nature and focus of the headwords and the provenance of the manuscripts it seems likely that the context for the special tables is pedagogic. In the rest of this essay I propose to examine the English *tabula* in manuscripts of Trevisa's translation of the *Polychronicon* in relation to a tradition of double tables and the *tabula specialis*.

The English Table in Trevisa's Polychronicon*: Function and Form*

The English table in the Trevisa manuscripts shares many of the characteristics of the Latin *tabulae speciales* that we have examined, but it also modifies the tradition. Like the common table and the special tables, it gives location references in the form of book and chapter. It maintains the referencing model of the common table, not adding a letter indicating position in the chapter, unlike Magdalen Lat. 147. Like the Latin special tables, it too is alphabetised to one letter. However, unlike the Latin special tables and the common table, letter sections are arranged by the order of the location reference, that is, chronologically.[37] It further modifies the alphabetisation of its Latin models by incorporating letters and letter sections not found in the Latin, reflecting the alphabets used in Middle English (different scribes modify the alphabet differently).[38] So, whereas the Latin table runs from "*Abraham*" to "*Zorobabel*", the English *tabula* runs from "*Appolyne Delphicus his temple*" to "*Wynchell see i-brend*" (MS Princeton University Library, Taylor 6, ff. 1r, 8r).[39]

The entries under *O* will serve as an example of the character of the English table entries.[40] The Latin table in Trevisa *Polychronicon* MS Cambridge, Trinity College R.5.25 comprises thirty-seven entries, while the English table in Taylor 6 has thirty-four. About a third of the Latin entries have corresponding entries

---

[37] However this is not unprecedented in the Latin tradition; some of the tables supplied with manuscripts that contain Book 7 only are in chronological rather than alphabetical order: see FREEMAN, "The manuscript dissemination and readership of the *Polychronicon*", pp. 199-200.

[38] For examples of the different alphabets in the English table see W. SCASE, *Visible English: Graphic Culture, Scribal Practice, and Identity, c. 700-c. 1550* (Turnhout, 2022: *Utrecht Studies in Medieval Literacy* 54), pp. 331-349.

[39] As the English table is unedited, it is necessary to quote from manuscript. I use the text of the English table in Princeton, Taylor 6. I have chosen this manuscript because it contains a full text and is readily available online.

[40] For previous discussion of the nature of the entries see STEINER, *John Trevisa's Information Age*, pp. 122-132. Steiner compares the practice of the English table with that of modern indexes, finding the compiler's grasp of indexing principles wanting.

The A *to* Z *of Middle English Indexing?* 171

in the English *O* section, i.e. entries that correspond both in location referenced and headword:

Olimpias ordeined/ De Olimpiade, 2.32
Origenes and his dedes/ De Origene doctore, 4.18
Osewaldis bones at Gloucestre/ De Osuualdo Rege, 5.14 (the Latin table also references 5.12)
Offediche/ De Offa Rege Merciorum, 5.25
Osewald translated to Gloucestre/De translacione ossium eius (i.e. "*De Osuualdo rege*", above), 6.4
Oto 'Mirabilia Mundi'[41]*/ De Othone qui dictus est 'Mirabilia'*, 6.13
Oliuer wol flee as a birde/ De Oliuero monacho Malmesburiensis, 6.28[42]
Ordre of Chartrehous/ De ordine Cartusiensi, 7.4
Ordre of White Monkes/ De ordine Cisterciensi, 7.10
Ordre of White Chanons/ De ordine Premonstrasensi, 7.16
Owen goth to purgatorie/ De Oweno et eius purgatorio, 7.20
Ordre of Frere Prechours begynneth/ De ordine Predicatorum, 7.33
Ordre of the Templeres dampned/ De ordine Templariorum, 7.16

Princeton, Taylor 6, f. 5 r-v [English];
Cambridge, Trinity R.5.24, f. viii r [Latin]

These common references share headwords that work in both languages. Some of these English entries have headwords that are proper nouns or include proper nouns ("*Origen*", "*Oswald*", "*Offa*", "*Oliver*", "*Charterhouse*", "*Owain*", "*Templars*") but many headwords are not names, notably "*De ordo*" / "*Ordre*". As in the Latin special tables, there is a tendency in the English table to foreground key words and to reduce the number of proper nouns. Latin *O* entry proper nouns that are missing from the English table but could in principle have been carried over into it are:

De Otho rege Persarum, 3. 22
De Ottomano Augusto, 3. 43
De Octovio [sic] *rege Britonum*, 4. 30
De Odone archiepiscopo, 6. 10
De Odone barocensi, 7. 5
De Olmero monacho Malmesburiensis, 6. 26, 24
De Oreb monoculo, 2. 14

---

[41] The English text referenced reads: "*Otho* [...] *hadde a wonder surname, and was i-cleped Otho þe wondres of þe world, Mirabilia mundi*" (*Polychronicon*, 7, p. 45).
[42] Cf. *Polychronicon*, 6, p. 223, "*he fondede forto flee as a bridde wyþ wynges*".

De Orosio presbitero, 4. 32
De Oswyno rege Northimrorum, 5. 15, 16
De Oswyno rege, 5. 15
De Osmundo episcopo Sarum, 7. 3
De Othoniel duce, 2. 16
De Othone cesare, 4. 10
Item, de Othone imperatore, 6. 6
De Othone legato, 7. 15
De Ovidio poeta, 4. 4
De Ottobono legato, 7. 37
De Oxonie scolis, 6. 1

A few entries in the Latin *O* section have equivalent entries under a different letter in the English *tabula*:

De orbis mensura, 1, 5 / *Mette and mesure of th'erth aboute*, 1.5
De orbis partibus, 1. 6, 7 / *Erth is deled a thre*, 1.6

Princeton, Taylor 6, ff. 4v, 2v [English];
Cambridge, Trinity R.5.24, f. viii r [Latin])

Largely, though, the picture is one of avoiding proper nouns. This aligns with the tendency in the Latin special tables.

Some twenty *O* section entries in the English table do not have an easily recognisable equivalent in the Latin *O* section or elsewhere in the Latin table:

O man louȝ in hys burthe day, 2.1
Oliphauntes clawed in þe forhede, 3.31
Oliphaunt i-þrowe, 3.34
Orchades þe ilondes i-wonne, 4. 8
Obley ordeined litel, 4. 13
Ordenaunce of Lente, 4. 26
On vers i-lurned, 4. 29
Oill for sike men, 4. 31
Office of þe masse, 4. 32
Oliuere and Rolond is ded, 5. 26
On hym ic trowe, 5. 27
Obedyens axed and i-werned, 7. 1
Ordinal imad, 7. 3
Ooste lad in to Wales, 7.22
Oon wiþ cristes woundes, 7.34

Oon woll slee the king, 7.35
Occasion of þe barons werre, 7.36
Oste liþ at Stretforde, 7.37
Oon woll winne Irlond, 7.41
Ordinaunce of Hebreu, Grew and Latyn, 7.42

While the Latin special tables depart from the norm of the proper noun to compile material under more general keywords, the English table entries supplement general keywords with enticing narrative snippets.[43] In the *O* section, "*O man louȝ in hys burthe day*, 2.1" refers to a passage about marvels of the body.[44] "*Oliphauntes clawed in þe forhede*, 3.31" refers to the story of Pirrus being conquered and his elephants being overcome by horsemen.[45] "*Oliphaunt i-browe*, 3.34" refers to a story in which an elephant is conquered by a prisoner and Hannibal puts him to death anyway.[46] "*Oon woll slee the king*, 7.35", refers to a passage about the deaths of several named Scottish kings.[47] Similarly enticing, in the *M* section, are several entries that concern strange transformations of men:

Men becomen briddes, 2. 25
Men becomen wolues, 2. 25
Mynstral bycometh an asse, 2. 25
Man becomen an hors, 2. 25

Princeton, Taylor 6, f. 4v

The chapter referenced concerns what happened to some of the Greeks after the fall of Troy.[48] The followers of Diomedes are turned into birds ("*foules*", in Trevisa's translation), the Arcades into wolves, and some witches turn a minstrel into a horse, and a man dreams that he is turned into a horse. These examples are assembled in the main text as part of a discussion as to whether such stories of transformation as the one about Diomedes' followers should be believed. The entries in the English table state the events as fact but anyone ven-

---

[43] For Steiner, the entries in the English table are like modern "tabloid" headlines, and she argues that their purpose is to make the *Polychronicon* sound "exciting" (STEINER, *John Trevisa's Information Age*, pp. 124, 126).
[44] *Polychronicon*, 2, p. 193.
[45] *Polychronicon*, 4, pp. 23-25.
[46] *Polychronicon*, 4, pp. 95-97.
[47] *Polychronicon*, 7, pp. 273-283.
[48] *Polychronicon*, 2, pp. 421-429.

turing into the text would then be invited to review that impression. Under *P* occurs the entry "*Pissing men sitting*, 1. 34" (Taylor 6, f. 5v). The compiler has selected this detail from a lengthy list in the text of the notable habits of the Irish. The detail that women urinate standing is omitted, suggesting a male perspective and anticipated male readers.[49] Many intriguing narrative snippets about women are found among the entries under *W*:

Wommen bicomen hares, 1. 34
Wommen selleth winde, 1. 44
Wommen becomen men, 2. 1
Wommen with men in bataille, 2. 19
Wenche buried quik aliue, 3. 13
Wyues wode for loue, 3. 25
Wenche sleeth hire self, 3. 33
Womman yeueth gode counseil, 4. 3

Princeton, Taylor 6, ff. 7v-8r

These entries confirm gender stereotypes and again perhaps imagine male readers.

Just as the Latin special tables are devised for local audiences, so a few entries in the English table may have been of particular interest to a local audience. Some entries in the English table reference matters of clerical controversy that are thought to have been of special interest to Trevisa.[50] However, these references, such as "*Pluralite of benefices dampned*, 7. 41" (Taylor 6, f. 7v) are relatively few. The table compiler also highlights local stories. A local compiler would have every right to expect that the entry for "*Wicche at Barkeleye*, 6.25" (Taylor 6, f. 8r) under *W* which refers to a story of a woman "*wont and customed to evel craftes*" would have been specially interesting to an audience associated with Berkeley, the seat of Thomas Berkeley, Trevisa's patron. (The text relates how, despite being secured in her grave covered by a stone fastened with iron bands, she is sprung from her grave by devils and taken away on a black horse.)[51] The Latin table does not have an equivalent entry. In the English *O* section the entries, "*Oswaldis bones at Gloucestre*" and "*Oswald translated*

---

[49] "*Among hem many men pisseþ sittynge and wommen stondynge*" (*Polychronicon*, 1, p. 359).

[50] STEINER, *John Trevisa's Information Age*, p. 126, finds that the English table has an "antipapal slant".

[51] *Polychronicon*, 7, pp. 195, 197.

The A to Z of Middle English Indexing? 175

to Gloucestre" (Taylor 6, f. 5r), are parallelled in the Latin table, which suggests that they were held to be of more general interest, but notably only the English table flags the location of Gloucester, close to Berkeley.

We have seen that comparison with the tradition of the special table illuminates some of the characteristics of the English table entries, in particular the preference for common nouns over proper nouns and the assembly of material of interest to a local audience. Trevisa's *Dialogue between a Lord and a Clerk* and his *Epistola* to his patron shed further light on the audience anticipated for the English table and its special needs. The Lord (who represents Trevisa's patron, Thomas Berkeley, or at least his pro-translation views) summarises the content of the *Polychronicon*:

> Ranulph, monk of Chester, wrot yn Latyn hys bookes of cronykes þat discreveþ þe world aboute yn lengthe and in brede, and makeþ mencyon and muynde of doyngs and of dedes, of mervayls and of wondres, and rekneþ þe ȝeres to hys laste dayes fram þe vurste makyng of hevene and of erþe. And so þarynne is noble and gret informacion and lore to hem þat can þarynne rede and vnderstonde. Þarfore ich wolde have þeus bokes of cronyks translated out of Latyn ynto Englysch, for þe mo men scholde hem understonde and have þereof konnyng, informacion and lore.[52]

This summary of the work is reflected in the headwords of the English table, which, as we have seen, highlight geography, deeds, and "marvels and wonders". The organisation of the letter entries also reflects this summary, since, listed in order of appearance in the text, they follow the chronological organisation of the text, and are therefore ordered within each letter section from "creation to the end of the world". The enlarged audience ("*mo men*") imagined for the translation in Trevisa's *Dialogue between a Lord and a Clerk* does not understand Latin and has not been able to learn for various reasons: "*som vor elde, som vor defaute of wyt, som vor defaute of katel oþer of frendes to vynde ham to scole*", and so on.[53] A further special need associated with this audience emerges when the Clerk (who represents the translator, Trevisa, or at least the

---

[52] WALDRON, "Trevisa's original prefaces on translation", p. 290. When quoting from this edition, I have removed Waldron's editorial brackets. The attribution of views in favour of translation to the Lord and views against to the Clerk is an elegant way of complimenting the patron and displaying the deference of the translator (cf. R. HANNA, *Pursuing History: Middle English Manuscripts and their Texts* (Palo Alto, CA, 1996), p. 66). It engages the project with contemporary debates about translation that had been intensified by the pro-translation arguments put forward by the followers of John Wyclif, judged a heretic. We should not assume that Trevisa, translator of many thousands of words of Latin, actually held the views of the Clerk.

[53] WALDRON, "Trevisa's original prefaces on translation", p. 291.

case against translation) suggests that "*hy þat understondeþ no Latyn mowe axe and be informed and ytauȝt of ham þat understondeþ Latyn*": uneducated people do not need a translation, for they can ask questions of clerks.[54] The Lord is scathing in his reply:

> Þou spekst wonderlych, vor þe lewd man wot noȝt what a scholde axe, and namelych of lore of dedes þat come nevere in hys muynde, noþer wot comynlych of whom a scholde axe.[55]

The Lord points out that an uneducated man – someone like those whom the translation project is designed to include in the audience for the *Polychronicon* – does not know what questions to ask, especially when it comes to learning about events in history of which he has never heard. As well as providing a defence of the English translation of the text, this comment points to the rationale for not translating the common table, but making a special table in English. The common table, with its preponderance of obscure names, would be useless for these users, since many of its headwords would not be meaningful to them. Further light is shed on the problem of the proper nouns by the *Epistola* to Lord Berkeley. Here, in an account of his translation practices, Trevisa explains that many personal and placenames in the main text such as "*Asia, Europa, Africa and Siria, Mont Athlas, Syna and Oreb, Marach, Iordan and Arnon, Bethleem, Nazareth, Ierusalem and Damascus, Hanybal, Rasyn, Assuerus and Cirus*" must be left to stand for themselves in a translation ("*mot be yset and stonde vor hem sylf in here oune kuynde*").[56] In relation to this list of examples of obscure and untranslatable names, it is noticeable that "*De Oreb monoculo, 2. 14*" is one of the Latin *O* entries omitted from the English table, while the English entry "*Oliphaunt i-þrowe, 3.34*" focuses on the subject of an elephant, avoiding use of the name Hannibal. Many proper nouns are useless as finding aids for the imagined audience of the English table, since they are not translatable into English, both because they are not found in English and because they are not meaningful to those who have never heard of them.

It is notable that several of the headwords in the *O* section are not terms on which anyone would be likely to search: they are grammatical rather than lexical words such as the pronoun "*one*" and the preposition "*on*". Other terms are very unspecific: "*occasion*" ('cause'); "*ordinaunce*"; "*office*". None of these

---

[54] WALDRON, "Trevisa's original prefaces on translation", p. 291.
[55] WALDRON, "Trevisa's original prefaces on translation", p. 291.
[56] WALDRON, "Trevisa's original prefaces on translation", p. 294.

headwords is the obvious word in the entry that someone might seek. It is often difficult to pinpoint what content in a given chapter is being referred to, and in some cases impossible, especially when the table paraphrases rather than using the same vocabulary as the text. Subject to their phrasing, these entries are only arbitrarily placed under *O*. But this, I suggest, is part of the point. An alternative and less onerous way of presenting the more general headings of the English table would have been structured under books and chapters, rather than under books and chapters in an alphabetical frame. It is clear that the alphabetical structure is important to the enterprise, even though it causes the compiler and scribes serious difficulty.[57] The entries function to make a table text that fits the visual model of the Latin one, adapted to the Middle English alphabet, and at the same time provide as many portals into discovery of the text as there are letters in that alphabet. The English table is in this way a *tabula specialis*, because it reproduces its alphabetical tabular model and its function as a mode of non-linear discovery of the text for a special audience. These entries, I suggest, provide access to the *Polychronicon* for readers for whom the proper nouns and many of the concepts of the common table would not be meaningful, but for whom the alphabetical structure of the special table and its affordances for reader discovery were held by the compiler or compilers to have value.

The common *Polychronicon* table is arranged for reading horizontally and vertically, and many entry points are available for the reader: the reader can read horizontally from entry to reference, or down the entries for content or down the columns for chapter and book references, and the eye is supported in navigation of the table by visual devices that highlight the beginnings of new entries, the beginnings of letter sections, and the content of the columns (book and chapter). The table supports rapid, selective, and non-linear access to the text itself. We saw that the scribes of the Latin special tables took pains to replicate the visual model of the common table to some extent, while also adapting it. The importance of replicating the model of the Latin table in the English table is also clear from the attention paid to replication of it by the scribes. To discuss layout and other visual aspects of the double tables that accompany the Trevisa text, I propose to focus on MS Manchester, Chetham's Library 11379 (Mun. A.6.90), where both tables appear.[58] The Chetham's manuscript is one of the earliest surviving witnesses of Trevisa's translation of

---

[57] For the difficulties and how scribes and decorators dealt with them see SCASE, *Visible English*, pp. 331-349, and WALDRON, "Dialect aspects", pp. 67-88.

[58] For some comments on the layout of the English table in some of the other manuscripts see LIIRA, *Paratextuality in Manuscript and Print*, pp. 136-138.

Higden, dated to the late fourteenth or early fifteenth century, and the language of the scribes is marked by features that suggest a Gloucestershire provenance, meaning that the manuscript was copied, in Waldron's words, "in the Berkeley neighbourhood [seat of Trevisa's patron Sir Thomas Berkeley] and probably at an early stage in transmission".[59] Ralph Hanna has suggested that the Chetham's manuscript "seems to represent a second exemplar prepared to facilitate further copying" in contrast to the two other manuscripts in Gloucestershire dialect, MS London, British Library, Cotton Tiberius D.vii and MS London, British Library, Stowe 65, that appear to have been prepared for local distribution.[60] The tables are now bound in the middle of Book One. The Latin *tabula* (ff. 19r-28v) is imperfect at the end; it contains *A, B, C, D, E, F, G, H, I, K, L, M, N, O, P, Q, R, S, T, U/V*. The English *tabula* (ff. 29r-34v) has suffered losses at the beginning and in the middle; it now contains only *D* (partial), *E, F, G, H, I, L, M, N, O, P, T, U/V, Z, Þ, 3, W*. The Chetham's English *tabula* is modelled visually on the *tabula communis* but is not quite the same, recalling the Latin *tabulae speciales*.

The two tables follow similar two-column layouts. The start of the Latin table is signalled by a four-line penwork initial *A* and subsequent letter sections in the Latin table are signalled by three-line penwork initials in blue with red flourishing. Each column is subdivided by ruling into three data columns, the first for the text of the entry, the second for the book number, and the third for the chapter number. In the line above where the text of the entries begins, these two narrower columns are headed "*Li*[*ber*]" and "*C*[*apitulum*]" in the same hand and script as the text. As noted, the start of the English table is missing, but from the beginning of the section for *E*, as in the Latin table, new letter sections are signalled by blue and red penwork initials.

There are, however, several differences between the two tables. Although they are both copied in Anglicana Formata, the English table has a slightly less regular aspect than the Latin one.[61] The tables differ in decoration: although as

---

[59] WALDRON, "Dialect aspects", p. 68. For the date see also LALME, citing N.R. Ker.
[60] HANNA, *Pursuing History*, p. 68.
[61] The hand of the Latin *tabula* is very consistent in the size, angle of, and spacing between letters, compared to the slightly less regular appearance of the hand of the English table. The less regular aspect of the English table is partly the result of its forms of minuscule *y*, where the descender curves to the left reaching beyond the body of the letter above the line before curling sweepingly to the right (see for example "*Olympias*" and "*Olyfaunt*", f. 32r), in contrast to the more restrained descender on *y* in the Latin table (see for example "*De Oswyno Rege*", f. 25r). Cf. *Late Middle English Scribes*, "the tail [on minuscule *y*] is an exaggerated curve counterclockwise". Both LALME and *Late Medieval English Scribes* attribute the work to one scribe: the latter refers to him as the "*Polychronicon* Scribe".

in the common table its initials are in blue and red penwork, in the English table they are two-line not three-line. Another difference between the Latin and English tables is that several lines are left blank at the end of each letter section. This recalls the practice that we observed in the special tables in Magdalen Lat. 147 and Benet's table. Two further differences appear to be attributable to a second hand in the English table. A third, unruled data column for referencing the entries is created from the space between the two text columns and the space in the right margin. In these columns a different hand with a slightly leftward-sloping minim stroke has inserted Roman numeral equivalents between points for the Arabic chapter numbers. The headers for the book and chapter columns also appear to have been supplied after the main text of the table was written, possibly by this second hand. They follow the format of those in the Latin *tabula* but 'C[*apitulum*]' is written differently. It seems from these differences that the English table has been visually modelled on the Latin one, but the model has been modified – possibly by different scribal hands. Another aspect of modelling may be the allocation of space to each letter section. Latin *E* is ruled for 89 lines. English *E* is ruled for 78 lines. Latin *G* is ruled for 60 lines. English *G* is ruled for 43 lines. The numbers of lines ruled for each section are not the same, but the proportion of space allocated is similar. If the proportions of space allocated to each English letter section were decided before the text of the table was available, that would at least partly explain the gaps at the ends of the sections in the English – perhaps they were based on the Latin model. But of course this would only partly be a guide. Unlike the *tabulae speciales* in Harley 3671 and Magdalen Lat. 147, the entries in the English *tabula* are brief enough to fit within one line so that the visual appearance of the table is very similar to that of the Latin *tabula*. The scribes' brief is arguably to create an English table that is modelled visually on the *tabula communis* while adapting it for special purposes.

    Carefully modelled in form, the English table offers its audience a key functionality of the alphabetical table: it makes available to the relatively unlearned and unknowledgeable a mode of reading hitherto limited to those who had encountered the scholastic reading practices associated with the energetic tabulation of books found in late medieval England. The conventional order of the alphabetical table makes available non-linear, rapid modes of access to the text, modes of access that are at least to some extent subject to reader selection and preference. The special table offers a version of that experience for those to whom many of the proper names in the common table would not have been familiar. Each letter section offers a different set of opportunities for discovering in the main text content of interest to the user. Translating the *tabula communis* could not have achieved the same end, but creating a *tabula specialis* in the pedagogic tradition of double tables could.

Conclusion

In this essay I have argued that the alphabetical tables associated with Trevisa's translation of the *Polychronicon* are examples of the pairing of *tabulae communes* and *speciales* found in some manuscripts of the Latin text and that their inclusion in the manuscripts is aligned with the rationales for the translation project set out in Trevisa's *Dialogue between a Lord and a Clerk* and in his *Epistola*. The tradition of the special table and its pairing with the common table offer a new framework for interpreting the propensity of the English table to dwell on the sensational and curious, and its lack of proper noun headwords. The relationship to the tradition of double tables in the manuscripts of the Latin *Polychronicon* and its clear enactment in the manuscripts of Trevisa's *Polychronicon* mean that the English table cannot have been compiled independently of the Latin table or in ignorance of its conventions. The appearance of the English special table without the common table in three manuscripts of the Trevisa *Polychronicon* is parallelled by the Benet example of a Latin special table that is dependent on the common model but not physically bound with it. The examples of *tabulae speciales* in the Latin manuscripts show that the alphabetical tabulation of material was not in these cases designed for quick retrieval of information from the text using headwords, but was a means of compiling material and providing access to the text to suit the needs of particular audiences, and probably it had pedagogic purposes. The English *tabula specialis* is likewise a special resource for those with minimal education. The common table enables readers to find the material they are already interested in and know about, and to read selectively and accretively. The special English table also empowers readers to benefit from the literacy practices afforded by tabulation, in their case to find both weird and wonderful and edifying matter in the text even if their knowledge of the past and the world is rudimentary. The English table is not an index, but a reflex of the *tabula specialis* tradition devised for the new kind of reader that Trevisa and his patron Berkeley evidently hoped could be brought to the translated *Polychronicon*.

A Visual and Linguistic Interpretation of the *Pater Noster* Table of the Vernon Manuscript[*]

OLGA TIMOFEEVA

Introduction

The famous Vernon manuscript (MS Oxford, Bodleian Library, Eng. poet. a. 1), dated to *c.* 1390 and produced by two West Midland scribes, is a luxurious collection of over 350 religious texts spread over more than 400 folios. Among them, we find copies of Middle English anonymous bestsellers (e.g. *South English Legendary*, *Northern Homily Cycle*, *Prick of Conscience*, *Ancrene Riwle*), minor verse and prayers, as well as English translations of and works by Aelred of Rievaulx, Robert Grosseteste, Walter Hilton, William Langland, and Richard Rolle. The main language of this assemblage is English, but several texts also comprise quotations and other text elements in

---

[*] I gratefully acknowledge Wendy Scase's critical comments and suggestions to investigate literary connections of chess and visual associations of the Exchequer cloth. I have also profited greatly from the patient support of the volume editor Matti Peikola and my untiring copy-editor Rahel Huwyler. The usual disclaimers apply.

....

Graphic Practices and Literacies in the History of English, ed. Matti PEIKOLA, Jukka TYRKKÖ, and Mari-Liisa VARILA, *Utrecht Studies in Medieval Literacy*, 61 (Turnhout: Brepols, 2025), pp. 181-200.

BREPOLS PUBLISHERS DOI 10.1484/M.USML-EB.5.143826

Latin and Anglo-French.[1] The manuscript contains plentiful decoration and illumination, including a *Pater Noster* table on f. 231v, referred to in a rubric on f. IIv as "*Pater noster in a table ypeynted*". The table presents the Lord's Prayer in a diagrammatic way, linking its seven petitions to the Seven Gifts of the Holy Spirit, the Seven Virtues, and the Seven Deadly Sins (Figures 1 and 2). Mixing Latin and Middle English, it is organised into sixteen horizontal rows and nine vertical columns (if the initials are counted as a separate column; but see Figure 2), along the following schema: a large initial introducing petitions of the *Pater Noster*, "*þis preiere*" ("this prayer"), petition of the *Pater Noster* in Latin and English, "*leduþ a man to*" ("leads a man to"), a gift of the Spirit in Latin and English, "*leduþ a man to*", a virtue in Latin and English, "*is a3enst*" ("is against", a vice in Latin and English (a full transcription is available in Figure 2). The key to how to read the table horizontally is found in the sixteenth row, "*Per peticiones peruenitur ad dona, per dona ad uirtutes & uirtutes sunt contra uicia*" ("through the petitions one arrives at the gifts, through the gifts at the virtues, and the virtues are against the vices"),[2] although the table can also be read vertically, using the headings at the top of the columns: "*vij Peticiones*" ("seven petitions"), "*vij Dona spiritus sancti*" ("seven gifts of the holy spirit"), "*vij Uirtutes*" ("seven virtues"), "*vij Uicia*" ("seven vices").

Visually, the grid has been compared to a "banner",[3] a "maze",[4] and even a "schoolboy's square wax tablet",[5] while its purpose has been described as

---

[1] <https://medieval.bodleian.ox.ac.uk/catalog/manuscript_4817>; *The Vernon Manuscript: A Facsimile Edition of Oxford, Bodleian Library, MS Eng. poet.a.1*, ed. W. SCASE (Oxford, 2011); *The Making of the Vernon Manuscript*, ed. W. SCASE (Turnhout, 2013).

[2] A. HENRY, "'The Pater Noster in a table ypeynted' and some other presentations of doctrine in the Vernon Manuscript", in: *Studies in the Vernon Manuscript*, ed. D. PEARSALL (Cambridge, 1990), pp. 89-113, at p. 90.

[3] HENRY, "'The Pater Noster in a table ypeynted'", p. 92.

[4] A. GOTTSCHALL, "The Lord's Prayer in circles and squares: An identification of some analogues of the Vernon Manuscript's Pater Noster table", *Marginalia* 7 (2008), <http://merg.soc.srcf.net/journal/08confession/circles.php>; cf. HENRY, "'The Pater Noster in a table ypeynted'", p. 102.

[5] F. BOURGNE, "Vernacular engravings in late medieval England", in: *Palimpsests and the Literary Imagination of Medieval England*, ed. L. CARRUTHERS, R. CHAI-ELSHOLZ, and T. SILEC (New York, 2011), pp. 115-136, at p. 131, <https://doi.org/10.1057/9780230118805_7>.

Fig. 1   The *Pater Noster* table in the Vernon MS (MS Oxford, Bodleian Library, Eng. poet. a. 1, f. 231v, *c.* 1390). © Bodleian Libraries, University of Oxford.

both mnemonic and didactic and / or contemplative.[6] Anna Gottschall, in particular, has argued that the purpose of such tabular diagrams was "to enable the viewer to engage with the theology and to perhaps contemplate or meditate on the relationships between the *Pater Noster* and the septenaries" (i.e. catechetical concepts, such as the Seven Gifts, arranged into groups of seven).[7] In this

---

[6] K.R. VULIC, "Prayer and vernacular writing in late-medieval England", unpublished doctoral thesis (University of California, Berkeley, 2004); A. GOTTSCHALL, "The *Pater Noster* and the laity of England, c. 700-1560, with special focus on the clergy's use of the prayer to structure basic catechetical teaching", unpublished doctoral thesis (University of Birmingham, 2014), <https://etheses.bham.ac.uk//id/eprint/6535/1/Gottschall16PhD.pdf>.

[7] GOTTSCHALL, "The *Pater Noster* and the laity of England", p. 89.

	1	2	3	4	5	6	7	8
1		vij Peticiones		vij Dona spiritus sancti		vij Uirtutes	contra	vij Uicia
2	PAter noster qui es in celis sanctificetur nomen tuum			Timor domini		Humilitas		Superbia
3	þis preiere	fadur þat art in heuene þi nome be halewed	leduþ a man to	Drede of god	leduþ a man to	mekenesse and lounesse	is aȝenst	Pruide & stow(t)nesse
4	ADueniat regnum tuum			Pietas		Caritas		Inuidia
5	þis preiere	lor(d) thi kyndam mote come amongus us	leduþ a man to	Pite of his neyȝbore	leduþ a man to	loue & charite	is aȝenst	Enuie
6	FIat uoluntas tua sicut in celo & in terra			Sciencia		Pax		Ira
7	þis preiere	lord þi wille be do in erþe as it is in heuene	leduþ a man to	knowing & wite þat he be not as a lyft	leduþ a man to	Pes & reste in herte	is aȝenst	Wrathe & angur
8	PAnem nostrum cotidianum da nobis hodie			Fortitudo		Leticia spiritualis		Accidia
9	þis preiere	lord oure uche dayes bred ȝeue us to day	leduþ a man to	strengþe aȝenst his gostli enemees	leduþ a man to	murthe & lykinge in godus seruise	is aȝenst	Slowthe & heuinesse in godus seruise
10	ET dimitte nobis debita nostra sicut & nos dimittimus debitoribus nostris			Concilium		Paupertas spiritus		Auaricia

A Visual and Linguistic Interpretation of the Pater Noster Table

11	þis p*r*e-ier*e*	lord for-Heue us oure dette of sy*n*ne as we forHeue our*e* det-ter*e*s	<u>leduþ a man to</u>	Counsel a3enst p*er*eles of sy*n*ne & þ*is* world	<u>leduþ a man to</u>	Pouer*t*e of soule þ*at* is to dispise wordili-che rich-es i*n* her*t*e	<u>is a3e*n*st</u>	Couetise
12	**ET** ne nos inducas in temptacionem			<u>Intellec-tus</u>		<u>Mensura & sobr*ie*-tas</u>		Gula
13	þis p*r*ei-er*e*	lord suffere us not to falle i*n* to sy*n*ne be te*m*p-tac*i*on	<u>leduþ a man to</u>	vndursto-ndi*n*g wat is good & wat is euel	<u>leduþ a man to</u>	mesure i*n* mete and soburnes-se i*n* drinke	<u>is a3e*n*st</u>	Glotonie
14	**S**Et libera nos a malo	Amen		<u>Sapiencia</u>		<u>Castitas</u>		Luxuria
15	þis p*r*ei-er*e*	lord þ*ou* deliuere us from wikidne sse	<u>leduþ a man to</u>	Sauour & liki*n*g in his god	<u>leduþ a man to</u>	Chastite & clan-nesse	<u>is a3e*n*st</u>	Lecherie
16	**PE**r peticiones peruenitur ad dona, p*er* dona ad uirtutes & uirtutes sunt contra uicia							

Fig. 2 Transcription of the *Pater Noster* table (expansions of abbreviations given in italics; underlined text is written in red ink in the original).

paper, I suggest one such contemplation path, comparing the layout of the Vernon diagram to a chessboard and offering a visual and linguistic reading of the septenaries.

While recent scholarship has concentrated on the visual elements of the table, its meditative and devotional purposes, and the literacy modes available to its readers,[8] little attention has been given so far to the relation of the vernac-

---

[8] HENRY, "'The Pater Noster in a table ypeynted'"; VULIC, "Prayer and vernacular writing in late-medieval England"; GOTTSCHALL, "The Lord's Prayer in circles and squares"; GOTTSCHALL, "The *Pater Noster* and the laity of England".

ular glosses in the roundels of the table (e.g. "*Drede of god*" 4:3,[9] Figure 2) to contemporaneous Middle English lexical usage. The aim of the paper is twofold: to analyse how the visual aids of the table can help us interpret its lexical parts and how the vocabulary of the roundels can enlighten us about the purpose, audience, and readings of the table. In particular, I concentrate on the binomials (here, coordinated noun phrases)[10] employed in the roundels containing the Seven Gifts, Virtues, and Vices (columns 4, 6 and 8, Figure 2), examining their relation to the lexicon of virtues and vices of the second half of the fourteenth century and using the *Corpus of Middle English Prose and Verse* (CME) and *Early English Books Online* (EEBO) as reference tools. This examination uncovers both neologisms (or possible copying mistakes) in the Vernon table, such as "*Pruide & stow(t)nesse*" ("pride" 8:3, Figure 2), and commonplace usage, such as "*loue & charite*" (6:5, Figure 2). Previous research has seen these double glosses as interpretative tools,[11] while this paper investigates them as binomial phrases undergoing freezing and idiomatisation. For ease of reference, the whole table is reproduced in Figure1 and transcribed in Figure 2 in full.

All the World's a Chessboard

The Vernon Pater Noster table is not unique in representing the septenaries in a concise diagrammatic way. For example, MS British Library, Arundel 83, dated to between *c.* 1308 and *c.* 1340, is famous for its collection of theological diagrams on ff. 123r-135. One of these, f. 128v, presents the Seven Deadly Sins as a tree ("*Arbor uiciorum*", "the tree of sins"), which stems out of Pride ("*Radix uiciorum Superbia*", "pride, the root of sins") and has seven branches. Each branch, in turn, contains seven subcategories of the respective sins, the whole tree using the same set of visual metaphors as the roughly contemporary treatise, the *Ayenbite of Inwyt*. Folio 129v is a wheel diagram, in which the petitions of the *Pater Noster*, seven sacraments, seven gifts of the Holy Spirit, seven spiritual weapons of the virtues, seven works of mercy, seven virtues, and seven vices are arranged into circles, starting with the Pater Noster in the

---

[9] Here and below the first figure refers to the column number and the second to the row number.

[10] S. MOLLIN, *The (Ir)reversibility of English Binomials: Corpus, Constraints, Developments* (Amsterdam, 2014).

[11] "GOTTSCHALL, "The Lord's Prayer in circles and squares".

A Visual and Linguistic Interpretation of the Pater Noster *Table* 187

Fig. 3 Lancelot playing chess. From the British Library Collection: MS London, British Library, Add. 10293, f. 302r, early fourteenth century.

outer ring. The wheel can be read clockwise, i.e. reading round the whole septenary (cf. the Vernon columns), or in radial segments, i.e. reading a single petition and the elements from each septenary that are associated with it, in a way reminiscent of the Vernon rows, although using a different visual schema.[12] While diagrammatic arrangement of the catechetical material is not without parallels, what makes the Vernon table stand out is the particular combination of the squares, circles embedded in squares, and decorative inlays,[13] which make the whole visual resemble, I argue, a chessboard. I would like to explore what this visual association may offer by way of interpreting the Vernon *Pater Noster*.

[12] GOTTSCHALL, "The *Pater Noster* and the laity of England", pp. 73-88.
[13] GOTTSCHALL, "The *Pater Noster* and the laity of England", pp. 91-96.

The tabular form is among the most basic memory tools in the Middle Ages. As Mary Carruthers has observed: "treating the memory as though it were a flat area divided linearly into columns within a grid seems clearly medieval".[14] The earliest grids were canon tables devised to cross-reference sections in the Gospels, but tables were also used in e.g. calendars and genealogies.[15] The chessboard was arguably the most famous grid in medieval culture, with chess arriving in the West in *c.* 1000.[16] By the late thirteenth century, chess had gained such widespread popularity that it could serve as an allegorical model to describe contemporary society, with chess pieces representing the different estates and classes. The anonymous *Moralitas de scaccario* is one of the best-known examples of such allegories.[17]

> This whole world is a kind of chessboard, of which one square is white but another black on account of the twofold state of life and death, of grace and sin. Moreover, the pieces of this chessboard are the people of this world, who are drawn out of one bag – a mother's womb [...]
> Moreover, in this game the Devil says "check", insulting or destroying someone with the dart of sin. When someone is stricken, unless he quickly says "delivered", passing over to penitence and remorse of the heart, the Devil says to him "mate", leading off his soul with him to hell, where he will not be freed by entreaty or payment because in hell there is no redemption.[18]

This chessboard is black and white, but we know numerous depictions of game boards that also display other colours: red and white, red and black, green and white, etc.,[19] with the ornamental elements that are not unlike those in the Vernon table (cf. Fig. 3: Lancelot holding a blue and yellow decorated board).

---

[14] M. CARRUTHERS, *The Book of Memory: A Study of Memory in Medieval Culture*, 2nd edn. (Cambridge, 2008), p. 162.

[15] CARRUTHERS, *The Book of Memory*, pp. 324-325.

[16] H.J.R. MURRAY, *A History of Chess* (Oxford, 1913), pp. 25-29.

[17] A. CLASSEN, "Chess in medieval German literature: A mirror of social-historical and cultural, religious, ethical, and moral conditions", in: *Chess in the Middle Ages and Early Modern Age: A Fundamental Thought Paradigm of the Premodern World*, ed. D.E. O'SULLIVAN (Berlin, 2012), pp. 17-44, <https://doi.org/10.1515/9783110288810.17>.

[18] S. FEIN, "109. Mundus iste totus quoddam scaccarium est / All the world's a chess board", in: *The Complete Harley 2253 Manuscript*, ed. and trans. S. FEIN with D. RAYBIN, and J. ZIOLKOWSKI, 3 vols. (Kalamazoo, MI, 2015), 3, <https://d.lib.rochester.edu/teams/text/fein-harley2253-volume-3-article-109>.

[19] Cf. S. MUSSER GOLLADAY, "Images of medieval Spanish chess and captive damsels in distress", in: *Chess in the Middle Ages and Early Modern Age: A Fundamental Thought Paradigm of the Premodern World*, ed. D.E. O'SULLIVAN (Berlin, 2012), pp. 135-167, at p. 150, n. 34 <https://doi.org/10.1515/9783110288810.135>.

In the *Liber de moribus hominum vel officiis nobilium sive super ludo scacchorum* (*c*. 1300) by the Dominican Jacopo da Cessola, the chessboard is used both as a social allegory and a mnemonic clue to the organisation of exempla in this highly popular collection.[20] Into the late fifteenth century, so-called chess moralities continue to use the trope of playing chess with the Devil. In these exempla, vices and virtues act as chess pieces, and their moves and counter-moves are described in minute detail. For example, in the *Jeu des esches de la dame moralisé* (MS London, British Library, Add. 15820), the Devil's pieces are black, with the king being *orgueil* 'pride', the queen *ambition*, and the other pieces and pawns representing various sins and temptations. His opponent is a lady who plays white, with the king *charité* and the queen *humilité* on her side of the board, along with other good qualities and virtues.[21] The allegory of war between the virtues and vices itself goes back to at least the *Psychomachia* ('Battle of the Soul') by Prudentius (348-*c*. 410) and was extremely popular in the Middle Ages.[22] As demonstrated in Fig. 3, chess and chess allegories are also widespread in courtly romances. The Knight in Chaucer's *Book of the Duchess* compares his life to a game of chess, in which Fortuna checkmated him when he lost his beloved queen. Both allegories (playing with the Devil and playing with Fortune) connect chess to game and gamble, in themselves morally questionable activities, as well as to the notions of chance and mutability in human life, broken down into black and white periods.

The popularity of chess and chess allegories as visual, didactic, and mnemonic tools suggests that an association of the Vernon table with the game board would have been available to medieval readers / contemplators of this manuscript. Progression from the petitions of the Lord's prayer to the Seven Gifts of the Holy Spirit and Seven Virtues fighting against ("*is aȝenst*") the Seven Deadly Sins and ousting them into the periphery of the board was part of

---

[20] CARRUTHERS, *The Book of Memory*, p. 179; CLASSEN, "Chess in medieval German literature"; A. MUSSOU, "Playing with memory: The chessboard as a mnemonic tool in medieval didactic literature", in: *Chess in the Middle Ages and Early Modern Age: A Fundamental Thought Paradigm of the Premodern World*, ed. D.E. O'SULLIVAN (Berlin, 2012), pp. 187-198, <https://doi.org/10.1515/9783110288810.187>.

[21] K. JUEL, "Defeating the Devil at chess: A struggle between virtue and vice in *Le Jeu des esches de la dame moralisé*", in: *Chess in the Middle Ages and Early Modern Age: A Fundamental Thought Paradigm of the Premodern World*, ed. D.E. O'SULLIVAN (Berlin, 2012), pp. 87-108, <https://doi.org/10.1515/9783110288810.87>.

[22] M.W. BLOOMFIELD, *The Seven Deadly Sins: An Introduction to the History of a Religious Concept, with Special Reference to Medieval English Literature* (Michigan University, 1967), pp. 64-65, at pp. 101-104.

the linear, left-to-right reading of the table and might have evoked the allegorical battle known from the written sources and popular sermons and poetry.

At the visual and semantic levels, another table type could also come to mind. In Medieval Latin, the family of words that denote chess and chess pieces or boards also has a number of derived senses, among them "table for accounts", "fiscal department of the English crown, incl. treasury and court of accounts, Exchequer".[23] These lexemes are reflected in the titles of the works cited above as well as in the late-twelfth-century *Dialogus de Scaccario* ('Dialogue of the Exchequer'), an administrative manual on the principles and practice of the English Exchequer written by Richard FitzNeal. In the prologue to his book, Richard makes the connection between the two senses of *scaccarium* explicit, by comparing the interaction between the sheriffs, who collected royal revenue from the counties, and himself, the treasurer, who audited them, to a game of chess. The comparison is facilitated by the design of the Exchequer table, covered by a chequered black-and-white cloth to allow consistent value record in pence, shillings, and pounds. The chess pieces on the board are counters, and the battle can sometimes be joined by the king.[24] An early-fifteenth-century depiction of the Exchequer (green-and-white) cloth is known from the *Red Book of the Irish Exchequer* (Fig. 4), while smaller counting boards and tables would be familiar to anyone involved in commerce and administration.[25] Thus, the Vernon table would allude not only to allegorical wars between good and evil and the precariousness of fortune, but also to bookkeeping and to human accountability before God, who holds a tally of one's vices and virtues. The roundels of the table might remind its reader of the beads of the abacus or counters of the checkerboard.

---

[23] *Dictionary of Medieval Latin from the British Sources* [DMLBS], compiled by R. ASHDOWNE et al. (University of Oxford, 2012 –) <http://clt.brepolis.net/dmlbs/Default.aspx> / <https://logeion.uchicago.edu/> [accessed 26 October 2023], s.vv. *scacca, scaccarium*, etc.

[24] P. MILLIMAN, "*Ludus scaccarii*: Games and governance in twelfth-century England", in: *Chess in the Middle Ages and Early Modern Age: A Fundamental Thought Paradigm of the Premodern World*, ed. D.E. O'SULLIVAN (Berlin, 2012), pp. 63-86, <https://doi.org/10.1515/9783110288810.63>.

[25] W.T. BAXTER, "Early accounting: The tally and checkerboard", *The Accounting Historians Journal* 16.2 (1989), pp. 43-83, at pp. 64-68.

Fig. 4 The Exchequer of Ireland at work. *Facsimiles of Irish Manuscripts*, vol. 3, plate XXXVII, early fifteenth century. Accessed on Virtual Record Treasury of Ireland <https://virtualtreasury.ie/item/VRTI-FAX-2>.

Binomials

As we now turn to the linguistic analysis of the Vernon roundels (columns 4, 6 and 8, Figure 2), it is worth pointing out that the polysemy of Latin *scaccarium* has parallels in Anglo-Norman and Middle English. In both vernaculars, the term *table* can be used to denote both "a table, columnar arrangement of words and numbers" and "a chess- or game board".[26] When the Vernon rubricator referred to the grid on f. 231v as "*Pater noster in a table ypeynted*", he might have noticed a possible ambiguity of 'a decorated table' / 'a decorated checkerboard'. The decorations and the overall design of the table seem to make such ambiguities and contrasts quite pronounced. The colours of the ink, the sizes and types of the scripts used for Latin and English, and the ornamental inlays around and between roundels (Fig. 1) certainly invite visual attention and contemplation.

On a different level, we can observe that the lexemes that take part in the semantic fields of vices and virtues engage with one another in various semantic and etymological relationships: most of the Latin abstract nouns appear as single entities in the table, as *Humilitas* (6:2) and *Superbia* (8:2), while the majority of English terms show up in pairs, as *mekenesse and lounesse* (6:3) or

---

[26] *Anglo-Norman Dictionary (AND² Online Edition)* (Aberystwyth University, 2023) <https://anglo-norman.net/> [accessed 26 October 2023], s.v. *table*, cf. s.v. *eschecker*; *Middle English Dictionary* [MED] online, compiled by F. MCSPARRAN *et al.* (University of Michigan, 2019) <https://quod.lib.umich.edu/m/middle-english-dictionary/dictionary> [accessed 26 October 2023], s.v. *table*, cf. s.vv. *checker* n.1 and n.2.

Pruide & stow(t)nesse (8:3). Another layer of juxtaposition, that between the source languages of these lexical fields, demonstrates that some terms are placed next to their reflexes, as Latin *Inuidia* (8:4) and French-derived *Enuie* (8:5), while others take on an English equivalent along with a reflex, as *Castitas* (6:14) / *Chastite & clannesse* (6:15; see Fig. 5), or two English equivalents, as *Ira* (8:6) / *wrathe & angur* (8:7). This section explores these lexical doublets, or binomials, in more detail.

Earlier scholarship has focused on the functions and hierarchies of Latin and English in the Vernon table. Henry has argued that the grid can be read in both Latin and English individually,[27] while Vulic has seen the pairing of the two languages as "one of the motivating forces behind this table's creation".[28] Drawing on insights from the psychology of visual perception, Gottschall has pointed out that it is the roundels with Middle English material that

Fig. 5   The *Pater Noster* table, detail, *Castitas / Chastite & Cleannesse*, MS Oxford, Bodleian Library, Eng. poet. a. 1, f. 231v, *c.* 1390. © Bodleian Libraries, University of Oxford.

should attract the eye and, therefore, be interpreted as "the main elements of the table"[29] (see Figures 1 and 5). Overall, however, all three approaches agree that the English roundels could be read as a kind of gloss or commentary upon Latin. In what follows, I aim to contribute to this discussion by concentrating on the roundels containing such lexical doublets, analysing their contents from a lexicalisation perspective and in relation to other word pairs in the Vernon manuscript and the Middle English lexicon, more generally.

The data for this case study come from the septenary columns containing Gifts of the Holy Spirit (4), Virtues (6), Vices (8) and comprise eleven binomials:

- *knowing & wite* (4:7) 'knowledge and reason; science';
- *Sauour & liking* (4:15) 'wisdom and content; sapience';
- *mekenesse and lounesse* (6:3) 'meekness and lowness; humility';
- *loue & charite* (6:5) 'love and charity; charitable love';

[27] HENRY, "'The Pater Noster in a table ypeynted'", p. 93.
[28] VULIC, "Prayer and vernacular writing in late-medieval England", p. 107.
[29] GOTTSCHALL, "The Lord's Prayer in circles and squares".

- *Pes & reste* (6:7) 'peace and rest; patience';
- *murthe & lykinge* (6:9) 'mirth and eagerness; spiritual joy';
- *mesure and soburnesse* (6:13) 'measure and soberness; moderation in food and drink';
- *Pruide & stow(t)nesse* (8:3) 'pride and stoutness; pride';
- *wrathe & angur* (8:7) 'wrath and anger; wrath';
- *Slowthe & heuinesse* (8:9) 'sloth and heaviness; sloth';
- *Chastite & clannesse* (8:15) 'chastity and cleanness; chastity'.

I refer to such pairs as *binomials*, that is "coordinated word pairs whose lexical elements share the same word class".[30] In my data, most binomial pairs contain close synonyms and are coordinated by *and* (whether abbreviated or not), but generally such units can also include many other levels of synonymy (*health **and** safety*; *sick **and** tired*) and antonymy (*the quick **and** the dead*; *master **and** servant*), as well as other types of coordinators (*love **or** money*, *last **not** least*). Semantic repetition (or contrast) is not the only principle that creates correlation between the two members of a binomial. Normally, with established binomials several other levels are involved: structural (noun + noun, verb + verb, etc.), phonological (alliteration and / or rhyme), and frequency of occurrence. The greater the level of repetition, the more likely a binomial is to lexicalise, i.e. to develop irreversible word order and / or idiomatic meaning.[31]

The process by which the order of the two coordinated elements becomes fixed is called 'freezing'. About a third of binomials in Sandra Mollin's Modern English data undergo freezing, i.e. they develop irreversible word order: A & B *or* B & A > A & B *not* B & A ('safe and sound' *not* 'sound and safe').[32] In spite of their irreversibility, most binomials can still be analysed semantically, i.e. the meaning of the whole phrase can be derived from the meanings of its parts, as in 'sick and disabled'. A fraction of binomials (around 5 per cent), however, undergo idiomatisation, i.e. develop (new) idiomatic meanings and become unanalysable, as 'sick and tired' ('fed up').[33] Below, I am going to test the frequency and reversibility of the selected eleven binomials to find out where they stand in relation to Middle English phraseology and lexicalisation processes. What I hope to demonstrate is that not all of them should be seen as mere glosses of the Latin material in the Vernon table but rather as established or emerging lexical units. Comparative data come from the *Corpus of Middle*

[30] MOLLIN, *The (Ir)reversibility of English Binomials*, p. 1.
[31] J. KOPACZYK and H. SAUER, "Defining and exploring binomials", in: *Binomials in the History of English: Fixed and Flexible*, ed. J. KOPACZYK and H. SAUER (Cambridge, 2017), pp. 1-24, at pp. 15-17.
[32] MOLLIN, *The (Ir)reversibility of English Binomials*, pp. 135-137.
[33] MOLLIN, *The (Ir)reversibility of English Binomials*, pp. 34-39, 56-58, 152-155.

English Prose and Verse (CME), the largest Middle English corpus to date with a collection of about 300 primary texts, and from the *Early English Books Online* (EEBO), a collection of 25,368 texts (or 755 million words) from the 1470s to the 1690s. The discussion of binomials is divided into two subsections, arranged by increasing frequency of occurrence in Middle English.

From Glosses to Emerging Binomials

The distinction between gloss binomials and established binomials is not clear cut. Some lexemes occur repeatedly in Middle English but not in the same order as in the Vernon manuscript, some appear frequently in binomials but with other synonymous partners, yet another group are infrequent in Middle English but gain momentum in the Early Modern English period. The distinction, thus, is a cline, especially if we look at it from a diachronic perspective. In the analysis below, this perspective is framed by three sources: the OED is used to establish the first attestations of the individual lexemes and their potential to appear in binomials, the CME points to their distributions in Middle English, while EEBO, with its vast database, tests the survival of the binomials in the two centuries that are not covered by the CME. This framework shows that the majority of the Vernon binomials, seven in total, tend towards the gloss end of the cline, two seem to be in the middle and can be called 'emerging binomials', and two more are established phrases (see next section).

"*Mekenesse and lounesse*" (6:3 – "meekness and lowness") is the only rhyming binomial in the data set. Outside the Vernon manuscript, the sequence occurs only twice in CME, both times in the verse *Life of St. Edith* (first half of the fifteenth century) as "*mekenesse & lowenesse*" (line 1237) and "*mekenes & lowenes*" (l. 1262). The reverse order has a single attestation, "*lowenes / and mekenes*" in the *Mirrour of the blessed lyf of Jesu Christ* dated to *c.* 1410. This text is a translation from Latin, which seems to strengthen the link between this binomial and its origin as a gloss.[34] Both sources are later than the Vernon

---

[34] Cf. M. KRYGIER, "Binominal glosses in translation: The case of the Wycliffite Bible", in: *Binomials in the History of English: Fixed and Flexible*, ed. J. KOPACZYK and H. SAUER (Cambridge, 2017), pp. 159-172; E. KUBASCHEWSKI, "Binominals in Caxton's *Ovid* (Book 1)",

manuscript. Apart from the present binomial, *meekness* features frequently in combination with other virtue-lexemes, e.g. *charity*, *cleanness*, or *patience*. *Lowness*, on the other hand, occurs several times alongside *humility*. The earliest record of *meekness* in the OED is *c*. 1175, while the first attestation of *lowness* is much closer in date to Vernon, at 1340.[35] Perhaps it is not coincidental that the older lexeme has more binomial partners, and that the combination is infrequent given that *lowness* was still a relatively new addition to the Middle English lexicon. EEBO has no record of either *meekness and lowness* or *lowness and meekness* sequences. So, this binomial must have remained an occasional poetic or translation device.

"*Murthe & lykinge*" (6:9 – "mirth and delight") are infrequent partners. The binomial occurs one more time in the Vernon manuscript, augmented with possessive pronouns, "*his murþe and his lykyng*",[36] and another time as *in myrthe & in grette lykynge* in the verse *Life of St. Edith*, the text that also shares *mekenesse and lounesse* with the Vernon. Although both constituents of the binomial are recorded from the Early Old English period onward,[37] they form more frequent collocations with other abstract nouns: *mirth* with *solas*, *joy*, *jollity*, and *gladness*, and *liking* with *lust*, *love*, and *joy*. Accordingly, EEBO has no records for either of the word orders.

The next binomial, "*mesure in mete and soburnesse in drinke*" (6:13 – "moderation in food and soberness in drink") is equally idiosyncratic, even though the combination seems to be suggested by the Latin virtue-lexeme itself, "*Mensura & sobrietas*" (6:12).[38] Of the two French-derived Middle English lexemes, *measure* is the older. In the sense 'limited extent, quantity', *measure* is recorded in a1200, but the sense 'moderation, restraint' is not much later, *c*. 1225.[39] *Soberness* arrives about a century later and is perceived as the opposite of *gluttony* from its earliest appearances, as in this quotation from the *Cursor Mundi*: "*Gains glotory* [sic] *soburnes o mete*".[40] *Measure* and *soberness* never collocate outside of the Vernon table, and *soberness* does not generally take

---

in: *Binomials in the History of English: Fixed and Flexible*, ed. J. KOPACZYK and H. SAUER (Cambridge, 2017), pp. 141-158.

[35] *Oxford English Dictionary* [OED] online (Oxford University Press, 2022) <https://www.oed.com/> [accessed 26 October 2023], s.vv. *lowness* n, *meekness* n.

[36] *Barlaam & Josaphat*, f. 100.

[37] OED, s.vv. *liking* n, *mirth* n.

[38] Siegfried Wenzel observes that in late medieval sermons the proportion of binomials is much higher in Middle English texts than in Latin ones. Cf. S. WENZEL, "Lexical doublets (binomials) in sermons from late medieval England", *Neuphilologische Mitteilungen* 123.1 (2022), pp. 157-170, esp. pp. 165-168.

[39] OED, s.v. *measure*.

[40] CM 27408; OED, s.v. *soberness* n.

part in binomials. *Measure*, on the other hand, has several partners: *weight*, *number*, *manner*, *order*, and *reason*. Of these only the latter two are relevant for the domain of virtue. There are no records of *measure and soberness* (or the reverse) in EEBO.

"*Chastite & clannesse*" (6:15 – "chastity and cleanness") displays both word orders in CME. Of these "*chastity and cleanness*" (A & B) features one more time outside the Vernon manuscript, while B & A can be found four times, with the earliest attestation in the *Ayenbite of Inwyt* (1340): "*þine klennesse and þine chastete*" (205 / 28). The adjectival binomial "*clene and chaste*" (4 occurrences in total, including one in the Vernon manuscript) could have provided further support for the spread of "*cleanness and chastity*". An even earlier semantic association between the two lexemes is suggested by the MED quotation from the *Vices and Virtues* (c. 1225): "*castitas is þe clannesse of ðe likame*" ("castitas is the cleanness of the body"). The earliest instance of *cleanness* is dated to the late ninth century, while 'chastity' is first attested in c. 1225.[41] EEBO does not record any instances of "*chastity and cleanness*" (or the reverse), so this pair, too, did not diffuse outside translation contexts.

"*Sauour & liking*" (4:15) "wisdom and content" appears to be an equally unproductive pair. In fact, the sense 'knowledge, wisdom' is not attested for *savour* in the OED and the MED until a few decades after the production of the Vernon manuscript (in *Medulla c.* 1425). So, we are likely dealing with a nonce phrase here. It comes as no surprise that EEBO has no record of this binomial.

"*Slowthe & heuinesse*" (8:9) "sloth and negligence" is also likely to be a gloss. The first element, 'sloth', is dated to c. 1175,[42] but it is very seldom used within a binomial, its occasional partners including *sin*, *idleness*, and *long sleep*. The attestations of the *i*-mutated form *sleuþ(e*, however, go back to the late ninth century. This earlier form collocates more frequently with *sleep* as well as with other sin-lexemes. *Heaviness*, too, is first attested in the late ninth century. Among its figurative senses, we find 'displeasure', 'anger'; 'dullness', 'despair'; 'sadness', 'grief'.[43] Accordingly, its binomial partners are 'sorrow', 'care', and 'pain', but not 'sloth'. The shift from 'despair' or 'sadness' to 'spiritual sloth, negligence; the vice of sloth' is recorded in the MED.[44] The quotations in the relevant subsection in the MED point to a close semantic association between 'sloth' and 'heaviness' around the time when the Vernon manuscript was compiled. Chaucer uses "*by cause / of hir slouthe and of hir heuynesse*" in

---

[41] OED, s.vv. *chastity* n, *cleanness* n.
[42] OED, s.v. *sloth* n, cf. OED, s.v. † *sleuth* n. 1.
[43] OED, s.v. *heaviness* n.
[44] MED, s.v. *hevines(se* n, 3d.

the 'Parson's Tale', while in the *Medulla Grammatice* (*c.* 1425), we find both words translating Latin *Accidia: drerinesse, heuinesse, sloupe.* EEBO has only a thin record of both sequences: "*sloth and heaviness*" (1) and "*heaviness and sloth*" (1); so, this late-fourteenth-century innovation must have turned out to be unsuccessful.

"*Knowing & wite*" (4:7) "knowledge and reason" has a slightly higher attestation rate. It is found one more time as "*such knowynge and such wit*" in the Minor Poems of the Vernon manuscript. Further, two instances of "*wyt and knowenge*" come up in a metrical romance *Merlin* (*c.* 1450). The verbal binomial *wite and knowe* is used a number of times, especially by Gower and Hoccleve. Its currency could have given additional support to the noun pair, but EEBO records are not extensive – only two attestations of "*wit and knowing*".

My interpretation of the sin-lexeme "*Pruide & stow(t)nesse*" (8:3) is "pride and stoutness", with an insertion of a <t>. The scribe's mistake or slip is easy to explain for the term must have been a very recent derivation in Middle English. The earliest OED attestations of *stoutness* are in 1398 and 1400. The Vernon occurrence may suggest a slightly earlier date for this derivative of the North-eastern French *stout* (cf. German *stolz*). The base is recorded in English from *c.* 1315.[45] The lexeme *pride* is traced to Late Old English and is used profusely from the Early Middle English period onward.[46] In CME, the binomial "*pride and stoutness*" features only one more time, in the roughly contemporary prose *Brut*;[47] on three more occasions the adjectival binomial "*proude & stout*" is used. The order of the constituents in both collocations is always the same. Thus, as with "*meekness and lowness*", the older lexeme takes slot A, and the whole phrase is infrequent, possibly due to the recent innovation of *stoutness*. In EEBO, however, "*pride and stoutness*" seems to have gained some ground (21 occurrences), compared to just one instance of "*stoutness and pride*".

Finally, and somewhat surprisingly, the sequence "*wrathe & angur*" (8:7 – "wrath and anger") has only one attestation in CME, in the verse *Legend of St. Wolfade and Ruffyn*.[48] The MED records one attestation of "*Angur or wrathe*" in 1440.[49] The lexeme *wrath* has continuous attestations in English from *c.* 900, while *anger* is only recorded from 1325.[50] The adjectives from the same semantic domain make a more stable binomial: "*wroth & angry*", with A & B order

---

[45] OED, s.vv. *stout* adj, *stoutness* n.
[46] OED, s.v. *pride* n.
[47] MS Oxford, Bodleian Library, Rawlinson B. 171 (*c.* 1400).
[48] MS London, British Library, Cotton Nero C.xii (*c.* 1450).
[49] MED, s.v. *anger* n, 2c.
[50] OED, s.vv. *anger* n, *wrath* n.

and mostly in prose, has 26 occurrences in CME, even though the adjective *angry* is first recorded only in *c.* 1380. The more frequent Middle English collocation of the two adjectives could have supported the later spread of the noun binominal. EEBO has a spectacular tally of 302 occurrences of "*wrath and anger*" and 232 of "*anger and wrath*". So, what we observe in the Vernon manuscript must be an early sign of the pair's development towards an established binominal.

Established Binomials

With established binomials slot A seems to be favoured by the older term, while slot B is occupied by more recent loanwords / derivatives. "*Loue & charite*" (6:5) "love and charity" is a good case in point. In CME, the binomial occurs 63 times, including several texts from the Vernon manuscript. Of these, A & B order ("*love and charity*") *is attested 57 times, while B & A order comes* up only 6 times. The term love (Old English *lufu*) is common to all Germanic languages and is attested from the Early Old English period onward; *charity* can be traced to as early as *c.* 1175.[51] The binomial occurs exclusively in poetry. The high record of the binomial in Middle English is parallelled in EEBO: "*love and charity*" occurs a total of 722 times, while "*charity and love*" occurs a total of 121 times, which also confirms the Middle English trend towards the A & B order freeze.

"*Pes & reste*" (6:7 – "peace and rest") is more complicated. It is by far the most frequent binomial in CME, occurring 128 times, including several texts from the Vernon manuscript. Even though the term *rest* is attested from Early Old English onward, and *peace* from *c.* 1160, the order of the elements is still reversible in the Middle English period, with about 50/50 distributions of both A & B and B & A word order. Both feature predominantly in poetry. Given that the metrical pattern is trochaic in both, the distributions may be dictated more by rhyme than lexicalisation. In EEBO the tally is 578 instances of "*peace and rest*" vs. 709 of "*rest and peace*".

Conclusions

This paper has explored the tabular arrangement of the catechetical septenaries and suggested that the visual clues of the chequered design might

---

[51] OED, s.vv. *love* n, *charity* n.

trigger at least two associative paths. The first is a resemblance between the Vernon *Pater Noster* table and a chessboard. This association brings to mind the metaphorical battle between virtues and vices, well-known from the *Psychomachia* by Prudentius as well as chess moralities of the Middle Ages. At the lexical level, it is supported by *"contra"* and *"is a3enst"* found in column 7 (Figures 1 and 2). The second path connects the Vernon table to the Exchequer cloth and one's soul's tally of vices and virtues before earthly confessors and divine judgement. The alternation of shapes and colours behind both metaphors reminds the observer about the mutability of fortune and the moral accountability of every sinner. This multiformity of readings is ingrained in the polysemy of Latin *scaccarium* and French / English *table*.

Within the meditative context of the Vernon diagram linguistic variation might have been part of the intentional design, which invites us to consider juxtaposition between languages: the lexical stability of Latin against the changeability of English, native English terms against loanwords from Anglo-Norman (*chastity*, *charity*) and Old Norse (*anger*), emerging terms against their more common counterparts, and recent phrasal innovations against established poetic clichés. In the second part of the present analysis, the lexical composition of the Vernon binomials appears quite innovative. Some binomials (*"mekenesse and lounesse"* (6:3)) are not attested before 1390 when the Vernon collection was compiled, while others (*"Pruide & stow(t)nesse"* (8:3) or *"Sauour & liking"* (4:15)) may even provide the earliest attestations of an individual lexeme or sense. The majority of the pairs are probably nonce binomials as their subsequent low or non-existent attestations in the fifteenth century and EEBO show. Yet another category (*"loue & charite"* (6:5); *"Pes & reste"* (6:7), as well as *"wrathe & angur"* (8:7)) consists of established or emerging set phrases with high frequency scores but varying levels of freezing. This study suggests that slot A is generally favoured by an older term and slot B by a more recent derivation or borrowing, which may be an indirect corroboration of Mollin's semantic observations for Modern English: slot A is associated with broader meanings, while slot B with more specific meanings, a divide that tends to go along chronological lines.[52] Several scholars have undertaken comparisons of native- vs. foreign-origin lexemes in slot A vs. B at the level of individual texts;[53] what is still missing, however, is a comprehensive survey of how the order within binomials and its relation to source languages develop over time.

---

[52] MOLLIN, *The (Ir)reversibility of English Binomials*, pp. 95-97.
[53] E.g. KUBASCHEWSKI, "Binominals in Caxton's *Ovid* (Book 1)"; H. SAUER, "Flexible and formulaic: Binomials and multinomials in the Late Middle English: *The Wise Book of Philosophy and Astronomy*", *Acta Philologica* 50 (2017), pp. 62-78.

The use of EEBO and other historical corpora may offer a solution to this question.

Visual Chronologies in Early Modern English Historiography*

AINO LIIRA, MATTI PEIKOLA, and MARJO KAARTINEN

Introduction

Early Modern English books addressing chronology frequently commented on the visual aspects of ordering events. The theme of visuality was not unique to vernacular works: a well-known metaphor of chronology and geography as the 'eyes' of history was popular across sixteenth-century Europe and appears in English as well.[1] However, the visual aspect of conceptualising time becomes even more apparent in authors' and other text

---

* Research for this chapter has been supported by the Research Council of Finland, grant number 340005.

[1] For instance, Thomas Pie writes in his dedication to John Whitgift, Archbishop of Canterbury: "HOW necessarie and requisite Chronologie is in the studie of all Historie, Diuine or Humane, it being the right eye thereof, as Geographie is the left", T. PIE, *An Houreglasse* (London, 1597: STC 19900), *A*3r. Stephen Boyd Davis traces the origin of the metaphor to the Lutheran theologian David Chytraeus (1563, *De lectione historiarum recte instituenda*: "duos velut oculos historiae"); see S. BOYD DAVIS, E. BEVAN, and A. KUDIKOV, "Just in time: Defining historical

---

Graphic Practices and Literacies in the History of English, ed. Matti PEIKOLA, Jukka TYRKKÖ and Mari-Liisa VARILA, *Utrecht Studies in Medieval Literacy*, 61 (Turnhout: Brepols, 2025), pp. 201-225.

producers' frequent references to tables and other graphic devices. Emphasis is placed on how easily the reader can access the chronological information and draw comparisons when the information is presented in visual form.

The emphasis on visuality reflects the increasing use of graphic devices in conveying chronological information during the early modern period. Although visual means such as tabularisation were used in the ancient and medieval periods, the increasing visuality of chronological discussion in the early modern period may be linked to a shift in historiography. The rise of empirical sciences played a part in the emergence of chronology as a separate field – auxiliary to historiography, as reflected in the eye metaphor – while historiography became more interdisciplinary.[2] Eventually, the new methods as well as new discoveries made in natural sciences led to the conceptualisation of time as following a universal, absolute timeline instead of specific timelines that were relative and tied to certain persons or events.[3] Advancing printing technologies in the course of the early modern period may also have contributed to the types of visualisations.

The aim of the present chapter is to find out how time was represented visually in early modern English printed books (1473-1700) addressing chronology, and how these representations were communicated to the reader. We focus on two aspects: Firstly, we ask what kind of visualisations (such as tables or timelines) English authors, translators, and book producers employed. What kinds of dating systems were used and how were the visualisations structured? It should be noted that our intention is not to replace existing accounts of the broader developments of the history of the timeline, or to focus on the timeline

---

chronographics", in: *Electronic Visualisation in Arts and Culture*, ed. J.P. BOWEN, S. KEENE, and K. NG (London, 2013), pp. 243-257, at p. 246; S. BOYD DAVIS, "May not duration be represented as distinctly as space? Geography and the visualization of time in the early eighteenth century", in: *Knowing Nature in Early Modern Europe*, ed. D. BECK (London, 2015), pp. 119-137. Anthony Grafton notes that François Baudouin used this metaphor "[l]ike all writers on the *ars historica*", A. GRAFTON, *What Was History? The Art of History in Early Modern Europe* (Cambridge, 2012 [2007]), p. 92. Grafton, however, does not comment on its origin.

[2] See e.g. D.R. KELLEY, "Between history and system", in: *Historia: Empiricism and Erudition in Early Modern Europe*, ed. G. POMATA and N.G. SIRAISI (Cambridge, MA, 2005), pp. 211-238; L. JANSSEN, "The rise of 'auxiliary sciences' in early modern national historiography: An 'interdisciplinary' answer to historical scepticism", *History of European Ideas* 43 (2017), pp. 427-441.

[3] On relative timelines, see e.g. D.J. WILCOX, *The Measure of Times Past: Pre-Newtonian Chronologies and the Rhetoric of Relative Time* (Chicago, IL, 1987); D.E. GREENWAY, "Dates in history: Chronology and memory", *Historical Research* 72 (1999), pp. 127-139.

format alone.[4] Rather, we explore the variety of different visual displays available to English book producers in order to see what prototypical or innovative types can be found. Secondly, we ask how authors and book producers referred to these visualisations when instructing the reader in their use and promoting the value of their books.

Graphic devices, i.e. the various means of expressing information which are situated between text and image, are an understudied feature of early modern books, yet they are important for the transmission of knowledge (see the introductory chapter in this volume by Peikola, Tyrkkö, and Varila). We aim to shed light on early modern English reading practices by focusing on the interplay of the devices themselves and the book producers' reader-oriented discussion around them.

Chronological Accounts and the Visualisation of Time

Historiography and Chronology in England

The medieval period had witnessed its "golden age" of historiography in the thirteenth century, with numerous Latin authors addressing the question of chronology and truth in their prologues.[5] Comparison of several works was seen as crucial in establishing a reliable chronology of events and achieving truth.[6] In Britain, English started to gain ground from Latin as the language of history writing in the course of the fifteenth century. By this time, the chronicle genre had already begun to decline, despite a brief revival of secular and lay chronicles.[7] Chronicles may be distinguished from histories in that they generally consist of brief entries organised year by year.[8] Their open-endedness was

---

[4] The invention of the timeline format is generally attributed to Joseph Priestley in 1769; see D. ROSENBERG and A. GRAFTON, *Cartographies of Time: A History of the Timeline* (New York, 2010), pp. 117-126; DAVIS, "May not duration be represented', p. 136.

[5] A. GRANSDEN, *Legends, Traditions and History in Medieval England* (London, 2010 [1992]), p. 130. This development was potentially linked to the proliferation of written documents after the Norman conquest; see M.T. CLANCHY, *From Memory to Written Record, England 1066-1307*, 2nd edn (Oxford, 1993), pp. 1-2, see also esp. ch. 2.

[6] GRANSDEN, *Legends, Traditions and History*, pp. 142-143.

[7] GRANSDEN, *Legends, Traditions and History*, pp. 222-223.

[8] This is a simplification; in practice there was overlap between categories. For a discussion of the distinctions, see e.g. GRANSDEN, *Legends, Traditions and History*, pp. 199-201. On medieval usage, see D.M. DELIYANNIS, "Introduction", in: *Historiography in the Middle Ages*, ed. D.M. DELIYANNIS (Leiden, 2003), pp. 2-14, at p. 5. For a fuller account of the meaning of

perhaps less suited to print, and in fifteenth-century England, audience interests shifted towards thematic histories.[9]

The emergence of chronology as a scholarly discipline has its roots in Renaissance culture, and in the widespread interest in the concept of time across Europe. The attempt to understand the past resulted in what Anthony Grafton calls "technical chronology", which aimed at "reconstructing the calendars and dating the main events of ancient and medieval history".[10] At the heart of this change was the shifting understanding of the concept of history, as illustrated by Daniel R. Woolf.[11] New discoveries about the world and a growing awareness of multiple timelines resulted in a keen interest in chronology in the sixteenth century.[12]

The shifting sense of history in the early modern period was also affected by emerging empirical sciences. The accuracy of history and historical sources were increasingly debated. As Donald R. Kelley shows, the term *historia* underwent changes in the sixteenth and seventeenth centuries: the term was no longer applied solely to the acts and events of the past or the description of such events, but also to encompass the chronological organisation of knowledge in any discipline; the role of natural history was considerable in this process.[13] The new writing of history drew from various disciplines, or 'auxiliary sciences', beginning with chronology and geography and extending to a number of scholarly disciplines, from philology to climatology, that aided in interpreting historical sources and material evidence.[14] As Lydia Janssen argues, early modern historiographers judged their contemporaries by their ability to incorporate evidence from these other disciplines.[15] In other words, chronological methods and the 'new' writing of history and chronology could be viewed as a more

---

'chronicle' in Antiquity, see R.W. BURGESS and M. KULIKOWSKI, *Mosaics of Time: The Latin Chronicle Traditions from the First Century BC to the Sixth Century AD, vol. 1: A Historical Introduction to the Chronicle Genre from its Origins to the High Middle Ages* (Turnhout, 2013), pp. 278-287.

[9] GRANSDEN, *Legends, Traditions and History*, pp. 223-224. On the open-endedness of chronicles, see BURGESS and KULIKOWSKI, *Mosaics of Time*, p. 28.

[10] A. GRAFTON, *Joseph Scaliger. A Study in the History of Classical Scholarship, vol. II: Historical Chronology* (Oxford, 1993), p. 4.

[11] D.R. WOOLF, "From hystories to the historical: Five transitions in thinking about the past, 1500-1700", *Huntington Library Quarterly* 68 (2005), pp. 33-70.

[12] WOOLF, "From hystories to the historical", p. 40.

[13] KELLEY, "Between history and system", pp. 214-215.

[14] JANSSEN, "The rise of 'auxiliary sciences'"; on 'auxiliary sciences', see also KELLEY, "Between history and system", p. 222.

[15] JANSSEN, "The rise of 'auxiliary sciences'", p. 438.

'scientific', rather than scholarly, enterprise.[16] In the following section, we outline how this affected visual representations.

Visualising Time

The interest in conceptualising and measuring time in the Renaissance period has been shown to have led to an increasing visuality of chronological material.[17] Visual representations, of course, did not emerge in the early modern period; we can see examples of a visual culture already in Antiquity and the early Middle Ages, the rise of what Ildar Garipzanov calls "graphicacy", where the textual and the visual modes were deeply intertwined.[18] However, while the early Renaissance period still followed medieval traditions, the concept of time itself was gradually changing in the course of the period. The change was from relative timelines, based upon persons and periods of reign, to an absolute, universal timeline.[19] Hans-Werner Goetz points out that while classical and medieval historians were concerned with accuracy in dating events of the past, at the same time they approached historical facts as "timeless" and frequently employed them to reflect on current events.[20] Relative timelines were suitable for building the necessary context for moral teachings. In a similar vein, Richard K. Emmerson reminds us of the inescapable intertwining of the 'past' and the 'future' in the medieval notion of history: universal history was concerned with a time frame extending from the biblical Creation until the end of the world, the Last Judgement.[21]

The changing conceptualisation of time and its relation to the past drove the emergence of chronology as a discipline in the early modern period. Further-

---

[16] JANSSEN, "The rise of 'auxiliary sciences'", p. 428.

[17] ROSENBERG and GRAFTON, *Cartographies of Time*; B. STEINER, *Die Ordnung Der Geschichte: Historische Tabellenwerke in Der Frühen Neuzeit* (Köln, 2008).

[18] I. GARIPZANOV, "The rise of graphicacy in Late Antiquity and the Early Middle Ages", *Viator* 46.2 (2015), pp. 1-21.

[19] The gradual conceptual change has been traced by WILCOX, *The Measure of Times Past*, who connects the groundbreaking turn with Sir Isaac Newton (see esp. pp. 4, 208-214); see also GREENWAY, "Dates in history".

[20] H.-W. GOETZ, "The concept of time in the historiography of the eleventh and twelfth centuries", in: *Medieval Concepts of the Past: Ritual, Memory, Historiography*, ed. G. ALTHOFF, J. FRIED, and P.J. GEARY, reprint (Washington, DC, 2003), pp. 139-165, at p. 155.

[21] R.K. EMMERSON, "Apocalypse and / as history", in: *Medieval Historical Writing: Britain and Ireland, 500-1500*, ed. J. JAHNER, E. STEINER, and E.M. TYLER (Cambridge, 2019), pp. 51-66, at p. 51.

more, the gradual shift from relative timelines to a single, universal timeline could not have happened without the early modern interest in making time 'visible'. It could be argued that the simple arrangement of events in a chronological order, or within "a chronographic frame",[22] to quote R.W. Burgess and Michael Kulikowski, is the first step in visualising the passage of time. However, the focus of the present chapter is on visual representations that go beyond the annalistic year-by-year format used in chronicles. Furthermore, even though the passing of time can be illustrated through this method, annalistic structure alone does not help with recording events which occur simultaneously. The desire for 'synchronisation' – which is required especially when attempting to shed light on biblical events – is what eventually led to attempts to visualise this information.

The earliest use of a clearly tabular format in historiography can be traced back to the *Chronici canones* of Eusebius of Caesarea in the fourth century AD.[23] In England these chronological tables were generally known through the Latin translations of St. Jerome, and they remained a standard reference tool until the late sixteenth century.[24] The history of western chronology is essentially the history of biblical chronology, which had a dual purpose: to determine the precise date of the creation of the world and to calculate the probable date of its end.[25] As J. D. North summarises, the endeavour was to "strengthen Faith in a literal reading of scripture", although this was done by synthesising biblical information with parallel chronologies of non-Christian nations.[26] Advances made in the early modern period in constructing parallel chronologies, and in measuring time with clocks and calendars, gradually resulted in abandoning the ties to Scripture.[27]

---

[22] BURGESS and KULIKOWSKI, *Mosaics of Time*, p. 190.

[23] See e.g. R.W. BURGESS, *Studies in Eusebian and Post-Eusebian Chronography* (Stuttgart, 1999), p. 21; A. GRAFTON and M. WILLIAMS, *Christianity and the Transformation of the Book: Origen, Eusebius, and the Library of Caesarea* (Cambridge, MA, 2006), pp. 133-177; M.R. CRAWFORD, *The Eusebian Canon Tables: Ordering Textual Knowledge in Late Antiquity* (Oxford, 2019), pp. 75-78.

[24] GREENWAY, "Dates in history", p. 130. For medieval responses, see GOETZ, "The concept of time", pp. 147-153.

[25] For biblical chronology, see e.g. J. BARR, "Pre-scientific chronology: The Bible and the origin of the world", *Proceedings of the American Philosophical Society* 143 (1999), pp. 379-387; J.D. NORTH, "Chronology and the age of the world", in: *Cosmology, History, and Theology*, ed. W. YOURGRAU and A.D. BRECK (Boston, MA, 1977), pp. 307-333.

[26] NORTH, "Chronology", p. 92.

[27] The fundamental scholarly contribution of Joseph Scaliger (d. 1609) to this development is discussed by GRAFTON, *Joseph Scaliger, vol. II*.

The linking of history to emerging empirical sciences, as discussed in the previous section, resulted in more systematic approaches to synchronising knowledge of the past.[28] Tables and other graphic devices which enable the comparison or synchronisation of events are important tools for establishing chronologies. Synchronisation of chronological information became increasingly popular throughout Europe, especially in the university context. The tabularisation of information allowed the comparison of separate timelines, eventually leading to synchronism: the practice of comparing separate timelines to find unifying elements. This tabularisation of history has been studied, e.g. by Benjamin Steiner and Helge Jordheim.[29] The practice was especially tied to the writing of universal or world history, and to university teaching in the seventeenth century; Jordheim notes that

> from the seventeenth century onward, no attempt to write universal history, and hence to create a universal temporal framework, could do without the so-called chronographic, synoptic, or in the term most commonly used, 'synchronistic' tables.[30]

Visual Representation of Chronology in English Books

Our aim is to gain a more fine-tuned understanding of the developments described so far by focusing on books and book producers in a vernacular environment. We approach our material from a primarily philological perspective. This entails situating graphic practices of the past in their communicative contexts of meaning-making. While we are interested in books and texts as transmitters of knowledge, we study them as multimodal items in which book producers' communicative choices are made with their intended audiences in mind, constrained by factors arising from the technology of production and historical conventions of written discourse. We are interested not only in tables but in all the different ways to visualise chronological information. We are also interested in the anticipated readership of the books, and the expected skills of readers in interpreting the visual information. To obtain evidence of this, we

---

[28] JANSSEN, "The rise of 'auxiliary sciences'", pp. 427-441; KELLEY, "Between history and system", pp. 211-238. See also GRAFTON, *What Was History?*, p. 28.

[29] STEINER, *Die Ordnung der Geschichte*; H. JORDHEIM, "Making universal time: Tools of synchronization", in: *Universal History and the Making of the Global*, ed. H. BJØRNSTAD, H. JORDHEIM, and A. RÉGENT-SUSINI (New York, 2018), pp. 133-151, esp. at pp. 145-150.

[30] JORDHEIM, "Making universal time", p. 146.

examine book producers' comments on the graphic devices and the phraseology and vocabulary used in these comments.

To identify relevant primary sources, we conducted subject searches in the *Early English Books Online* (EEBO) database and the *English Short Title Catalogue* (ESTC) with the terms 'Chronology', 'World history' and 'Bible – Chronology' for the period up to the year 1700; all publications not written in English (mostly in Latin) were excluded from the results. Excluding multiple editions of the same work, these searches yielded altogether 49 unique titles in English. The relevant hits were manually checked for visualisations of chronology. We did not have a preconception of what counts as a 'visualisation'; instead, we considered all layouts from standard prose or verse text to prototypical tables and everything in between, and paid attention to how dates or other units of time were presented. The main focus was on the first (available) editions of works / titles, so that successive editions of the same title were not analysed systematically. The searches were then complemented with a manual check of approximately sixty additional volumes, including successive editions, searched by the keyword 'histor*' until the year 1600. The motivation behind this was to form a more comprehensive picture of potentially relevant material published in the early part of the period, before chronology was fully established as a specialised field. The primary sources were accessed via EEBO, supplemented with digital copies made available by individual repositories.

Types of Visual Representations

In this section, we explore the different types of layouts early modern book producers employed to visualise chronologies. We do not intend to impose a hierarchy, nor do we aim at creating a typology of chronological devices as such. However, to organise the discussion we group similar phenomena, and provide schematic illustrations of prototypical features.

Works addressing the question of chronology do not always contain visualisations, either by a conscious choice or convention, or due to technological constraints especially in the earliest printed works. Slightly over half of all books in the 'World history' subject category lack visualisations; in contrast, in the combined 'Chronology' and 'Bible – Chronology' category, 17 of the 21 books examined contain some visualisations. This quantitative difference highlights the close connection between visualisations and the more specialised

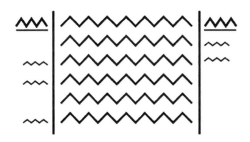

Fig. 1　Schematic illustration of marginal annotations.

field of chronology versus more general historiography in the Early Modern English period.

Some visual structure can be created through chapter titles or other subheadings. Examples of such graphic practices are found, for instance, in the anonymous *A Briefe Chronologie of the Holie Scriptures*, which contains no visualisations but discusses biblical chronology in verse and prose within an eschatological or apocalyptic framework, with subtitles summarising the time frame of each biblical book, e.g. "GENESIS. 2368. yeares".[31] The prose format appears to be common in seventeenth-century eschatological works, but is not limited to them. Basic visual structuring can be found, for instance, in the *Ductor historicus* of Thomas Hearne, where the discussion is somewhat visually organised by printing each item on one line, with dates placed on each side.[32] However, all text is contained in the main text area (as opposed to margins) and is more prose-like than the visualisations we explore below.

The first type that we consider an example of visualisation involves placing dates in the margins (cf. Fig. 1). In England, this method can already be attested in manuscript chronicles such as the English translation of Ranulf Higden's *Polychronicon*.[33] The printed editions retain the chronological system: many copies of William Caxton's first edition (1482) feature a handwritten apparatus, while in the two subsequent editions (1495, 1527) it is printed in the margins.[34]

[31]　ANON., *A Briefe Chronologie of the Holie Scriptures* (London, 1600: STC 14), A6.

[32]　T. HEARNE, *Ductor historicus, or, A Short System of Universal History* (London, 1698: WING H1309).

[33]　For discussion of the author's "marginal chronologies", see J. FREEMAN, "The manuscript dissemination and readership of the 'Polychronicon' of Ranulph Higden, c. 1330-c. 1500", unpublished doctoral thesis (University of Cambridge, 2013), pp. 168-182. For the English translation of John Trevisa, see A. LIIRA. *Paratextuality in Manuscript and Print: Verbal and Visual Presentation of the Middle English* Polychronicon. PhD thesis, University of Turku (Turku, 2020), pp. 222-224, 230-231, available at <https://urn.fi/URN:ISBN:978-951-29-8058-1>.

[34]　R. HIGDEN, *Prolicionycion* [sic] (Westminster, 1482: STC 13438); R. HIGDEN, *Policronicon* (Westminster, 1495: STC 13439); R. HIGDEN, *Polycronycon* (London, 1527: STC 13440). The rubrication was likely produced in Caxton's workshop, see L. HELLINGA and G.D. PAINTER, *Catalogue of Books Printed in the XVth Century Now in the British Library. BMC Pt. 11: England* ('t Goy-Houten, 2007), p. 128. See also K. TONRY, "Reading history in Caxton's

In the *Polychronicon*, headings at the top of the marginal columns refer to various relative chronologies, beginning from Abraham and other biblical patriarchs. Longer, more universal time frames are also used, such as years counted from the Exodus, from the founding of Rome (*ab urbe condita*),[35] and eventually, years of grace. A second row of dates runs parallel with the dating system: these mark the reigns of various rulers.

A step towards a more visual timeline is taken in Thomas Lanquet's *An Epitome of Chronicles* (1549).[36] Two parallel marginal columns are separated with a rule, one providing *anno mundi*[37] dates, the other counting years before and after Christ. The vertical line could be taken as a visual reminder of the passing of time. However, it seems more likely that the vertical line simply divides the margin into two columns for visual clarity, as in the anonymous *Chronographia*, an adaptation of the work of the German chronographer Lorenz Codomann.[38] In this book, the headings for the parallel columns are also separated with a horizontal rule, creating a tabular structure. The work also contains tables; these will be discussed below.

Presenting dates in the margins remains a popular technique in our materials throughout the seventeenth century. A somewhat tabular structure of two parallel columns and ruled column headings, not unlike the one found in *Chronographia*, is attested in James Ussher's *The Annals of the World* (1658).[39] The majority of the seventeenth-century works with this type of visualisation, however, simply record dates in the margins, as illustrated in Fig. 1. No clear difference of preference can be found between works translated from other languages and those originally published in English.

For a more visual approach, book producers could arrange the information in a list or a table. Their distinction is not clear-cut. Prototypically, a list[40] con-

---

Polychronicon", *Journal of English and Germanic Philology* 111 (2012), pp. 169-198, at p. 178. For other examples of rubrication organised by printers, see J. BOFFEY, *Manuscript and Print in London, c. 1475-1530* (London, 2012), pp. 70-71.

[35] 753 BC.

[36] T. LANQUET, *An Epitome of Chronicles* (London, 1549: STC 15217), from B2 onwards. See also subsequent editions: STC 15218, 15219, 15220.

[37] *Anno mundi* (AM), 'year of the world', is a reckoning of the years from the beginning of the world as understood in biblical chronology; different chronologies would have different calculations. In Lanquet's chronicle, year 1 AM is given as 3962 BC (STC 15217, B2r).

[38] ANON. *Chronographia. A Description of Time, from the Beginning of the World, vnto the Yeare of Our Lord 137* (London, 1590: STC 5471), from A1 onwards.

[39] J. USSHER, *The Annals of the World* (London, 1658: WING U149).

[40] For a recent definition, stressing "enumerative practices", see E. VON CONTZEN and J. SIMPSON, "Introduction: Enlistment as poetic stratagem", in: *Enlistment: Lists in Medieval and Early Modern Literature*, ed. E. VON CONTZEN and J. SIMPSON (Columbus, OH, 2022), pp. 1-13.

Visual Chronologies in Early Modern English Historiography 211

sists of items which are separated using typographical or visual means, such as punctuation marks or line breaks. Here we have only included lists which are visually distinguished from the surrounding text. The mode of reading is linear. In contrast, a table consists of cells, which are prototypically created by lines (rules) forming a grid. The mode of reading is not linear; instead, the reader moves along the x and y axes to locate the cell which carries the information the readers seek.[41] However, not all tables are ruled: cells can also be created through whitespace. There is thus overlap between tables and lists consisting of two or more columns (cf. Fig. 2).

Fig. 2   Schematic illustration of a list and table.

Lists are firmly tied to the domain of historiography, where, for instance, papal and regnal lists, along with genealogies, have been used to serve various functions: to record the chronology of rulers and office holders, but also to reinforce ideas of authority and, sometimes, to manipulate information.[42] In our materials, lists are frequent tools for arranging chronological knowledge. Typically, they are used for a specific purpose amidst discussion in prose format, and it could be argued that their visual arrangement reinforces the idea of chronology as a succession of times or events. The earliest example in our materials is *The Thre Bokes of Cronicles* of Johannes Carion (1550).[43] Lists in the section discussing Persian monarchs are concerned with accuracies of dating and differences between certain dating systems or sources, such as the difference of 191 years in the Jewish and Greek dating systems.[44] Carion's work also engages with questions of synchronisation: in Book 3, section headings are followed by brief lists which help synchronise different dating systems. For example, the chapter discussing the second Roman emperor Tiberius dates the events using

---

[41] On early tables, see F.T. MARCHESE, "Tables and early information visualization", in: *Knowledge Visualization Currents: From Text to Art to Culture*, ed. F.T. MARCHESE and E. BANISSI (London, 2013), pp. 35-61; A.M. RIGGSBY, *Mosaics of Knowledge: Representing Information in the Roman World* (New York, 2019), pp. 42-82.

[42] See D.N. DUMVILLE, "Kingship, genealogies and regnal lists", in: *Early Medieval Kingship*, ed. P.H. SAWYER and I.N. WOOD, reprint (Leeds, 1979), pp. 72-104. For the manipulation of genealogical tables in the early modern period, see GRAFTON, *What Was History?*, pp. 150-151.

[43] J. CARION, *The Thre Bokes of Cronicles* (London, 1550: STC 4626).

[44] CARION, *The Thre Bokes*, D5-6.

three systems: *anno mundi* ("The yeare of the worlde"), *ab urbe condita* ("The yeare of Rome") and AD ("The yeare of Christe").[45]

A specific type of list, presenting chronological information in account-like calculations (cf. Fig. 3), is found in some late seventeenth-century books. In William Nisbet's *A Golden Chaine of Time Leading unto Christ*, account-like lists walk the reader through the calculation of the years passed, for instance "From the Creation of *Adam* to the birth of *Seth*" (130 years).[46] Similar account-like lists, featuring sums of years presented under a horizontal line, are also found in *A Chronological Account* by George Keith.[47] The account format is perhaps intended to highlight accuracy and precision in the calculation of dates.

Some examples of the overlap between lists and tables in our materials include, for instance, the regnal and papal lists in Peter Heylyn's *Cosmographie in four bookes* and the regnal lists in the second part of John Swan's *Calamus mensurans*.[48] In *Cosmographie*, some lists consist of several columns. The majority of these are, despite their multi-column layout, unambiguously lists – such as the one listing the Dukes of Venice.[49] *Calamus mensurans* has multi-column lists entitled either "lists" or "catalogues"; the column for dates (years of the Julian period[50]) is ruled while other columns are separated by whitespace only. The

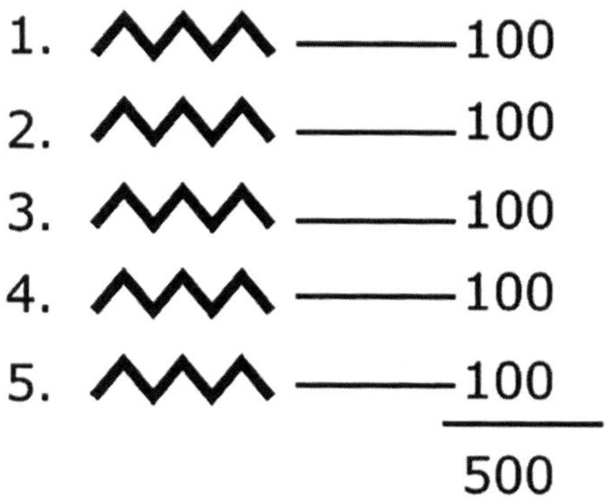

Fig. 3 Schematic illustration of an account-type list.

---

[45] CARION, *The Thre Bokes*, M1.

[46] W. NISBET, *A Golden Chaine of Time Leading unto Christ* (Edinburgh, 1650: WING N1171), A7v.

[47] G. KEITH, *A Chronological Account of the Several Ages of the Vvorld from Adam to Christ* (New York, 1694: WING K223), e.g. A4; according to the ESTC the work was issued together with the *Truth advanced in the correction of many gross & hurtful errors* by the same author.

[48] P. HEYLYN, *Cosmographie in Four Bookes* (London, 1652: WING H1689); J. SWAN, *Calamus mensurans: The Measuring Reed*, 2 vols. (London, 1653: WING S6235).

[49] HEYLYN, *Cosmographie*, M5v-6.

[50] An interval of 7980 years; this chronological system was invented by Scaliger.

Visual Chronologies in Early Modern English Historiography 213

author's comment following the list instructs the reader on the interpretation of the Julian Period:

> This is the first List; in which we have not onely the number of yeares that each King reigned, but also the very year of the *Julian Period* when any of them began his reigne: out of which if you take 709. you have the year of the world in the stead thereof as exactly as may be.[51]

Information presented in a list format appears to fall mainly into two types: regnal lists (including e.g. office-holders) and chronological calculations. However, tabular arrangements – going back to the Eusebian tradition – were the standard format for visualising chronological information. In our materials, tables take different forms. Some tables were ruled (cf. Fig. 4) while others were not (cf. Fig. 5); sometimes either vertical or horizontal rules were used solely instead of the prototypical grid format (cf. Fig. 6).[52]

One of the most famous English examples of an extensive chronological table is found in Sir Walter Ralegh's *The History of the World* (first edition 1614; see the following section).[53] Yet, large chronological tables are found well before Ralegh. They seem to have become popular from the late 1550s onwards. A significant example from 1558, William Rastell's *A Table Collected of the Yeres of Our Lorde God, and of the Yeres of the Kynges of England* is a publication devoted to this one table

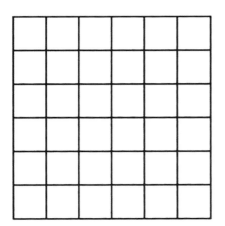

Fig. 4   Schematic illustration of a table with horizontal and vertical rulings.

---

[51] SWAN, *Calamus mensurans*, 2, C3.
[52] Eleanor Robson calls tables without rulings "informal tables", while ruled tables are "formal tables"; see E. ROBSON, "Tables and tabular formatting in Sumer, Babylonia, and Assyria, 2500 BCE-50 CE", in: *The History of Mathematical Tables: From Sumer to Spreadsheets*, ed. M. CAMPBELL-KELLY, M. CROARKEN, R. FLOOD, and E. ROBSON (Oxford, 2003), pp. 19-48, at p. 20.
[53] W. RALEGH, *The History of the World* (London, 1614: STC 20637).

only.[54] Its various (at least twelve) reprints until 1639 reflect the popularity of this visualisation form. The multi-page table consists of four parallel columns, ruled vertically (cf. Fig. 6).

Tables formed parts of many later sixteenth-century chronicles, such as John Foxe's *Acts and Monuments*, which presents tables for "the vii kyngdomes of the Saxons", or Edward Lively's *A True Chronologie of the Times of the Persian Monarchie*, which contains an extensive chronological table of some 127 pages at the end of the volume.[55] Lively's detailed table is intended to shed light on the prophecy of seventy weeks in the Book of Daniel, mapping these so-called weeks with Greek olympiads and the years of Rome. The dates are not collated with *anno mundi* or AD, although the life and death of Christ are marked in the table and discussed in several instances in the prose work.[56] A more modest table of eight pages, focused on the biblical Book of Kings and Book of Chronicles, is appended to Thomas Pie's *An Houreglasse*.[57] Three narrow columns are ruled for the dates: the regnal years of the kings of Judaea

Fig. 5 Schematic illustration of a table without rules.

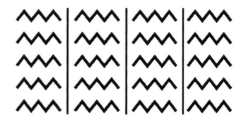

Fig. 6 Schematic illustration of a vertically ruled table.

---

[54] W. RASTELL, *A Table Collected of the Yeres of Our Lorde God, and the Yeres of the Kynges of England* (London, 1558: STC 20732.5).

[55] J. FOXE, *The First Volume of the Ecclesiasticall History Contaynyng the Actes and Monumentes of Thynges Passed in Euery Kynges Tyme in This Realme* (London, 1570: STC 11223), N3-4; E. LIVELY, *A True Chronologie of the Times of the Persian Monarchie* (London, 1597: STC 16609), S1-Cc8.

[56] LIVELY, *A True Chronologie*, K5 and elsewhere.

[57] PIE, *An Houreglasse*, P1-4v.

Visual Chronologies in Early Modern English Historiography

and the kings of Israel, with *anno mundi* dates running in the middle. None of these examples is as ambitious as Ralegh's table in coverage, however.[58]

Tables without rulings (cf. Fig. 5) in our material are generally less complex in that they do not attempt to cover as much information as ruled tables. Like lists, unruled tables are often used to visualise a specific point, such as the succession of ancient Persian monarchs illustrated in tabular arrangements in Pierre d'Avity's *The Estates, Empires, & Principallities of the World*.[59] These arrangements, collectively referred to as a "Catalogue", consist of numbered lists, which, however, can be interpreted as tables because the columns have headings. *Anno mundi* dates, although sparse, are given on the left side, while regnal years and months are given in separate columns on the right.

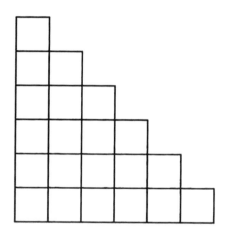

Fig. 7 Schematic illustration of a 'mileage-type' table.

Occasionally, chronological information is presented in a table reminiscent of mileage tables found in modern road atlases, with a stair-step-like design (cf. Fig. 7).[60] In our material, this type of table is exclusively used to convey genealogical information, and in most cases, specifically the life spans of biblical patriarchs from Adam to Abraham. The earliest examples of such genealogical tables in our material can be found in Hugh Broughton's *A Concent of Scripture* (1588/1589), where the chronological tables begin with a 'mileage-type' layout. The table is divided into three parts: the first runs from Adam until the Flood, the second from Arpachshad (one of the sons of Shem,

---

[58] A notable sixteenth-century table that fell outside our keyword searches is the Chronographie of Meredith Hanmer, published as part of his Eusebius translation and reissued several times between 1577 and 1663. For the first edition, see EUSEBIUS OF CAESAREA, *The Auncient Ecclesiasticall Histories of the First Six Hundred Yeares after Christ*, transl. M. HANMER (London, 1577: STC 10572). We are grateful to Dr Angela Andreani for bringing this table to our notice.

[59] P. D'AVITY, *The Estates, Empires, & Principallities of the World*, transl. E. GRIMESTON (London, 1615: STC 988), 4B2v-4A3 [sic].

[60] See ROSENBERG and GRAFTON, *Cartographies of Time*, p. 70, who note the similarity of the format to the road atlas design.

son of Noah) until the "Promise", i.e. the Abrahamic covenant (Gen. 12). The third part, indicating the years after the Promise, no longer follows the mileage format, however: vertically ruled parallel columns form the rest of the table.[61]

Tables are added to the third edition of *Chronographia* (1596). The first mileage-type table outlines the patriarchs from Seth down until the Flood, and *anno mundi* dates run along the left side.[62] The table only has vertical rulings separating the columns. The second table has a similar layout but adds more running columns to the left. The *anno mundi* dates are now accompanied by separate ruled columns for Noah, Shem, and the Flood. Two further tables continue the pattern, although the fourth is ruled in a way that somewhat obscures the mileage-type layout.[63] All of these tables derive from Lorenz Codomann's work; the producer of the English adaptation has left out Codomann's extensive astronomical tables, and has brought together a simplified version of the chronological tables, which were dispersed in Codomann's Latin edition.[64]

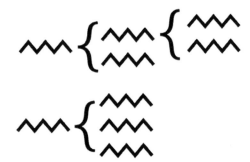

Fig. 8   Schematic illustration of a tree diagram.

The flexible use of mileage-type tables alongside other kinds of tables can be witnessed in other sixteenth- and seventeenth-century books. Extensive and complex tables are found in Thomas Allen's *A Chain of Scripture Chronology*. Most noteworthy are the large ruled tables which have been inserted as foldouts. These are accompanied by mileage-type tables and other visualisations, such as tree diagrams.[65]

---

[61] H. BROUGHTON, *A Concent of Scripture* (London, 1588/89: STC 3850), A1. For the dating of the work, see K. MACFARLANE, *Biblical Scholarship in an Age of Controversy: The Polemical World of Hugh Broughton (1549-1612)* (Oxford, 2021), p. 41.

[62] ANON., *Chronographia. A Description of Time, from the Beginning of the World, vnto the Yeare of Our Lord, 137* (London, 1596: STC 5472), G2.

[63] ANON., *Chronographia*, G3v-4.

[64] L. CODOMANN, *Quatuor libri chronologiae*, issued together with *Annales sacrae scripturae* (Wittenberg, 1581: USTC 611615), 2N3v-2O, 2P4v-2Q, 3F4. See also ROSENBERG and GRAFTON, *Cartographies of Time*, p. 70. They draw their example from the English *Chronographia*; however, they do not discuss its differences from Codomann's work.

[65] T. ALLEN, *A Chain of Scripture Chronology* (London, 1659: WING A1048).

Visual Chronologies in Early Modern English Historiography

The horizontal tree diagram has its origins in the scholastic culture of the Middle Ages.[66] Its function is to indicate hierarchical relationships between concepts. In printed books, braces are used to create the branches of the 'tree' (cf. Fig. 8). This type of visualisation is fairly common in our material, and like mileage-type tables, tree diagrams often illustrate the early biblical chronology of the patriarchs. Such content is found in Pie's *An Houreglasse*, Allen's *A Chain of Scripture Chronology*, and Arthur Hopton's *A Concordancy of Yeares*.[67] Other uses of tree diagrams occasionally occur, for instance in John Prideaux's Synopsis of Councels, added to the third edition of Mathias Prideaux's *An Easy and Compendious Introduction for Reading All Sorts of Histories*.[68] The use of braces in this work, however, is not directly related to chronological discussion.

To conclude, early modern English book producers had a variety of visualisation formats at hand to support their discussion of chronology. Technological aspects and aesthetic reasons may have played a part in choosing the types. In our material, ruled tables appear at the end of the sixteenth century: these tend to be extensive tables which occur at the end of the book, or make up the majority of the work. In the former case, we may perhaps think of chronological tables as index-like paratextual elements which allow the reader to navigate the prose discussion preceding them; such an approach is taken by Ralegh, as shown in the following section. Unruled tables in our materials are found in the seventeenth century; typically more limited in scope compared to ruled tables, they often function rather as complex lists instead of tables. Their use may reflect an aesthetic preference, but it may also be related to practical questions of print technology.

Communicating Visual Representations to the Reader

In this section, we discuss how early modern English authors (and translators) communicated the function of chronological visualisations to their audiences. The focus lies on primarily tabular devices that convey synchronised chronologies. We examine the phraseology and vocabulary authors used to highlight the benefits of the visual mode of chronological representation, as

---

[66] A. EVEN-EZRA, *Lines of Thought: Branching Diagrams and the Medieval Mind* (Chicago, IL, 2021), see especially pp. 7 and 24.
[67] A. HOPTON, *A Concordancy of Yeares* (London, 1612: STC 13778).
[68] M. PRIDEAUX, *An Easy and Compendious Introduction for Reading All Sorts of Histories* (Oxford, 1654: WING P3441).

well as how the comparative and synchronistic thinking required by the operation of the graphic device was linguistically expressed. We also pay attention to how such comments may have been influenced by authors' understanding of the level of expertise of their target audiences. Empirical studies of image captions in modern professional communication and science education show that such linguistic elements may support the reader's engagement with the visual device, for example by attracting their attention to the device and by guiding interpretation.[69]

Historical visualisations of chronology are often accompanied by supporting text in which the device is labelled and its operating principles are communicated to the reader. Authorial discussions of the benefits of the table form for chronology go back to the Eusebian-Hieronymian *Chronicle*. Its preface highlights the virtues of simplicity and brevity of the parallel-column layout in addition to chronological exactness and selectivity.[70] Similar *topoi* occur in sixteenth- and seventeenth-century chronological writing in English when the tabular form is discussed by authors. Some aspects of these accounts undoubtedly echo broader discourse traditions about the virtues of the tabular format. While we expect to discern such broader discursive trends in future publications, the present study focuses on works of chronology without tracing further parallels.

In our material, one of the most comprehensive statements about the benefits of tables in chronological writing occurs in the preface to "A Chronologicall Table" in Ralegh's *The History of the World*. The 26-page table is placed after a nearly 800-page prose narrative. According to the author, the function of tables in works of general history can be compared to an index that allows the reader to navigate the book by highlighting synchronous events scattered in different locations in the prose narrative.[71] Other benefits of the table include its capacity to "free the Booke, and likewise the Reader (if but of meane iudgement) from anie notorious Anachronisme".[72] Ralegh defends the length of his description "touching the vse or explication of these Tables" by pointing out

---

[69] J. SMITH, "A content analysis of figure captions in academic journals from four disciplines", *IEEE Transactions of Professional Communication* 63.4 (2020), pp. 341-360, at p. 342.

[70] CRAWFORD, *The Eusebian Canon Tables*, pp. 76-77; GRAFTON and WILLIAMS, *Christianity and the Transformation of the Book*, p. 140.

[71] RALEGH, *The History of the World*, 6T5. See also N. POPPER, *Walter Ralegh's History of the World and the Historical Culture of the Late Renaissance* (Chicago, IL, 2012), pp. 113-115. Cf. CRAWFORD, *The Eusebian Canon Tables*, pp. 21-55, who discusses Eusebian Canon Tables as paratextual tools for the reader's interaction with the gospels.

[72] RALEGH, *The History of the World*, 6T5.

that "it sufficeth if hereby all be made plaine enough to the vulgar"; those readers, however, who already are "conuersant in workes of this kinde" would not need all that support.[73]

By singling out "vulgar" readers and those "of meane judgement", and emphasising the need to render the content "plaine" for them, Ralegh's preface highlights the perceived importance of historical chronology also to the uneducated and non-Latinate. Similar views also occur elsewhere in our material, especially in the seventeenth century. Some authors specifically emphasise the suitability of the table format for readers of this kind. Roger Drake, for example, points out that "without the helpe of these parallel Tables", the "almost infinite Truths" of Scripture chronology would be practically inaccessible to "meaner capacities".[74] Arthur Hopton notes that he has "drawne new Tables and methods" for the benefit of "such, whose vnderstanding liues in a lower Region, amongst the mists and clouds of ignorance".[75]

Highlighting the use of chronological tables to facilitate unlearned readers' comprehension may be viewed in the broader context of comments made by early modern authors and book-producers regarding enhanced reader-friendliness.[76] Lori Anne Ferrell argues that this kind of rhetoric – encountered especially in religious and secular "how-to" books – was fostered by the culture of English Protestantism, which included "a dependence upon vernacular texts loaded with diagrams and instructions".[77] A case in point are works by the biblical scholar and controversialist Hugh Broughton, who experimented with visual forms "to make even the most learned and esoteric scholarship accessible to the literate reader".[78] Broughton's *A Concent of Scripture* (1588/1589) is furnished with ambitious chronological visualisations that are probably among the earliest of their kind in English (see the previous section). In his preface, the author explains how to navigate the chronological tables and their parallel

---

[73] RALEGH, *The History of the World*, 6T5v.

[74] R. DRAKE, *Sacred Chronologie* (London, 1648: WING D2131), B1.

[75] HOPTON, *A Concordancy*, A3v.

[76] See H. SALMI, "'I write not to expert practitioners, but to learners': Perceptions of reader-friendliness in early modern printed books", in: *The Dynamics of Text and Framing Phenomena: Historical Approaches to Paratext and Metadiscourse in English*, ed. M. PEIKOLA and B. BÖS (Amsterdam, 2020), pp. 187-207.

[77] L.A. FERRELL, "Page *techne*: Interpreting diagrams in Early Modern English 'how-to' books", in: *Printed Images in Early Modern Britain: Essays in Interpretation*, ed. M. HUNTER (Farnham, 2010), pp. 113-126, at p. 115.

[78] MACFARLANE, *Biblical Scholarship*, p. 21.

columns.[79] The reader is alerted to the importance of constructing information by means of horizontal reading across the columns:

> touchyng the Columne, vnderstande that you shalbe often to marke by the matter, that the sayinges depend not vpon the next aboue them, but vpon those that be on the other Columne oueragaynst them.[80]

Broughton's preface emphasises the comparative method to establish a harmonious biblical chronology; according to the author, "For euery partition of these tymes [i.e. different historical periods], auncient concent of *Hebrevves* and *Grekes* may be brought".[81] The noun 'concent' / 'consent' ("[a]greement, accord, harmony") features prominently already in the title of the work, and the form of visual presentation is clearly designed to serve the comparative approach that will arrive at such an agreement.[82]

Overall, historians and chronographers use a rich variety of lexical items and phrases when they refer to the synchronised visual mode of presenting their data. In addition to 'concent' / 'consent', nouns that convey a similar idea of harmonised datasets comprise 'concordancy' / 'concordance', 'correspondence', 'conference' and 'concurrence'. Learned latinate loanwords formed with variants of the prefix *com-* clearly seem to have been considered appropriate choices for such expressions.

According to the OED, the sense in which 'concordancy' is used in the title of Hopton's *A Concordancy of Yeares* (first edition 1612) corresponds to the primary sense of the closely related and more widely attested noun 'concordance': "the fact of agreeing or being concordant; agreement, harmony".[83] In this case, a chronological table devised by Hopton is essentially intended to bring the AD reckoning into agreement with the regnal years of the post-conquest English monarchs. The author's description of the device reveals that although the whole publication is presented as a "concordancy", this label specifically applies to the table: "The Description and vse of this New Table, called A Concordancy of Yeares".[84] A shorter chronological table modelled

---

[79] BROUGHTON, *A Concent*, π2.
[80] BROUGHTON, *A Concent*, π2v.
[81] BROUGHTON, *A Concent*, π2.
[82] OED online (henceforth OED), Oxford University Press, April 2023, OED3, s.v. *concent*, n., sense 2; see also OED2, s.v. *consent*, n., sense 2a. Although the OED presents 'concent' and 'consent' as two different lexemes, it also points out that their early uses are often difficult to distinguish from each other.
[83] OED2, s.v. *concordancy*, n., sense 2; *concordance*, n., sense 1.
[84] HOPTON, *A Concordancy*, P7.

after Hopton's device came to be appended to various kinds of seventeenth-century practical books. The title pages of some of these publications mention the presence of the device, which suggests that it was expected to add some value to the book. In the 1630s, for example, several editions of Frig Winter's almanac mention "a compendious concordance of yeares" as one of its additional items.[85]

Of the other nouns used to describe the chronological apparatus, 'correspondence' appears in the first edition of *Chronographia* (1590), in which Codomann's chronological research is rendered into English. In the preface, the compiler / translator mentions that "*The tables containing a correspondence of yeares [...] I haue for breuitie sake omitted*".[86] While 'correspondence' may simply denote a relationship, i.e. "[t]he action or fact of corresponding", it may also more evaluatively suggest "congruity, harmony, [and] agreement" between the items (as in 'concent' / 'consent' and 'concordancy' / 'concordance').[87]

The nouns 'conference' and 'concurrence' appear together in the preface to the 1596 edition of *Chronographia*: "I haue now translated certaine tables of Codomannu<s> wherein thou mayest at once see a conference and concurrence of times in the storie of the Patriarkes, Iudges, and Kings".[88] In this context, 'conference' suggests both the actions of bringing together and comparison; on the basis of the OED, this mid-sixteenth-century loanword was first used in philological contexts of textual collation.[89] The meaning of 'concurrence' attested here is best viewed as an example of the sense "[o]ccurrence together in time", for which the first attestation provided by the OED is from 1605.[90] On the whole, the compiler / translator's prefatory comment using both 'conference' and 'concurrence' expresses the idea that the table brings together multiple "times" (chronologies) and allows their synchronic observation.

In addition to nouns, the synchronic operation of the chronological apparatus may be conveyed through adjectives, adverbs, and verbs. Drake characterises the tables of his *Sacred Chronologie* as "parallel".[91] As an adjective, 'paral-

---

[85] F. WINTER, *Winter, an Almanack for the Yeare of Our Lord 1634* (Cambridge, 1634: STC 530.3), A1. In addition to almanacs, the chronological concordance is mentioned as an additional item for example on the title pages of the anonymous *The Compleat Clark* (London, 1655: WING C5633) and J. HERNE, *The Law of Conveyances* (London, 1656: WING H1570).
[86] ANON., *Chronographia*, A2v.
[87] OED2, s.v. *correspondence*, n., sense 1.
[88] ANON., *Chronographia*, A2v-3.
[89] OED2, s.v. *conference*, n., senses 1 and 3; the first recorded attestation in the OED for sense 1 is from 1610.
[90] OED2, s.v. *concurrence*, n., sense 2a; ANON., *Chronographia*, G2v.
[91] DRAKE, *Sacred Chronologie*, B1.

lel' was first used in English in the mid-sixteenth century, in contexts of cosmography and geometry, for elements "lying or extending alongside each other and always at the same distance apart".[92] In addition to referring to the layout of the data on the page in this primary sense, Drake's usage possibly anticipates the slightly later meaning of 'parallel' to denote similarities or analogies between datasets beyond their spatial alignment.[93] Drake also uses the corresponding adverb when he describes chronological data in columns "which run parallel with" each other.[94] The first citation recorded by the OED for 'parallel' as an adverb (in the phrase 'to run parallel') is from 1646, so Drake (1648) appears to have belonged to its early adopters.[95] Based on a full-text search in EEBO, 'parallel' (as an adjective, adverb or noun) occurs 46 times in Drake's 150-page book, which suggests major topical relevance of the concept for his work.

In our material, verbs that highlight the synchronisation of tabular datasets are attested already well before the proliferation of vernacular chronologies in the seventeenth century. The title page of Rastell's 1558 chronological table announces the device to be "shewynge how the yeres of our Lord god and the yeares of the Kynges of Englande *concurre* and *agree* togyther."[96] The OED dates the first attestation of 'concur' in the chronological sense "[t]o fall, happen, or occur together; to coincide" to 1596, so it is possible that Rastell's usage of the verb here seeks to convey the idea of the datasets running alongside each other visually rather than their strict coincidence.[97] In any case, the second element of the binomial ('agree') clearly emphasises the synchronisation of the datasets.

The caption of the chronological table in Pie's *An Houreglasse* illustrates the use of the verb 'couple' to express the presentation of synchronised data: "A Table coupling the yeares of the Kings *of* Iuda *with the Kinges of* Israel, *and them both* with the yeares of the world".[98] The same caption also makes use of 'compare' in demonstrating how data are treated in the table: "and also some middle yeares compared together".[99]

---

[92] OED3, s.v. *parallel*, n., adj., adv.; see adj., sense 1a.
[93] OED3, s.v. *parallel*, n., adj. and adv.; see adj., sense 2a, "Having a similar or analogous objective, tendency, development, method, etc.; having a similar function, role, or structure; corresponding, equivalent, or equal (*to*)".
[94] DRAKE, *Sacred Chronologie*, B1v.
[95] OED3, s.v. *parallel*, n., adj. and adv., see adv., sense 1.
[96] RASTELL, *A Table*, A1; our emphasis.
[97] OED2, s.v. *concur*, v., sense 2d.
[98] PIE, *An Houreglasse*, P1.
[99] PIE, *An Houreglasse*, P1; OED2, s.v. *compare*, v.1, sense 2a.

Visual Chronologies in Early Modern English Historiography 223

Pie's caption ends by stating that the overall *modus operandi* of the table is to communicate to the visual sense: "as here is represented to the eye".[100] In another location, the author points out that certain computations concerning biblical time periods "are confirmed to the eie in the chronological table".[101] In this case, the table is thus also understood to have an epistemic function in corroborating knowledge visually.[102] There are also other instances in which chronological tables are presented as visual devices for knowledge validation. In Swan's *Calamus mensurans*, the author first presents prose arguments concerning the regnal years of certain kings, but then concedes that a table establishes the information more effectively: "for a more cleare demonstration, see the Table following".[103]

As visual devices, tables are said to allow readers to perceive chronological information instantaneously and comprehensively.[104] This notion is expressed already in the title page of Rastell's mid-sixteenth-century table.[105] It is also prominently present in Broughton's *A Concent of Scripture*. A medallion at the top centre of the title-page border invites the reader to "Come and see": to enter into the book and perceive the harmony of scriptural chronology.[106] Several seventeenth-century authors convey the idea more explicitly by using expressions that involve the noun 'cast' in the sense "[a] throwing or turning of the eye in any direction; a glance, a look, expression".[107] Such phrases include 'in the cast of an eye' (e.g. "by virtue of these Tables you may in the cast of an eye know [...]"[108]) and 'upon the cast of the eye' ("there is another Generall *Table*, to show presently upon the cast of the eye [...]"[109]). The corresponding verb 'cast' is also used to the same effect: "an *Historical Chronology*; in which, if

---

[100] PIE, *An Houreglasse*, P1. See OED3, s.v. *represent*, v.1, sense category II, especially sense 8a.

[101] PIE, *An Houreglasse*, E3v.

[102] See OED2, s.v. *confirm*, v., sense 7a: "To corroborate, or add support to (a statement, etc.); to make certain, verify, put beyond doubt".

[103] SWAN, *Calamus mensurans*, Q4. See OED3, s.v. *demonstration*, n., sense 2: "A sign or indication that something is true; a thing or circumstance which establishes the truth of a claim or theory; (a piece of) evidence or proof".

[104] See also L. DASTON, "Super-vision: Weather watching and table reading in the early modern Royal Society and Académie Royale des Sciences", *Huntington Library Quarterly* 78 (2015), pp. 187-215.

[105] RASTELL, *A Table*, A1.

[106] BROUGHTON, *A Concent*, engraved title page.

[107] See OED2, s.v. *cast*, n., sense 6.

[108] DRAKE, *Sacred Chronologie*, B4.

[109] ALLEN, *A Chain*, E4.

the *Reader* cast an Eye, he will without trouble discern [...]".[110] Adverbs such as 'quickly', 'readily', 'at once', 'presently', and 'suddenly' (immediately) emphasise how tables allow instantaneous perception of information.[111]

Conclusion

Our survey of early modern English works addressing chronology gives an overview of the different types of visualisations used to convey chronological information, and of their linguistic presentation. A few caveats are needed. We have here focused on books in English, although some of them are translations from other languages. Systematic comparison between original publications and the translated English editions was not possible within the scope of the research, but notes have been made where the origin of the devices could be traced to an earlier publication.

Our study shows that visual elements were frequent in early modern histories and chronologies: half of the 49 titles examined contained one or more types of visualisations. In the first part of the study, we grouped the different types of visualisations based on their formal characteristics. These types include marginal annotations, lists, tables (ruled and unruled), and tree diagrams. Further subtypes can be identified, such as 'mileage-type' tables or 'account-type' lists. It should be noted that we excluded purely genealogical information; additional types could be found where material of that kind could be considered. Most visualisation types appear to feature parallel dating systems, such as *anno mundi* and / or years before and after Christ alongside possible relative datings.

The second part of our study focused on the linguistic expressions book producers use to refer to these visualisations. It is clear that book producers were aware of their audiences' differing levels of experience in using graphic devices. This trend appears to be connected to a wider early modern interest in catering for uneducated or non-Latinate readers. The references to visualisations also make clear the attempts at synchronising or 'harmonising' chronological data, which was increasingly presented in various tabular forms. We hope

---

[110] N. FONTAINE, *The History of the Old and New Testament* (London, 1691: WING F1406A), π3v.

[111] 'quickly' and 'readily': RASTELL, *A Table*, A1; 'at once': BROUGHTON, *A Concent*, A3; 'presently': ALLEN, *A Chain*, E4; 'suddenly': ALLEN, *A Chain*, in table caption on foldout after leaf Hh4.

that our study will open up new avenues for tracing concurrent developments in a wider European context and in genres other than chronology or history, and thus help shed further light on early modern graphic practices.

Visual Representation of Information in Medical Texts, 1500-1700[*]

MARI-LIISA VARILA, CARLA SUHR, and JUKKA TYRKKÖ

Introduction

This chapter examines variation in the use of graphic devices (such as tables and diagrams) across printed medical books addressing different topics and written for different audiences ranging from physicians, apothecaries and surgeons to laypeople. We first set out to determine what kinds of graphic devices were used in early modern English printed medical books.[1] We then compare the use of graphic devices between different categor-

---

[*] Research for this chapter has been supported by the Research Council of Finland, grant number 340005.

[1] For graphic devices in medical texts, see e.g. I. PANTIN, "Analogy and difference: A comparative study of medical and astronomical images in books, 1470-1550", in: *Observing the World through Images: Diagrams and Figures in the Early-Modern Arts and Sciences*, ed. N. JARDINE and I. FAY (Leiden, 2013), pp. 9-44; C. PENNUTO, "From text to diagram: Giambattista Da Monte and the practice of medicine", in: *Inscribing Knowledge in the Medieval Book: The Power of Paratexts*, ed. R. BROWN-GRANT, P. CARMASSI, G. DROSSBACH, A.D. HEDEMAN, V. TURNER, and I. VENTURA (Berlin, 2020), pp. 95-116.

....

Graphic Practices and Literacies in the History of English, ed. Matti PEIKOLA, Jukka TYRKKÖ, and Mari-Liisa VARILA, *Utrecht Studies in Medieval Literacy*, 57 (Turnhout: Brepols, 2025), pp. 227-257.

BREPOLS PUBLISHERS   DOI 10.1484/M.USML-EB.5.143828

ies of medical texts ranging from specialised treatises to popular health guides to see how the text topic influenced the information design of the books.

Our selection of material is based on the linguistic corpus Early Modern English Medical Texts (EMEMT), which contains a representative set of medical texts from 1500 to 1700. Our analysis focuses on five different categories of medical writing as defined in the EMEMT corpus:

1) General treatises or textbooks;
2) Treatises on specific topics;
3) Recipe collections and *materia medica*;
4) Regimens and health guides; and
5) Surgical and anatomical treatises.

We examine what kinds of graphic devices were used in medical texts and for what purposes, and whether differences can be observed in the use of graphic devices across the five categories of medical writing. Our results show how book producers designed medical texts and shed light on the role of graphic devices in the transmission and circulation of medical knowledge.

Graphic Devices in Medical Texts

Already Plato and Aristotle mention tables and diagrams in some of their works, but graphic elements borrowed from logic and mathematics were adopted to visualise and explain Galenic and Aristotelian medical theories only from the fourteenth century onwards.[2] Tables, squares of opposition, wheels, and various kinds of tree diagrams were used to divide, define and classify concepts and to represent relationships between concepts.[3] At their simplest, diagrams could use braces to divide discursively described concepts into their several parts – at times forming layered and complex diagrams – but they could also be turned into elaborate images produced by artists. According to Concetta Pennuto, diagrams were useful pedagogical tools in medical textbooks for three reasons: they recapitulated and explained medical information, they synthesised

---

[2] I. MACLEAN, "Diagrams in the defence of Galen: Medical uses of tables, squares, dichotomies, wheels, and latitudes, 1480-1574", in: *Transmitting Knowledge: Words, Images, and Instruments in Early Modern Europe*, ed. S. KUSUKAWA and I. MACLEAN (Oxford, 2006), pp. 136-164, at pp. 135-137.

[3] J.E. MURDOCH, *Album of Science: Antiquity and the Middle Ages* (New York, 1984); MACLEAN, "Diagrams in the defence of Galen", p. 138.

information that could then be memorised, and they were a way to recall knowledge to memory. Furthermore, theoretical information organised into diagrams could be connected to medical practice: after linking the signs of a disease with the symptoms of a patient, the doctor could prognosticate the progress of the disease and prescribe suitable therapies.[4] In addition to pedagogical purposes, Ian Maclean speculates that diagrams were also used during the Renaissance to "dignify medical theory by association with natural philosophy".[5] As noted by Maclean, such diagrams assumed previous knowledge in natural philosophy and medicine, which places their readership firmly among university students and university-trained physicians.[6] Some authors claimed that the clarity and brevity of diagrams were helpful for the "less intelligent" reader, but they were likely not referring to uneducated readers with this claim.[7]

Medical images also have a long, and, as Peter Murray Jones has shown, complicated history.[8] In the Middle Ages, medical images were not always connected to a text, and they could become detached from a text to circulate independently and even end up attached to a different text.[9] During the Renaissance, anatomical images circulated perhaps mainly as separate sheets rather than as part of a book.[10] In these cases, there is clearly a disconnect between text and image, though there are also examples where the text instructing the interpretation of the image has become part of the image itself.[11] Medical images often carried religious and moral messages as well as (or rather than) scientific information.[12] Perhaps most importantly, the ancient authorities' emphasis on first-hand visual observation in anatomy meant that images were not considered trustworthy witnesses to describe part of the body or medicinal plants.[13] Rather, images often functioned as aids to memory, as was the case

[4] PENNUTO, "From text to diagram", pp. 106, 114.
[5] MACLEAN, "Diagrams in the defence of Galen", p. 137.
[6] MACLEAN, "Diagrams in the defence of Galen", p. 162.
[7] Cf. I. MACLEAN, *Logic, Signs and Nature in the Renaissance* (Cambridge, 2002), p. 62.
[8] P.M. JONES, "Image, word, and medicine in the Middle Ages", in: *Visualizing Medieval Medicine and Natural History, 1200-1550*, ed. J.A. GIVENS, K.M. REEDS, and A. TOUWAIDE (Aldershot, 2006), pp. 1-24.
[9] JONES, "Image, word, and medicine in the Middle Ages", p. 3; V. NUTTON, "Representation and memory in Renaissance anatomical illustration", in: *Immagini per conoscere: Dal Rinascimento alla Rivoluzione scientifica*, ed. F. MEROI and C. POGLIANO (Firenze, 2001), pp. 61-80, at pp. 78-79.
[10] PANTIN, "Analogy and difference", p. 20.
[11] JONES, "Image, word, and medicine in the Middle Ages", pp. 4-5.
[12] JONES, "Image, word, and medicine in the Middle Ages", p. 5; PANTIN, "Analogy and difference", p. 11.
[13] PANTIN, "Analogy and difference", p. 15.

with, for example, wound-men, zodiac men and phlebotomy men; this meant that they could be replaced with diagrams that served the same function.[14] Images also did not need to be realistic when their function was simply to remind the reader of information they already knew.[15] In our study, we consider zodiac men and phlebotomy men to be diagrams rather than images, as they indicate a relationship between certain body parts or veins and the zodiac signs (cf. our definitions of images and diagrams in the Methodology section below).

During the Renaissance, images were mostly found in surgeries, anatomies and herbals, but they were not in widespread use. Vivian Nutton has noted that anatomical description was only one aspect of anatomical teaching; explanations of the body's structure and its relationship to medicine did not need visual aids. Furthermore, the primary method of instruction was the commented lecture, which could be combined with a dissection that illustrated the set readings and thereby rendered images unnecessary.[16]

The use of images in the sixteenth century was often criticised and needed to be defended.[17] Sachiko Kusukawa argues that both Leonhard Fuchs and Andreas Vesalius, whose images of plants and human anatomy were copied extensively, aimed for idealised images of the objects they described in the text and intended the images to be used together with the text and first-hand observation rather than replacing dissections or viewing of original plants.[18] Other sixteenth-century authors who included images with their texts also stressed the pedagogical purpose of the images, and increasingly included explanatory captions or commentaries that connect the text with the images.[19] Especially illustrations of female reproductive organs could be associated with pornography, and at least one English author, Helkiah Crook, turned that fact into a marketing tool by apologising in his preface to his "proper" readers for the didactic necessity of providing such images while at the same time admonishing his "improper" readers who would use the images for non-medical purposes, thereby advising readers of the presence of such images in his book.[20]

---

[14] PANTIN, "Analogy and difference", p. 20.

[15] NUTTON, "Representation and memory in Renaissance anatomical illustration", p. 70.

[16] NUTTON, "Representation and memory in Renaissance anatomical illustration", pp. 67, 77-78.

[17] PANTIN, "Analogy and difference", pp. 15-19.

[18] S. KUSUKAWA, "The uses of pictures in the formation of learned knowledge: The cases of Leonhard Fuchs and Andreas Vesalius", in: *Transmitting Knowledge: Words, Images, and Instruments in Early Modern Europe*, ed. S. KUSUKAWA and I. MACLEAN (Oxford, 2006), pp. 75-96.

[19] PANTIN, "Analogy and difference", pp. 32-38.

[20] H. NEWMAN, "'[P]rophane fiddlers': Medical paratexts and indecent readers in early

Some irregular practitioners used images to market their medical skills in handbills passed out on the street.[21] It was only in Germany that larger numbers of medical books with images were produced, and they were addressed to barbers and surgeons and a wider lay readership rather than to learned physicians.[22] This was a major break from authors such as Vesalius and Fuchs, whose illustrated medical books required a university education and knowledge of Latin.[23]

The preceding discussion of the history and functions of various graphic elements in medical books is based mainly on studies of continental medical textbooks written in Latin, whereas our study investigates a broader range of vernacular medical texts written in England. Nonetheless, the continental Latin models were undoubtedly familiar to learned English authors either directly or through translations, and they could be appropriated for texts intended for more general audiences as well. England has been shown to be a spearhead in the vernacularisation of medical knowledge starting in the late medieval period.[24] In the Early Modern period, medical texts in English were written for a wide range of audiences from lay people to learned physicians.[25] Previous linguistic research on paratextual material in medical books has shed light on the readers and users of these books, but graphic devices, especially those other than images, are seldom considered in linguistic analyses.[26] Yet by examining

---

modern England", in: *Medical Paratexts from Medieval to Modern: Dissecting the Page*, ed. H.C. TWEED and D. G. SCOTT (Cham, 2018), pp. 15-41.

[21] R. MULLINI, "Graphic surgical practice in the handbills of seventeenth-century London irregulars", in: *Medical Paratexts from Medieval to Modern: Dissecting the Page*, ed. H.C. TWEED and D.G. SCOTT (Cham, 2018), pp. 57-73.

[22] PANTIN, "Analogy and difference", p. 26.

[23] S. KUSUKAWA, "The uses of pictures in the formation of learned knowledge", pp. 76-77.

[24] See e.g. I. TAAVITSAINEN and P. PAHTA, "Vernacularisation of medical writing in English: A corpus-based study of scholasticism", *Early Science and Medicine* 3.2 (1998), pp. 157-183; *Medical and Scientific Writing in Late Medieval English*, ed. P. PAHTA and I. TAAVITSAINEN (Cambridge, 2004).

[25] *Early Modern English Medical Texts: Corpus Description and Studies*, ed. I. TAAVITSAINEN and P. PAHTA (Amsterdam, 2010); *Medical Writing in Early Modern English*, ed. I. TAAVITSAINEN and P. PAHTA (Cambridge, 2011).

[26] J. TYRKKÖ, "'Halles Lanfranke' and its most excellent and learned expositive table", in: *Words in Dictionaries and History: Essays in Honour of R. W. McConchie*, ed. O. TIMOFEEVA and T. SÄILY (Amsterdam, 2011), pp. 17-39; M. RATIA and C. SUHR, "Verbal and visual communication in title pages of early modern English specialised medical texts", in: *Verbal and Visual Communication in Early English Texts*, ed. M. PEIKOLA, A. MÄKILÄHDE, H. SALMI, M.-L. VARILA, and J. SKAFFARI (Turnhout, 2017), pp. 67-93; M.V. DOMÍNGUEZ-RODRÍGUEZ and A. RODRÍGUES-ÁLVAREZ, "'All which I offer with my own experience': An approach to persuasive advertising strategies in the prefatory matter of 17th-century English midwifery treatises", in: *The*

graphic devices we can learn more about prospective readers' graphic literacies: which audiences were expected to need, 'read', and understand the various different devices? Our interest in the current chapter is to investigate systematically how widespread the use of graphic devices such as tables, diagrams and images is in this period, and whether their use has been extended to audiences beyond the learned physicians and texts outside surgical and anatomical treatises (our category 5) and herbals (part of our category 3, recipe collections and *materia medica*).

Materials

The primary data for the study come from facsimile images derived from Early English Books Online (EEBO), a well-known resource that provides access to over 125,000 volumes of early printed material in English.[27] The data set of the present study replicates the contents and, for the most part, the structure of Early Modern English Medical Texts (EMEMT), a linguistic corpus released in 2010.[28] The corpus aims to accurately represent different kinds of printed medical writing of the period, and it includes a wealth of contextual information about the texts and their authors, which makes it a suitable data set for this study. However, unlike EMEMT, which was limited to keyed-in extracts of 10,000 words per book, the present data set uses facsimiles and includes the books *in toto*. The subcorpus of EMEMT containing medical articles published in the journal *Philosophical Transactions of the Royal Society* was excluded from the present study, as our focus is on publications in book format. It should be noted that some potentially relevant material is nevertheless missing from our data set. Importantly, astro-medical material such as calendars was not

---

Dynamics of Text and Framing Phenomena: Historical Approaches to Paratext and Metadiscourse in English, ed. M. PEIKOLA and B. BÖS (Amsterdam, 2020), pp. 163-185; E. LONATI, "Paratextual features in 18th-century medical writing: Framing contents and expanding the text", in: *The Dynamics of Text and Framing Phenomena: Historical Approaches to Paratext and Metadiscourse in English*, ed. M. PEIKOLA and B. BÖS (Amsterdam, 2020), pp. 233-266. However, see E. ROWLEY-JOLIVET, "The emergence of text-graphics conventions in a medical research journal: *The Lancet* 1823-2015", *ASp [Online]* 73 (2018), pp. 5-24, and contributions in H.C. TWEED and D.G. SCOTT ed., *Medical Paratexts from Medieval to Modern: Dissecting the Page* (Cham, 2018).

[27] *Early English Books Online*, <https://www.proquest.com/eebo>.

[28] *Early Modern English Medical Texts*, compiled by I. TAAVITSAINEN, P. PAHTA, T. HILTUNEN, M. MÄKINEN, V. MARTTILA, M. RATIA, C. SUHR, and J. TYRKKÖ (Amsterdam, 2010), CD-ROM.

included in the EMEMT corpus because such books contain very little text and mostly consist of tables. Yet calendars were one of the most sold kinds of texts in the early modern period, and would definitely merit more research on the graphic practices and literacies involved in their production and use. Despite its limitations, the EMEMT selection of texts offers a balanced starting point for examining medical writing. Altogether, the primary data contains 181 medical books. Importantly for the present study, nearly all of the books were printed by different printing houses, which helps guard against possible skewing that could result from the practices or specialisms of individual printers.

The EMEMT corpus is divided into several *categories*, or sub-corpora, which are used to represent contemporaneously meaningful types of medical writing during the Early Modern period.[29] The corpus categories are based on the text-external criterion of topic on the premise that medical topics remain much the same even when writing styles change. Different genres cut across category boundaries; recipes, for example, are common in all categories. The corpus categories make it easy to consider the influence of topic on the use of graphic devices, but contextual information such as target audience has to be collected separately from the corpus catalogue. Our analysis focuses on five different categories of medical writing as defined in the EMEMT corpus:

1) General treatises and textbooks;
2) Treatises on specific topics (divided into five sub-categories: specific substances, specific methods, specific illnesses, midwifery and children's diseases, and the plague);
3) Recipe collections and *materia medica*;
4) Regimens and health guides; and
5) Surgical and anatomical treatises.

In the few cases when the book as a whole represents a category different from the short corpus extract, the book was shifted to its primary category for the purposes of this study.

---

[29] See P. PAHTA and I. TAAVITSAINEN, "Introducing Early Modern English medical texts", in: *Early Modern English Medical Texts: Corpus Description and Studies*, ed. I. TAAVITSAINEN and P. PAHTA (Amsterdam, 2010), pp. 1-8; J. TYRKKÖ and I. TAAVITSAINEN, "The field of medical writing with fuzzy edges", in: *Early Modern English Medical Texts: Corpus Description and Studies*, ed. I. TAAVITSAINEN and P. PAHTA (Amsterdam, 2010), pp. 57-62. The compilation principles, detailed descriptions of corpus categories, and editorial conventions of EMEMT are discussed in detail in individual chapters in *Early Modern English Medical Texts: Corpus Description and Studies*, ed. I. TAAVITSAINEN and P. PAHTA (Amsterdam, 2010). The volume also contains a list of all editions appearing in the corpus.

As the corpus categories represent the contemporary textual reality, they are not equal in size, nor is the distribution of texts in each category always spread evenly across time. Categories 3 and 5 (Recipe collections and *materia medica*; Surgical and anatomical treatises) have the most texts, and the texts are often very long. Regimens and health guides (category 4) and books focusing on specific topics (category 2) are usually fairly short, whereas texts in category 1 (General textbooks and treatises) are a mix of long and short texts. Especially category 2 is characterised by gaps in the timeline that represent a dip in the number of publications (cf. Fig. 1 in our Analysis and Discussion section below).

The use of EEBO images as the basis of paratextual and book historical studies is naturally not without challenges. The commonplace understanding among scholars is that remediated facsimile images can never entirely replace the original artefact, and depending on the research question, issues such as the quality and consistency of photography,[30] the condition of the specific artefact that was used to represent the book, the use of coloured inks, and manuscript annotations on the page may all affect the accuracy at which a facsimile represents the original.[31] Consequently, it is advisable for researchers relying on facsimile data to have prior hands-on experience with authentic early printed books.[32] In the specific case of the present study, our view is that EEBO facsimiles do serve adequately as primary data. Since the study focuses on the frequency, distribution and characteristics of printed illustrations and graphic devices, it is sufficient for our purposes that the illustrations and graphic devices are almost always easy to identify from the facsimile images.

---

[30] It is worth noting that the EEBO images were largely digitised from microfilms; see S. MARTIN, "EEBO, microfilm, and Umberto Eco: Historical lessons and future directions for building electronic collections", *Microform & Imaging Review* 36.4 (2007), pp. 159-164. The original photographing of early modern books by Eugene Power began in 1938, and the quality of photography, though of a high quality for the time, naturally falls short of modern high definition digital imagery. Further degradation and loss of detail occurs when the microfilms were digitised in the 1990s.

[31] See D. KICHUK, "Metamorphosis: Remediation in Early English Books Online (EEBO)", *Literary and Linguistic Computing* 22.3 (2007), pp. 291-303; S. WERNER, "Where material book culture meets digital humanities", *Journal of Digital Humanities* 1.3 (2012), available online at <http://journalofdigitalhumanities.org/1-3/where-material-book-culture-meets-digital-humanities-by-sarah-werner/>.

[32] Cf. A. PRATT, "Talking about early digital facsimiles with Sarah Werner", *Ransom Center Magazine*, interview published January 31, 2018. Available online at <https://sites.utexas.edu/ransomcentermagazine/2018/01/31/talking-about-early-digital-facsimiles-with-sarah-werner/>.

Methods

In the first stage of the analysis, we examined the EEBO facsimile images of books in the EMEMT corpus, excluding the *Philosophical Transactions of the Royal Society* articles, as noted above. We recorded all instances of graphic devices in the books using a threefold typology, dividing the graphic devices into general images, diagrams, and tables. This typology is based on an early version of the classification model developed by the Early Modern Graphic Literacies (EModGraL) project at the University of Turku.[33]

Briefly put, the categories of graphic devices in the EModGraL typology can be described as follows:

1) The category of *general images* (G) contains representational, pictorial, or symbolic illustrations. It also has one subcategory, Gt, for images containing text. In the present study, we include in Gt also images with a caption or caption-like element appearing outside the image proper but in close proximity to it.
2) *Diagrams* (D) represent objects, relationships, or processes in a schematic manner, and they may also contain alphanumeric information. There are three subcategories under diagrams used for special cases, the first two of which are relevant for the present study: Da (arithmetic notation), Db (braces), and Dn (musical notation, including staves and tabulatures).
3) *Tables* (T) organise information in rows and columns, often with labels. This category is divided into four subcategories. The first subcategory is for calendars (Tc), which we consider a special type of table. The other three are for different sizes of tables, based on the number of cells: small (Ts, ≤ 25 cells), medium (Tm, 26 to 100 cells), and large (Tl, >100 cells).

The EModGraL typology also contains a category for unclear or hybrid cases (U) that are relevant to the analysis but do not easily fall into any of the three main categories. In the present study, we were able to place all devices in the three main categories and their subcategories, although there were some cases that required negotiation between the authors.

In our study we disregarded layout features frequently found in recipes (found in all corpus categories), in which the ingredients and the amounts needed of each ingredient could be laid out in ways that resemble the columns

---

[33] The present study is part of the Early Modern Graphic Literacies project. The project methodology and classification are presented in S. RUOKKEINEN, A. LIIRA, M.-L. VARILA, O. NORBLAD, and M. PEIKOLA, "Developing a classification model for graphic devices in early printed books", *Studia Neophilologica* 96.1 (2024), pp. 69-93.

of a table. Although these layouts function to organise information and would merit further investigation, they did not fulfil our criteria for tables. We did, however, record braces that were often used in this semi-tabular layout to indicate that the same amount was needed of several different ingredients.

In keeping with the EModGraL methodology, we also excluded from our analysis primarily paratextual elements (e.g. title pages, printers' devices, tables of contents) and decorative elements (e.g. borders and vignettes). This was done in order to focus on graphic devices that are placed alongside the main text to illustrate and / or complement it. However, we recognise that the boundary between textual and paratextual elements is fuzzy, and our decisions regarding some individual ambiguous cases are therefore necessarily subjective.

After the initial mapping of graphic devices in our material, we proceeded to conduct a quantitative survey. The data set contained some books that were clearly outliers in terms of the high number of graphic devices found in them. To mitigate the influence of such rare cases on our overall survey, instead of using the actual numbers of devices per book we treated each type of graphic device as a separate ordinal categorical variable with three levels that correspond to the number of devices in the books:[34]

0 = no graphic devices
1 = up to five graphic devices
2 = more than five graphic devices.

In an Excel spreadsheet, we filled in the metadata on each book in our data set, including their EMEMT category or sub-corpus. We then added the values for the number of graphic devices (0, 1, 2) in each book, divided into the categories and subcategories of the EModGraL classification model. This resulted in an overview of the distribution of graphic devices in the data set. Although the main focus of this study is on the uses of different types of graphic devices in medical writing, the systematic classification that was carried out also allows for some general observations of diachronic trends and differences across categories. However, the small size of the data set (181 texts) is not conducive to full-blown statistical analysis.[35]

---

[34] The cutoff point of five occurrences was essentially heuristic in nature.

[35] Categorical variables allow for classifying data into categories. Ordinal categorical variables are used when categories can be ranked according to an inherent order, for example lowest to highest or smallest to largest. To study the factors that might predict the use of graphic devices, we fit a series of ordinal logistic regression models, one for each type of graphic device

Visual Representation of Information in Medical Texts, 1500-1700 237

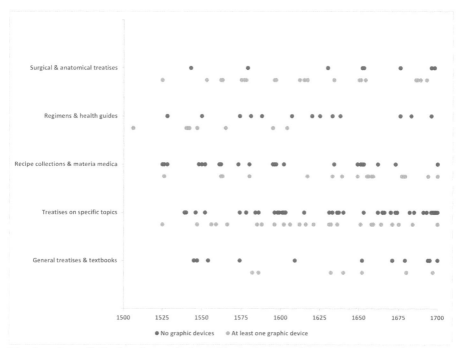

Fig. 1   Overall diachronic trend of graphic devices; markers represent texts in EMEMT.

On the basis of the quantitative overview we then analysed the data qualitatively, focusing on those EMEMT categories that show a tendency for utilising graphic devices. We investigated what kinds of graphic devices appear in each EMEMT category, how they are used, and how they are referred to in the text. In the following section, we first present the results of the quantitative survey before discussing the use of devices category by category.

Analysis and Discussion

The overall picture of the use of graphic devices in Early Modern medical texts suggests that they were a relatively common feature in our data set, with

as the dependent variable, and year, EMEMT category (with subcategories collapsed into one category of "special treatises"), and translation status (whether the text was a translation into English or not) as the independent variables. The relative scarcity and distribution of the graphic devices, together with the small size of the EMEMT corpus, resulted in very limited statistically significant results.

one or more devices occurring in 79 out of 181 texts (44%). A somewhat surprising finding was that there was rather little overall change over the two centuries (Fig. 1).

The categories and subcategories of medical writing differ from each other to some extent in their use of graphic devices (see Table 1). Overall, 79 out of 181 texts (44%) contain graphic devices. The category with the highest ratio of texts with graphic devices (21/30, 70%) contains surgical and anatomical treatises, which have previously been identified as most commonly containing images. In addition, the subcategory of specific methods (2b) has a ratio of 11/19 (58%) texts with graphic devices. In contrast, only 6/19 (32%) of general treatises and textbooks have graphic devices. The category of plague texts (2e) only contains one text with graphic devices, and those devices are actually images of coats of arms, not medical illustrations.

Table 1 The numbers and ratios of texts with graphic devices in each text category.

EMEMT category	Texts in category (n)	Texts with devices (n)	Texts with devices (%)
1 General treatises & textbooks	19	6	32
2a Specific illnesses	16	5	31
2b Specific methods	19	11	58
2c Specific substances	15	4	27
2d Midwifery & children's diseases	10	5	50
2e Plague	9	1	11
3 Recipe collections & *materia medica*	41	18	44
4 Regimens and health guides	22	8	36
5 Surgical & anatomical treatises	30	21	70
Total	**181**	**79**	**44**

Table 2 The numbers of texts with different types of graphic devices in each text category. D = Diagram, Da = Diagram (arithmetic), Db = Diagram (brace), Tc = Table (calendar), Ts = Table (small), Tm = Table (medium), Tl = Table (large), G = general image, Gt = General image with text.

EMEMT category	Texts (n)	D	Da	Db	Tc	Ts	Tm	Tl	G	Gt
1 General treatises & textbooks	19	2	0	4	0	1	0	1	1	0
2a Specific illnesses	16	0	0	5	0	0	0	0	0	0
2b Specific methods	19	2	3	5	0	3	1	4	8	2
2c Specific substances	15	0	0	4	0	0	0	0	0	0
2d Midwifery & children's diseases	10	1	0	1	0	0	0	1	4	3
2e Plague	9	0	0	0	0	0	0	0	0	1
3 Recipe collections & *materia medica*	41	5	2	12	0	1	4	1	2	6
4 Regimens and health guides	22	2	0	1	1	0	0	1	4	0
5 Surgical & anatomical treatises	30	8	0	10	0	2	2	2	11	7
Total	**181**	**20**	**5**	**42**	**1**	**7**	**7**	**10**	**30**	**19**

The observed differences could perhaps be interpreted in part as reflecting a contrast between the often abstract natural philosophy, which the university-trained physicians and student physicians read in general treatises and textbooks, and the more hands-on texts aimed for the medical practitioners trained through apprenticeship. Some of the more theoretical texts contain fewer graphic devices than some of the more practice-oriented texts, in which images could help the readers understand and practically identify features of human anatomy, surgical instruments, medicinal herbs, etc. The information found in regimens and health guides, which also do not make much use of graphic devices, was often based on classical medical theories (such as humoral theory and the six non-naturals), even if that kind of specialised medical knowledge was not expected of the middling and more elite readers that mainly made up the readership of these advice books for maintaining health.[36] In our data, using diagrams in theoretically oriented texts to "dignify medical theory", as suggested by Maclean, seems to be less salient a practice than illustrating practically oriented texts with images – or perhaps it is medical practice that is being dignified by the use of diagrams.[37]

Breaking down the use of different graphic devices (Table 2), we can see that braces and general images were the predominant device types used in early modern English medical books. Braces appear in 42 out of 181 books (23%) and general images (with and without text) in 49 out of 181 books (27%). Diagrams other than braces or arithmetic calculations only appear in 20 books (11%) and tables of various sizes in 25 books (14%). In terms of the EMEMT categories, braces were most common in recipe collections and *materia medica* and surgical and anatomical texts, mainly occurring in medicinal recipes, which are found in both categories. Diagrams are also mostly found in these two categories. General images are often used in surgical and anatomical treatises, books on specific methods, and books on midwifery and children's diseases. They also occur in recipe collections and *materia medica*.

In terms of the variety of different graphic devices used, there are three categories that stand out. In books on specific methods (category 2b) and recipe collections and *materia medica* (3), all types of devices except calendar tables appear in our data set; surgical and anatomical treatises (5) use all kinds of devices apart from calendars and arithmetical operations.

Next, we turn to a qualitative analysis of the use of graphic devices in each of the five text categories.

General Treatises and Textbooks

Books in this category (19 texts) include both authoritative and comprehensive textbooks on the theory and practice of medicine as well as texts for heterogeneous lay audiences and households. Seven of the texts contain graphic devices. Stephen Batman's *Batman vppon Bartholome* (1582), which reworks the medieval encyclopaedic text of Bartholomeus Anglicus, contains several full-page generic images at the beginnings of some of the books. For example, the book on animals opens with an image of different

---

[36] A. WEAR, *Knowledge and Practice in English Medicine, 1550-1680* (Cambridge, 2000), pp. 159-160.
[37] MACLEAN, "Diagrams in the defence of Galen", p. 137.

kinds of animals.[38] Such images can work as markers for different sections of the book, but since images are not used systematically at the beginning of each book, it is more likely that the images were simply decorative in function. Batman's text also has two diagrams indicating the functioning of the eye. Another text, Thomas Brugis's *Marrow of Physicke* (1640), which was targeted for household use, especially for women, contains a diagram of "a Stove to sweat in", with letters marking its various parts and functions, which are explained in the text.[39] This text also contains a small table describing the natures of the twelve zodiac signs. The only other table in this category, which is also astrological, is found in John Durant's *Art and Nature* (1697).[40] It lists the reigns of planets for every hour of the week.

Several of the sixteenth-century treatises in this category draw on classical and medieval medical authorities, and thus it is perhaps surprising that only two of the texts make use of braces to classify and describe medical concepts. Both texts are translations. Thomas Gale's translation of Galen's *Methodus medendi* (1566, reprinted in 1586) was intended for non-Latinate medical students of surgery and physick, and it uses braces to organise, classify, and summarise the basic concepts of medical theory.[41] Some of these diagrams are quite intricate, while others are very simple. The simplest ones could just as easily be written out, but formatting the information as a diagram makes it stand out from the surrounding text. A later text, Brugis's *Marrow of Physicke* (1640), also uses braces for the purpose of organising and summarising information, but the text also contains a complex diagnostic flow chart that has been attached between the pages and is to be folded out by the user (see Fig. 2).[42] Two other texts show occasional use of braces. In Walter Bruele's *Praxis medicinae* (1632), braces only appear in a list of medicinal weights and measures on the last page, not in the recipes in the text as might have been anticipated.[43] In Nicholas Culpeper's *Galen's Art of Physick* (1652), braces occur in Culpeper's commentary of Galen in Chapter 85.[44] Although braces are not employed elsewhere in this

---

[38] S. BATMAN, *Batman vppon Bartholome [...]*, STC 1538 (London, T. East, [1582]), between ff. 332-333.
[39] T. BRUGIS, *The Marrovv of Physicke [...]*, STC 3931 (London, R. Hearne, [1640]), p. 103.
[40] J. DURANT, *Art and Nature Joyn Hand in Hand [...]*, WING D2681A (London, for S. Clark, 1697), p. 13.
[41] GALEN, *Certaine Vvorkes of Galens, Called Methodus medendi [...]*, transl. T. Gale, STC 11531 (London, T. East, 1586).
[42] BRUGIS, *The Marrovv of Physicke*, between pp. 38-39.
[43] G. BRUELE, *Praxis medicinae [...]*, STC 3929 (London, J. Norton for W. Sheares, 1632), p. 411.
[44] GALEN, *Galens Art of Physick [...]*, transl. N. CULPEPER, WING G159 (London, P. Cole, 1652 [1653]), pp. 89-101.

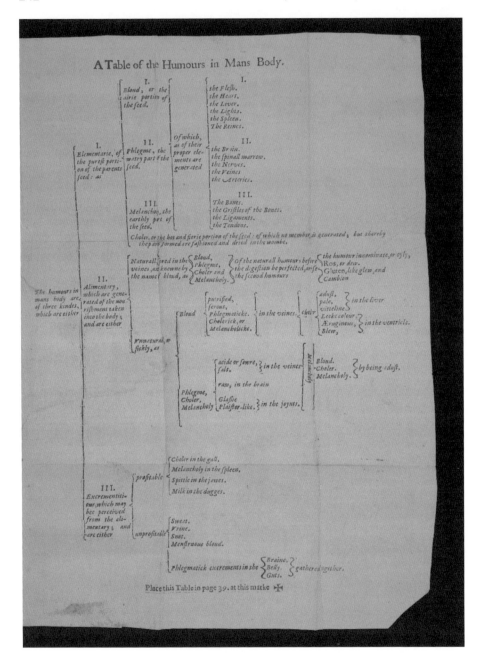

Fig. 2 A fold-out flowchart explaining humours attached to Thomas Brugis, *Marrow of Physick* (1640). STC 3931. Image: Wellcome Collection / Public Domain Mark.

work, it makes extensive use of numbered lists, which could be seen as a practice related to the use of graphic devices.

Treatises on Specific Topics

The five subcategories of treatises on specific topics in EMEMT are

1) texts on specific illnesses;
2) texts on specific methods of diagnosis or treatment;
3) texts on specific therapeutic substances;
4) texts on midwifery and children's diseases; and
5) texts on plague.

The number of graphic devices used varies considerably between the different subcategories and also between books in the same subcategory.

The texts on specific diseases (EMEMT category 2a, 16 texts) deal with the nature of single diseases, such as gout or syphilis, or types of diseases (e.g. agues, diseases typical to mariners). Plague texts are in their own subcategory (2e, 9 texts), as they are quite numerous and also distinctive from other texts on specific diseases in their moral and religious argumentation. The texts in these categories contain very few graphic devices. Only five texts in category 2a contain braces; they are used in diagnostic flowcharts in two texts from 1566 and 1621, and, less interestingly, in recipes in three other texts to denote shared quantities of ingredients. No tables or images are found in texts on specific diseases. In plague texts, there are no graphic devices apart from two coats of arms in one text, the Royal College of Physicians' *Certain Necessary Directions* (1636).[45] Discussing specific diseases was apparently not thought of as something requiring medical illustrations, tables, or diagrams.

The texts on specific methods (EMEMT category 2b, 19 texts) cover a wide range of methods for diagnosing and treating illnesses, including for example uroscopies, astrological treatises, and treatments such as phlebotomy, baths, warming stones, purges and emetics. Though the audiences in this category range from general readers to highly educated physicians, the texts with graphic devices are more often than not meant for practical use by surgeons and other non-university-educated practitioners of medicine. There is a gap of almost 40

---

[45] ROYAL COLLEGE OF PHYSICIANS IN LONDON, *Certain Necessary Directions [...]*, STC 16769.5 (London, R. Barker, 1636).

years in the texts in the sixteenth century, which seems to be meaningful. Of the five texts printed between 1525 and 1559, four contain images (with and without text), whereas only four of the 14 texts printed between 1596 and 1700 contain images – and in two of these texts, the images are frontispiece portraits of Nicholas Culpeper.

The earlier set of texts includes two uroscopies and a physiognomical text, where it is easy to include images of bottles and heads as generic illustrations. The images could just as easily have been left out, as is the case with the later uroscopy *Pisse-Prophet* (1637), which contains no graphic elements at all. In the early set of texts, one uroscopy contains an anatomical diagram with various parts of the urinary system indicated by letters that are explained next to the graphic device. There is only one text, Gesner's *Treasure of Evonymus* (1559), that makes repeated and sophisticated use of diagrams; it is one of only four translations in this category. The text explains how to distil medicines, and many of the images show the distilling process, the furnace, tools and vessels needed for distilling, or the herbs to be used for preparing medicines. The diagrams are clearly intended to be additional practical aids for the reader: "although me thinks I have described the matter plain inough [...] yet wil I ad[d] sum figure, that I may lay the thinge before the eyes mooste clerely".[46]

The seventeenth-century texts in category 2b that contain graphic elements other than images are dominated by astrological texts (5 out of 14), and it is not surprising to find arithmetical diagrams and tables of varying sizes in them. In some cases, the tables include braces used to indicate shared information. Often authors refer to these graphic elements explicitly in the text and explain how to read them or use them for instance for calculating critical days. Of the remaining texts of the seventeenth century, only Cock's *Miscelanea medica* (1675) contains a general image of a bath (accompanied by an instruction for the typesetter to "Place here the Figure") and the translation of Tauvry's *Treatise of Medicines* (1700) uses braces to indicate shared doses of various anti-emetic medicines.[47]

EMEMT category 2c (15 texts) focuses on specific substances used as medicines or as ingredients for medicines (pepper, tobacco, water from particular locations). The only graphic device found in these texts is braces, used to indicate identical quantities to be used in recipes or in the composition

---

[46] K. GESNER, *The Treasure of Euonymus, Conteyninge the Vvonderfull Hid Secretes of Nature [...]*, transl. Peter MORWYN, STC 11800 (London, John Day, 1559), p. 246.

[47] T. COCK, *Miscelanea medica [...]*, WING C4793 (London, [s. n.], 1675, p. 24; D. TAUVRY, *A Treatise of Medicines [...]*, WING T247 (London, for R. Wellington, A. Bettesworth, and B. Lintott, 1700), p. 147.

of a particular substance. The majority of the texts describe in prose the properties and uses of what would today be called proprietary medicines, that is, ready-made pills, elixirs and ointments sold by the 'owner' of the secret recipe and approved vendors.

In texts on midwifery and children's diseases (EMEMT category 2d, 10 texts), there are no graphic devices in the earliest two books from the 1540s – the only sixteenth-century books in this category. However, both contain an example where the layout would allow for a horizontal tree diagram if braces were printed or drawn in to connect the parts. In the seventeenth century, three of the eight books in our data contain no graphic devices. The translation of Guillemeau's *Childbirth* (1612) is exceptional in that it contains eleven illustrations of foetuses in the womb in specific positions, with the text advising the practitioner on the best way to deliver the baby in each situation.[48] In addition, the work contains images of instruments accompanied with caption-like passages within the body text, distinguished by the use of italic font. The translation of Guillemeau's *Nursing of Children* (1612) also contains two images of instruments. One of these is not named in the surrounding text but referred to as "such an instrument as you see heere".[49] The image thus helped in identifying the instrument.

In contrast to the detailed images in Guillemeau, Culpeper's *Directory for Midwifes* (1651) only contains one full-page image of a foetus in the womb, opposite to the first page of Book II, titled 'Of the Formation of the Child in the Womb'.[50] Some thirty pages later, the text notes: "Lastly, I here insert you the Figure taken out of *Spigelius*, who quotes it but of a Child prepared for the birth, or when the birth is near; and as far as I remember that which I saw was like this".[51] There is also a placeholder on this page that instructs the printer to "Insert the Figure here". However, there is no figure at this location, so it is unclear whether this refers to the image on p. 41 or whether another figure was intended to be added here. In addition, this edition contains one astrological table and one horizontal tree diagram with a brace, but the latter lists the

---

[48] J. GUILLEMEAU, *Child-Birth or, The Happy Deliuerie of Vvomen [...]*, STC 12496 (London, A. Hatfield, 1612). This is a translation of *De l'hereux accouchement des femmes* and *De la nourriture et gouvernement des enfants*, with distinct title pages and pagination for the two parts. The illustrations are in the first treatise, e.g. on p. 155.

[49] GUILLEMEAU, *Child-Birth*, p. 86 of the latter treatise in the volume.

[50] N. CULPEPER, *A Directory for Midwives [...]*, WING C7488 (London, P. Cole, 1651), p. 41.

[51] N. CULPEPER, *A Directory for Midwives*, p. 74.

contents of the following sections and is thus in practice paratextual rather than medical.

Sharp's *Midwives Book* (1671) contains a foldout diagram of a dissection of the womb, with alphabetical tie marks (letters linking parts of the image to relevant text) and explanations under the heading "The Figure Explained".[52] There is also a foldout plate containing a series of eight numbered pictures of a foetus in the womb in different positions (between pp. 198 and 199), which offers more detailed information to the practitioner. The anonymous *Aristoteles Master-Piece* (1684) is somewhat different in tone, as it only contains a handful of images of 'monstrous births' at the end of the book.[53] To sum up, the majority of images in midwifery books appear to be more or less specific images of foetuses in the womb.

Recipe Collections and Materia medica

The texts in the recipe collections and *materia medica* (texts on medicinal substances) category (EMEMT category 3, 41 texts) vary considerably in their use of graphic devices. Overall, 23 out of 41 books have no graphic devices. In the sixteenth century, only 4 out of the 17 books contain graphic devices, whereas in the seventeenth century there are devices in 15 out of 24 books. It thus seems that including at least some graphic devices in books of this category became more common in the seventeenth century.

Some of the books in this category are especially image-heavy. These include the *Grete Herball* (1526), which typically contains two to five images of plants per opening (with some images used more than once in the book), and Gerard's *Generall Historie of Plantes* (1633), with a typical opening containing one to eight captioned images of plants.[54] Apart from these two large volumes, there are perhaps surprisingly few images of plants in texts of this category. Monardes' *Ioyfvll Newes* (1580), for example, only contains eleven such images despite being a volume of nearly 400 pages.[55]

---

[52] J. SHARP, *The Midwives Book [...]*, WING S2969B (London, for Simon Miller, 1671), between pp. 152 and 153.

[53] ANON., *Aristoteles Master-Piece [...]*, WING A3689 (London, for J. How, 1684), pp. [193-203].

[54] ANON., *The Grete Herball [...]*, STC 13176 (London, P. Treveris, 1525); J. GERARD, *The Herball or Generall Historie of Plantes [...]*, STC 11751 (London, A. Islip, J. Norton and R. Whitakers, 1633).1

[55] N. MONARDES, *Ioyfull Newes out of the Newfound World [...]*, STC 18006.5 (London, [T. Dawson for] W. Norton, 1580).

Visual Representation of Information in Medical Texts, 1500-1700

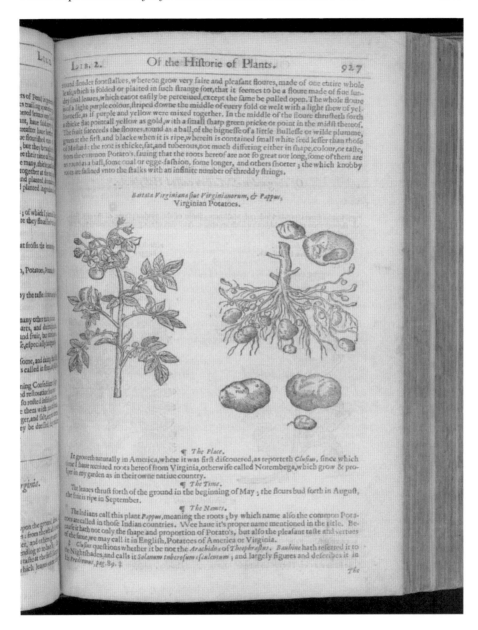

Fig. 3 Example of plant illustrations from the 1636 edition; the same illustrations appear on the same page in the 1633 edition discussed above. *The Herball, or General Historie of Plantes / Gathered by John Gerarde [...] Very Much Enlarged and Amended by Thomas Johnson.* STC 11752, p. 927. Image: Wellcome Collection / Public Domain Mark.

Illustrations of medical plants had the potential to serve a real functional purpose. In the early modern period, a mixture of vernacular, classical, and so-called apothecary lexis was in use for herbs and plants, resulting in confusion and uncertainty that was widely mentioned by apothecaries and surgeons.[56] The same plant or herb might be called by several different names in various parts of the country and by members of different professions, and to compound the problem many of the major herbals such as the *Grete Herball* and Gerard's *Generall Historie of Plantes* were translations, which added another layer of linguistic complexity. The generous illustrations in these books thus served an important function in helping readers identify the plant in question. This usefulness naturally depended on the quality of the illustrations, and the features of the plants that were depicted. While illustrations of the shoot system, flowers, and leaf blades may feel like the obvious choice for a lay person, a professional may benefit more from seeing the roots, for example. This attention to detail is best exemplified by the *General Historie of Plantes*,[57] which provides hundreds of woodcuts featuring the entire plant (see Fig. 3).

Illustrations of something other than plants occur in Porta's *Natural Magick* (1658), which has seven images depicting distillation and "burning-glasses".[58] There are also some diagrams and diagrammatic elements in recipe collections and *materia medica*. The earliest diagram in this category is in the *Grete Herball* (1526), showing a human skeleton with Latin labels for the bones.[59] This illustration is known to have previously appeared elsewhere, for example in Brunschwig's *Noble Aperyence of Surgeri* (1525) and the original *Buch der cirurgia* (Strasbourg, 1497, USTC 743717). This skeleton is the only example of a clear diagram in our sixteenth-century data in this category.[60]

---

[56] See TYRKKÖ, "'Halles Lanfranke'".

[57] Although ostensibly written by London gardener John Gerard, the book was mostly a translation of *Cruydeboeck* (1554) by Flemish botanist Rembert Dodoens. The 1633 edition included in EMEMT was the second edition, corrected and enlarged by apothecary Thomas Johnson. While Gerard had procured the woodcuts from Nicolaus Bassaeus in Frankfurt, Johnson acquired the original, higher quality woodcuts used in the Latin version of Dodoens' *Cruydeboeck* (1583), printed by the famed Plantin Press in Antwerp. The woodblocks used in important books could be stored for decades and then brought back into use.

[58] G. DELLA PORTA, *Natural Magick [...]*, WING P2982 (London, for T. Young and S. Speed, 1658).

[59] ANON., *The Grete Herball [...]*, sig. *6r.

[60] Folio 99r of Monardes' *Ioyfvll Newes* contains an illustration of bezoar stones that we have labelled a diagram since it depicts the relationship between objects, but the picture also has features of a general image.

In the seventeenth century, there are more examples of diagrams in the same category. The 1655 edition of Paracelsus' *Supreme Mysteries of Nature* contains over twenty images of occult signs and symbols to be engraved by the practitioner.[61] Since the placement of the symbols and letters in relation to each other is essential here, we have classified these illustrations as diagrams. Culpeper's *School of Physick* (1659) contains the author's nativity chart.[62] Porta's *Natural Magick* (1658) has seven geometrical diagrams, parts of which are alphabetically labelled and referred to in the accompanying text. Similar alphabetical labels connect the instruments and their parts to textual explanations in the five plates of Charas' *Royal Pharmacopoea* (1678).[63]

Braces are used in the recipes of Gale's *Antidotarie* (1563) to illustrate that one must take the same amount of several different ingredients.[64] There are typically several braces per opening. The only other sixteenth-century work in this category with braces is Turner's *Book of Baths* (1562).[65] In the seventeenth century, 10 out of the 24 texts contain one or more braces, mainly used in horizontal tree diagrams and to connect lists or sets of things.

Tables only appear in this category in the latter half of the seventeenth century. Paracelsus' *Supreme Mysteries of Nature* (1655) uses a table to show the suitable times for transmuting metals. Porta's *Natural Magick* (1658) contains two mathematical tables accompanying the images and geometric diagrams in its section on "burning-glasses". In Culpeper's *School of Physick* (1659), some of the information regarding his nativity is presented in a table. *The Compleat Servantmaid* (1677) contains a "table of numeration" showing the places and values of digits up to hundreds of millions.[66] Finally, Salmon's *Phylaxa medicinae* (1700) contains a table showing the price per ounce of various medical substances.[67] In the preface (dated 27 March 1684), Salmon notes:

---

[61] PARACELSUS, *Of the Supreme Mysteries of Nature [...]*, WING B3544 (London, by J. C. for N. Brook and J. Harison, 1656 [1655]).

[62] N. CULPEPER, *Culpeper's School of Physick [...]*, WING C7544 (London, for N. Brook, 1659), sig. B3v.

[63] M. CHARAS, *The Royal Pharmacopoea [...]*, WING C2040 (London, for J. Starkey and M. Pitt, 1678).

[64] T. GALE, *Antidotarie Conteyning Hidde and Secrete Medicines Simple and Compounde*, in *Certaine Vvorkes of Chirurgerie*, STC 11529 (London, by R. Hall [for T. Gale], [1563/64]).

[65] W. TURNER, *The Seconde Part of Vuilliam Turners Herball [...]*, STC 24366 (Collen [Köln], by A. Birckman, 1562).

[66] ANON., *The Compleat Servant-Maid [...]*, WING W3273A (London, for T. Passinger, 1677), p. 21.

[67] W. SALMON, *Phylaxa medicinae [...]*, WING S443 (London, I. Dawks, 1700), p. 3.

although we every where give you the *Price* of each Medicine in particular, as we hereafter severally treat of them: Yet for your farther ease, that you might see them all at one View, We have taken the pains to collect the same together in the following Catalogue, being *the Value of each Medicine by the Ounce.*[68]

This comment explicitly stresses the value of gathering similar information together and presenting it as a table, where it can be consulted "at one View".[69]

Regimens and Health Guides

Regimens and health guides generally instruct readers on healthy living, for example in terms of diet. There are 22 texts in this category, and only 8 of them contain graphic elements, which indicates that authors found the traditional prose format to be sufficient for this genre. The texts with graphic devices can be divided into two groups, and they are all from the sixteenth century or the very first years of the seventeenth century. The texts from the first half of the sixteenth century contain images of a person or persons at the beginning of the text and occasionally also at the very end of the text. These images seem to function as early frontispieces, as many of them also contain labels identifying the persons as Ptolemy or Galen, for example. The images did not convey any medical information for the readers. One of the texts, Thomas Elyot's *Castel of Helth* (1541) also contains a high number of braces; they connect lists of symptoms with various humoral conditions, making it easy for a medical practitioner to skim the text to find a condition that matches their patient's symptoms.[70]

The second group of three texts are from the period 1565-1604. The texts contain 1-3 graphic elements each. One text has two calendars and a diagram for calculating the golden number, one text has a large table, and one text has a diagram of a zodiac man. What the texts in this group have in common is the fact that in all of them graphic elements are an integral part of the text, as the functions of the graphic elements are explained in the running text. For example, Manning's *Complexions Castle* (1604) contains a large, full-page table introduced in the following manner:

---

[68] SALMON, *Phylaxa medicinae [...]*, p. 2; roman and italic inverted for ease of reading.
[69] For similar expressions, see also LIIRA, PEIKOLA and KAARTINEN, this volume.
[70] T. ELYOT, *The Castel of Helth [...]*, STC 7644 (London, T. Berthelet, [1541]).

Here insueth a table collected out of Pythagoras, with certaine breife notes added therevnto, whereby may be knowne in all humorall diseases (without sight of vrin or patient) what part of the body is ill affected, what humor aboundeth, & causeth the passion. Which beeing knowne, you may looke vnto the discourse of the complexion, there shall you find what is to correct the offending humours, and to purge the peccant matter: what diet is to be vsed, and what hurtfull things are to be auoided.[71]

The reader is instructed on what information they need to acquire from the patient and is given detailed instructions for using that information to read the table to find out "the cause, and the affected place", after which they can consult the correct place in the book to determine the required treatment. The table thus has a clear function as an aid to speed up the diagnosis of patients. The author assumes that the reader is not familiar with this kind of diagnosis, which is why they provide the table and instructions for using it. Similar instructions are included for reading the two calendars in Moore's *Hope of Health* (1565).[72] The zodiac man diagram in William Bullein's *Gouernement of Health* (1595) also collects together in a visual form information on letting blood from the correct vein according to sickness and the heavenly signs, but the reader is not instructed how to decipher the image. Bullein simply tells the reader to "first marke this figure of the Anatomie here present before thee, with the heauenly signes, because I haue not painted at large the seuerall parts of the said Anatomie".[73] Contrary to the other two authors, Bullein assumes that the readers have enough previous knowledge about the topic for it to be condensed into an image that needs no further elaboration.

Surgical and Anatomical Treatises

Surgical and anatomical treatises (30 texts) were written by established surgeons for other surgeons and apprentice surgeons rather than for lay audiences or university-trained physicians. The texts drew on continental and Latin traditions, and many (12) of them are translations of continental works. The ratio of graphic devices per text is highest in this category: 70% of the texts in this category contain at least one graphic device.

---

[71] J. MANNING, *A New Booke, Intituled, I Am for You All, Complexions Castle [...]*, STC 17257 (Cambridge, J. Legat, 1604), p. 38.
[72] P. MOORE, *The Hope of Health [...]*, STC 18060 (London, J. Kingston, [1565]).
[73] W. BULLEIN, *The Gouernment of Health [...]*, STC 4042 (London, V. Sims, 1595), p. 17.

A third (10) of the texts contain braces for classifying and organising information. The simplest graphic devices reformat lists into a horizontal layout with the heading separated by a brace from the listed items. The information is much more easily located than if it were written as running text, making the text a working aid for a practising surgeon. Braces also work to visualise complex systems of information (see Fig. 2 for an example from a textbook). The 1634 translation of the works of Ambroise Paré, a famous French surgeon, makes copious use of braces to build flowcharts detailing information about basic medical concepts such as humours and temperaments.[74] Paré is also one of the handful of texts that contain tables. He introduces a table collecting information about the nature, consistency, colour, taste, and use of the four humours with the following words: "It may easily appear by the following scheme, of what kind they all are, and also what the distinction of these foure humors may be".[75] Apart from Paré, only William Brugis (*Vade Mecum*, 1651) uses a table more than five times.[76]

Just under half of the surgical and anatomical texts (14) contain general images with or without text, often in large quantities. In most cases, the images depict parts of the human anatomy or medical instruments needed by a surgeon, and any accompanying text is usually a caption for the image. The anatomical images commonly depicted the systems of the bones, arteries, veins, nerves, and muscles, along with the head and brain, internal organs, and genitals. There are also a few instances of the traditional diagrams of the zodiac man or the bone man. The 1525 translation of Hieronymus Brunschwig's manual for surgeons contains numerous images that range from purely decorative trees and human figures to anatomy and surgical instruments and procedures.[77] Interestingly, the images are different from the ones in the original German text; for example, the original text included one image of several surgical tools, but the English translation contains numerous images of various surgical tools and braces for healing fractures; not surprisingly, the images are not referred to in the text itself in any way. Though the more specific images are placed alongside discussions of the same topic, they nonetheless seem to function as generic illustrations rather than as support for the text.

---

[74] A. PARÉ, *The Workes of that Famous Chirurgion Ambrose Parey [...]*, STC 19189 (London, T. Cotes and R. Young, 1634).

[75] PARÉ, *The Workes of that Famous Chirurgion Ambrose Parey [...]*, p. 13.

[76] T. BRUGIS, *Vade mecum [...]*, WING B5225 (London, T. H. for T. Williams, 1652 [1651]).

[77] H. BRUNSCHWIG, *The Noble Experyence of the Vertuous Handy Warke of Surgeri [...]*, STC 13434 (London, P. Treveris, [1525]).

Another early text, William Bullein's *Bulleyns Bulwarke of Defēce gainste all Sickness, Sornes, and Woundes* (1562), also contains a rather eclectic collection of diagrams and images.[78] For example, Bullein concludes his section on bloodletting and announces that he will move on to the next topic, only to introduce a diagram of a human figure and the veins for bloodletting, with extensive annotations explaining the tie marks on both sides of the diagram. The large diagram is clearly recycled from another text. The book of simples (medicines consisting of a single ingredient) ends with captioned illustrations of herbs and distilling equipment. Between two parts of the book is placed a diagram of a skeleton, with Latin labels for each bone (see Fig. 4). The figure is headed by a caption:

> In this place good reader, but that infortunate happe haue preuented me with lettes, els assuredly, I would haue written at lēgth, the whole large *Anatomie* of the bodie of mankind: but here I do ende, onely with the names of these bones, at this present time, vntill hereafter, if God will suffer me to doe more, I am then yours.[79]

Again, the diagram is a recycled one. Perhaps the diagrams are ones the printer already possessed or could get his hands on, and they were simply incorporated into the book with tenuous textual links. The most whimsical example of the use of a graphic device is found in the dialogue between Soreness and Chirurgy, when Soreness says, "I would knowe howe to heale my sores, whiche you doe see here present, before and behinde".[80] The request is followed by two large images of a man with sores on his body, shown from the front and the back, and a comment from Chirurgy, "I see them very well, and I truste by Gods grace, to teache you those things, whiche I haue learned my self of others, for cure".[81] The diagrams and images in Bullein's text are not fully integrated into the contents of the text, though there are metatextual references to them. Thus they do not seem to function as visualisations of verbal descriptions, and even their value as memory aids is questionable at times.

This contrasts heavily with the systematic and comprehensive anatomical illustrations found in Thomas Geminus' *Compendiosa totius anatomie delineatio* (1553) and the majority of the texts with images and diagrams in this

---

[78] W. BULLEIN, *Bulleyns Bulwarke of Defe(n)ce [...]*, STC 4033 (London, John Kingston, [1562]).
[79] BULLEIN, *Bulleyns Bulwarke of Defe(n)ce*, sig. 2I4r.
[80] BULLEIN, *Bulleyns Bulwarke of Defe(n)ce*, sig. 2A3r-v.
[81] BULLEIN, *Bulleyns Bulwarke of Defe(n)ce*, sig. 2A3v.

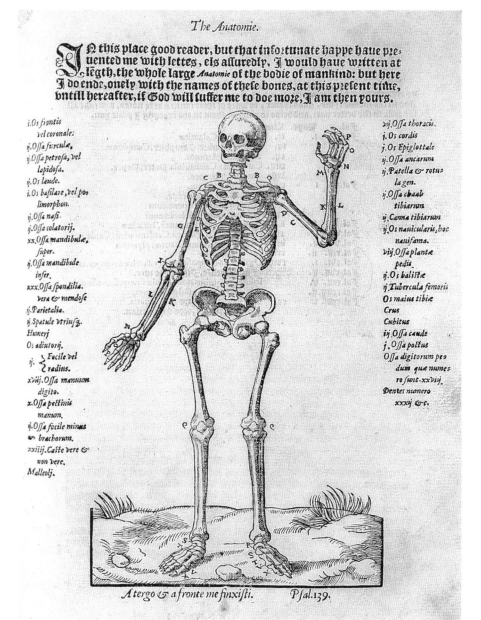

Fig. 4 Image of a skeleton with tie marks to the Latin names of the bones. William Bullein, *Bulwarke of Defence against All Sickness [...]* (1562). STC 4033, no folio number. Image: Wellcome Collection / Public Domain Mark.

category.[82] These diagrams are overwhelmingly anatomical illustrations with letters indicating various smaller parts of a larger whole, for example individual bones of a skeleton. In Geminus' book, the anatomical diagrams and images – based on Andreas Vesalius' images – and the explanations of the diagrams' tie marks are separate from the main text, which describes the functions of the parts of the body (the text comes mostly from Thomas Vicary's 1548 manuscript *Anatomy of the Bodie of Man*). The explanations of tie marks give some additional information, but they are not referred to in the main text. In these texts, the graphic devices, along with the possible annotations, are highly functional, as they replace information presented in verbal form.

The images and the explanations of tie marks are often rather separate from the main text: they are placed at the beginning or end of the work. In fact, the images often seem to function like the anatomical fugitive sheets that circulated independently from texts in the sixteenth century.[83] Students as well as practising surgeons could use the images for learning and remembering the anatomical information or the selection of instruments that was necessary for the practice of their craft.

A number of texts in this category discuss and describe anatomy and surgical procedures without the support of images. Texts without images fall into two categories. On the one hand, we find translations of established older texts such as Johannes de Vigo (1543) and Guy de Chauliac (1579) that were originally printed before Vesalius produced his anatomical illustrations and that represent the older traditions of medical writing; Braunschweig's 1525 translation mentioned above is an anomaly in changing and adding images to the original text. On the other hand, especially in the second half of the seventeenth century, surgical texts started to specialise towards wound treatment as a part of naval and military surgery, which was explained only verbally, thus leading to a downturn in the number of anatomical and surgical texts with images or diagrams.[84] This turn towards the practical applications of anatomy can also be seen in the kinds of images still found in the texts, as

[82] T. GEMINUS, *Compendiosa totius anatomie delineatio [...]*, STC 11716 (London, [N. Hill for T. Geminus], 1553).

[83] JONES, "Image, word, and medicine in the Middle Ages", p. 3; NUTTON, "Representation and memory in Renaissance anatomical illustration", pp. 78-79; A. CARLINO, *Paper Bodies: A Catalogue of Anatomical Fugitive Sheets, 1538-1687* (London, 1999); R. MOORE, "Paper cuts: The early modern fugitive print", *Object: Graduate Research and Reviews in the History of Art and Visual Culture* 17.1 (2015), pp. 54-76.

[84] There is an exception to this trend: James Cooke's 1593 *Mellificium chirurgiae, or, The Marrow of Chirurgerie* contains a multitude of anatomical diagrams as well as images of surgical instruments and procedures.

illustrations of the multitude of instruments needed by a surgeon become more prevalent alongside and, by the end of the seventeenth century, instead of anatomical illustrations and diagrams.

Conclusion

According to our analysis, graphic devices were relatively commonly used in English medical books of the sixteenth and seventeenth centuries. Overall, 44% of all books in our data set contain at least one graphic device. However, there is variation in terms of the type of device and the sub-genre of the work. Tables are found in very few books, which is possibly a reflection of the types of texts that were selected into the EMEMT corpus. Widening the scope beyond the EMEMT categories, for example to astro-medical material such as calendars, would shed more light on the use of tables in this period.

In terms of diagrams, braces were commonly used in recipes to mark that the same amount was needed of several medical substances. Braces were also used to classify and organise information, as they could be used to build elaborate flowcharts to portray a diagnostic process or to describe different medical concepts. This kind of classifying function for braces stems from medieval logic, which implies that they were associated more with the learned spectrum of medical texts. Other types of diagrams are very rare in our material, but there are individual instances such as zodiac men and bone men, diagrams depicting distillation processes, and models for creating occult engravings.

As for images, their relative scarcity, even in most herbals and anatomical and surgical texts, is in line with the findings of earlier research on continental medical texts.[85] German surgical books remain the exception in their increasing use of images in texts meant for surgeons.[86] In textbooks, specialised texts, recipe collections and health guides, images are most commonly generic images that contribute no medical information and are rarely commented on in the text. Even in surgical and anatomical texts, the images and their potential explanations are often kept separate from the text by placing them at the beginning or end of sections rather than integrating them into the discussion.

---

[85] For example KUSUKAWA, "The uses of pictures in the formation of learned knowledge"; NUTTON, "Representation and memory in Renaissance anatomical illustration"; PANTIN, "Analogy and difference".

[86] PANTIN, "Analogy and difference", p. 26.

This seems to indicate that the potential of images as didactic tools was not yet realised in early modern English medical texts, at least in codex form. However, the influence of more ephemeral forms of print production, such as anatomical fugitive sheets, should also be considered in order to fully understand the use of graphic devices in the context of early modern medicine.

Verbal and Visual Instruction in Early Dance Manuals: The Curious Case of John Playford's Tables

HANNA SALMI

Introduction

John Playford (1623-1686?) is a central source of knowledge about dance in England in the mid-seventeenth century. His popular volume, *The English Dancing Master*, was successful enough to appear in some eighteen editions within the eighty years after it was first published in 1651 (and this count excludes the supplemental volumes). In this chapter, I will examine the innovative tabular format he adopted for presenting his dance instructions, and its continuing development through the different editions.

Dance manuals first started to appear in Italy in the fifteenth century, and Playford's manual is one of the earliest in England. However, while terminology was somewhat standardised, there was no standard way of notating dance steps in the seventeenth century. In 1589, the Frenchman Thoinot Arbeau had published a volume detailing a notation system that found favour among the theoretically-minded professionals, but it took some time and effort to learn.

Graphic Practices and Literacies in the History of English, ed. Matti PEIKOLA, Jukka TYRKKÖ, and Mari-Liisa VARILA, *Utrecht Studies in Medieval Literacy*, 61 (Turnhout: Brepols, 2025), pp. 259-279.

BREPOLS ⚜ PUBLISHERS   DOI 10.1484/M.USML-EB.5.143829

When writing for wider audiences, each manual-writer would therefore have to find their own way of explaining the different movements in the most reader-friendly way they could devise. In many cases, this simply meant a long verbal description; other authors used a combination of images and verbal explanations. As already mentioned, Playford chose to use an informal tabular arrangement in combination with the tune's musical notation.

When well designed, tables take advantage of Gestalt principles such as closure, proximity and continuation;[1] Francis Marchese has noted that the table is "a format that promotes associations among diverse data elements, and facilitates exploration of relationships among them".[2] Indeed, Playford's clever tables allow the reader to quickly identify how the dance figures flow with the music. The format allows not only "receptive reading", defined by A.K. Pugh as reading sequentially for the purpose of understanding the author's message, but also skimming (overviewing the structure) and searching (locating particular information in a text when its "precise symbolic representation is not known").[3] Facilitating the latter two reading strategies is of considerable assistance to the reader who actually wants to use the book for dancing, since remembering the steps themselves is not a major chore in country dances: the main difficulty lies in remembering the figures and their order. It would be fairly common for a dancer to forget a particular figure, which could easily be looked up in a manual such as Playford's.

Playford's tables must therefore have been a great help for many dancers. Despite this, in the later editions, there seems to be a gradual movement away from a strictly tabular presentation. In the following pages, I will examine this development in detail, shedding light on an interesting example of a publisher's evolving graphic practices at the time.

Background

In this section, I will first discuss dance manuals as an example of the broader flowering of instructional and technical writing in the early modern

---

[1] P. MOORE and C. FITZ, "Using Gestalt theory to teach document design and graphics", *Technical Communication Quarterly* 2.4 (1993), pp. 389-410.

[2] F.T. MARCHESE, "Tables and early information visualization", in: *Knowledge Visualization Currents: From Text to Art to Culture*, ed. F.T. MARCHESE and E. BANISSI (London, 2013), pp. 35-61.

[3] T. PUGH, "The development of silent reading", in: *The Road to Effective Reading*, ed. W. LATHAM (London, 1975), pp. 110-119, at pp. 112-113.

period. I will then move on to describe what is known of the social context in which these manuals would have been used, and who may have been their intended audience. I will close the section with a brief review of John Playford's career as a music publisher.

Dance Manuals as Instructional / Technical Writing

During the Renaissance and the early modern period, the new possibilities created by the printing press started something of a boom in popular education. In fact, Ian Gordon described the fifteenth century as the "age of instruction", with an "insatiable" demand for instructional manuals on various topics.[4] These topics covered practical skills such as gardening or taking care of horses, but at the same time, manuals on various art forms started to be written down. In some cases, such as gardening, an everyday activity developed into an art form practised for aesthetic purposes as well as practical ones.[5] The fifteenth century is also the time when the first written dance manuals started to appear, first in Italy and soon all across Europe.

Elizabeth Tebeaux notes that a key difference between "traditional texts" (literary, religious, historical) and technical ones was the way in which the text was read.[6] She points out that traditional texts were read slowly, for the purpose of internalising their knowledge and possibly meditating on it. Technical writing, on the other hand, was read selectively, for the purpose of performing a practical task of some kind. This difference in reading strategies, according to Tebeaux, also led to innovations in book presentation. While tables had been known and used for a long time at this point, Tebeaux comments on the "continued struggle" of English printers when using tables especially in books of smaller format[7] – an interesting point given that Playford chose precisely tables as the presentation method for his manual.

Dance undoubtedly presented challenges of its own: in addition to providing music notation, which was already challenging enough to print with mov-

---

[4] I.A. GORDON, *The Movement of English Prose* (Longman, 1966), p. 63, as cited in T.H.J.B. LUBBERS, *Towards Profiles of Periodic Style: Discourse organisation in modern English instructional writing* (Edinburgh, 2017), p. 5.
[5] J. MUNROE, "Gender, class, and the art of gardening: Gardening manuals in early modern England", *Prose Studies* 28.2 (2006), pp. 197-210.
[6] E. TEBEAUX, *The Flowering of a Tradition: Technical Writing in England, 1641-1700* (Amityville, NY, 2014), p. 92.
[7] TEBEAUX, *The Flowering of a Tradition*, p. 109.

able type and required special high-quality paper, the movements had to be described as well. This, too, is no simple task, as a perfect dance notation system would cover movement in three dimensions and in different parts of the body, while showing the relationship of the dancer to both the physical space and the musical time in which they move – in addition to the exact movement quality (sharp, lingering). Inevitably, most notation systems make compromises, assuming that the reader will be able to fill in some details from their pre-existing knowledge of dance.

Given this difficulty of describing dance in writing, it is perhaps not very surprising that before the fifteenth century dance masters were apparently not interested in writing down the basic steps and principles of their art; when they started doing so, it was partly with the goal of showing that dance was a liberal art and shared the norms and values of the Italian humanists.[8] Indeed, almost 300 years later a similar motivation is likely to have been behind John Weaver's dance treatise, which contains pearls of wisdom such as "The Hand is the Length of a Face" and "The longest Toe is a Nose long".[9] This rather mind-numbing discussion of anatomy and correct proportions served the purpose of connecting dance to other arts such as painting, and it is in fact significantly longer than the part of the book that covers actual dance positions and moves. We should therefore not assume that instruction in dance was always the only purpose of these manuals. Yet manuals could and did also serve as genuine pedagogical tools, and Playford certainly did not dedicate much space to the philosophy or artistic significance of dance.

It can therefore be said that dance manuals are not a unified genre. At least three subgenres can be distinguished: manuals describing dance technique (for example, the foot positions of classical ballet), manuals describing individual dances or choreographies, and finally manuals on dance notation. In addition, there are more academic treatises, such as Weaver's. While all of these are clearly related and would count as instructional writing, the precise goals of each are different. Manuals on dance technique focus on posture, basic steps and foot positions, but above all, a visually pleasing presentation of the dancer's body. Manuals describing individual dances, on the other hand, focus on the spatial location of the dancer in relation to the dance space and / or other dancers. Playford's manual, along with other manuals on country dances, be-

---

[8] J. NEVILE, *Eloquent Body: Dance and Humanist Culture in Fifteenth-Century Italy* (Bloomington, IN, 2004), p. 58.

[9] J. WEAVER, *Anatomical and Mechanical Lectures Upon Dancing* (London, 1721), p. 88, available at <https://www.libraryofdance.org/manuals/>.

longs in the latter group: the instruction focuses on the formations created by a group of dancers, and there is no discussion of how the individual dancer is expected to move. This could simply be a matter of prioritising the most important information, but it is also likely that nuances of technique were not a central issue for performing such dances.

The Social Context and Intended Audience of Dance Manuals

The first known dance manual is Domenico da Piacenza's treatise *De arte saltandi et choreas ducendi* (*c.* 1450), which was soon followed by a number of others in various languages. As Jennifer Nevile notes, it seems fair to assume that before the first manuals started to appear, dance teaching was largely an oral endeavour based on embodied demonstration.[10] After all, this is still the default way of learning to dance. However, there was surely an internationally recognised shared culture around dance, since local practices were intertwined with international networks. At first, Italy was the leader in these networks, but soon French dance masters became more influential.

Dance masters would teach at dance schools, but sometimes also at the homes of their students, especially in the case of female pupils. It was common for students to take lessons for a period while travelling: for example, Prince Charles took dance lessons in Madrid when he visited in 1623.[11] In 1610, Sir John Puckering's son studied in Paris, where an hour's dance lesson each afternoon formed part of the syllabus.[12] Humanistic educational curricula generally considered dance to be an important skill: for example, in *The Book Named the Governour,* Thomas Elyot argued that practising dance was an appropriate way to teach impatient young children moral virtues such as the eight branches of prudence.[13] In England, the members of the Inns of Court were known for their dancing skills, which they gained in classes organised by London dancing

---

[10] J. NEVILE, *Footprints of the Dance: An Early Seventeenth-Century Dance Master's Notebook* (Leiden, 2018), p. 102.

[11] NEVILE, *Footprints of the Dance*, pp. 105-06.

[12] NEVILE, *Footprints of the Dance,* p. 107.

[13] T. ELYOT, *The Boke Named the Governour,* (London, 1531: STC 7635), f.83v; see Ch. XXII in the online edition available at <https://www.luminarium.org/renascence-editions/gov/gov1.htm>.

schools. Such classes could cost as much as the fees for academic institutions;[14] this is an indication of the social importance of the ability to dance.

There were many dance schools in London in the sixteenth and seventeenth centuries, but as some of them were in disreputable neighbourhoods, in 1574 a monopoly to teach in London was granted to three dance masters for twenty-one years.[15] The idea of dance schools being disreputable is common. Indeed, dance masters themselves often mentioned this trope. Speaking of fifteenth-century Italian dance masters, Nevile notes that "[t]he opposition between a group of informed viewers and an uninformed group was central to both the dance masters and the humanists".[16] Their work was intended for the elite, those who had the education and nobility to appreciate it intellectually. This point is important, since any evidence of morally questionable behaviour could be deflected by arguing that such cases were examples of abuse by the uneducated.[17]

The authors who focus on describing individual dances rarely give much detail on the intended audience or the role which they expect dance to play in their readers' social lives. On the title page of the first edition (1651), Playford frames his book as containing "[p]laine and easie Rules", and in his note to the "Ingenious Reader" on the following page, he associates the art with ancient Greeks, young children, and the "Gentlemen of the Innes of Court". The number of new editions in the following decades suggests that the work soon proved immensely popular among readers, and scholars in general agree that music publishing in this period was aimed at a broad popular audience (see the section 'John Playford and His Works' below). However, it is not immediately clear who these enthusiastic readers would have been.

Some of the more technical manuals, which demonstrated dance positions and actual steps, were published with the help of a subscription model. Sometimes the names of the subscribers were printed as part of the front matter. For example, Kellom Tomlinson's manual from 1735 contains an alphabetical list containing 169 names.[18] This rather extensive list serves to give us some idea of the potential readership of dance manuals at the time. Out of this total, 57

---

[14] B. RAVELHOFER, "Dancing at the Court of Queen Elizabeth", in: *Queen Elizabeth I: Past and Present*, ed. C. JANSOHN (Münster, 2004), pp. 101-116, at p. 102.

[15] NEVILE, *Footprints of the Dance,* p. 107.

[16] NEVILE, *Eloquent Body,* p. 67.

[17] NEVILE, *Eloquent Body*, p. 68.

[18] K. TOMLINSON, *The Art of Dancing Explained by Reading and Figures; Whereby the Manner of Performing the Steps is Made Easy by a New and Familiar Method* (London, 1735), available at <https://www.libraryofdance.org/manuals/>.

subscribers were women; 19 were dancing-masters (all men). Out of the remaining men, 14 are titled as "Gent.", 39 as "Esq." The list also contains titles of nobility and people in the book trade, music, and other arts. A few are given the title of dancer, and there is a "John Rich, esq; master of the Theatres Royal in Lincoln's-Inn-Fields, and Covent-Garden". It has been estimated that only five percent of the population could afford to consume elite culture at the time;[19] many, if not all, of these subscribers would have been part of this minority.

However, there is reason to be careful about assuming an identical audience for all dance manuals. Tomlinson finishes his book by noting that his main focus is only on "genteel dancing",[20] suggesting that the distinction between this form and country dances may have been important at least to some practitioners. Furthermore, it is hardly likely that a small minority of the population could have supported a new edition of Playford's book every few years: his strategy as a publisher was to focus on the needs of popular audiences.

John Playford and His Works

John Playford (1623-1686?) was a bookseller and music publisher; his work forms the "principal source of knowledge of English country dance steps and melodies".[21] He has been called "the foremost music publisher of his generation".[22] A competent musician and composer himself, he was also acquainted with many composers and professional musicians of the time.[23] However, the first few years of his career as a publisher focused mostly on political tracts. These publications, together with his choice of themes and the composers he worked with, suggest that he had clear Royalist sympathies.[24] After Playford's death, his son Henry (1657-1709) continued the family trade.

---

[19] R.D. HUME, "The economics of culture in London, 1660-1740", *Huntington Library Quarterly* 69.4 (2006), pp. 487-533.

[20] TOMLINSON, *The Art of Dancing,* at p. 156.

[21] EDITORS OF ENCYCLOPAEDIA BRITANNICA, "John Playford", in: *Encyclopedia Britannica* (2022), available at <https://www.britannica.com/biography/John-Playford>.

[22] P. LINDENBAUM, "John Playford: Music and politics in the Interregnum", *Huntington Library Quarterly* 64.1-2 (2001), pp. 125-138, at p. 125.

[23] S. CARTER, "Published musical variants and creativity: An overview of John Playford's role as editor", in: *Concepts of Creativity in Seventeenth-Century England*, ed. R. HERISSONE and A. HOWARD (Woodbridge, 2013), pp. 87-104.

[24] K. WHITLOCK, "John Playford's *The English Dancing Master* 1650/51 as cultural politics", *Folk Music Journal* 7.5 (1999), pp. 548-578; LINDENBAUM, "John Playford".

As a music publisher, John Playford's strategy was to focus on the needs of a growing audience of enthusiastic amateur musicians. Rebecca Herissone describes music publications in this era as having two different and competing functions or goals:

> on the one hand catering to a music-buying public that wanted cheap copies of popular tunes to sing and play at home or in the tavern; on the other serving as a medium through which individuals – including composers – could make a statement about themselves or their creation.[25]

Achieving the second goal generally required patronage, but Playford chose to focus on the first goal as the more financially viable option. As Herissone notes, he was one of the first pioneers of such an approach, which is reflected, for example, in the complete lack of dedications in his publications.[26] His introductory works on music, for example *A Briefe Introduction to the Skill of Musick*, were also designed to increase musical literacy, thereby growing his potential audience.[27]

Materials and Methods

As mentioned above, there are many different subgenres under the label 'dance manuals'. This creates some methodological challenges for studying these texts, since the material is so heterogeneous: different authors chose very different approaches to the problem of explaining dance in writing. This means that it would be very hard to cover more than one approach in the space of a single book chapter. I have therefore chosen to conduct an in-depth case study of a single subgenre, in the interest of having a set of materials with relatively comparable aims and audiences. I will focus mostly on Playford's manual, although I will later briefly compare it to Thomas Bray's 1699 volume, which also focuses on country dances.

---

[25] R. HERISSONE, "Playford, Purcell, and the functions of music publishing in Restoration England", *Journal of the American Musicological Society* 63.2 (2010), pp. 243-290, at p. 280.

[26] HERISSONE, "Playford, Purcell, and the functions of music", p. 249.

[27] S. CARTER, "'Yong Beginners, who live in the Countrey': John Playford and the printed music market in seventeenth-century England", *Early Music History* 35 (2016), pp. 95-129, at p. 95.

Verbal and Visual Instruction in Early Dance Manuals 267

The materials for this project have been accessed through the list of manuals at the Library of Dance online collection.[28] The analysis will focus on the editions by the two Playfords, listed in Table 1. There were six additional editions by John Young, published between 1706 and 1728, but as most of these were not available through the Library of Dance, they have been left out of the analysis. The ESTC describes the bibliographical form as an "obl. 12" from the second through to the tenth edition.

Table 1 The editions considered for this chapter. The third edition is only partially available through the Library of Dance, and the eleventh not at all. For this reason, they are not included in the current analysis. The number of dances follows the publisher's numbering in the book.

Edition number	Date	Wing number	Publisher	Number of dances
1st	1651	WING (2nd ed.), P2477	John Playford	104
2nd	1652	WING (2nd ed.), P2468	John Playford	112
4th	1670	WING (2nd ed.), P2470	John Playford	155
5th	1675	WING (2nd ed.), P2471	John Playford	160
6th	1679	WING (2nd ed.), P2472	John Playford	182
7th	1686	WING (2nd ed.), P2473	John Playford	208 + 18
8th	1690	WING (2nd ed.), P2474	Henry Playford	220
9th	1695	WING (2nd ed.), P2475	Henry Playford	194 + 24
10th	1698	WING (2nd ed.), P2476	Henry Playford	215
12th	1703	–	Henry Playford	354
2nd Part	1696	WING (2nd ed.), P2499A	Henry Playford	24
2nd Part	1698	WING (2nd ed.), P2499B	Henry Playford	47

The first edition of *The English Dancing Master* (1651) contained 104 dances and corresponding tunes. While the title page describes the volume as

---

[28] N. ENGE, *Vintage Dance Manuals* (n.d.), available at <https://www.libraryofdance.org/manuals/>.

containing "Country Dances", one should not necessarily assume that Playford collected folk dances for his manual: Whitlock has convincingly argued that many of the dances have clear connections to the stage, and that Playford may have had access to unpublished notes from Ben Jonson's masques and the dances included in their performance.[29]

Analysis: The Development of the Tables in Playford's Manual

In this section, I will begin by describing the first edition of Playford's manual in some detail, beginning with the front matter and going on to the dance descriptions themselves. I will then present descriptive statistics on how the tabular format was gradually abandoned in the later editions. I will go on to discuss potential explanations for the reasons behind this development, using evidence from Playford's paratexts and a comparison with Bray's volume of country dances from 1699.

The Front Matter: The First Edition (1651)

The title page of the first edition contains a print showing a large hall where people are conversing and a cherub plays a lute. The full title is given as *The English Dancing master: or, Plaine and easie Rules for the Dancing of Country Dances, with the Tune to each Dance*. The title page stays very similar throughout the following fifty years of new editions, and the image is later labelled "the dancing schoole". The title page is followed by a single-page foreword to "the Ingenious Reader". Although it is signed by "J.P.", it has been suggested that the foreword may in fact have been written by the playwright Richard Brome.[30] In any case, the foreword justifies dance as a respectable art form with roots in the Greek period, serving to strengthen the body. The intended audience is not specified beyond listing associations with princely courts and noting that the art form develops "a quality very much beseeming a Gentleman".

The following four pages are dedicated to an alphabetical index of dances, with page numbers for each dance. After this index, there is a one-page table explaining the symbols used. Before the table proper, three common step combinations are explained verbally: a double or four steps, a single or two steps,

---

[29] WHITLOCK, "John Playford's *The English Dancing Master* 1650/51".
[30] WHITLOCK, "John Playford's *The English Dancing Master* 1650/51".

and finally a "set and turne single". These are the only explanations of actual dance steps in the book; under individual dances, the descriptions assume that the user of the book will already know how to perform more complicated manoeuvres such as "fall back and slip up" (dance 3) or perform the Single Hey (dance 4) – an interlacing pattern where the timing can be tricky.

The brevity of these initial instructions means that the volume was hardly suited for complete beginners. For example, directional conventions like 'up' and 'down' would need explanations if the book was intended for beginners, and the same applies to step combinations like the Hey. However, the lack of such instructions is not surprising, since it would be rare for a complete beginner to rely solely on a book to learn such matters. As these are not solo dances, more experienced dancers are always likely to be present to demonstrate the correct performance of a particular detail. Further, it has recently been shown that the most common keywords and collocations found in the "Old Measures", a set of manuscripts recording dances from the Inns of Court, are also very frequent in early modern English plays.[31] This would imply that even non-experts would have had at least some familiarity with dance terminology and conventions, and the keywords discussed in Fabio Ciambella's analysis include many words that are also common in Playford's dance descriptions (such as 'double' and 'single'). All in all, then, a thorough explanation of all the steps seems to have been considered unnecessary, suggesting that the intended function of the book was more as an aide-memoire for particular dances, as opposed to a manual for learning basic steps.

After this extremely brief introduction to the most basic steps, the following table lists abbreviations for them (S. for single, D. for double). In addition, there are abbreviations referring to the participants (Wo. for women etc.). These abbreviations are in practice mainly used in the verbal descriptions, but the table also lists alternative symbols for men and women: a sickle moon shape for men and a dotted circle for the women. These symbols are borrowed from astrology, where the dotted circle traditionally represents the sun. However, the signs were apparently incorrectly used in the first edition – of course, it is the moon which is traditionally associated with femininity. In any case, the symbols are used for describing the formation of the dancers, which is provided in graphic form for each dance (see Figure 1). In dances where couples take turns performing the same figure, the couples can be identified by ordinal numbers,

---

[31] F. CIAMBELLA, "A corpus linguistic analysis of dance lexis in eight early modern manuscripts: From the Inns of Court to drama", *SKENÈ Journal of Theatre and Drama Studies* 7.2 (2021), pp. 231-250.

also listed in the table of abbreviations. Finally, there are also symbols for repetitions in music. These consist of dots arranged above a horizontal line: one dot for a strain played once, two dots for a strain played twice, and so on (see Figure 1 below for examples).

The Dance Descriptions

In her discussion of how dance may have been taught during the preparations for sixteenth and early seventeenth century court masques, Barbara Ravelhofer cites Justinian Pagitt, a lawyer, who recommended in 1633: "Write the marks of the stepps in euery daunce under the notes of the tune, as the words are in songs".[32] To Ravelhofer's dismay, this recommendation was rarely followed in descriptions of courtly dancing. However, this is in fact roughly the approach Playford seems to have adopted. His descriptions of the dances follow a very formulaic structure. I will begin here by describing the structure used in the first edition of 1651. At the top of each page, the number of the dance (or page) is given in parentheses.

Underneath the page number is the name of the dance in Roman letters. The same line contains two other items. First, there is a brief verbal description in italics of the general formation of the dance and the number of dancers (e.g. *Longwayes for six* [dance 1], *Round for eight* [dance 20]), and finally a diagrammatic presentation of the exact way in which the dancers line up to form the figure. This diagram uses the astrological symbols previously defined in the "Table explaining the Characters", showing the positions of men and women in the figure. In most dances, all men line up on one side of the room facing the women; in some others they alternate. The figure is therefore a very important graphic resource, since the following instructions may not produce the desired outcome if the formation is incorrect. Fig. 1 reproduces the layout of a simple dance.

After this general information about the dance, the detailed description begins. The first part in all of the descriptions consists of a musical staff showing the tune to be played for the dance. Most tunes in the 1651 first edition consist of two parts, so the structure of the tune can be represented as AB. There are almost seventy tunes in this format. About thirty tunes consist of only a

---

[32] GB-Lo Brit. Lib. MS Harl. 1026, fol. 7; as cited in B. RAVELHOFER, "Memorable movements: Rhetoric and choreography in early modern courtly entertainment", *Internationales Archiv für Sozialgeschichte der Deutschen Literatur* 22.1 (1997), pp. 1-18, at p. 1.

Verbal and Visual Instruction in Early Dance Manuals 271

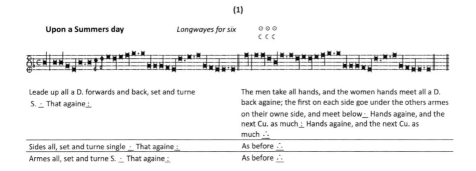

Fig. 1   A transcription of the first dance, conserving key aspects of the layout and visual elements (Playford 1651, first edition). Font sizes, column widths, and so on are rough approximations, and white space at the bottom of the page has not been reproduced. The musical notation is reproduced using Elam Rotem's specialist font EMS Serenissima; ties were left out, however, since they are not integrated in the font and are not relevant for the argumentation in this chapter.

single part, while nine tunes have three or more parts (ABC or ABCD). In the first edition, the musical line gives a visual appearance similar to the first row of a table, forming implied headers for the following rows. The columns of descriptions are generally carefully lined up to agree with the divisions between the musical parts.

After the musical line, descriptions of the movements are given. The main difficulty of country dances such as these, where the choreographic material is relatively simple, is in remembering the different combinations and their order in relationship to the musical material. In Playford's presentation, this is visually simplified by separating the movements done to each part of a tune with a horizontal line, so that the reader can easily distinguish between each figure and see how they relate to the music. Repeated parts in the figures are explained with a short "that againe" or "as before", combined with a symbol showing how many times the "strain" (of music) is to be played. Within each horizontal section of the verbal description, there can be up to four columns separated by a space, each column corresponding to a part in the dance tune. There are no vertical borders between the columns.

Nowhere does Playford refer to this rather clever manner of organising the material as a table, but it can clearly be described as one. According to Eleanor

Robson, tables can be defined as 'formal' if they have "both vertical and horizontal rulings to separate categories of information", while 'informal' tables rely on spatial arrangement (i.e. layout) only.[33] It is not entirely clear from her brief discussion how to categorise tables which have rulings across the horizontal axis only. Perhaps such cases can be described as semi-informal tables. There is in any case some fairly clear evidence that a table format is indeed what Playford wanted to achieve in the edition of 1651. First of all, the musical line almost always fits onto a single 'row', which is a prerequisite for its functioning as an unnamed header for the informal columns. In the seven dances (out of 104) where the music cannot be made to fit onto a single line, the last few notes of the tune are generally added as a short second line close to the right-side margin of the page, as opposed to starting a new line on the left as usual (e.g. dance No. 30). This allows the verbal descriptions to line up with the music: while columns are not separated by vertical lines, empty space between columns generally coincides with the double bars marking the division between musical structures.

This manner of presentation has both advantages and disadvantages. The main advantage is that it allows the reader to see the structure of the dance at a glance ('skim', in Pugh's terminology[34]): the number of 'strains', the number of repetitions of the whole tune, and most importantly, the relationship between the different movements and the tune. It is this last part that makes Playford's system innovative. It can also be seen as a navigational aid: since the borderlines between the different figures are immediately obvious, it is easy to use the description as an aide-memoire. Perhaps the reader remembers the movements for the first and third repetitions of the tune, but needs a reminder of what is supposed to happen during the second repetition. The tabular format allows the reader to search for the information much more efficiently.

Nor does such a use of the tables necessarily assume a high degree of musical literacy, since the only thing the reader really needs to know in order to grasp the relationship between music and movement is that the music in most cases consists of repeated sections, and that the dance needs to keep time with these. Many modern folk dancers manage to operate perfectly well with essentially this knowledge and no more, timing their steps to the tune which they know by ear. A basic knowledge of musical notation would of course make it

---

[33] E. ROBSON, "Tables and tabular formatting in Sumer, Babylonia, and Assyria, 2500 BCE-50 CE", in: *The History of Mathematical Tables: From Sumer to Spreadsheets*, ed. M. CAMPBELL-KELLY, M. CROARKEN, R. FLOOD, and E. ROBSON (Oxford, 2003), pp. 19-48, at p. 20.

[34] PUGH, "The development of silent reading", pp. 112-113.

Verbal and Visual Instruction in Early Dance Manuals 273

even easier to make sense of the table format. However, perhaps the biggest potential benefit of Playford's page organisation is that it would make it easier for the musicians also to keep track of where the dancers are. It would even have been possible for them to 'call' the figures, as is the custom in, for example, American square dancing.

The disadvantages, on the other hand, are related to the limited space available. This applies both to the musical notation and the dance descriptions. The music, as mentioned above, has to fit into a single line of staff, which does not always lead to high readability. The space available for the dance description, on the other hand, is determined by the length of the musical strain. However, where the music is simple, the movement is not necessarily so at the same time. This means that if a section is very busy in terms of movement – as opposed to musically – the description will take up several lines inside the table cell, the vertical borders of which are determined by the simple musical line. Conversely, if the musical line contains more notes than average but the dance is simple, there may be a considerable amount of empty space in the cells of the table.

There is some evidence that such situations gave the publisher some trouble. For example, dance 116 in the 1675 edition is presented with the two first rows of dance description neatly lining up with the repeats in the music. However, on the bottom row, the vertical space dividing the columns has been moved slightly to the right, to give space for a longer description of the movements in the A part of the tune. Similarly, there are cases where a partial notation line is squeezed into the first cell of the table together with the description (e.g. No. 14 in the 1686 edition).

The Development of the Tables in Later Editions

Since Playford's book is focused on dance rather than music, one might expect the clarity of the dance presentation to take priority over the needs of the musician. Certain features, such as the astronomical symbols showing the dance formation, were indeed preserved in all editions. However, when examining the development of the table format in later editions of the book, it soon becomes clear that this system of organising the dances was not consistently followed. Indeed, there are two related developments that show a consistent movement away from this system. First of all, the average length of the music notation keeps growing: while the overwhelming majority of tunes in the first edition fit on a single line, the average length of the notation in later editions is well over two lines. This is probably due at least in part to added white space between the notes. At the same time, the number of cells goes down so that especially in the last few editions, it is not unusual to see three or four lines of music linked to a dance description which fits in a single cell. Of course, such an arrangement can no longer really be described as a table. Table 2 shows how these changes progressed from one edition to the next.

Table 2 The development of the table format between 1651 and 1703. The column labelled 'Average lines notation' shows the length of the musical notation in lines; the column 'Average no. of cells' shows the average number of cells in the table.

Edition	Average lines notation	Average no. of cells
1651	1.08	6.74
1652	1.07	6.56
1670	1.62	6.07
1675	1.63	5.89
1679	1.68	5.52
1686	1.77	4.80
1690	1.86	4.60
1695	2.13	3.13
1698	2.06	3.21
1703	2.34	1.89
1696 Second Part	2.46	1.00
1698 Second Part	2.43	1.00

It is clear, based on Table 2, that the change was gradual, and although it accelerated as Henry took over the family business, it seems to have started already with the third edition of 1670. A closer examination of individual examples shows that the dances described in the first edition kept their tabular formatting even in later editions. For example, *Goddesses* (No. 52 in the first

Verbal and Visual Instruction in Early Dance Manuals 275

edition) starts out with the two-part tune on a single line, with no fewer than 22 cells in the table – the two parts of the tune were to be repeated eleven times, which makes it one of the more complicated examples. The dance stays in the manual until 1698, where it is presented in essentially the same way (now No. 46). However, an examination of the new dances in the same edition shows that these overwhelmingly follow an arrangement with multiple lines of music notation but a dance description that fits within a limited number of cells. This trend is particularly clear in the supplemental "Second Part" volumes from 1696 and 1698, where none of the dance descriptions are given in a tabular format.

Even before these late additions, there are cases where there is only a single column and a single horizontal line to separate the sections in the description (e.g. No. 185, 1686 edition). At that point, it is questionable whether the horizontal line adds any clarity at all, since it is not at all immediately obvious from the page how the different sections relate to the music, which appears to consist of four different sections. In yet other cases (Nos. 193 and 195, 1686 edition), the single horizontal line comes only at the end of the description, where it serves no purpose in terms of organising the text; perhaps it was added simply to keep the visual appearance of the page more consistent.

A Comparison with Bray (1699)

It seems odd that such a useful and easily understandable presentation style as Playford's tabular format was simply abandoned. One way to assess the potential reasoning behind this presentation of the material is to compare it with other writers' approaches. His manual was so successful that he does not seem to have had many competitors but, in 1699, Thomas Bray prepared a collection of twenty country dances.[35] It does not appear to have been nearly as popular as Playford's manual: apparently there was only one edition. The volume was actually available at Playford's shop, among other places. The title page advertises the contents to be "entirely NEW, and the whole Cast Different from all that have yet been publish'd; with Bass and Treble to each Dance". In addition to country dances, the volume is said to include the latest French dances and some dancing tunes. By this time, Playford's volume had been circulating for

---

[35] T. BRAY, *Country Dances: Being a Composition Entirely New; And the Whole Cast Different from All That Have Yet Been Publish'd; with Bass and Treble to Each Dance* (London, 1699: WING B4291B), available at <https://www.libraryofdance.org/manuals/>.

nearly half a century, so it is probably safe to assume that Bray would have been familiar with it. However, judging by Bray's volume, he did not consider the tabular format worth emulating. Instead, he incorporated various features designed to assist musicians in playing for the dancers.

The decision to include a polyphonic version of the music (as advertised on the title page) means that it was impossible for Bray to fit the music onto the same page as the dance instructions, let alone onto one line as Playford did in the first edition. Instead, the music is presented on alternate pages with the descriptions. There is a clever detail designed to make the music more usable in the dance context: the bass clef is printed upside down at the bottom of the page, which means that the musicians could set the book on a table between them, and could read their own parts the right way up.

However, the cost of this design decision is that the relationship between the dance and the music is much harder to understand at a glance. In the description of the first dance, there are headings indicating the beginning of the second and third "Part"; it is not immediately clear whether these "parts" refer to subdivisions in the music or in the dance itself. It is also rather hard to work this out, since the description does not include the formation or the number of dancers. An experienced dancer can make an educated guess about the number of bars it takes eight dancers to (for example) exchange places or 'cast off' to the side; it is much harder to estimate this when neither the number nor the formation of dancers is clearly stated. Perhaps the author himself was aware of the potential for misunderstandings: in his single-sentence note to the reader on page A3r, he says he tried to make his new dances "as easie as possible, to evary ingenious Reader, but if any Gentleman or Lady finds any difficulty in the performance of any of them, he shall be ready, when ever commanded, to wait upon them with his Instructions".

The main method which Bray seems to use to show the relationship to the music is a pair of symbols: a dot and a colon, both underlined to distinguish them from normal punctuation signs, signifying a part of the tune repeated once and twice, respectively. These are similar to the symbols used by Playford for the same purpose. In addition, there are some brief headings and occasional short notes in italics (e.g. "*Second passage thus*", in the third dance, combined with a paragraph division which visually reinforces the structural break between passages). In sum, it seems safe to say that the focus of Bray's book lies overwhelmingly on the clarity and ease of use of the musical notation, with very few visual aids for the dance descriptions.

Discussion

We have seen that Playford's tabular format facilitated several different types of reading. Yet Bray, who must have been familiar with Playford's manual, did not choose to emulate the format in his book, and the Playfords themselves did not apply the system consistently in later editions. Paratextual evidence may help to explain why this was the case. It is interesting to note that the table format is not mentioned on the title page. Yet it was not unusual to highlight such things on the title page at the time. For mathematical, astronomical and navigational works this seems to have been very common, but it is possible to find examples within less mathematical genres as well. For example, Thomas Porter published a book of maps in 1655, and the title page contained a list of the three types of tables provided, noting specifically that these tables were a useful and easy way to find information.[36] The title page of John Wilkins's dictionary of 1668 mentions the use of "philosophical tables" for the word definitions, and indeed the word 'tables' is printed in a much larger size than any other word on the title page.[37] The lack of such mentions suggests that the Playfords hardly viewed their table as a key innovation. The dance descriptions themselves are mentioned in only the briefest manner: starting with the 1670 edition, the title page notes that the manual includes both "the Figure and Tunes to each Dance". Prior to this, only the tunes were mentioned. However, other features of the book were repeatedly advertised on the title pages of the various editions.

Apparently, new tunes were a major part of the commercial appeal of such books – at least, they are mentioned prominently on the title pages, as in Bray's manual. For example, the 1665 edition mentions adding tunes for French dances in addition to English ones. The title page of the 1686 edition similarly notes the "[a]ddition of several new Dances, and Tunes of Dances, never before printed". The preface separately draws attention to the presence of forty-seven

---

[36] T. PORTER, *A New Booke of Mapps being a Ready Guide Or Direction for any Stranger, Or Other, Who is to Travel in any Part of the Comon-Wealth of England, Scotland, & Ireland.* (London, 1655: WING P2998B), available at ProQuest, <https://www.proquest.com/books/new-booke-mapps-being-ready-guide-direction-any/docview/2240861294/se-2.>.

[37] J. WILKINS, *An Alphabetical Dictionary wherein All English Words According to Their Various Significations, Are Either Referred to Their Places in the Philosophical Tables, Or Explained by Such Words as Are in Those Tables* (London, 1668: WING W2196), published in the same volume with Wilkins's *An Essay towards a Real Character, and a Philosophical Language*, available at ProQuest, <https://www.proquest.com/books/alphabetical-dictionary-wherein-all-english-words/docview/2264199555/se-2>.

"new Dances, and many new Dance Tunes". The 1670 edition announces "many new Dances, never Printed before", while the 1675 edition simply mentions "additions". The seventh edition, from 1686, even marks all the new dances with an asterisk in the table of contents, so that the reader can locate them more easily. This is also done in the following 1690 edition, while in the 1695 and 1698 editions there was a separate "Second Part" for new dances. Overall, then, it seems that novelty was an important consideration for the audience.

The details of the musical notation could also be used as a selling point. For example, the 1686 title page specifies that the tunes are intended "for the Treble-Violin", and from 1665, the foreword mentions that Playford "barred every Semibrief" to make it easier to play the tunes (i.e. he added bar lines to the notation after the equivalent of one semibreve or whole note to make it more readable). It is probably not a coincidence that 1665 is also when the average number of lines of notation starts to grow for the first time: the more spacious formatting would naturally lead to longer lines. This would indeed have made the notation easier to read than in the 1651 edition. However, it also means that the implicit 'header' of the semi-informal table no longer lines up as easily with the columns in the dance descriptions.

While new tunes and innovations were highlighted on the title page, and the notated tunes increased in length, a close reading of the later dance descriptions does not suggest that these were developed with corresponding care. For example, *The Happy Millet* (No. 22 in the 1696 Second Part) consists of a single movement: "The 1. man change places with the 2. wo. and the 1. wo. change places with the 2. man, then cross over into your own places and clap hands with your own Partners, then lead up above and cast off". The dance is designed for "as many as will", meaning that this simple sequence would probably have been repeated until every couple had performed it. Aaron Macks, who compared some of the Playford's later dances with the versions of the same dances surviving in the Ward Dance Manuscript, found that the Playford versions were significantly simplified compared to the manuscript.[38] Such simplicity is a double-edged sword: more experienced dancers would probably find the dance tedious, while beginners would benefit from the easy combinations. Since the same dances existed in more complex versions, it is tempting to see the simplified forms as an indication that the Playfords were developing already existing material for less skilled dancers.

---

[38] A. MACKS, "The Ward Dance Manuscript: A new source for seventeenth-century English country dance", *Harvard Library Bulletin* 27.3 (2018), pp. 141-166, at p. 145.

It is also possible that the audience had more need for readability in the music notation than in the dance descriptions. After all, dance depends on music, and even the clearest description of the steps is useless if the musician is unable to play the accompanying tune. Indeed, for many people the only way to secure musical accompaniment would have been to play it themselves or invite an amateur friend to play: not everyone had the means to hire a professional. John Playford was a skilled amateur musician himself, so his personal preferences may also have tended towards focusing on the musical side.

Conclusion

It seems clear that it is the readability of the music notation that drives the format of the page, rather than the accuracy and ease of use of the dance descriptions. The innovative table format for describing the dances was watered down to some degree already fairly early, with the addition of more songs where the notation spread onto two or more lines. Perhaps this was simply a learning process: in 1650, Playford had only just begun working as a publisher of music, having started his career printing political tracts.

In any case, the tabular format must have been labour-intensive to produce. Using movable type to print music was a challenge in itself, and only specialised music publishers were up to the task. Although the Playfords were precisely such specialists, adding tables to the mix must have added to the workload, since getting the tables to align was demonstrably tricky (see the section 'The Dance Descriptions' above). If it was possible for readers to follow the dance descriptions without this form of additional visual organisation, surely it would have been tempting to leave the tables out, especially when there was a constant call for new tunes, but the dances themselves kept getting simpler.

In this chapter, I have examined the evolving graphic practices of an early modern music publisher faced with the challenging task of presenting dance in written form. The gradual erosion of the table format in the different editions of John Playford's famous dance manual shows the trial-and-error nature of evolving conventions. Similar analyses would be a fruitful area for further work: there appears to be very little research on the linguistic and visual aspects of dance manuals for now, and the same applies to other instructional genres dealing with movement.

Graphic Elements in Early Printed Grammar Books

JANNE SKAFFARI and JUKKA TYRKKÖ

Introduction

When we look into a grammar book today – be it a textbook for beginners or a descriptive grammar intended for use at university – we typically expect more than just prose descriptions and instructions: the book is likely to contain a variety of tables and perhaps other visualisations explaining patterns of grammatical structures. Such graphic devices are not a feature of the grammars of the last few generations only but can be traced back to the early modern period (*c.* 1500 to *c.* 1700) and beyond. In this chapter, we consider grammar books from the first century of English-language grammars of English. In addition to analyses of a mid-seventeenth-century book by Jeremiah Wharton and a grammar from the end of the seventeenth century by Joseph Aickin, we also make observations about some of their predecessors and contemporaries.[1]

While there is no shortage of studies on the history of English grammars,

---

[1] J. WHARTON, *The English Grammar* (London, 1655); 1st edn 1654. J. AICKIN, *The English Grammar* (London, 1693).

....

Graphic Practices and Literacies in the History of English, ed. Matti PEIKOLA, Jukka TYRKKÖ, and Mari-Liisa VARILA, *Utrecht Studies in Medieval Literacy*, 61 (Turnhout: Brepols, 2025), pp. 281-307.

BREPOLS PUBLISHERS   DOI 10.1484/M.USML-EB.5.143830

grammatical theories and grammarians in the early and particularly late modern periods,[2] few have paid attention to the graphic or visual dimension of grammar books.[3] Graphic features are not, however, in any way irrelevant. For example, Hedwig Gwosdek points out that in the visual arrangement of early Latin grammars, information about nominal and verbal morphology "leaps to the eye".[4] Of the early English grammars, Ian Michael notes that the most essential content – for learning by heart – could be printed in a larger size and thus separated from "amplifications".[5] Such an arrangement thus served a practical pedagogical purpose. However, a scholarly discussion of the layout of grammar books may mention footnotes containing additional explanations, rules, or references to Latin, and manicules pointing to important content, but not discuss tables or other graphic devices.[6] In general, it is the eighteenth-century grammars that seem to have received more attention from scholars than those of the previous century, perhaps at least partly because there were more of them: for example, the number of new titles and reprinted grammars in the 1710s is roughly twice

---

[2] For example: I. MICHAEL, *English Grammatical Categories and the Tradition to 1800* (Cambridge, 1970); E. VORLAT, *The Development of English Grammatical Theory, 1586-1737: with Special Reference to the Theory of Parts of Speech* (Leuven, 1975); J. ALGEO, "The earliest English grammars", in: *Historical and Editorial Studies in Medieval and Early Modern English for Johan Gerritsen*, ed. M.-J. ARN and H. WIRTJES (Groningen, 1985), pp. 191-207; U. DONS, *Descriptive Adequacy of Early Modern English Grammars* (Berlin, 2004); I. TIEKEN-BOON VAN OSTADE, "Grammars, grammarians and grammar writing: An introduction", in: *Grammars, Grammarians and Grammar-Writing in Eighteenth-Century England*, ed. I. TIEKEN-BOON VAN OSTADE (Berlin, 2008), pp. 1-14; I. TIEKEN-BOON VAN OSTADE, *The Bishop's Grammar: Robert Lowth and the Rise of Prescriptivism* (Oxford, 2011); and M.V. DOMÍNGUEZ-RODRÍGUEZ and A. RODRÍGUEZ-ÁLVAREZ, "'The reader is desired to observe ...': Metacomments in the prefaces to English school grammars of the eighteenth century", *Journal of Historical Pragmatics* 16.1 (2015), pp. 86-108.

[3] See J. TYRKKÖ, "Notes on eighteenth-century dictionary grammars", *Transactions of the Philological Society* 111.2 (2013), pp. 179-201, at pp. 190-192. For Latin grammars, see R. SCHRIRE, "Shifting paradigms: Ideas, materiality and the changing shape of grammar in the Renaissance", *Journal of the Warburg and Courtauld Institutes* 84 (2021), pp. 1-31.

[4] *Lily's Grammar of Latin in English: An Introduction of the Eyght Partes of Speche, and the Construction of the Same*, ed. H. GWOSDEK (Oxford, 2013), p. 67. SCHRIRE, "Shifting paradigms", p. 1, notes that grammars of Latin typically made use of linear arrangements until the Renaissance.

[5] I. MICHAEL, *The Teaching of English: From the Sixteenth Century to 1870* (Cambridge, 1987), pp. 320-321.

[6] E. VORLAT, "On the history of English teaching grammars", in: *Sprachtheorien der Neuzeit* III/2, ed. P. SCHMITTER (Tübingen, 2007), pp. 500-525, at pp. 518-519.

that of the 1680s or the 1690s.[7] The start of the rapid rise in new grammars has been traced to the second quarter of the eighteenth century.[8]

Our study focuses on the purpose and use of graphic elements in grammar books: which topics were deemed to benefit from, or deserve, information visualisation? The particular graphic features we investigate organise content so that it stands out graphically from the justified body text: thus, rather than investigating differences in font size (see above) or occasional switches to blackletter, we observe the use of such graphic devices as tables and diagrams in connection with particular grammar topics. To answer the question above, we also need to consider the range of graphic devices used and to understand what the books that were called grammars contained. The first of these points is the main concern of the present volume. As for the second point, research on early grammars has shown that the contents of the books covered more ground than grammars do today.[9] We will see that in addition to inflectional morphology and syntax – which to today's readers represent 'grammar proper', unlike "the more peripheral topics"[10] – the books discussed, for example, word-formation, sound-letter correspondence and versification.[11] A further question relates to graphic literacy and expectations thereof: that grammars were often marketed as learning tools for young learners would suggest that their graphic practices were pedagogically useful and easy to understand, especially with the help of schoolmasters teaching grammar. It is therefore necessary to consider supporting metadiscourse and the embedding of the graphic devices in the prose of the grammar.

This chapter first briefly introduces the history of grammar writing in the early modern period and then the main primary sources. We will subsequently present the findings from our case studies, also considering the graphic devices in selected contemporaries and predecessors of Wharton's and Aickin's grammars. The last section before the conclusion reviews the findings and further discusses their potential implications, also touching upon matters of graphic literacy.

---

[7] TIEKEN-BOON VAN OSTADE, *Grammars, Grammarians*, p. 2.
[8] MICHAEL, *Teaching of English*, p. 12. Rote learning was important in early modern education; for a recent overview of education and pedagogy in the period, see A. MÄKILÄHDE, *The Philological-Pragmatic Approach: A Study of Language Choice and Code-Switching in Early Modern English School Performances*. PhD thesis, University of Turku (Turku, 2019), pp. 21-25. See also SCHRIRE, "Shifting paradigms", pp. 26-28.
[9] For example, MICHAEL, *Teaching of English*; VORLAT, "On the history".
[10] MICHAEL, *Teaching of English*, p. 317.
[11] Syntax was, however, "poorly treated" in the early books (VORLAT, "On the history", p. 505).

Grammar Books in the Early Modern Period

Although our focus is on the seventeenth century, there were of course grammars also in the pre-modern or pre-print period: for example, Ælfric's († 1010) efforts in producing English-language materials for learning Latin are well-known.[12] Description of English was not, however, a major concern until the vernacular surpassed Latin as the language of a range of genres from the end of the Middle English period onwards, and the printing press made more texts available to an increasing number of readers. As part of the standardisation of the vernacular, codification[13] – which in concrete terms relates to the publication and use of dictionaries as well as grammars – is an important feature of the Early Modern English period. The first printed dictionaries of English were bilingual, including William Caxton's English-French one from 1480; many early grammars of English were not monolingual either, but written in Latin. The association of English grammars with Latin is clearly visible in our data as well.

Latin grammars, although not within the scope of the present chapter, had of course been available before grammars of English appeared, and those involved with writing the latter must have been familiar with the former; Michael underlines that "[t]he influence of Latin pervades every aspect of the English grammars".[14] Extremely influential was the grammar by Lily and Colet, which became obligatory in teaching Latin in the mid-sixteenth century.[15] This grammar, attributed to William Lily, contains an introductory part in English for the younger learners and a Latin part for more advanced learners.[16] Later in the sixteenth century, in 1586, William Bullokar published his *Pamphlet for Grammar*, recognised as the first English-language grammar of English.[17] However, the idea of writing about the vernacular in the vernacular itself did not instantly supplant the more traditional practice in learned writing, as new grammars of English were still published in Latin in the next 99 years. Particularly notable

---

[12] See, for example, MICHAEL, *English Grammatical Categories*, p. 153; *Lily's Grammar*, pp. 30-41.

[13] Since E. HAUGEN, "Dialect, language, nation", *American Anthropologist* 68.4 (1966), pp. 922-935.

[14] MICHAEL, *Teaching of English*, p. 318.

[15] V. SALMON, *Language and Society in Early Modern England: Selected Essays 1981-1994* (Amsterdam, 1996), pp. 13-14.

[16] *Lily's Grammar*, pp.vii-x.

[17] For example, VORLAT, *Development*, p. 12; DONS, *Descriptive Adequacy*, p. 13. Gwosdek (*Lily's Grammar*, pp. 133-139) traces the impact of Lily's Latin grammar on Bullokar's English one.

are the *Grammatica Linguæ Anglicanæ* by John Wallis (1653), and the last grammar of English in Latin by Christopher Cooper in 1685.[18]

After Bullokar, the seventeenth century was marked by small but steady increases in the number of grammars of English produced and reprinted – the 1660s being the only notable exception in this trend – but the numbers remained small, with never more than three new grammars or four reprints per decade.[19] From the 1630s onwards, the English-language grammar books outnumbered those in Latin, and the need for such grammar books must have increased in the second half of the century, when English started to emerge as a subject in schools.[20] The two case studies in the present chapter focus on books from the latter period.

The grammars of English are known to have resembled those of Latin in many ways. In Michael's words, the grammar of Latin "*was* grammar",[21] which suggests that other languages could not differ from it. Vorlat describes the grammar writers of English until the mid-1650s as "beginners; they have only Latin to go by".[22] Early vernacular grammars were thus modelled after Latin grammars, and they also contained, for example, orthographical information. The Latinate structure of English grammars and their relationship to Latin grammar in terms of content have been acknowledged for example by John Algeo, who underlines the importance of "contrastive grammar" in these books: the early modern grammars of the vernacular were to benefit the students by priming them with the same grammatical concepts they would encounter when learning to read and translate Latin texts.[23] English grammars were thus not meant to be tools for learning or analysing English alone. However, John Wallis wished to write about the structures of English without modelling his grammar on those of Latin.[24] We shall return to the Latin connections in the Findings and Discussion sections below.

---

[18] DONS, *Descriptive Adequacy*, p. 16.
[19] TIEKEN-BOON VAN OSTADE, *Grammars, Grammarians*, p. 2, drawing on the bibliography by R.C. Alston.
[20] DONS, *Descriptive Adequacy*, p. 6.
[21] MICHAEL, *English Grammatical Categories*, p. 492; original italics.
[22] VORLAT, *Development*, p. 10.
[23] ALGEO, "The earliest English grammars", pp. 202-203. See also, for example, SALMON, *Language and Society*, p. 14. In the eighteenth century, Robert Lowth, an influential prescriptivist, had the same English-before-Latin motivation for his grammar (TIEKEN-BOON VAN OSTADE, *Bishop's Grammar*, pp. 54-55).
[24] DONS, *Descriptive Adequacy*, p. 13; VORLAT, "On the history", pp. 506-506. VORLAT, *Development*, actually divides her general discussion of pre-1738 grammars of English into two parts, 'pre-Wallis' and 'Wallis and thereafter'.

Material and Methods

As it was in the second quarter of the seventeenth century that English grammars of English began to outnumber those in Latin, we have selected two books from the last two quarters of that century for close reading and analysis, one from the beginning of the half-century, the other from the end. Both are called, aptly, *The English Grammar*, and contain a wealth of tables, diagrams, and / or other comparable graphic elements, a requisite feature for our study. The earlier book was written by Jeremiah Wharton and published in 1654 (reprinted in 1655), the later one by Joseph Aickin in 1693.[25] Both were printed in London, originally published privately ("for the author") and contain roughly the same number of pages. We have examined the books as image files downloaded from the Early English Books Online database.[26]

To compare the choices made by Wharton and Aickin with those of their contemporaries and predecessors, we have consulted another four grammars from the seventeenth century. These also include two Latin grammars of English, those of Cooper and Wallis.[27]

Wharton

Jeremiah Wharton became a Bachelor of Arts at Cambridge in 1625 and a Master of Arts in 1633;[28] his grammar was published twenty years after his graduation. *The English-Grammar: Or, The Institution of Letters, Syllables, and Words in the English-Tongue* (on the title page of the 1654 book) contains 109 pages, preceded by front matter (from the title page to the table of contents), including an eight-page preface called 'To the Courteous Reader'. It is not until Chapter 7 that Wharton begins addressing what we would call grammatical topics (see below), after six chapters on letters, spelling, and pronunciation. Chapters 8 and 9 focus on word-formation, while the final chapter is on

---

[25] With "[a]nother issue" in the same year, according to R.C. ALSTON, *A Bibliography of the English Language from the Invention of Printing to the Year 1800. A Corrected Reprint of Volumes I-X* (Ilkley, 1974), p. 11.

[26] For analysing Wharton, we used the file of the 1655 reprint in EEBO because of its better quality. Images produced by ProQuest as part of Early English Books Online, <www.proquest.com>.

[27] For a full list of grammars of the seventeenth century, in English and in Latin, see ALSTON, *Bibliography*.

[28] R.D. SMITH, "Wharton, Jeremiah", in ODNB (Oxford, 2004).

punctuation. The last 21 pages present an appendix with sample sentences containing (near) homophones, such as *deer / dear* and *jointer / jointure*. Not untypically, the book was aimed at young learners, particularly those who had not yet begun to learn Latin; foreigners were also identified as a target audience. In his preface, the author specifies that for the former audience it will be easier to become familiar with grammatical terms and rules in the mother tongue than in Latin; this is a common motivation for writers of English grammars. The latter audience, Wharton argues, will see that English is less complicated than Latin and Greek because of its lack of "variation" (inflections), but also that it is not a "barbarous, confused, and irregular" language.[29] For such "strangers", the title page claims, this book is "the most certain Guide, that ever yet was extant". Wharton lists several benefits for using his book, only one of which is directly connected with grammar proper; more prominent here seem to be the benefits related to word-formation. The link to learning Latin is also highlighted.

Wharton was not exactly original in his work: Dons notes that he compiled material for his book from various sources.[30] Wharton does acknowledge that his work was influenced by other grammarians, and he names Richard Mulcaster and Edmund Coote from the previous century, and Alexander Gill, Ben Jonson, and Charles Butler from the first half of his own.[31] Of these, we can only explore Butler (1633), a choice motivated by the close relationship between Butler's and Wharton's books.

Aickin

A little more is known about Joseph Aickin, the author of *The English Grammar: Or, the English Tongue Reduced to Grammatical Rules* (1693). He had a Master's degree and worked as a schoolmaster in London. It appears that Aickin moved to Ireland sometime before the grammar was published, because the title page notes that Aickin was "lately one of the masters of the Free-School in London Dery". Some of his other published work suggests that he was familiar with teaching Greek in addition to English and Latin.[32]

---

[29] WHARTON, *English Grammar*, A6r-v.
[30] DONS, *Descriptive Adequacy*, p. 14. Assessing the originality or quality of the grammars is outside the scope of our study.
[31] Their surnames are printed in the margin of A7r.
[32] R.D. SMITH, "Aickin, Joseph", in the ODNB.

Aickin's book is in many ways similar to Wharton's and other late-seventeenth-century grammars. Both the title page and the preface focus on children as the primary audience, though "youth and those of riper years" are also mentioned on the title page. The objective of teaching English grammar "without the assistance of Latine" is likewise stated there, and elaborated on in the eleven-page preface. This feature was common in the prefaces of school grammars, perhaps at least partly because the grammars' primary readership were schoolmasters, whom the grammarians naturally wanted to address.[33]

The book is divided into two major parts. The first 76 pages concern orthography, while the following 34 cover etymology, syntax, and prosody; this arrangement with four main topics was typical.[34] The orthographic section begins with the letters of the alphabet, their forms, and associated sounds, and then moves on to listing syllables. Words of one syllable, diphthongs, spelling rules and polysyllabic words are discussed with extensive tables (see below). The first part ends with punctuation, numbers and abbreviations. The first section of the second part of the book, on etymology – which at this time covered, importantly, parts of speech as well as word-formation and word provenance[35] – begins with a 17-page introduction to word classes (parts of speech), numbers, grammatical gender, prepositions, adjectival comparisons, pronouns, verbs, and adverbs. Dons notes that Aickin was "clearly influenced by the works of Wallis and Cooper",[36] both of whom – along with Wharton – are mentioned in a one-page long congratulatory greeting in the front matter, written by a friend called "S.H.".[37] Despite still publishing their grammars of English in Latin, both Wallis and Cooper were progressive in their views of English and how grammar should be taught. The second part of the book ends with prosody, taking the reader back to pronunciation and the rules of poetical versification.

Findings

After a brief introduction to visualising grammatical information and the challenges in analysing it, we will describe graphic features in the two main

---

[33] See DOMÍNGUEZ-RODRÍGUEZ and A. RODRÍGUEZ-ÁLVAREZ, "The reader", for such metadiscourse in prefaces to eighteenth-century grammars.
[34] VORLAT, "On the history", p. 504.
[35] MICHAEL, *English Grammatical Categories*, p. 185.
[36] DONS, *Descriptive Adequacy*, p. 17.
[37] AICKIN, *English Grammar*, A2r.

sources and then proceed to the broader context, with overviews of four other seventeenth-century grammar books.

On the Graphic Devices Used

When present-day readers open a grammar book, they may well expect the book to contain information not only in prose form but also arranged into *tables*. This type of arrangement is not uncommon in the seventeenth-century materials, but the tables look different: while columns and rows can be discerned, they are not always realised with horizontal and vertical lines or *rules*, nor is there often a frame for the table as a whole, but white space – though sometimes not much of it – surrounding the content of each 'cell' suffices to separate units. Due to the missing rules or grids, at least some of these tables could be regarded as *lists*, but we follow Aickin's practice and often refer to them as tables, since the tabular layout visually distinguishes them from any sequence of coordinated items laid out as prose within the body text. Therefore, the term *table* does not necessarily suggest that the horizontal and vertical axes should be utilised together in making sense of the information provided (as in Table 1 at the end of this chapter). From a present-day perspective, some list-like or vaguely tabular units could also be regarded as *diagrams* with *braces* (curly brackets; see images below). In addition to tables, diagrams and braces, we occasionally offer some observations on actual lists embedded in the paragraph and page layout. Some of them are lists of words printed in italics within paragraphs, which somewhat stand out from their surroundings; others are very short paragraphs, sometimes numbered, which are also easy to discern when viewing a page, although no additional graphic elements, such as rules or braces, are used.

It is important to note that graphic arrangement sometimes defies systematic classification: even within one book, a graphic or visual category with a particular definition which seems workable at first may turn out less than adequate in some subsequent chapters. We therefore do not intend to provide hard and fast definitions here. For example, as noted above, some gridless and unruled 'tables' – especially if they do not seem to have a rectangular shape – could also be called 'diagrams', particularly if they feature braces. We have attempted a very rough quantitative estimate of the frequency of graphic devices in connection with Wharton, but our focus is for the most part qualitative.

Tracing their history to Antiquity, Ferguson divides *tabulae* – broadly understood, ranging from charts to maps – into figural and non-figural, the former containing images, the latter involving numbers, words, or brackets.[38] Overall, the two grammars mainly have non-figural graphic devices: the tables and braced diagrams typically contain words and phrases, not images. However, we will show some exceptions to this, particularly in Aickin's grammar, which includes pictorial elements within some tables. Examining the history of non-figural and figural devices is outside the scope of this chapter.[39]

Wharton

Despite the difficulties in labelling and distinguishing between the different types of graphic devices discussed above, it is clear that Wharton's grammar is quite rich in such devices. Even the most casual reader is likely to observe table-like devices but without borders or grids; what could be called diagrams with braces (used in pairs or alone); and also various lists. Some of these appear together (see below), and a table or a list may contain a single brace added for clarity at some point (p. 66 is a case in point). While the choice of device and, more broadly, the need to visualise information must relate to the grammar topic discussed, the use of the table format and the like may also have been motivated by saving space: too much unused space on many pages would have made the book longer and therefore ultimately more expensive to print and to purchase, which may have made a table (or a list with two or more columns) an attractive alternative, as better use would be made of the space available.[40] Some of these choices may not have been the author's but the printer's.

Of the ten chapters in Wharton, only two are without tables and braces of the kind we are mainly concerned with here: chapters 3 and 4. However, chapter 3 contains a page of sentences providing examples, usually one line each, which looks like a list, even if it does not deviate from the paragraph layout,

---

[38] S. FERGUSON, "System and schema: Tabulae of the fifteenth to eighteenth centuries", *Princeton University Library Chronicle* 49 (1987), pp. 8-30, at pp. 11-13. See also W. SCASE, this volume.

[39] For an overview of different classifications of graphic devices and a proposal for a system designed for classifying Early Modern English data, see S. RUOKKEINEN, A. LIIRA, M.-L. VARILA, O. NORBLAD, and M. PEIKOLA, "Developing a classification model for graphic devices in early printed books", *Studia Neophilologica* 96.1 (2024), pp. 69-93. For a brief history of the transition from the linear to the tabular in Latin grammars, see SHRIRE, "Shifting paradigms", pp. 4-20.

[40] See A. LIIRA, M. PEIKOLA and M. KAARTINEN, this volume.

Graphic Elements in Early Printed Grammar Books 291

and chapter 4, on silent letters, is basically a list with each short paragraph beginning with a specific silent vowel or consonant. Both chapters are very short (only about five pages altogether) and deal with discrepancies between orthography and pronunciation. This broad topic alone, however, is not enough to account for not using graphic devices, as the slightly longer chapter 5 covers a related topic but is approximately one third tables, and graphic devices make up 1.5 pages of chapter 6, which also contains short sample sentences laid out as paragraphs.

The longest section in Wharton is chapter 7, which makes up almost one quarter of the book (pp. 32-60). It presents Wharton's description of the parts of speech: nouns (including adjectives as well as "substantives"), pronouns, verbs, participles (as a separate word class), adverbs, conjunctions, prepositions and interjections, discussed in this order. This division and order of the parts of speech hails from the Latin tradition; both Wharton's and Aickin's categories represent Michael's System 1, "the 'purest' of the Latin systems", along with those used in another ten seventeenth-century grammars, and previously Bullokar and Lily.[41] Part of speech as a concept is the only grammatical one mentioned by Wharton in the preface where he motivates the reader to make use of his book. The analysis below is mainly concerned with chapter 7. Altogether, this chapter contains tables or braces on 16 of its 28.5 pages; measured in lines, the tables cover more than five pages, and the share of diagrams with braces is similar. In addition, there are italicised lists within paragraphs that altogether correspond to more than one page, and other list-type layout solutions make up three pages. In sum, nearly two thirds of chapter 7 thus deviate from the unmarked paragraph and page layout. Counting the number of separate graphic devices is not feasible since sometimes a feature could be viewed either as a device in its own right or as part of a much larger element containing, for example, two or more tables united by a broader shared topic (see Fig. 1, which is more a series of devices than a single table). The large proportion of the space occupied by various non-prose-paragraph elements does, however, illustrate how prominent the elements are in this chapter.

The word class with the most graphic devices is that of verbs, which display variation in conjugations and in combinations with auxiliaries (as in Fig. 1). The longest units in the chapter are tables of irregular verbs: nearly four pages. The first of them, on pp. 49-50, contains five vertical rules with two different functions (Fig. 2): the purpose of the one in the middle seems to be to separate the two main parts of the table laid out side by side (thus saving space),

[41] MICHAEL, *English Grammatical Categories*, p. 214.

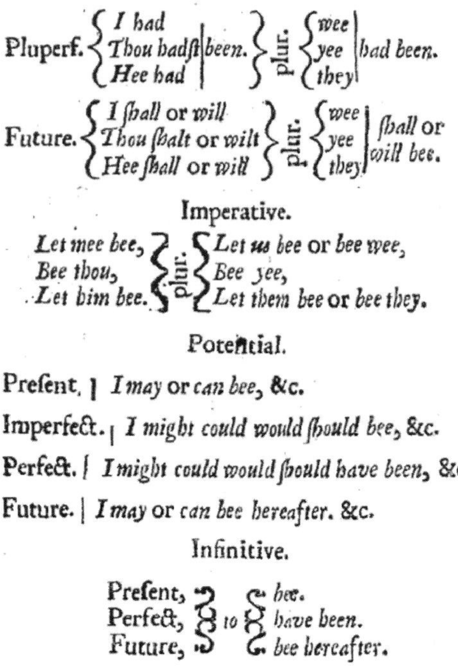

Pluperf. I had / Thou hadſt / Hee had | been. plur. wee / yee / they | had been.

Future. I ſhall or will / Thou ſhalt or wilt / Hee ſhall or will plur. wee / yee / they | ſhall or will bee.

Imperative.

Let mee bee, / Bee thou, / Let him bee. plur. Let us bee or bee wee, / Bee yee, / Let them bee or bee they.

Potential.

Preſent. | I may or can bee, &c.

Imperfect. | I might could would ſhould bee, &c.

Perfect. | I might could would ſhould have been, &c.

Future. | I may or can bee hereafter. &c.

Infinitive.

Preſent, / Perfect, / Future, to bee. / have been. / bee hereafter.

Fig. 1 Variation in the arrangement of the indicative, imperative, potential and infinitive moods (Wharton, p. 47) under the general header 'A Verb Neuter with his Moods, Tenses, and Persons'. From the British Library collection. Image published with permission of Pro-Quest. Further reproduction is prohibited without permission.

while on either side there is a pair of lines, and between them the words "is formed" are printed vertically in the middle of the column; on opposite sides there are the base form of the verb and its past tense form. Thus, the first pair of verb forms in the table reads "[of] *make* is formed *made*", and so on. The five rules appear to distinguish six columns, which do not have headings. The rectangular impression makes this more a table than a diagram.

In order to understand the graphic practices better, we may attempt some form-to-function mapping here.[42] Similar to Fig. 2, vertical rules separate – also elsewhere in the chapter – lists of structures from words or phrases shared between them, so that repetition is avoided. For example, on p. 48, "I am", "Thou art", and "Hee is" are printed on different lines but share "loved", printed after a vertical rule. This form – i.e., a vertical line – can also function as a separator (as in the middle of Fig. 2) when space is saved by printing the same type of information side by side rather than consecutively. Instead of or in addition to vertical lines, many graphic devices show braces, which seem to outnumber vertical rules in chapter 7. These braces seem to serve at least three functions. Firstly, a single brace may link a larger unit, concept or category with its constituents or sub-

[42] See, for example, R. CARROLL, M. PEIKOLA, H. SALMI, M.-L. VARILA, J. SKAFFARI, and R. HILTUNEN, "Pragmatics on the page: Visual text in late medieval English books", *European Journal of English Studies* 17.1 (2013), pp. 54-71, at p. 64.

Of a Verb. 45

From this general rule many Verbs are excepted, for of

make	made	ſpend	ſpent	
lead	led	wend	went	
read	red	lean	lent	
ſpread	ſpred	mean	ment	
mete	met	ſel	ſold	
ſweat	ſwet	tel	told	
leav	left	ſlide	ſlid	
bereav	*bereft	ſtride	ſtrid	*bereaved 3
bleed	bled	pitch	*pitht	*pitched 3
breed	bred	catch	caught	
feed	fed	teach	taught	
ſpeed	ſped	fetch	faught	
flee	fled	ſeek	ſought	
meet	met	beſeech	beſought	
feel	felt	bring	brought	
ſpil	ſpilt	think	thought	
ſmel	*ſmelt	work	wrought	*ſmelled 2.
keep	kept.	buy	bought	
creep	crept	gird	*girt	*girded 3.
weep	wept	mis	miſt	
ſleep	ſlept	kis	*kiſt	*kiſſed 3.
ſweep	ſwept	wis	wiſt	
bend	bent	binde	bound	
lend	lent	finde	found	
rend	rent	grinde	ground	
ſend	ſent	winde	wound	
ſhend	ſhent	ſtand	ſtood	

is formed — is formed

E ſit

Fig. 2 Irregular verbs in two main columns, with base form and "imperfect tens" linked with the vertically printed "is formed" (Wharton, p. 49). "Of a Verb", the phrase at the top, is a running head, not part of the graphic device. From the British Library collection. Image published with permission of ProQuest. Further reproduction is prohibited without permission.

types (for example, "A Pronoun is of three sorts" on p. 39 is followed by a single left-facing brace in front of the three categories "1 Personal, 2 Demonstrative, 3 Relative", each printed on a line of its own). Secondly, the purpose of a pair of braces may be to link together a series of forms whose grammatical label is presented in front of the left brace (see top of Fig. 1). The right brace may also double as a separator between two categories laid out side by side (see "Imperative" in Fig. 1, where the right brace – potentially confusingly – seems to group together also singular forms, although the label says "plur."). Thirdly, an inward-looking pair of braces can also be used around a shared word or term, similarly to the pair of tall vertical rules in Fig. 2. Moreover, curly brackets, particularly the right-hand brace, also seem to be decorative elements; some of them are very ornate compared to the majority of the braces, which have a more straightforward appearance. This is illustrated by the last pair of braces in Fig. 1. Finally, braces do not seem to be used for actual horizontal tree-diagrams branching out to the right but could sometimes be replaced with vertical rules without losing clarity or informativeness.

A noteworthy feature of the graphic devices in Wharton's grammar is that he does not refer to them as such in the preface or the text. His devices often do

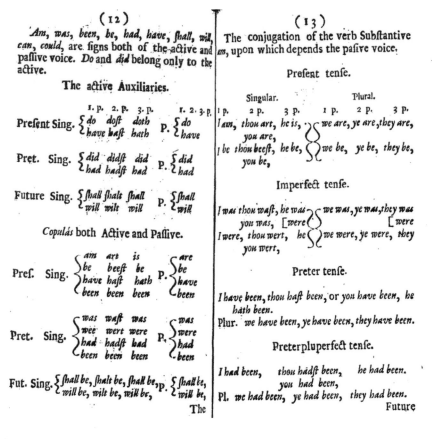

Fig. 3 Auxiliaries and tenses (Aickin, Part II, pp. 12-13). From the Lambeth Palace Library collection. Image published with permission of ProQuest. Further reproduction is prohibited without permission.

not have actual titles or headings, but they simply follow the preceding paragraph or sentence, not always ending in a full stop but in a colon or a comma, as if the sentence continued without interruption, only laid out differently.[43] Sometimes, however, the previous sentence could be viewed as a heading, as in Fig. 2.

---

[43] Such an arrangement – placing core content in a table without treating it separately in the body text – raises the question of whether these devices can be called *paratextual* "constituents [...] that serve to reinforce and support" the grammar at all (DOMÍNGUEZ-RODRÍGUEZ and A. RODRÍGUEZ-ÁLVAREZ, "The reader", p. 89).

Aickin

Aickin's grammar features lists, tables, braces, diagrams and imprints of a woodcut. Of these, the preface mentions the long lists of words and syllables and the illustrated tables. In general, Aickin has a wider range of graphic devices than Wharton, but there are many similarities as well.

The core grammar appears in the second part of Aickin's book, which is much shorter than the first. Its first graphic device (p. 2) introduces the word classes in four unruled columns, the first one specifying "Four which change their endings", followed by a brace and, in a somewhat larger size, a four-line list of "Noun, Pronoun, Verb, Participle". The remaining two columns similarly introduce the other four parts of speech and their shared morphological characteristics. On p. 6, the two graphic elements used next to two columns listing six noun and prepositional phrases in the singular and plural, corresponding to the Latin nominal cases, look more like vertical rules than braces. While four short braces accompany the first and second-person personal pronouns (p. 9), the graphically richest grammatical categories are the verbs in chapter 3 (see Fig. 3). Unruled tables of "active Auxiliaries" and the verb *be*, arranged by tense and person, contain braces with "Sing." or "P." on the left and the relevant verb forms or verb phrases on the right, whereas the inward-looking pairs of braces between various pronoun subject + *be* combinations rather seem to separate the singular and plural groups. The "Preterpluperfect" and "Future tense" are printed in three columns without rules or braces.

Within the grammar proper, Aickin's use of tables or diagrams with braces is thus relatively limited and straightforward, with the exception of the next two tables on conjugation, which are included as an insert (see Fig. 4). The table shows the singular and plural verb forms for each person in the active and the passive voice, indicative mood, "Preterit Time", and imperative mood. The arrangement of the first table suggests a possible conflict between what was intended to be included, and what could be practically fit on the page. Two of the five 'rows' end with a brace and a sign for "etc.", rather than following through the whole conjugation schema. In the second to last line, we see the auxiliary *been* spelled as "bin", this variant possibly preferred to the other form used three times on the same line in order for the final brace to align vertically with the one above. The braces are not explicitly mentioned or explained.

Instead of the use of braces, a possibly more striking feature in Aickin's grammar – and certainly so if we compare it with Wharton's – is the inclusion of figural devices: that there are three separate tables containing the "Symboli-

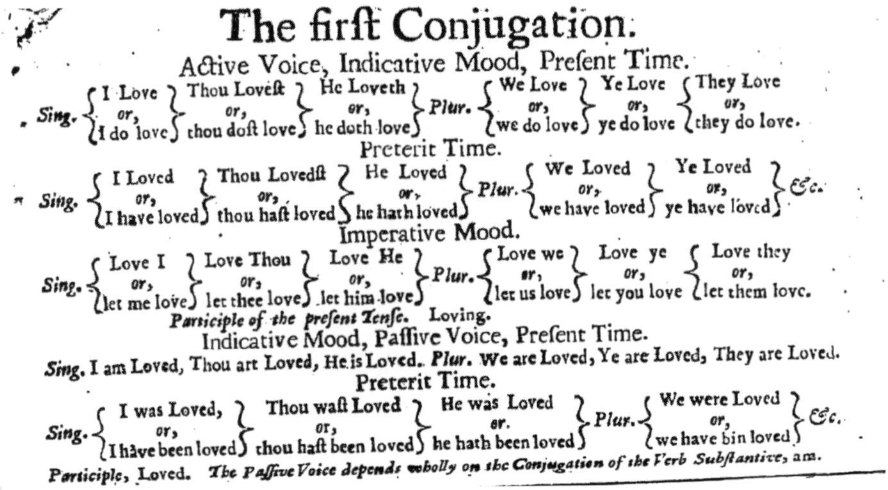

Fig. 4 The first conjugation in Aickin's Part II, between pp. 14-15. From the Lambeth Palace Library collection. Image published with the permission of ProQuest. Further reproduction is prohibited without permission.

cal Alphabet", that is, tables intended to teach children the connection between letters and sounds by associating each letter with a small image of a familiar concept, such as an animal or natural phenomenon. The largest of them appears quite early in the first part of the book (Fig. 5).

On p. 66, close to the last of the tables in the grammar, Aickin refers to "*Commenius's Orbis visibilium pictus*" as the inspiration behind the tables. This is a reference to John Amos Comenius's *Orbis sensualium pictus*, an illustrated children's textbook first published in 1658 in Latin and German, and almost immediately after publication translated into several European languages; the English edition was published in 1659. Comenius (1592-1670) was a Czech educator whose new principles of humane and inspirational teaching gained widespread attention, and the *Orbis pictus* was reprinted and translated around the Continent for well over a century.[44] Aickin notes that he planned to use more images in his grammar, but that the printing proved too difficult and he will leave that task of producing a picture book to "a more ingenious Person to effect".[45] He was not, however, a pioneer in including tables with images in

---

[44] See M.E. AGUIRRE, "Teaching through texts and pictures. A contribution of Jan Amos Comenius to education", *Revista Electrónica de Investigación Educativa* 3.1 (2001).

[45] AICKIN, *English Grammar*, p. 66.

Graphic Elements in Early Printed Grammar Books   297

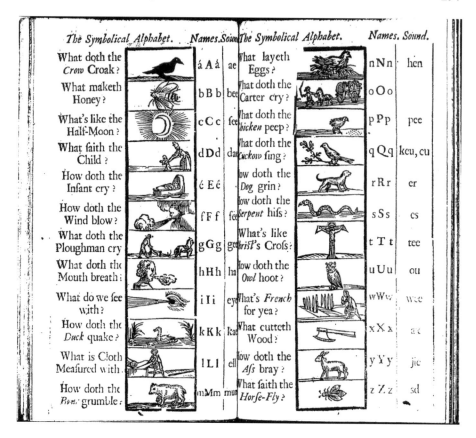

Fig. 5   Symbolic alphabet in Aickin, Part I, between pp. 16-17. From the Lambeth Palace Library collection. Image published with permission of ProQuest. Further reproduction is prohibited without permission.

an English grammar, as we shall see below. In addition to the three alphabetical tables, Aickin's book includes two imprints of the same woodcut of a seated schoolmaster, a young boy standing in front of him, and two pupils seated in the background. Both images introduce short sections, one at the beginning of the book and the other at the end, in which the schoolmaster and the young student engage in dialogue.

In addition to the woodcuts and the alphabet tables, another graphic feature of note in the first part of Aickin's grammar is that there are several extremely long unruled tables of syllables. For example, a series of tables listing syllables, double consonants, terminating syllables, and so forth, in up to ten columns begins on p. 19 and continues until p. 30 in Part I of the book, and tables of disyllables and trisyllables begin at the bottom of p. 54 and occupy the next ten pages, each page listing four columns of syllables in alphabetical order. In the preface, Aickin notes that one of the tables contains 1360 syllables, which the reader, presumably a schoolmaster or parent, "must cause the children to learn perfectly".[46] Like many other grammarians, including Bullokar over a hundred years earlier, Aickin believed that the system of English spelling was problematic in many ways, and according to the long discussions in the preface and in the body text, it would be more effective to teach spelling and pronunciation using syllables, rather than by printing hyphens at syllable boundaries, as many contemporary spelling books did.

Other Grammars Consulted for Comparison

After these detailed case studies of the two grammars, what follows is an overview of another four books and their graphic devices. With Wharton, the most obvious grammar for comparison is by Charles Butler, acknowledged by the author himself; it was published approximately twenty years earlier.[47] A similar temporal distance can be found between Aickin and another grammar book intended for young learners, by Thomas Lye.[48] Lye's system of word classes is similar to Wharton's as well as Aickin's, while Charles Butler's is simpler and quite different from its contemporaries.[49] Of Latin grammars of English, we consult the important book by John Wallis and the very late one by Christopher Cooper;[50] the former's parts of speech are the sole member of Michael's System 25, while the latter's represent System 28, although in an unclear manner.[51] It is noteworthy that like Wharton's and Aickin's, many of these grammars were reprinted several times. Reprinting signals popularity, and

---

[46] AICKIN, *English Grammar*, p. A6v.

[47] C. BUTLER, *English Grammar* (Oxford, 1633); the image below is from the 1634 reprint.

[48] T. LYE, *The Childs Delight. Together with an English Grammar* (London, 1671). Lye's is the only grammar consulted in the present chapter that is not discussed in VORLAT, *Development*.

[49] System 1 is prominent in MICHAEL, *English Grammatical Categories*, p. 214. Butler's is System 23 (MICHAEL, *English Grammatical Categories*, p. 238).

[50] J. WALLIS, *Grammatica Linguæ Anglicanæ* (Oxford, 1653); C. COOPER, *Grammatica linguæ Anglicanæ* (London, 1685).

[51] MICHAEL, *English Grammatical Categories*, p. 241 and pp. 251-253.

Pronoun. § II. Of a Noun. 41
3. Sing. {himself, her self, it self, } plur. demselvs.
{hee himself, shee her self, } plur. dey demselvs.
{his own self, hir own self, its own self, } plur. deir own selvs.
Pronouns Demonstrativ' ar three:
Sing. {Dis, dat, de sam', } plur. {des', dos', de sam'.

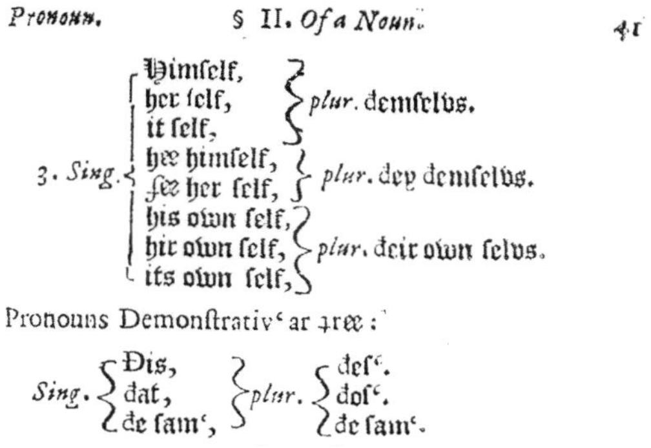

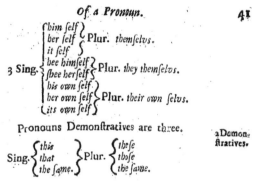

Fig. 6a Butler (p. 41) on reflexive and demonstrative pronouns. From the Huntington Library collection. Image published with permission of ProQuest. Further reproduction is prohibited without permission.

Of a Pronoun. 41
3 Sing. {him self, her self, it self} Plur. themselvs.
{hee himself, shee herself} Plur. they themselvs.
{his own self, her own self, its own self} Plur. their own selvs.
Pronouns Demonstratives are three. 2 Demonstratives.
Sing. {this, that, the same.} Plur. {these, those, the same.

Fig. 6b Wharton (p. 41) on reflexive and demonstrative pronouns. From the British Library collection. Image published with permission of ProQuest. Further reproduction is prohibited without permission.

Wallis is a case in point: this Latin grammar of English is the only item with six seventeenth-century editions,[52] and it continued to be reprinted until 1765.[53]

Printed in the author's reformed spelling, Charles Butler's *English Grammar* is a little shorter than Wharton's book: 92 pages, including a lengthy "Index of woords like and vnlike" – not unlike Wharton's – which takes up the final quarter of the book. In addition to the reformed orthography, another feature immediately catching the eye is the use of blackletter for the words and word forms under discussion. The grammar begins with chapters on letters and syllables, including pronunciation, after which chapter 3 focuses on word classes. As for the visualisations used, we may first of all observe that tables, diagrams and braces appear on thirteen of the 22 pages in this chapter. Nouns – substantives and adjectives – do not seem to merit graphic devices, the first of which appear in the section on pronouns. Here the similarities between Butler and Wharton become apparent, in wording and in order of topics but also in graphic presentation. Vertical rules are more characteristic of Wharton than Butler, who, moreover,

[52] ALSTON, *Bibliography*, Vol. I, pp. 7-8.

[53] TIEKEN-BOON VAN OSTADE, *Grammars, Grammarians*, pp. 1-2.

acknowledges fewer cases than Wharton (see below), which prompts different graphic arrangements. Again, one of the word classes that stand out graphically is that of pronouns. Perhaps the most striking visual similarity between Wharton and Butler are the figures presenting the reflexive and demonstrative pronouns (for the third-person forms and demonstratives, see Figs. 6a and 6b). Even the page number is the same, although the contents are not organised identically in the two books: for example, pronouns are part of chapter 7 in Wharton and preceded by six chapters on the topics described above, while Butler covers this word class as part of chapter 3 ("Of Woords"), preceded by chapters on letters and spelling.[54]

As for verbs, the two authors discuss them in a somewhat different order – Wharton's first device deals with 'love' in the indicative mood, which Butler illustrates only after the various patterns of auxiliary verbs and 'be' – but the visuals often look quite similar. Braces group examples together, and next to the left brace there is a grammatical label for tense or number; braces are a typical graphic feature, whereas there are just two diagrams with some vertical rules. Butler does not have a graphic device corresponding to that in Fig. 2, but a similar list of verbs is printed as a regular paragraph (pp. 47-48). Towards the end of chapter 3, Butler discusses prepositions without any tables or diagrams, unlike Wharton, who provides a five-column list that looks much like a table, and a diagram with a layout similar to that in Fig. 2. Despite a number of differences, Butler and Wharton seem a closer match, visually, than Wharton and Aickin.

The other English-language grammar we consider here, *The Childs Delight* by Thomas Lye, bears the subtitle *Together with an English Grammar*. The longest of the English-language books consulted, it contains 162 pages after twelve pages of front matter and the first table. Visual similarities with Aickin immediately become obvious, as this first graphic device is a four-page series of tables on vowels, diphthongs and consonants, with a letter or sound in each cell accompanied by a noun, such as 'goose' or 'urinal', illustrated by a matching image. What follows are dozens of pages of unruled tables on letters, letter combinations and syllables of varying length, with barely any explicatory prose; there are also two minor figures with some braces or vertical rules. On pp. 69-162, the "Essay towards an English Grammar" contains the grammatical core of the volume. Word classes or "eight sorts of words" are discussed in chapters XI to XIX. Nouns are presented in a not untypical diagram with braces,

---

[54] VORLAT, *Development*, p. 432, regards Wharton's work as "mere plagiarism", with Butler and Lily as his sources.

with singulars and plurals separated, each line starting with the abbreviated Latin name of the corresponding case, from 'Nom.' to 'Abl.'. Pronouns are discussed unusually briefly on p. 118, without any more complicated graphic elements than a numbered list which does not really seem to stand out from its context. The visually most prominent part of the grammar are the two openings on pages 122-125: both contain six columns separated by vertical rules, with braces near the outer margins on either side accompanied by the appropriate grammatical category, such as "Present Tense" and "Future". The cells contain examples of active and passive verb phrases (VPs) arranged by mood, person and number. After the verbs, the remaining word classes are treated as list-like sequences of paragraphs, sometimes just single lines, apart from the more tabular arrangement of prepositions as affixes on pages 134-135. Otherwise, the "Essay" is characterised by numbered paragraphs on letters, syllables and sounds before the 26-page description of parts of speech, and, after it, on abbreviations, punctuation, numbers symbolising truths such as "Two Testaments" and "XII Monseths in the year", and finally proverbs. Overall, the long tables of syllables alone make it feasible to associate Lye with Aickin, but Lye's table of verbs and illustrated tables of sounds and letters also bear a family resemblance to Figures 4 and 5 above.

As English grammatical description was typically modelled on Latin, and Latin was still used for writing grammars of the vernacular, it is also useful to consider some important Latin grammars of English. After some twenty pages of front matter, Wallis, in 128 pages, covers the kinds of topics encountered in other grammars as well: sounds, letters, pronunciation and word classes, the last of which are addressed in the second half of the book. On p. 36 we find the first graphic device, under the prominent title '*Literarum omnium Synopsis*', which consists of a table of vowels above a table of consonants, both with grids and altogether eight braces used for grouping terms and classes. The next device, on p. 88, is in the word classification part of the book and arranges the personal and interrogative pronouns in a table with a grid and seven braces. On p. 97, there are some braces in the representation of the conjugations of the verb 'be', but these are the only notable graphic devices in the book, whose layout is otherwise characterised by different types of content printed in different sizes. As this important work was in print for a long time, we checked if the same devices remained in the later books. In the fourth edition (1674), which contains "substantial changes",[55] a table very similar to the first device of the first edition appears on p. 26, with the same content and the same number of cells

---

[55] ALSTON, *Bibliography*, p. 8.

and braces, the only difference being that the later edition does not abbreviate the grammatical terminology. The pronoun table on p. 78 bears an even greater resemblance to that in the 1653 book; and the braces reappear in connection with the forms of *be*. Unlike the first edition, the 1674 edition also contains over fifty pages of *Praxis grammatica*, including, for example, the Lord's Prayer with each English line followed by the corresponding Latin one printed in italics. In sum, graphic devices seem rarer in Wallis than in Wharton or Aickin, but what the reader gets are quite carefully designed tables.

Published some thirty years after Wallis's and Wharton's grammars, Cooper's grammar is acknowledged by Aickin and therefore merits a note here; though somewhat later, Aickin is deemed by Dons to be "more conservative" than Cooper and Wallis.[56] The last of the Latin grammars of English[57] is 200 pages long (excluding some thirty pages of front matter) but does not contain a particularly large number of graphic devices. The first of these is a gridless list-like table of the English alphabet, placed between the table of contents ('Index') and the '*Pars Prima*', which contains not only some braces and tabularly laid-out lists (without grids), but also a fold-out insert with a table on vowels and consonants, printed with a grid and labels for both (groups of) columns and rows. In the '*Pars Secunda*', the most prominent visual feature is the way numerous lists of examples are arranged, usually, into three unruled columns. Following nearly a hundred pages on sounds and spelling, the '*Pars Tertia*' discusses word classes. Chapter 1 presents some examples of English words, with Latin glosses, in small gridless tables with labels for the columns ("Concreta. Abstracta") and the rows ("Neutrum. Activum. Passivum."). In chapter 2, information on pronouns is presented by similar graphic means, with a few braces added for clarity. There are also some numbered lists of prepositions, in one column. The fourth chapter, on verbs, contains some tabular devices with up to six columns for VPs with 'be' as the main verb, illustrating variation by number, person, and tense. In addition, some other elements resemble the ones seen in the preceding sections, but on pages 150-151 there are two tables with grids providing the forms of some modal and primary verbs. After the section on verbs, the rest of the book does not contain any elements that stand out visually, apart from some topics treated with the help of numbered lists in one column. It is thus mainly the by now 'usual suspects' that receive graphic support; a visually important feature is the use of grids in the layout of tables.

---

[56] DONS, *Descriptive Adequacy*, p. 17.
[57] VORLAT, *Development*, p. 28.

Graphic Elements in Early Printed Grammar Books 303

Discussion

Above, we have seen that both the grammars selected for the case studies and their (near) contemporaries, described more briefly, discussed some of the content they provided with the help of graphic devices. We found that the word classes most typically accompanied by graphic devices were verbs and pronouns. Verbs – lexical, primary and modal – make up the part of speech with the most morphological variation also in Present-Day English, and the complexity of the VP increases when auxiliaries are added to the main verb. This is clearly an area of grammar which grammarians have recognised as such a complex one that conjugations and combinations of verbs into VPs are best described with the help of tables and diagrams. In the six grammars, even Wallis did this, although he limited his use of graphic elements in the verb-related parts of his grammar to presenting the forms of 'be' with some braces. In addition to variation in tense and aspect, inflection according to person and number is also relevant, which links verbs with pronouns. Pronouns could be presented graphically in connection with verbs, but visualisation was also helpful when the focus was solely on the pronominal system. The different dimensions of the personal pronoun system – number, gender, and case – invited graphic support,

Table 1 The six grammars in chronological order, with tabular or diagram-type graphic devices per word class. ✓ devices used; – devices not used; an empty cell signifies a topic not covered in a section of its own.

	Butler	Wallis	Wharton	Lye	Cooper	Aickin
Noun	–	–	✓	✓	✓	✓
Pronoun	✓	✓	✓	–	✓	✓
Verb	✓	✓	✓	✓	✓	✓
Participle			–	–		
Adverb	–	–	–	–	–	–
Conjunction	–	–	✓	–	–	–
Preposition	–	–	✓	✓	–	–
Interjection			–	–	–	–

as did the variation in the forms of, for example, reflexive pronouns; Wallis's table, notable for its grid, featured interrogative pronouns as well as personal pronouns.

The other word classes seemed to be less prominent in this respect: the authors or typesetters did not always make the same or similar graphic choices although they needed to cover the same ground in their books. Table 1 presents a comparison of the grammars in tabular format. For example, Wharton displays more graphic solutions for discussing prepositions than Butler, as observed under Findings. The grammarians also differed in the analyses and classifications they presented, which led to graphic elements of varying complexity: where Butler acknowledged only two cases for personal pronouns, Wharton arranged his pronouns into nominatives and five other cases from the genitive to the ablative (instead of Butler's oblique case). The six-case model, reflecting Latin grammar, was applied by Wharton to nouns as well, although he did specify that in English, "there is no variation in Nouns by Cases" (p. 34), unlike in Latin. The same model for nouns also showed in the tables by Aickin and Lye.[58]

The Latin model – in terms of organisation of the book as well as grammatical categories assigned to English words and phrases – was quite clearly present in the English books. As noted above, word classes were a prominent topic discussed under 'Etymology'. This term appeared in the section titles of Cooper and Aickin, but not of Wallis, Butler, Wharton or Lye. The Latin model must have guided the graphic choices as well. For example, William Lily's 1542 *Introduction of the Eyght Partes of Speche*, introducing Latin grammar to younger English learners, contains a wealth of graphic devices with braces; these were not unlike the ones that would appear in grammars of English in the seventeenth century. In a recent edition of Lily, each of the four "declyned" parts of speech is described with the help of tables or diagrams – and verbs, with their numerous conjugations and paradigms, are particularly prominent – whereas of the other word classes only prepositions are arranged into columns with braces.[59]

In addition to word classification, spelling – and / or its connection to pronunciation – was prominent in the grammars. The idea that English spelling was problematic can be seen not just in the number of pages devoted to the

---

[58] For a book-length discussion of grammatical categories and efforts to reform them in the early modern period, see MICHAEL, *English Grammatical Categories*. VORLAT, "On the history", p. 508, calls the Latin model "an ill-fitting straightjacket for the English language".

[59] *Lily's Grammar*.

topic in many grammars of the period – and many of the early grammarians were interested in spelling reform[60] – but also in the orthography of some of the books: Butler used his reformed spelling, and Bullokar had already introduced an orthographic system of his own in 1586. In the books consulted, there was variation in the ways in which information on spelling and pronunciation was provided. The most striking solutions include the long lists of syllables found in Aickin and Lye, whose audiences may have been younger learners in need of better reading skills, as also suggested by, for example, the inclusion of illustrated tables.

What we have seen so far suggests that a range of graphic devices was used in seventeenth-century grammar books. It also seems that the graphic choices made within each grammar were not completely coherently applied throughout the book: using both braces and vertical rules as separators is a case in point. All this also points to a level of familiarity with graphic practices that was expected of potential and actual readers by those who wrote and printed books. Grammars were often intended for young learners and, potentially, foreigners. Although the pedagogical needs of the two target audiences must have been different, it was advantageous to market a grammar as useful for more than one type of customer. However, the younger learners needed access to grammatical information that would help them in learning Latin, whereas the foreign readers probably sought more practical English language skills – whether passive or active – and benefited from the classifications similar to Latin, which they may have known.[61] The graphic arrangements may also have looked familiar.

In addition to the ability to read, some graphic literacy also seems to have been expected of the readers. Since we cannot directly access their views on the usefulness or accessibility of graphic devices, we instead need to review what paratextual and other cues are traceable in the books. In the two case studies, Aickin is more explicit about the graphic features of his grammar: he refers to the graphic devices in the first part of the book as tables both in the text and in the table headings, and elaborates on their use in the preface. This is not typical of the second part, and in connection with the complex table presented as Fig. 4 above, Aickin does not mention or explain braces, which may suggest that he

---

[60] VORLAT, *Development*, p. 10.

[61] The Latin and monolingual English ones were not the only grammars of English in the seventeenth century: the third edition of P. BERAULT, *A New, Plain, Short, and Compleat French and English Grammar* (London, 1693; 1st edn 1688), for example, contains an English grammar in French, although its length is only one twentieth of the French part of the book. For more on English grammars in other languages from the early modern period, see ALSTON, *Bibliography*, Vol. II.

either did not regard their interpretation as problematic, that he did not really consider the issue of graphic literacy or that, possibly, some of the solutions visible to us are the printer's (typesetter's) rather than the author's. Many of Aickin's tables in the first part have headings, whereas Wharton's graphic devices often seem to continue organically after a comma or a word or phrase such as "as" or "as followeth". Unlike Aickin, Wharton does not provide any metadiscourse on the devices in the preface or elsewhere, although the 1655 title page suggests that the book contains "Directions for the use of this Book in Schools". Aickin addresses "the School-masters of the English Tongue and other Candid Readers" in his preface. This highlights the feature of grammar learning that children did not study the books independently but were taught by teachers, and it is therefore perhaps the teachers' graphic literacy skills rather than the children's alone that should be considered. Indeed, even the woodcut imprints at the beginning and end of Aickin's grammar remind us that a key role must have been played by the schoolmaster, seated in the image with a book in front of him, who assisted the young student in learning grammar and making sense of the graphic arrangement of grammatical content and, for example, the endless tables of syllables to be memorised – or who at least tested the student's ability to recite from the teaching materials by heart.

Concluding Remarks

In addition to grammatical information, arranged according to word class, early modern printed grammars covered other topics related to language use, including orthography. A single book was expected to serve multiple purposes; Ian Michael refers to "linguistic hold-alls".[62] Our survey of two seventeenth-century grammars and additional overview of four others indicates that in their coverage of such varied topics, the books displayed many kinds of graphic elements, whose numbers varied considerably from book to book and topic to topic. Their type also varied, but various devices for listing items were common, sometimes diagrams which grouped items with the help of braces, at other times tables, which tended not to have grids, apart from some illustrated tables of the alphabet and a few devices in some of the later books.

It thus seems that using graphic devices for arranging grammatical information for pedagogical purposes was quite common in the seventeenth century. Despite variation in the use of devices, certain topics were deemed useful to lay out in some other way than prose. Word classification is a case in point; of the parts of speech, particularly verbs and various types of pronouns were often

---

[62] MICHAEL, *Teaching of English*, p. 162.

presented in a visually distinct manner. However, the variation inherent in these grammatical categories does not, perhaps, suffice as an explanation for this; the model of Latin grammars was also important.

As the use of graphic elements in grammatical description is characterised by variation, more work on the visual dimension of early modern grammar books would be welcome. In addition to qualitative descriptions of small sets of books, there would be much to gain from a quantitative approach applied to a larger number of grammars. This would help to trace patterns and diachronic changes in the use of graphic devices, such as non-figural tables with proper grids, which are rare in the books we examined. The present study and the volume in which it appears will, we hope, serve as a stepping-stone for establishing methods for defining the forms and functions of graphic devices in the early modern period and, subsequently, for discovering patterns of use. In addition to this step forward, research on the graphic features of early modern grammars of English will also benefit from looking back, considering more thoroughly the impact of grammars of Latin on those of the vernacular.

Afterword

JEREMY J. SMITH

The rise of pragmatics, the study of how language works in interactive situations, has in recent decades transformed the nature of linguistic enquiry. Researchers working within the pragmatic paradigm focus on how language works through social interaction and investigate how formal features of language align with socio-cultural contexts. As the late Geoffrey Leech put it in a pioneering and still valuable study, "formalists study language as an autonomous system, whereas functionalists study it in relation to its social function",[1] and this summary was echoed some thirty years later by Andreas Jucker and Irma Taavitsainen: "a shift seems to be taking place in linguistics towards pragmatic approaches (...) with context playing a more prominent role than before".[2] It would seem that, for many scholars, the linguistics of *parole* or 'performance' has productively displaced the earlier dominant disciplinary mode that concentrated on 'competence' or *langue*.[3] Transmitters, receivers and

---

[1] G. LEECH, *Principles of Pragmatics* (London, 1983), p. 46.
[2] A.H. JUCKER, and I. TAAVITSAINEN, *English Historical Pragmatics* (Edinburgh, 2013), p. 43.
[3] See further W. KRETZSCHMAR, *The Linguistics of Speech* (Cambridge, 2013).

mediators of language are seen to exist within wider social frameworks: dyna-dynamically shifting socio-cultural communities of practice and discourse communities, influenced by overlapping ideological engagements with religion, social structure, and national and / or local identity. As Norman Fairclough put it, "language is a part of society, and not somehow external to it (...) language is a social process".[1]

Early work in linguistic pragmatics, with special reference to English, focused on very recent data, drawing on the increasing availability of large electronic corpora such as the pioneering *Brown Corpus of Standard American English* or the *British National Corpus*. Such research continues on specialised topics such as theolinguistics,[2] or – more massively – the study of computer-mediated communication. However, from the late 1980s important initiatives in corpus linguistics by scholars such as the late Matti Rissanen made possible detailed historical investigation, a tradition still pursued by Finnish scholars associated with the renowned Helsinki-based VARIENG research-cluster.

Much of this historical work concentrated at first, for operational reasons to do with the availability of transcriptions, on grammatical and lexical features. However, more recently English historical pragmatics has developed – drawing especially on different kinds of analysis made possible because of technological innovation – in exciting, more capacious directions. Particularly important in this regard was the work of other Finnish scholars, notably the 'Pragmatics on the Page' group centred on the University of Turku, whose impact can be seen in all the chapters of this book. The case studies that form its core engage with genres that have often been regarded as culturally marginal, such as medical writings, churchwardens' accounts, recipe books, letters and dance-manuals, or with paratextual features such as indices, tables and diagrams. They also cross periodic boundaries that have often meant researchers in (say) eighteenth-century studies are unaware of the valuable insights to be derived from engaging with (for instance) medievalists, and indeed vice versa; the extraordinary scope of the book means that data discussed range from the appearance of the ampersand in Pompeii to the deployment of hyphens by Bishop Lowth.

But the papers are also innovative in that they demonstrate convincingly how meaning can be expressed not only through lexis and grammar but also – as the Turku team has drawn attention to – through features that have tradition-

---

[1] N. FAIRCLOUGH, *Language and Power*, 3rd edn (London, 2015), p. 22.
[2] See e.g. V. HOBBS, *An Introduction to Religious Language* (London, 2021) and references there cited.

ally been seen as non-linguistic, part of scholarly domains such as palaeography and bibliography. All such "written-language" features are shown to "function as markers of difference and belonging, and [are] involved in the creation of identities at different levels of social organisation".[3] The case-studies are framed and informed by major theoretical interventions – always comprehensively exemplified from real data – that address directly the relation between form and function, and offer exciting and productive ways in which the book's research-agenda might be pursued in the future. Substantial bibliographical information adds to the volume's value as an essential – indeed primary – point of reference for all scholars in this growing field.

As flagged in the book's introduction, its concerns link with "the material turn in philology":

(...) a paradigm shift that highlights the importance of the material context of the book for historical linguistics and textual scholarship (...) philologists are now increasingly seen to include non-textual or supra-textual features of the physical book (artefact) as contextual variables in their analyses (...) In doing so, they are informed by research in codicology and palaeography to scrutinise the physical structure, handwriting, layout, decoration and provenance of manuscripts.[4]

Many of the current leaders in the extension of historical pragmatics are represented in this book, which represents an original and methodologically rigorous reimagining of traditional philology. This reimagining requires, this book argues, the breaking down of boundaries between disciplines, such as book history (including such subjects as palaeography, codicology, and bibliography), textual editing (or, as I would prefer, 'criticism'), and historical linguistics, and an enhanced dialogue between them. This book thus offers a distinctive and very exciting model for interdisciplinary and collaborative scholarship, something that has been a challenge – still often unresolved, despite many institutional attempts at organisational refashioning – to the present-day academic landscape.

---

[3] M. SEBBA, "Sociolinguistic approaches to writing systems research", *Writing Systems Research* 1 (2009), pp. 35-49, at p. 36.

[4] M. DROUT and S. KLEINMAN, "Doing philology 2: Something 'old', something 'new': Material philology and the recovery of the past", *The Heroic Age* 13 (2010), available online at <http://www.heroicage.org/issues/13/pi.php>, last consulted 10th September 2023, in section 8, cited in M. KYTÖ and M. PEIKOLA, "Philology on the move: Manuscript studies at the dawn of the 21st century", *Studia Neophilologica* 86 (2014), Special Issue: Manuscript Studies and Codicology: Theory and Practice, ed. M. PEIKOLA and M. KYTÖ, pp. 1-8, at p. 1.

Bibliography

Manuscripts

Aberdeen, University Library, 21
Aberystwyth, National Library of Wales, Brogynton II.24
Boston, MA, Collectanea medica, Boston Medical Library, Francis A. Countway Library of Medicine, Ballard 19
Cambridge, Corpus Christi College, 354
Cambridge, Emmanuel College, 69
Cambridge, Fitzwilliam Museum, 261
Cambridge, Gonville & Caius College, 336/725
Cambridge, Magdalene College, Pepys 878
Cambridge, Peterhouse, 177
Cambridge, St. John's College, A.12 (12)
Cambridge, St. John's College, H.1 (204)
Cambridge, Trinity College, O.8.29
Cambridge, Trinity College, R.5.25
Cambridge, Trinity College, R.14.52
Cambridge, University Library, Ii.2.24
Cambridge, University Library, Ii.4.22
Cambridge, University Library, Ll.1.18
Dublin, Trinity College, 516
Durham, University Library, Cosin V.IV.1
Glasgow, University Library, Ferguson 7
Glasgow University Library, Hunter 64
Glasgow, University Library, Hunter 328
Glasgow, University Library, Hunter 367
Leiden, University Library, SEM 45
Lincoln, Cathedral Library, 85
Lincoln, Cathedral Library, 91 ('Lincoln Thornton')
Liverpool, Public Libraries, f909 HIG

London, British Library, Addit. 10293
London, British Library, Addit. 24194
London, British Library, Addit. 43405
London, British Library, Arundel 83
London, British Library, Arundel 334
London, British Library, Cotton Nero C.xii
London, British Library, Cotton Nero D.viii
London, British Library, Cotton Tiberius D.vii
London, British Library, Egerton 871
London, British Library, Egerton 1624
London, British Library, Egerton 2572 ('Barber-Surgeons')
London, British Library, Harley 1026
London, British Library, Harley 1900
London, British Library, Harley 3671
London, British Library, Lansdowne 285
London, British Library, Sloane 776
London, British Library, Sloane 965
London, British Library, Sloane 1588
London, British Library, Sloane 2320
London, British Library, Sloane 2507
London, British Library, Stowe 65
London, Inner Temple, Petyt 511.5
London, Lambeth Palace, 112
Manchester, Chetham's Library, 11379 (Mun.A.6.90)
New Haven, CT, Yale Center for British Art, Paul Mellon Collection, John Porter Manuscript
Oxford, Bodleian Library, Eng. lett. c. 572
Oxford, Bodleian Library, Eng. poet. a. 1 ('Vernon')
Oxford, Bodleian Library, Lyell 21
Oxford, Bodleian Library, Rawlinson A.393
Oxford, Bodleian Library, Rawlinson A.429
Oxford, Bodleian Library, Rawlinson B.171
Oxford, Bodleian Library, Wood D.8
Oxford, Magdalen College, Lat. 147
Oxford, Oxfordshire History Centre, PAR211/4/F1/1/70
Oxford, Oxfordshire History Centre, PAR211/4/F1/2/78
Oxford, Oxfordshire History Centre, PAR211/4/F1/2/100
Paris, Bibliothèque nationale de France, fonds français, nouvelle acquisition 4516
Princeton, NJ, University Library, Garrett 151
Princeton, NJ, University Library, Taylor 6
San Marino, CA, Huntington Library, HM 129
San Marino, CA, Huntington Library, HM 132
San Marino, CA, Huntington Library, HM 28561

Bibliography

Tokyo, Senshu University Library, 1 (formerly Oslo / London, Schøyen Collection, 194)

Printed Books from the Hand Press Period (short titles)

AICKIN, J., *The English Grammar* (London, 1693). WING A799A.
ALLEN, T., *A Chain of Scripture Chronology* (London, 1659). WING A1048.
ANON., *Aristoteles Master-Piece* (London, 1684). WING A3689.
ANON., *A Briefe Chronologie of the Holie Scriptures* (London, 1600). STC 14.
ANON., *Chronographia. A Description of Time, from the Beginning of the World, vnto the Yeare of Our Lord 137* (London, 1590). STC 5471.
ANON., *Chronographia. A Description of Time, from the Beginning of the World, vnto the Yeare of our Lord, 137* (London, 1596). STC 5472.
ANON., *The Compleat Clark* (London, 1655). WING C5633.
ANON., *The Compleat Letter Writer*, 3rd edn (London, 1756).
ANON., *The Compleat Servant-Maid* (London, 1677). WING W3273A.
ANON., *A Grammar of the English Tongue* (London, 1711).
ANON., *The Grete Herball* (London, 1525). STC 13176.
ANON., *A Passing Gode Lityll Boke Necessarye [and] Behouefull a[g]enst the Pestilence* (London, 1485). STC 4591.
ANON., *The Second Part of a Literary Correspondence, between the Bishop of Gloucester and a Late Professor of Oxford* ([Oxford, 1766]).
BATMAN, S., *Batman vppon Bartholome* (London, [1582]). STC 1538.
BERAULT, P., *A New, Plain, Short, and Compleat French and English Grammar* (London, 1693). WING B1954.
BRAY, T., *Country Dances* (London, 1699). WING B4291B.
BROUGHTON, H., *A Concent of Scripture* (London, 1588/89). STC 3850.
BRUELE, G., *Praxis medicinae* (London, 1632). STC 3929.
BRUGIS, T., *The Marrovv of Physicke* (London, [1640]). STC 3931.
BRUGIS, T., *Vade mecum* (London, 1652 [1651]). WING B5225.
BRUNSCHWIG, H., *The Noble Experyence of the Vertuous Handy Warke of Surgeri* (London, [1525]). STC 13434.
BULLEIN, W., *Bulleyns Bulwarke of Defe(n)ce* (London, [1562]). STC 4033.
BULLEIN, W., *The Gouernment of Health* (London, 1595). STC 4042.
BUTLER, C., *English Grammar* (Oxford, 1633). STC 4190.
CARION, J., *The Thre Bokes of Cronicles* (London, 1550). STC 4626.
CARPENTER, T., *The Scholar's Spelling Assistant* ([London], 1796).
CARTER, J., *A Practical English Grammar* (Leeds, 1773).
CHARAS, M., *The Royal Pharmacopoea* (London, 1678). WING C2040.
COCK, T., *Miscelanea medica* (London, 1675). WING C4793.

CODOMANN, L., *Quatuor libri chronologiae*, issued together with *Annales sacrae scripturae* (Wittenberg, 1581). USTC 611615.
COOPER, C., *Grammatica linguæ Anglicanæ* (London, 1685). WING C6051B, C6052.
CULPEPER, N., *A Directory for Midwives* (London, P. Cole, 1651). WING C7488.
CULPEPER, N., *Culpeper's School of Physick* (London, 1659). WING C7544.
D'AVITY, P., *The Estates, Empires, & Principallities of the World,* transl. E. GRIMESTON (London, 1615). STC 988.
DELLA PORTA, G., *Natural Magick* (London, 1658). WING P2982.
DIGGES, L., *A Prognostication Euerlasting of Right Good Effect* (London, 1564). STC 435.41.
DRAKE, R., *Sacred Chronologie* (London, 1648). WING D2131.
DURANT, J., *Art and Nature Joyn Hand in Hand* (London, 1697). WING D2681A.
ELYOT, T., *The Boke Named the Governour* (London, 1531). STC 7635.
ELYOT, T., *The Castel of Helth* (London, [1541]). STC 7644.
EUSEBIUS OF CAESAREA, *The Auncient Ecclesiasticall Histories of the First Six Hundred Yeares after Christ*, transl. M. HANMER (London, 1577). STC 10572.
FONTAINE, N., *The History of the Old and New Testament* (London, 1691). WING F1406A.
FOXE, J., *The First Volume of the Ecclesiasticall History Contaynyng the Actes and Monumentes of Thynges Passed in Euery Kynges Tyme in This Realme* (London, 1570). STC 11223.
GALE, T., *Antidotarie Conteyning Hidde and Secrete Medicines Simple and Compounde*, in *Certaine Vvorkes of Chirurgerie* (London, [1563/64]). STC 11529.
GALEN, *Certaine Vvorkes of Galens, Called Methodus medendi*, transl. T. GALE (London, 1586). STC 11531.
GALEN, *Galens Art of Physick*, transl. N. CULPEPER (London, 1652 [1653]). WING G159.
GEMINUS, T., *Compendiosa totius anatomie delineatio* (London, 1553). STC 11716.
GERARD, J., *The Herball or Generall Historie of Plantes* (London, 1633). STC 11751.
GESNER, K., *The Treasure of Euonymus, Conteyninge the Vvonderfull Hid Secretes of Nature*, transl. P. MORWYN (London, 1559). STC 11800.
GUILLEMEAU, J., *Child-Birth or, The Happy Deliuerie of Vvomen* (London, 1612). STC 12496.
HEARNE, T., *Ductor historicus, or, A Short System of Universal History* (London, 1698). WING H1309.
HERNE, J., *The Law of Conveyances* (London, 1656). WING H1570.
HEYLYN, P., *Cosmographie in Four Bookes* (London, 1652). WING H1689.
HIGDEN, R., *Prolicionycion* (Westminster, 1482). STC 13438.
HIGDEN, R., *Policronicon* (Westminster, 1495). STC 13439.
HIGDEN, R., *Polycronycon* (London, 1527). STC 13440.
HOPTON, A., *A Concordancy of Yeares* (London, 1612). STC 13778.
KEITH, G., *A Chronological Account of the Several Ages of the Vvorld from Adam to Christ* (New York, 1694). WING K223.

LANQUET, T., *An Epitome of Chronicles* (London, 1549). STC 15217.
LIVELY, E., *A True Chronologie of the Times of the Persian Monarchie* (London, 1597). STC 16609.
LOWTH, R., *A Short Introduction to English Grammar* (London, 1762).
LOWTH, R., *De sacra poesi Hebræorum* (London, 1753), 2nd edn (Oxford, 1763).
LOWTH, R., *A Letter to the Right Reverend Author of the Divine Legation of Moses Demonstrated* (Oxford, 1765).
LYE, T., *The Childs Delight. Together with an English Grammar* (London, 1671). WING L3530.
MANNING, J., *A New Booke, Intituled, I Am for You All, Complexions Castle* (Cambridge, 1604). STC 17257.
MONARDES, N., *Ioyfull Newes out of the Newfound World* (London, 1580). STC 18006.5.
MOORE, P., *The Hope of Health* (London, [1565]). STC 18060.
NISBET, W., *A Golden Chaine of Time Leading unto Christ* (Edinburgh, 1650). WING N1171.
PARACELSUS, *Of the Supreme Mysteries of Nature* (London, 1656 [1655]). WING B3544.
PARÉ, A., *The Workes of That Famous Chirurgion Ambrose Parey* (London, 1634). STC 19189.
PIE, T., *An Houreglasse* (London, 1597). STC 19900.
PORTER, T., *A New Booke of Mapps* (London, 1655). WING P2998B.
PRIDEAUX, M., *An Easy and Compendious Introduction for Reading All Sorts of Histories* (Oxford, 1654). WING P3441.
RALEGH, W., *The History of the World* (London, 1614). STC 20637.
RASTELL, W., *A Table Collected of the Yeres of Our Lorde God, and of the Yeres of the Kynges of England* (London, 1558). STC 20732.5.
ROYAL COLLEGE OF PHYSICIANS IN LONDON, *Certain Necessary Directions* (London, 1636). STC 16769.5.
SALMON, W., *Phylaxa medicinae* (London, 1700). WING S443.
SHARP, J., *The Midwives Book* (London, 1671). WING S2969B.
SMITH, J., *The Printer's Grammar* (London, 1755).
SWAN, J., *Calamus mensurans: The Measuring Reed*, 2 vols. (London, 1653). WING S6235.
TAUVRY, D., *A Treatise of Medicines* (London, 1700). WING T247.
TOMLINSON, K., *The Art of Dancing Explained by Reading and Figures* (London, 1735).
TOWNE, J., *Remarks on Dr. Lowth's Letter to the Bishop of Gloucester* (London, 1766).
TURNER, W., *The Seconde Part of Vuilliam Turners Herball* (Collen [Köln], 1562). STC 24366.
USSHER, J., *The Annals of the World* (London, 1658). WING U149.
WALLIS, J., *Grammatica linguæ Anglicanæ* (Oxford, 1653). WING W584.
WEAVER, J., *Anatomical and Mechanical Lectures upon Dancing* (London, 1721).

WHARTON, J., *The English Grammar* (London, 1655). WING W1572. 1st edn is Wing W1571 (London, 1654).
WILKINS, J., *An Alphabetical Dictionary* (London, 1668). WING W2196.
WINTER, F., *Winter, an Almanack for the Yeare of Our Lord 1634* (Cambridge, 1634). STC 530.3.

Editions and Corpora

Byrhtferth's Manual (A.D. 1011), ed. S.J. CRAWFORD (Oxford, 1929: EETS O.S. 177).
A Corpus of Middle English Local Documents – MELD version 2017.1 [MELD], comp. M. STENROOS, K.V. THENGS, and G. BERGSTRØM (University of Stavanger) <http://www.uis.no/ meld>.
Corpus of Middle English Prose and Verse [CME] (University of Michigan) <https://quod.lib.umich.edu/c/cme/>.
Early Modern English Medical Texts [EMEMT], compiled by I. TAAVITSAINEN, P. PAHTA, T. HILTUNEN, M. MÄKINEN, V. MARTTILA, M. RATIA, C. SUHR, and J. TYRKKÖ (Amsterdam, 2010), CD-ROM.
The Guild Book of the Barbers and Surgeons of York (British Library, Egerton MS 2572): Study and Edition, ed. R.D. WRAGG (York, 2021).
Jane Austen's Letters, 4th edn, ed. D. LE FAYE (Oxford, 2011).
Liber de Diversis Medicinis, ed. M. OGDEN (London, 1938: EETS O.S. 207).
Lily's Grammar of Latin in English: An Introduction of the Eyght Partes of Speche, and the Construction of the Same, ed. H. GWOSDEK (Oxford, 2013).
The Málaga Corpus of Early English Scientific Prose <http://hunter.uma.es> – <http://modernmss.uma.es>.
Mandeville's Travels, Translated from the French of Jean d'Outremeuse. Edited from MS. Cotton Titus C. xvi, in the British Museum, 2 vols, ed. P. HAMELIUS (London, 1919: EETS O.S. 153, 154).
Muchelney Memoranda, ed. B. SCHOFIELD (Somerset, 1927).
Polychronicon Ranulphi Monachi Cestrensis with English Translations of John Trevisa and of an unknown Writer of the Fifteenth Century, ed. C. BABINGTON (vols. 1-2) and J.R. LUMBY (vols. 3-9), 9 vols. (London, 1865-1886: *Rolls Series* 41).
The Vernon Manuscript: A Facsimile Edition of Oxford, Bodleian Library, MS Eng. poet.a.1, ed. W. SCASE (Oxford, 2011).

Dictionaries, Catalogues and Reference Works

ALSTON, R.C., *A Bibliography of the English Language from the Invention of Printing to the Year 1800. A Corrected Reprint of Volumes I-X* (Ilkley, 1974).

Anglo-Norman Dictionary (AND² Online Edition) (Aberystwyth University, 2023) <https://anglo-norman.net/>.

British History Online (Institute of Historical Research, School of Advanced Study, University of London) <https://www.british-history.ac.uk/>.

CAPPELLI, A., *Lexicon abbrevaturarum. Dizionario di abbreviature latine ed italiane*, 6th edn (Milan, 1990 [1929]).

CARLINO, A., *Paper Bodies: A Catalogue of Anatomical Fugitive Sheets, 1538-1687* (London, 1999).

COXE, H.O., *Catalogus Codicum MSS qui in Collegiis Aulisque Oxoniensibus Hodie Adservantur*, 2 vols. (Oxford, 1852).

Dictionary of Medieval Latin from British Sources [DMLBS], ed. R.K. ASHDOWNE, D.R. HOWLETT, and R.E. LATHAM (Oxford, 2018).

DOYLE, A.I. *Catalogue of Durham University Library Cosin MS V.iv.1: Medical Recipes* <https://reed.dur.ac.uk/xtf/view?docId=ark/32150_s19s1616306.xml>.

Encyclopedia Britannica <https://www.britannica.com>.

HELLINGA, L., and G.D. PAINTER, *Catalogue of Books Printed in the XVth Century Now in the British Library. BMC Pt. 11: England* ('t Goy-Houten, 2007).

JOLLIFFE, P.S., *A Check-List of Middle English Writings of Spiritual Guidance* (Toronto, 1974).

MCINTOSH, A., M.L. SAMUELS, and M. BENSKIN, with the assistance of M. LAING and K. WILLIAMSON, *A Linguistic Atlas of Late Mediaeval English* [LALME], 4 vols. (Aberdeen, 1986).

MCKITTERICK, R., and R. BEADLE, *Catalogue of the Pepys Library at Magdalen College*, 7 vols. (Bury St. Edmunds, 1992).

Middle English Dictionary [MED], ed. R.E. LEWIS et al. (Ann Arbor, MI, 1952-2001). Online edition in *Middle English Compendium*, ed. F. MCSPARRAN et al. (Ann Arbor, MI, 2000-2018). <https://quod.lib.umich.edu/m/middle-english-dictionary/dictionary>.

MOONEY, L., S. HOROBIN, and E. STUBBS, *Late Medieval English Scribes, Version 1.0*, (2011) <http://www.medievalscribes>.

Oxford Dictionary of National Biography [ODNB] (Oxford University Press) <http://www.oxforddnb.com>.

Oxford English Dictionary online [OED] (Oxford University Press) <https://www.oed.com>.

Oxford Reference (Oxford University Press) <https://www.oxfordreference.com>.

POLLARD, A.W., and G.R. REDGRAVE, *A Short-Title Catalogue of Books Printed in England, Scotland, and Ireland, and of English Books Printed Abroad 1475-1640* [STC], 2nd edn, comp. W.A. JACKSON, F.S. FERGUSON, and K.F. PANTZER, 3 vols. (London, 1976-1991).

Universal Short Title Catalogue [USTC] (University of St. Andrews) <https://www.ustc.ac.uk/>.

WING, D.G., *Short-Title Catalogue of Books Printed in England, Scotland and Ireland, Wales, and British America and of English Books Printed in Other Countries,*

1641-1700 [WING], 2nd edn, revised and enlarged by J.J. MORRISON and C.W. NELSON, with the assistance of M. SECCOMBE, 4 vols. (New York, 1972-1998).

Literature

ACHESON, K., *Visual Rhetoric and Early Modern English Literature* (Farnham, 2013).
AGUIRRE, M.E., "Teaching through texts and pictures. A contribution of Jan Amos Comenius to education", *Revista Electrónica de Investigación Educativa* 3.1 (2001).
AIJMER, K., "The interface between grammar and discourse: 'The Fact is That.'", in: *Connectives as Discourse Landmarks*, ed. A. CELLE and R. HUART (Amsterdam, 2007), pp 31-46.
AIJMER, K., and A.-M. SIMON-VANDERBERGEN, "Pragmatic markers", in: *Discursive Pragmatics*, ed. J. ZIENKOWSKI, J.-O. ÖSTMAN, and J. VERSCHUEREN (Amsterdam, 2011), pp. 223-247.
ALGEO, J., "The earliest English grammars", in: *Historical and Editorial Studies in Medieval and Early Modern English for Johan Gerritsen*, ed. M.-J. ARN and H. WIRTJES (Groningen, 1985), pp. 191-207.
ALONSO-ALMEIDA, F., "'Gyf hyr þis medycyn': Analysing the Middle English recipe medical discourse", *Revista de lenguas para fines específicos* 5-6 (1998-99), pp. 48-81.
ALONSO-ALMEIDA, F., "Genre conventions in English recipes, 1600-1800", in: *Reading and Writing Recipe Books 1550-1800*, ed. M. DIMEO and S. PENNELL (Manchester, 2013), pp. 68-92.
ALONSO-ALMEIDA, F., and M. CABRERA-ABREU, "The formulation of promise in medieval English medical recipes: A relevance-theoretic approach", *Neophilologus* 86.1 (2002), pp. 137-154.
ANESA, P., and I. FORNASINI, "The modernity of Middle English manuscripts: A multimodal investigation", *Elephant & Castle* 17 (2017), pp. 5-41.
Approaches to Grammaticalization, ed. E. TRAUGOTT and B. HEINE (Amsterdam, 1991).
ARAKELIAN, P.G., "Punctuation in a Late Middle English manuscript", *Neuphilologische Mitteilungen* 76.4 (1975), pp. 614-624.
ARMSTRONG, G., "Coding continental: Information design in sixteenth-century English vernacular manuals and translations", *Renaissance Studies* 29 (2015), pp. 78-102.
ARONOFF, M., "The orthographic system of an early English printer: Wynkyn de Worde", *Folia Linguistica Historica* 8.1-2 (1989), pp. 65-97.
AUSTIN, F., "Epistolary conventions in the Clift family correspondence", *English Studies* 54 (1973), pp. 9-22, 129-140.
AVGERINOU, M.D., and R. PETTERSSON, "Toward a cohesive theory of visual literacy", *Journal of Visual Literacy* 30.2. (2011), pp. 1-19.

BAKER, P.S., "Byrthferth's *Enchiridion* and the computus in Oxford, St. John's College 17", *Anglo-Saxon England* 10 (1982), pp. 123-142.
BARR, J., "Pre-scientific chronology: The Bible and the origin of the world", *Proceedings of the American Philosophical Society* 143 (1999), pp. 379-387.
BARTON, D., *Literacy: An Introduction to the Ecology of Written Language*. 2nd edn (Malden, MA, 2007).
BARTON, D., and M. HAMILTON, "Literacy practices", in: *Situated Literacies: Reading and Writing in Context*, ed. D. BARTON, M. HAMILTON, and R. IVANIČ (London, 2000), pp. 7-15.
BATEMAN, J., J. WILDFEUER, and T. HIIPPALA, *Multimodality: Foundations, Research and Analysis. A Problem-Oriented Introduction* (Berlin, 2017).
BAXTER, W.T., "Early accounting: The tally and checkerboard", *The Accounting Historians Journal* 16.2 (1989), pp. 43-83.
BEADLE, R., "Cambridge University Library, MS LL.1.18: A Southwell miscellany", in: *Pursuing Middle English Manuscripts and Their Texts: Essays in Honour of Ralph Hanna*, ed. S. HOROBIN and A. NAFDE (Turnhout, 2017), pp. 99-112.
BEAL, J., "Standardization", in: *The Cambridge Handbook of English Historical Linguistics,* ed. M. KYTÖ and P. PAHTA (Cambridge, 2016), pp. 301-317.
BEAL, J., "Dialect and the construction of identity in the ego documents of Thomas Bewick", in: *Dialect Writing and the North of England*, ed. P. HONEYBONE and W. MAGUIRE (Edinburgh, 2020), pp. 51-74.
BERNARD, J., "Using extended captions to improve learning from instructional illustrations", *British Journal of Educational Technology* 21 (1990), pp. 215-225.
BIBER, D., *Variation Across Speech and Writing* (Cambridge, 1988).
BIBER, D., and S. CONRAD, *Register, Genre and Style* (Cambridge, 2009).
BLOOMFIELD, M.W., *The Seven Deadly Sins: An Introduction to the History of a Religious Concept, with Special Reference to Medieval English Literature* (Michigan University, 1967).
BOFFEY, J., *Manuscript and Print in London, c. 1475-1530* (London, 2012).
Books and the Sciences in History, ed. M. FRASCA-SPADA and N. JARDINE (Cambridge, 2000).
BOURGNE, F., "Vernacular engravings in late medieval England", in: *Palimpsests and the Literary Imagination of Medieval England*, ed. L. CARRUTHERS, R. CHAI-ELSHOLZ, and T. SILEC (New York, 2011), pp. 115-136.
BOYD DAVIS, S., "May not duration be represented as distinctly as space? Geography and the visualization of time in the early eighteenth century", in: *Knowing Nature in Early Modern Europe*, ed. D. BECK (London, 2015), pp. 119-137.
BOYD DAVIS, S., E. BEVAN, and A. KUDIKOV, "Just in time: Defining historical chronographics", in: *Electronic Visualisation in Arts and Culture*, ed. J.P. BOWEN, S. KEENE, and K. NG (London, 2013), pp. 243-257.
BRIGGS, C.F., "Late medieval texts and *tabulae*: The case of Giles of Rome, *De regimine principum*", *Manuscripta* 37.3 (1993), pp. 253-275.

BROWN, M.P., *Understanding Illuminated Manuscripts: A Guide to Technical Terms*, rev. E.C. TEVIOTDALE and N.K. TURNER (Los Angeles, CA, 2018 [1994]).

BROWN, M.P., I.H. GARIPZANOV, and B.C. TILGHMAN, "Introduction: The role of graphic devices in understanding the early decorated book", in *Graphic Devices and the Early Decorated Book*, ed. M.P. BROWN, I.H. GARIPZANOV, and B.C. TILGHMAN (Woodbridge, 2017), pp. 1-11.

BURGESS, R.W., *Studies in Eusebian and Post-Eusebian Chronography* (Stuttgart, 1999).

BURGESS, R.W., and M. KULIKOWSKI, *Mosaics of Time: The Latin Chronicle Traditions from the First Century BC to the Sixth Century AD, vol. 1: A Historical Introduction to the Chronicle Genre from its Origins to the High Middle Ages* (Turnhout, 2013).

BUSCHMANN-GÖBELS, A., "Bellum grammaticale (1712) – A battle of books and a battle for the market?", in: *Grammars, Grammarians and Grammar Writing in Eighteenth-Century England*, ed. I. TIEKEN-BOON VAN OSTADE (Berlin, 2008), pp. 81-100.

BUTTERFIELD, A., "'Mise-en page' in 'Troilus' manuscripts: Chaucer and French manuscript culture", *Huntington Library Quarterly* 58 (1995), pp. 49-80.

BYBEE, J., "Mechanisms of change in grammaticization: The role of frequency", in: *The Handbook of Historical Linguistics*, ed. B.D. JOSEPH and R.D. JANDA (Oxford, 2003), pp. 602-623.

BYBEE, J., "From usage to grammar: The mind's response to repetition", *Language* 82.4 (2006), pp. 711-733.

CALLE-MARTÍN, J., "'His maiestie chargeth, that no person shall engrose any maner of corne': The standardization of punctuation in Early Modern English legal proclamations", in: *Punctuation in Context – Past and Present Perspectives*, ed. C. CLARIDGE and M. KYTÖ (Bern, 2019), pp. 179-200.

CALLE-MARTÍN, J., and A. MIRANDA-GARCÍA, "Aspects of scribal punctuation in the Old English *Apollonius of Tyre*", *Folia Linguistica Historica* 26.1-2 (2005), pp. 95-113.

CALLE-MARTÍN, J., and A. MIRANDA-GARCÍA, "Editing Middle English punctuation. The case of MS Egerton 2622 (ff. 136-152)", *International Journal of English Studies* 5.2 (2005), pp. 27-44.

CALLE-MARTÍN, J., and A. MIRANDA-GARCÍA, "The punctuation system of Elizabethan legal documents: The case of G.U.L. MS Hunter 3 (S.1.3)", *Review of English Studies* 59.240 (2008), pp. 356-378.

CARROLL, R. "The Middle English recipe as a text-type", *Neuphilologische Mitteilungen* 100 (1999), pp. 27-42.

CARROLL, R., M. PEIKOLA, H. SALMI, J. SKAFFARI, M.-L. VARILA, and R. HILTUNEN, "Pragmatics on the page: Visual text in late medieval English books", *European Journal of English Studies* 17 (2013), special issue *Visual Text*, ed. J. KENDALL, M. PORTELA, and G. WHITE, pp. 54-71.

CARRUTHERS, M., *The Book of Memory: A Study of Memory in Medieval Culture*, 2nd edn (Cambridge, 2008).
CARTER, S., "Published musical variants and creativity: An overview of John Playford's role as editor", in: *Concepts of Creativity in Seventeenth-Century England*, ed. R. HERISSONE and A. HOWARD (Woodbridge, 2013), pp. 87-104.
CARTER, S., "'Yong Beginners, who live in the Countrey': John Playford and the printed music market in seventeenth-century England", *Early Music History* 35 (2016), pp. 95-129.
CHABÁS, J., and B.R. GOLDSTEIN, *A Survey of European Astronomical Tables in the Late Middle Ages* (Leiden, 2012).
CHRISTIE, J., *Some Account of Parish Clerks, More Especially of the Ancient Fraternity (Bretherne and Sisterne) of S. Nicholas, Now Known as the Worshipful Company of Parish Clerks* (London, 1893).
CIAMBELLA, F., "A corpus linguistic analysis of dance lexis in eight early modern manuscripts: From the Inns of Court to drama", *SKENÈ Journal of Theatre and Drama Studies* 7.2 (2021), pp. 231-250.
CLANCHY, M.T., *From Memory to Written Record, England 1066-1307*, 2nd edn (Oxford, 1993).
CLARIDGE, C., and M. KYTÖ, "Introduction: Multiple functions and contexts of punctuation", in: *Punctuation in Context – Past and Present Perspectives*, ed. C. CLARIDGE and M. KYTÖ (Bern, 2020), pp. 9-20.
CLASSEN, A., "Chess in medieval German literature: A mirror of social-historical and cultural, religious, ethical, and moral conditions", in: *Chess in the Middle Ages and Early Modern Age: A Fundamental Thought Paradigm of the Premodern World*, ed. D.E. O'SULLIVAN (Berlin, 2012), pp. 17-44.
CLEMENS, R., and T. GRAHAM, *Introduction to Manuscript Studies* (Ithaca, NY, 2007).
COLE, G., "The historical development of the title page", *The Journal of Library History (1966-1972)* 6.4 (1971), pp. 303-316.
COX, J.C., *Churchwardens' Accounts from the Fourteenth Century to the Close of the Seventeenth Century* (London, 1913).
CRAWFORD, M.R., *The Eusebian Canon Tables: Ordering Textual Knowledge in Late Antiquity* (Oxford, 2019).
CROFT, W., *Radical Construction Grammar: Syntactic Theory in Typological Perspective* (Oxford, 2001).
CULPEPER, J., and M. KYTÖ, *Early Modern English Dialogues. Spoken Interaction as Writing* (Cambridge, 2010).
CUSACK, B., *Everyday English 1500-1700: A Reader* (Edinburgh, 1998).
DANOS, X., and E.W.L. NORMAN, "The development of a new taxonomy for graphicacy", in *The Design and Technology Association International Research Conference 2009*, ed. E. NORMAN and D. SPENDLOVE (Wellesbourne, 2009), pp. 69-84.
DASTON, L., "Super-vision: Weather watching and table reading in the early modern Royal Society and Académie Royale des Sciences", *Huntington Library Quarterly* 78 (2015), pp. 187-215.

DE YOUNG, G., "Mathematical diagrams from manuscript to print: Examples from the Arabic Euclidean transmission", *Synthese* 186 (2012), pp. 21-54.

DELIYANNIS, D.M., "Introduction", in: *Historiography in the Middle Ages*, ed. D.M. DELIYANNIS (Leiden, 2003), pp. 2-14.

DELIYANNIS, D., H. DEY, and P. SQUATRITI, "Introduction: Things, matter and meaning in Late Antiquity and the Early Middle Ages", in: *Fifty Early Medieval Things: Materials of Culture in Late Antiquity and the Early Middle Ages*, ed. D. DELIYANNIS, H. DEY, and P. SQUATRITI (Ithaca, NY, 2019), pp. 1-32.

DENISON, D., "Log(ist)ic and simplistic S-curves", in: *Motives for Language Change*, ed. R. HICKEY (Cambridge, 2003), pp. 54-70.

Discourse Markers. Description and Theory, ed. A.H. JUCKER and Y. ZIV (Amsterdam, 1998).

DOMÍNGUEZ-RODRÍGUEZ, M.V., and A. RODRÍGUEZ-ÁLVAREZ, "'The reader is desired to observe ...': Metacomments in the prefaces to English school grammars of the eighteenth century", *Journal of Historical Pragmatics* 16.1 (2015), pp. 86-108.

DOMÍNGUEZ-RODRÍGUEZ, M.V., and A. RODRÍGUES-ÁLVAREZ, "'All which I offer with my own experience': An approach to persuasive advertising strategies in the prefatory matter of 17th-century English midwifery treatises", in: *The Dynamics of Text and Framing Phenomena: Historical Approaches to Paratext and Metadiscourse in English*, ed. M. PEIKOLA and B. BÖS (Amsterdam, 2020), pp. 163-185.

DONS, U., *Descriptive Adequacy of Early Modern English Grammars* (Berlin, 2004).

DOYLE. A.I.,"The work of a late-fifteenth century English scribe, William Ebesham", *Bulletin of the John Rylands Library, Manchester* 39 (1956), pp. 298-325.

DROUT, M., and S. KLEINMAN, "Doing philology 2: Something 'old', something 'new': Material philology and the recovery of the past", *The Heroic Age* 13 (2010) <http://www.heroicage.org/issues/13/pi.php>.

DUFFY, E., *Marking the Hours: English People and Their Prayers, 1240-1570* (New Haven, CT, 2006).

DUMVILLE, D.N., "Kingship, genealogies and regnal lists", in: *Early Medieval Kingship*, ed. P.H. SAWYER and I.N. WOOD, reprint (Leeds, 1979), pp. 72-104.

Early Modern English Medical Texts: Corpus Description and Studies, ed. I. TAAVITSAINEN and P. PAHTA (Amsterdam, 2010).

ECKERT, P., "Three waves of variation study: The emergence of meaning in the study of variation", *Annual Review of Anthropology* 41 (2012), pp. 87-100.

EGGINS, S., *An Introduction to Systemic Functional Linguistics* (London, 1994).

EGMOND, F., and S. KUSUKAWA, "Circulation of images and graphic practices in Renaissance natural history: The example of Conrad Gessner", *Gesnerus* 73 (2016), pp. 29-72.

EISENSTEIN, E.L., *The Printing Press as an Agent of Change: Communications and Cultural Transformations in Early-Modern Europe*, 2 vols. (Cambridge, 1979).

ELKINS, J., "Introduction: The concept of visual literacy, and its limitations", in: *Visual Literacy*, ed. J. ELKINS (New York, 2009), pp. 1-9.

EMANUEL, R., and S. CHALLONS-LIPTON, "Visual literacy and the digital native: Another look", *Journal of Visual Literacy* 32 (2013), pp. 7-26.

EMMERSON, R.K., "Apocalypse and / as history", in: *Medieval Historical Writing: Britain and Ireland, 500-1500*, ed. J. JAHNER, E. STEINER, and E.M. TYLER (Cambridge, 2019), pp. 51-66.

ENGE, N., *Vintage Dance Manuals* (n.d.) <https://www.libraryofdance.org/manuals/>.

Enlistment: Lists in Medieval and Early Modern Literature, ed. E. VON CONTZEN and J. SIMPSON (Columbus, OH, 2022).

EVEN-EZRA, A., *Lines of Thought: Branching Diagrams and the Medieval Mind* (Chicago, IL, 2021).

FAIRCLOUGH, N., *Language and Power*, 3rd edn (London, 2015).

FAIRMAN, T., "Strike-throughs: What textual alterations can tell us about writers and their scripts, 1795-1835", in *Studies in Late Modern English Correspondence: Methodology and Data*, ed. M. DOSSENA and I. TIEKEN-BOON VAN OSTADE (Bern, 2008), pp. 193-212.

FEIN, S., "109. Mundus iste totus quoddam scaccarium est / All the world's a chess board", in: *The Complete Harley 2253 Manuscript*, ed. and trans. S. FEIN with D. RAYBIN, and J. ZIOLKOWSKI, 3 vols. (Kalamazoo, MI, 2015), 3 <https://d.lib.rochester.edu/teams/text/fein-harley2253-volume-3-article-109>.

FENS-DE ZEEUW, L., "The letter-writing manual in the eighteenth and nineteenth centuries: From polite to practical", in: *Studies in Late Modern English Correspondence: Methodology and Data*, ed. M. DOSSENA and I. TIEKEN-BOON VAN OSTADE (Bern, 2008), pp. 163-192.

FERGUSON, S., "System and schema: Tabulae of the fifteenth to eighteenth centuries", *Princeton University Library Chronicle* 49 (1987), pp. 8-30.

FERRELL, L.A., "Page *techne*: Interpreting diagrams in Early Modern English 'how-to' books", in: *Printed Images in Early Modern Britain: Essays in Interpretation*, ed. M. HUNTER (Farnham, 2010), pp. 113-126.

FREEMAN, J., "The manuscript dissemination and readership of the 'Polychronicon' of Ranulph Higden, c. 1330-c. 1500", unpublished doctoral thesis (University of Cambridge, 2013).

FRIENDLY, M., and H. WAINER, *A History of Data Visualization and Graphic Communication* (Cambridge, MA, 2021).

FUNKHOUSER, H.G., "Historical development of the graphical representation of statistical data", *Osiris* 3 (1937), pp. 269-404.

GARIPZANOV, I., "The rise of graphicacy in Late Antiquity and the Early Middle Ages", *Viator* 46.2 (2015), pp. 1-21.

GARSIDE, R., and N. SMITH, "A hybrid grammatical tagger: CLAWS 4", in: *The Computational Analysis of English*, ed. R. GARSIDE, G. LEECH, and G. SAMPSON (London, 1997), pp. 102-121.

GENETTE, G., *Paratexts: Thresholds of Interpretation*, trans. J. LEWIN (Cambridge, 1997).

GOETZ, H.-W., "The concept of time in the historiography of the eleventh and twelfth centuries", in: *Medieval Concepts of the Past: Ritual, Memory, Historiography*, ed. G. ALTHOFF, J. FRIED, and P.J. GEARY, reprint (Washington, DC, 2003), pp. 139-165.

GORDON, I.A., *The Movement of English Prose* (Longman, 1966).

GOTTSCHALL, A., "The Lord's Prayer in circles and squares: An identification of some analogues of the Vernon Manuscript's Pater Noster table", *Marginalia* 7 (2008).

GOTTSCHALL, A., "The *Pater Noster* and the laity of England, c. 700-1560, with special focus on the clergy's use of the prayer to structure basic catechetical teaching", unpublished doctoral thesis (University of Birmingham, 2014).

GRAFTON, A., *Joseph Scaliger. A Study in the History of Classical Scholarship, vol. II: Historical Chronology* (Oxford, 1993).

GRAFTON, A., *What Was History? The Art of History in Early Modern Europe* (Cambridge, 2012 [2007]).

GRAFTON, A., and M. WILLIAMS, *Christianity and the Transformation of the Book: Origen, Eusebius, and the Library of Caesarea* (Cambridge, MA, 2006).

GRANSDEN, A. *Legends, Traditions and History in Medieval England* (London, 2010 [1992]).

GREENWAY, D.E., "Dates in history: Chronology and memory", *Historical Research* 72 (1999), pp. 127-139.

GRIFFIN, C., *Instructional Writing in English, 1350-1650: Materiality and Meaning* (Abingdon, 2019).

GRINDLEY, C.J., "Reading Piers Plowman C-text annotations: Notes towards the classification of printed and written marginalia in texts from the British Isles 1300-1641", in: *The Medieval Professional Reader at Work: Evidence from Manuscripts of Chaucer, Langland, Kempe and Gower*, ed. K. KERBY-FULTON and M. HILMO (Victoria, BC, 2001), pp. 73-141.

HAIMAN, J., "Ritualization and the development of language", in: *Perspectives on Grammaticalization,* ed. W. PAGLIUCA (Amsterdam, 1994), pp. 3-28.

HAMBURGER, J.F., *Script as Image* (Paris, 2014).

HAMBURGER, J.F., *Diagramming Devotion: Berthold of Nuremberg's Transformation of Hrabanus Maurus's Poems in Praise of the Cross* (Chicago, IL, 2020).

HAMILTON, M., "Expanding the new literacy studies: Using photographs to explore literacy as social practice", in: *Situated Literacies: Reading and Writing in Context*, ed. D. BARTON, M. HAMILTON, and R. IVANIČ (London, 2000), pp. 16-34.

HANNA, R., "Sir Thomas Berkeley and his patronage", *Speculum* 64.4 (1989), pp. 878-916.

HANNA, R. *Pursuing History: Middle English Manuscripts and their Texts* (Palo Alto, CA, 1996).

HART, A.T., *The Man in the Pew, 1558-1660* (London, 1966).

HAUGEN, E., "Dialect, language, nation", *American Anthropologist* 68.4 (1966), pp. 922-935.

HAUGEN, E., "Dialect, language, nation", in: *The Ecology of Language: Essays by Einar Haugen*, ed. A.S. DIL, (Stanford, CA, 1972 [1966]), pp. 237-254.
HECTOR, L.C., *The Handwriting of English Documents* (London, 1958).
HENRY, A., "'The Pater Noster in a table ypeynted' and some other presentations of doctrine in the Vernon manuscript", in: *Studies in the Vernon Manuscript*, ed. D. PEARSALL (Cambridge, 1990), pp. 89-113.
HENTSCHEL, K., *Visual Cultures in Science and Technology: A Comparative History* (Oxford, 2014).
HEPWORTH, B., *Robert Lowth* (Boston, MA, 1978).
HERISSONE, R., "Playford, Purcell, and the functions of music publishing in Restoration England", *Journal of the American Musicological Society* 63.2 (2010), pp. 243-290.
The History of Mathematical Tables: From Sumer to Spreadsheets, ed. M. CAMBELL-KELLY, M. CROARKEN, R. FLOOD, and E. ROBSON (Oxford, 2003).
HOBBS, V., *An Introduction to Religious Language* (London, 2021).
HONKAPOHJA, A., *Alchemy, Medicine, and Commercial Book Production: A Codicological and Linguistic Study of the Voigts-Sloane Manuscript Group* (Turnhout, 2017).
HONKAPOHJA, A., "Functions of punctuation in six Latin and English versions of the plague treatise by John of Burgundy", in: *Punctuation in Context – Past and Present Perspectives,* ed. C. CLARIDGE and M. KYTÖ (Bern, 2019), pp. 151-178.
HONKAPOHJA, A., "Tracing the early modern John of Burgundy", in: *Genre in English Medical Writing, 1500-1820: Sociocultural Contexts of Production and Use*, ed. I. TAAVITSAINEN, T. HILTUNEN, J.J. SMITH, and C. SUHR (Cambridge, 2022), pp. 68-88.
HONKAPOHJA, A., and L. JONES, "From *Practica Phisicalia* to *Mandeville's Travels*: Untangling the misattributed identities and writings of John of Burgundy", *Notes and Queries* 67.1 (2020), pp. 18-27.
HONKAPOHJA, A., and A. LIIRA, "Abbreviations and standardisation in the *Polychronicon*: Latin to English and manuscript to print", in: *The Multilingual Origins of Standard English*, ed. L. WRIGHT (Berlin, 2020), pp. 269-316.
HONKAPOHJA, A., and J. SUOMELA, "'Lexical and function words or language and text type?' Abbreviation consistency in an aligned corpus of Latin and Middle English plague treatises", *Digital Scholarship in the Humanities* 37.3 (2022), pp. 765-787.
HOPPER, P., and E. TRAUGOTT, *Grammaticalization* (Cambridge, 1993).
HOUSTON, K., *Shady Characters: The Secret Life of Punctuation, Symbols, & Other Typographical Marks* (New York, 2013).
HOWARD, U., *Literacy and the Practice of Writing in the 19th Century: A Strange Blossoming of Spirit* (Leicester, 2012).
HUME, R.D., "The economics of culture in London, 1660-1740", *Huntington Library Quarterly* 69.4 (2006), pp. 487-533.
HUNT, K., "Convenient characters: Numerical tables in William Godbid's printed books", *Journal of the Northern Renaissance* 6 (2014), n.p.

HUNT, T., *Popular Medicine in Thirteenth-Century England: Introduction and Texts* (Cambridge, 1990).

Investigations into the Meta-Communicative Lexicon of English: A Contribution to Historical Pragmatics, ed. U. BUSSE and A HÜBLER (Amsterdam, 2012).

JACOBS, A., and A.H. JUCKER, "The historical perspective in pragmatics", in *Historical Pragmatics: Pragmatic Developments in the History of English*, ed. A.H. JUCKER (Amsterdam, 1995), pp. 3-33.

JANSSEN, L., "The rise of 'auxiliary sciences' in early modern national historiography: An 'interdisciplinary' answer to historical scepticism", *History of European Ideas* 43 (2017), pp. 427-441.

JONES, L., "Itineraries and transformations: John of Burgundy's plague treatise", *Bulletin of the History of Medicine* 95.3 (2021), pp. 277-314.

JONES, L., "Bubo men? Repurposing medieval anatomic illustrations for plague therapy in the fifteenth and sixteenth centuries", in: *Death and Disease in the Medieval and Early Modern World: Perspectives from across the Mediterranean and Beyond*, ed. L. JONES and N. VARLIK (Cambridge, 2022), pp. 221-246.

JONES, L., *Patterns of Plague: Changing Ideas about Plague in England and France, 1348-1750* (Montreal, 2022).

JONES, P.M., "Image, word, and medicine in the Middle Ages", in: *Visualizing Medieval Medicine and Natural History, 1200-1550*, ed. J.A. GIVENS, K.M. REEDS, and A. TOUWAIDE (Aldershot, 2006), pp. 1-24.

JONES, P.M., "John Arderne's afterlife in manuscript and print", in: *Genre in English Medical Writing, 1500-1820: Sociocultural Contexts of Production and Use*, ed. I. TAAVITSAINEN, T. HILTUNEN, J.J. SMITH, and C. SUHR (Cambridge, 2022), pp. 13-31.

JORDHEIM, H., "Making universal time: Tools of synchronization", in: *Universal History and the Making of the Global*, ed. H. BJØRNSTAD, H. JORDHEIM, and A. RÉGENT-SUSINI (New York, 2018), pp. 133-151.

JOYCE, J. *Ulysses* (Minneapolis, MN, 2016).

JUCKER, A.H., and P. PAHTA, "Communicating manuscripts: Authors, scribes, readers, listeners and communicating characters", in: *Communicating Early English Manuscripts*, ed. P. PAHTA and A.H. JUCKER (Cambridge, 2011), pp. 3-10.

JUCKER, A.H., and I. TAAVITSAINEN, *English Historical Pragmatics* (Edinburgh, 2013).

JUEL, K., "Defeating the Devil at chess: A struggle between virtue and vice in *Le Jeu des esches de la dame moralisé*", in: *Chess in the Middle Ages and Early Modern Age: A Fundamental Thought Paradigm of the Premodern World*, ed. D.E. O'SULLIVAN (Berlin, 2012), pp. 87-108.

KAISLANIEMI, S., "Code-switching, script-switching, and typeface-switching in Early Modern English manuscript letters and printed tracts", in: *Verbal and Visual Communication in Early English Texts*, ed. M. PEIKOLA, A. MÄKILÄHDE, H. SALMI, M.-L. VARILA, and J. SKAFFARI (Turnhout, 2017), pp. 165-200.

KAY, P., and C. FILLMORE, "Grammatical constructions and linguistic generalizations: The what's X doing Y? construction", *Language* 75.1 (1999), pp. 1-33.

KEISER, G.R., "MS. Rawlinson A. 393: Another Findern manuscript", *Transactions of the Cambridge Bibliographical Society* 7.4 (1980), pp. 445-448.

KEISER, G.R., "Practical books for the gentleman", in: *The Cambridge History of the Book in Britain*, ed. L. HELLINGA and J.B. TRAPP, 7 vols. (Cambridge, 1999), 3, pp. 470-494.

KEISER, G.R., "Two medieval plague treatises and their afterlife in early modern England", *Journal of the History of Medicine and Allied Sciences* 58.3 (2003), pp. 292-324.

KELLEY, D.R., "Between history and system", in: *Historia: Empiricism and Erudition in Early Modern Europe*, ed. G. POMATA and N.G. SIRAISI (Cambridge, MA, 2005), pp. 211-238.

KER, N.R. "From 'above top line' to 'below top line': A change in scribal practice", in: *Books, Collectors, and Libraries: Studies in Medieval Heritage*, ed. A.G. WATSON (London, 1985), pp. 71-74.

KICHUK, D., "Metamorphosis: Remediation in Early English Books Online (EEBO)", *Literary and Linguistic Computing* 22.3 (2007), pp. 291-303.

KOPACZYK, J. *The Legal Language of Scottish Burghs. Standardisation and Lexical Bundles 1380-1560* (Oxford, 2013).

KOPACZYK, J., "Textual standardization of legal Scots *vis a vis* Latin", in: *The Multilingual Origins of Standard English*, ed. L. WRIGHT (Berlin, 2020), pp. 487-514.

KOPACZYK, J., and H. SAUER, "Defining and exploring binomials", in: *Binomials in the History of English: Fixed and Flexible*, ed. J. KOPACZYK and H. SAUER (Cambridge, 2017), pp. 1-24.

KRETZSCHMAR, W., *The Linguistics of Speech* (Cambridge, 2013).

KRYGIER, M., "Binominal glosses in translation: The case of the Wycliffite Bible", in: *Binomials in the History of English: Fixed and Flexible*, ed. J. KOPACZYK and H. SAUER (Cambridge, 2017), pp. 159-172.

KUBASCHEWSKI, E., "Binominals in Caxton's *Ovid* (Book 1)", in: *Binomials in the History of English: Fixed and Flexible*, ed. J. KOPACZYK and H. SAUER (Cambridge, 2017), pp. 141-158.

KÜMIN, B., "Late medieval churchwardens' accounts and parish government: Looking beyond London and Bristol", *The English Historical Review* 119 (2004), 87-99.

KUSUKAWA, S., "The uses of pictures in the formation of learned knowledge: The cases of Leonhard Fuchs and Andreas Vesalius", in: *Transmitting Knowledge: Words, Images, and Instruments in Early Modern Europe*, ed. S. KUSUKAWA and I. MACLEAN (Oxford, 2006), pp. 75-96.

KWAKKEL, E., "medievalbooks" <https://medievalbooks.nl/2014/12/19/the-medieval-origins-of-the-modern-footnote/>.

KWAKKEL, E., "Cultural residue in medieval manuscripts", in: *The Medieval Manuscript Book*, ed. M. JOHNSTON and M. VAN DUSSEN (Cambridge, 2015), pp. 60-76.

KYTÖ, M., and M. PEIKOLA, "Philology on the move: Manuscript studies at the dawn of the 21st century", *Studia Neophilologica* 86 (2014), Special Issue: *Manuscript*

Studies and Codicology: Theory and Practice, ed. M. PEIKOLA and M. KYTÖ, pp. 1-8.

LABOV, W., *Principles of Linguistic Change, 1: Internal Factors* (Oxford, 1994).

LECKNER, S., "Presentation factors affecting reading behaviour in readers of newspaper media: An eye-tracking perspective", *Visual Communication* 11 (2012), pp. 163-184.

LEECH, G., *Principles of Pragmatics* (London, 1983).

LEHMANN, C., *Thoughts on Grammaticalization*, 3rd edn (Berlin, 2015).

LENNARD, J., "Punctuation: And – pragmatics", in: *Historical Pragmatics. Pragmatic Developments in the History of English*, ed. A.H. JUCKER (Amsterdam, 1995), pp. 65-98.

LIIRA, A., *Paratextuality in Manuscript and Print: Verbal and Visual Presentation of the Middle English* Polychronicon. PhD thesis, University of Turku (Turku, 2020). <https://urn.fi/URN:ISBN:978-951-29-8058-1>.

LINDENBAUM, P., "John Playford: Music and politics in the Interregnum", *Huntington Library Quarterly* 64.1-2 (2001), pp. 125-138.

LONATI, E., "Paratextual features in 18th-century medical writing: Framing contents and expanding the text", in: *The Dynamics of Text and Framing Phenomena: Historical Approaches to Paratext and Metadiscourse in English*, ed. M. PEIKOLA and B. BÖS (Amsterdam, 2020), pp. 233-266.

LUBBERS, T.H.J.B., *Towards Profiles of Periodic Style: Discourse Organisation in Modern English Instructional Writing* (Edinburgh, 2017).

LUCAS, P.J., "Sense-units and the use of punctuation-markers in John Capgrave's *Chronicle*", *Archivum Linguisticum* 2 (1971), pp. 1-24.

MCCONCHIE, R.W., "Some reflections on early modern printed title pages", in: *Principles and Practices for the Digital Editing and Annotation of Diachronic Data*, ed. A. MEURMAN-SOLIN and J. TYRKKÖ (Helsinki, 2013) <https://varieng.helsinki.fi/series/volumes/14/mcconchie/>.

MACFARLANE, K., *Biblical Scholarship in an Age of Controversy: The Polemical World of Hugh Broughton (1549-1612)* (Oxford, 2021).

MACHAN, T.W., "The visual pragmatics of code-switching in Late Middle English literature," in: *Code-Switching in Early English,* ed. H. SCHENDL and L. WRIGHT (Berlin, 2011), pp. 303-333.

MCINTOSH, A., "The analysis of written Middle English", *Transactions of the Philological Society* 55 (1956), pp. 26-55.

MCKAY, D., "The duties of the medieval parish clerk", *The Innes Review* 19 (1968), pp. 32-39.

MACKS, A., "The Ward Dance Manuscript: A new source for seventeenth-century English country dance", *Harvard Library Bulletin* 27.3 (2018), pp. 141-166.

MACLEAN, I., *Logic, Signs and Nature in the Renaissance* (Cambridge, 2002).

MACLEAN, I., "Diagrams in the defence of Galen: Medical uses of tables, squares, dichotomies, wheels, and latitudes, 1480-1574", in: *Transmitting Knowledge: Words,*

Images, and Instruments in Early Modern Europe, ed. S. KUSUKAWA and I. MACLEAN (Oxford, 2006), pp. 136-164.

MAK, B., *How the Page Matters* (Toronto, 2011).

MÄKILÄHDE, A., *The Philological-Pragmatic Approach: A Study of Language Choice and Code-Switching in Early Modern English School Performances* PhD thesis, University of Turku (Turku, 2019) <https://urn.fi/URN:ISBN:978-951-29-7888-5>.

MÄKINEN, M., "Efficacy phrases in Early Modern English medical recipes', in: *Medical Writing in Early Modern English*, ed. I. TAAVITSAINEN and P. PAHTA (Cambridge, 2011), pp. 158-179.

The Making of the Vernon Manuscript, ed. W. SCASE (Turnhout, 2013).

MARCHESE, F.T., "Tables and early information visualization", in: *Knowledge Visualization Currents: From Text to Art to Culture*, ed. F.T. MARCHESE and E. BANISSI (London, 2013), pp. 35-61.

MARTIN, S., "EEBO, microfilm, and Umberto Eco: Historical lessons and future directions for building electronic collections", *Microform & Imaging Review* 36.4 (2007), pp. 159-164.

MATHESON, L.M., "Medecin sans frontieres?: The European dissemination of John of Burgundy's plague treatise", *ANQ* 18 (2005), pp. 19-30.

MAXTED, I., "*Impressorie Arte*: The impact of printing in Exeter and Devon", in: *Print Cultures and Peripheries in Early Modern England*, ed. B.R. COSTAS (Brill, 2013), pp. 127-146.

Medical and Scientific Writing in Late Medieval English, ed. P. PAHTA and I. TAAVITSAINEN (Cambridge, 2004).

Medical Paratexts from Medieval to Modern: Dissecting the Page, ed. H.C Tweed and D.G. SCOTT (Cham, 2018).

Medical Writing in Early Modern English, ed. I. TAAVITSAINEN and P. PAHTA (Cambridge, 2011).

MEILLET, A., "L'évolution des formes grammaticales", *Scientia* (Rivista di Scienza) 12.26 (1912), pp. 130-148.

MELD Manual 2017.1 <https://www.uis.no/en/meld-corpus-files>.

MEURMAN-SOLIN, A. "Visual prosody in manuscript letters in the study of syntax and discourse", in *Principles and Practices for the Digital Editing and Annotation of Diachronic Data*, ed. A. MEURMAN-SOLIN and J. TYRKKÖ (Helsinki, 2013) <https://varieng.helsinki.fi/series/volumes/14/meurman-solin_a/>.

MICHAEL, I., *English Grammatical Categories and the Tradition to 1800* (Cambridge, 1970).

MICHAEL, I., *The Teaching of English: From the Sixteenth Century to 1870* (Cambridge, 1987).

MILLIMAN, P., "*Ludus scaccarii*: Games and governance in twelfth-century England", in: *Chess in the Middle Ages and Early Modern Age: A Fundamental Thought Paradigm of the Premodern World*, ed. D.E. O'SULLIVAN (Berlin, 2012), pp. 63-86.

MOLLIN, S., *The (Ir)reversibility of English Binomials: Corpus, Constraints, Developments* (Amsterdam, 2014).
MOONEY, L.R., "The scribe", in: *Sex, Aging, & Death in a Medieval Medical Compendium: Trinity College Cambridge MS.14.52, Its Texts, Language, and Scribe*, ed. M.T. TAVORMINA (Tempe, AZ, 2006), pp. 55-63.
MOORE, C., "The use of *videlicet* in early modern slander depositions: A case of genre-specific grammaticalization", *Journal of Historical Pragmatics* 7.2 (2006), pp. 245-263.
MOORE, C., *Quoting Speech in Early English* (Cambridge, 2011).
MOORE, C., "Talking about talk: *quethen, quoth, quote*", in: *The Pragmatics of Quoting Now and Then*, ed. J. ARENDHOLZ, W. BUBLITZ, and M. KIRNER (Berlin, 2015), pp. 255-270.
MOORE, C., "Visual pragmatics: Speech presentation and Middle English manuscripts", in: *The Cambridge Handbook of English Historical Linguistics*, ed. M. KYTÖ and P. PAHTA (Cambridge, 2016), pp. 481-496.
MOORE, C., "Discourse variation, *mise-en-page*, and textual organisation in Middle English saints' lives", in: *Verbal and Visual Communication in Early English Texts*, ed. M. PEIKOLA, A. MÄKILÄHDE, H. SALMI, M.-L. VARILA, and J. SKAFFARI (Turnhout, 2017), pp. 23-40.
MOORE, C., "The path not taken: Parentheses and written direct speech in early printed books", in: *Punctuation in Context – Past and Present Perspectives*, ed. M. KYTÖ and C. CLARIDGE, (Bern, 2019), pp. 85-101.
MOORE, C., "Paratext, information studies, and Middle English manuscripts", in: *The Dynamics of Text and Framing Phenomena: Historical Approaches to Paratext and Metadiscourse in English*, ed. M. PEIKOLA and B. BÖS (Amsterdam, 2020), pp. 289-307.
MOORE, P., and C. FITZ, "Using Gestalt theory to teach document design and graphics", *Technical Communication Quarterly* 2.4 (1993), pp. 389-410.
MOORE, R., "Paper cuts: The early modern fugitive print", *Object: Graduate Research and Reviews in the History of Art and Visual Culture* 17.1 (2015), pp. 54-76.
MULLINI, R., "Graphic surgical practice in the handbills of seventeenth-century London irregulars", in: *Medical Paratexts from Medieval to Modern: Dissecting the Page*, ed. H.C. TWEED and D.G. SCOTT (Cham, 2018), pp. 57-73.
The Multilingual Origins of Standard English, ed. L. WRIGHT (Berlin, 2020).
MUNROE, J., "Gender, class, and the art of gardening: Gardening manuals in early modern England", *Prose Studies* 28.2 (2006), pp. 197-210.
MURDOCH, J.E., *Album of Science: Antiquity and the Middle Ages* (New York, 1984).
MURRAY, H.J.R., *A History of Chess* (Oxford, 1913).
MUSSER GOLLADAY, S., "Images of medieval Spanish chess and captive damsels in distress", in: *Chess in the Middle Ages and Early Modern Age: A Fundamental Thought Paradigm of the Premodern World*, ed. D.E. O'SULLIVAN (Berlin, 2012), pp. 135-167.

MUSSOU, A., "Playing with memory: The chessboard as a mnemonic tool in medieval didactic literature", in: *Chess in the Middle Ages and Early Modern Age: A Fundamental Thought Paradigm of the Premodern World*, ed. D.E. O'SULLIVAN (Berlin, 2012), pp. 187-198.

NAFDE, A., "Hoccleve's hands: The mise-en-page of the autograph and non-autograph manuscripts", *Journal of the Early Book Society for the Study of Manuscripts and Printing History* 16 (2013), pp. 55-83, 314.

NEDELIUS, S., "Changed perspectives: On modernised punctuation in Middle English texts", unpublished doctoral dissertation (University of Oslo, 2021).

NEVALAINEN, T., "Processes of supralocalisation and the rise of Standard English in the Early Modern Period", in: *Generative Theory and Corpus Studies,* ed. R. BERMÚDEZ-OTERO, D. DENISON, R.M. HOGG, and C. MCCULLY (Berlin, 2000), pp. 329-371.

NEVALAINEN, T., "Descriptive adequacy of the S-curve model in diachronic studies of language change" (Helsinki, 2015) <https://varieng.helsinki.fi/series/volumes/16/nevalainen/>.

NEVILE, J., *Eloquent Body: Dance and Humanist Culture in Fifteenth-Century Italy* (Bloomington, IN, 2004).

NEVILE, J., *Footprints of the Dance: An Early Seventeenth-Century Dance Master's Notebook* (Leiden, 2018).

NEWMAN, H., "'[P]rophane fiddlers': Medical paratexts and indecent readers in early modern England", in: *Medical Paratexts from Medieval to Modern: Dissecting the Page*, ed. H.C. TWEED and D. G. SCOTT (Cham, 2018), pp. 15-41.

NICHOLSON, B., "The digital turn: Exploring the methodological possibilities of digital newspaper archives", *Media History* 19 (2013), pp. 59-73.

NORTH, J.D., "Chronology and the age of the world", in: *Cosmology, History, and Theology*, ed. W. YOURGRAU and A.D. BRECK (Boston, MA, 1977), pp. 307-333.

NUNBERG, G., *The Linguistics of Punctuation* (Menlo Park, CA, 1990).

NUNBERG, G., T. BRISCOE, and R. HUDDLESTON, "Punctuation", in: *The Cambridge Grammar of the English Language*, ed. R. HUDDLESTON and G.K. PULLUM (Cambridge, 2002), pp. 1723-1764.

NUTTON, V., "Representation and memory in Renaissance anatomical illustration", in: *Immagini per conoscere: Dal Rinascimento alla Rivoluzione scientifica*, ed. F. MEROI and C. POGLIANO (Firenze, 2001), pp. 61-80.

ONG, W.J., "From allegory to diagram in the Renaissance mind: A study in the significance of the allegorical tableau", *The Journal of Aesthetics and Art Criticism* 17 (1959), pp. 423-440.

OOMS, K., P. DE MAEYER, L. DUPONT, N. VAN DER VEKEN, N. VAN DE WEGHE, and S. VERPLAETSE, "Education in cartography: What is the status of young people's map-reading skills?", *Cartography and Geographic Information Science* 43 (2016), pp. 134-153.

OSSELTON, N.E., "Formal and informal spelling in the 18th century: Error, honour and related words", *English Studies* 44 (1963), pp. 267-275.

OSSELTON, N.E., "Informal spelling systems in Early Modern English: 1500-1800", in: *English Historical Linguistics: Studies in Development*, ed. N.F. BLAKE and C. JONES (Sheffield, 1984), pp. 123-137.

The Oxford Handbook of Latin Palaeography, ed. F.T. COULSON and R.G. BABCOCK (New York, 2020).

PAHTA, P., and I. TAAVITSAINEN, "Introducing Early Modern English medical texts", in: *Early Modern English Medical Texts: Corpus Description and Studies*, ed. I. TAAVITSAINEN and P. PAHTA (Amsterdam, 2010), pp. 1-8.

PANTIN, I., "Analogy and difference: A comparative study of medical and astronomical images in books, 1470-1550", in: *Observing the World through Images: Diagrams and Figures in the Early-Modern Arts and Sciences*, ed. N. JARDINE and I. FAY (Leiden, 2013), pp. 9-44.

PARKES, M.B., *English Cursive Book Hands 1250-1500* (Oxford, 1969).

PARKES, M.B., "The literacy of the laity", in: *The Mediaeval World*, ed. D. DAICHES and A. THORLBY (London, 1973), pp. 555-577.

PARKES, M.B., "The influence of the concepts of *ordinatio* and *compilatio* on the development of the book", in: *Medieval Learning and Literature: Essays Presented to Richard William Hunt*, ed. J.J.G. ALEXANDER and M.T. GIBSON (Oxford, 1976), pp. 115-141; repr. in: *Scribes, Scripts and Readers: Studies in the Communication, Presentation, and Dissemination of Medieval Texts* (London, 1991), pp. 55-74.

PARKES, M.B., "Punctuation, or pause and effect", in: *Medieval Eloquence: Studies in the Theory and Practice of Medieval Rhetoric*, ed. J.J. MURPHY (Berkeley, 1978), pp. 127-142.

PARKES, M.B., *Pause and Effect: An Introduction to the History of Punctuation in the West* (Aldershot, 1992).

PARKES, M.B., *Their Hands Before Our Eyes: A Closer Look at Scribes. The Lyell Lectures Delivered at the University of Oxford 1999* (Aldershot, 2008).

PATTWELL, N., "Providing for the learned cleric: Schemas and diagrams in *Sacerdos Parochialis* in British Library MS Burney 356", *Journal of the Early Book Society for the Study of Manuscripts and Printing* 10 (2007), pp. 129-149.

PEIKOLA, M., "Tables of lections in manuscripts of the Wycliffite Bible", in: *Form and Function in the Late Medieval Bible*, ed. E. POLEG and L. LIGHT (Leiden, 2013), pp. 351-378.

PEIKOLA, M., "Guidelines for consumption: Scribal ruling patterns and designing the mise-en-page in later medieval England", in: *Manuscripts and Printed Books in Europe 1350-1550: Packaging, Presentation and Consumption*, ed. E. CAYLEY and S. POWELL (Liverpool, 2014), pp. 14-31.

PEIKOLA, M., and M.-L. VARILA, "Multimodal and multilingual practices in late medieval English calendars", in: *Multilingualism from Manuscript to 3D: Intersections of Modalities from Medieval to Modern Times*, ed. M. WŁODARCZYK, J. TYRKKÖ, and E. ADAMCZYK (New York, 2023), pp. 93-118.

PEIKOLA, M., and M.-L. VARILA, "Presenting manuscript tables and diagrams to the Middle English reader", *Journal of Historical Pragmatics*, published ahead of print 27 August 2024.

PENNUTO, C., "From text to diagram: Giambattista Da Monte and the practice of medicine", in: *Inscribing Knowledge in the Medieval Book: The Power of Paratexts*, ed. R. BROWN-GRANT, P. CARMASSI, G. DROSSBACH, A.D. HEDEMAN, V. TURNER, and I. VENTURA (Berlin, 2020), pp. 95-116.

PETTI, A.G., *English Literary Hands from Chaucer to Dryden* (London, 1977).

POPPER, N., *Walter Ralegh's* History of the World *and the Historical Culture of the Late Renaissance* (Chicago, IL, 2012).

The Power of Images in Early Modern Science, ed. W. LEFÉVRE, J. RENN, and U. SCHOEPFLIN (Basel, 2003).

PRATT, A., "Talking about early digital facsimiles with Sarah Werner", *Ransom Center Magazine*, interview published January 31, 2018. <https://sites.utexas.edu/ransomcentermagazine/2018/01/31/talking-about-early-digital-facsimiles-with-sarah-werner/>.

PROOT, G., "The transformation of the typical page in the handpress era in the Southern Netherlands, 1473-c. 1800", in: *Impagination – Layout and Materiality of Writing and Publication: Interdisciplinary Approaches from East and West*, ed. K. CHANG, A. GRAFTON, and G.W. MOST (Berlin, 2021), pp. 237-272.

PUGH, T., "The development of silent reading", in: *The Road to Effective Reading*, ed. W. LATHAM (London, 1975), pp. 110-119.

PURCHASE, H.C., "Twelve years of diagrams research", *Journal of Visual Languages and Computing* 25 (2014), pp. 57-75.

QUIRK, R., S. GREENBAUM, G. LEECH, and J. SVARTVIK, *A Comprehensive Grammar of the English Language* (London, 1985).

RATIA, M., and C. SUHR, "Verbal and visual communication in titlepages of Early Modern English specialised medical texts", in: *Verbal and Visual Communication in Early English Texts*, ed. M. PEIKOLA, A. MÄKILÄHDE, H. SALMI, M.-L. VARILA, and J. SKAFFARI (Turnhout, 2017), pp. 67-93.

RAVELHOFER, B., "Memorable movements: Rhetoric and choreography in early modern courtly entertainment", *Internationales Archiv für Sozialgeschichte der Deutschen Literatur* 22.1 (1997), pp. 1-18.

RAVELHOFER, B., "Dancing at the Court of Queen Elizabeth", in: *Queen Elizabeth I: Past and Present*, ed. C. JANSOHN (Münster, 2004), pp. 101-116.

RIGGSBY, A.M., *Mosaics of Knowledge: Representing Information in the Roman World* (New York, 2019).

RISSANEN, M., "Language of law and the development of Standard English", in: *Writing in Nonstandard English*, ed. I. TAAVITSAINEN, G. MELCHERS, and P. PAHTA (Amsterdam, 1999), pp. 189-203.

ROBERTS, J., and P. ROBINSON, *The History of the Book in the West* (London, 2010).

ROBSON, E., "Tables and tabular formatting in Sumer, Babylonia, and Assyria, 2500 BCE-50 CE", in: *The History of Mathematical Tables: From Sumer to Spread-*

sheets, ed. M. CAMPBELL-KELLY, M. CROARKEN, R. FLOOD, and E. ROBSON (Oxford, 2003), pp. 19-48.

ROGOS-HEBDA, J., "The visual text: Bibliographic codes as pragmatic markers on a manuscript page", *Studia Anglica Posnaniensia* 51 (2016), pp. 37-44.

ROMERO-BARRANCO, J., "Early Modern English scientific text types: Edition and assessment of linguistic complexity of the texts in MS Hunter 135 (ff. 34r-121v)", unpublished doctoral thesis (Universidad de Málaga, 2017).

ROMERO-BARRANCO, J., "Punctuation in Early Modern English scientific writing: The case of two scientific text types in GUL, MS Hunter 135", *Studia Anglica Posnaniensia* 54.1 (2019), pp. 59-80.

ROSENBERG, D., and A. GRAFTON, *Cartographies of Time: A History of the Timeline* (New York, 2010).

ROUSE, R.H., and M.A. ROUSE, "*Statim invenire*: Schools, preachers, and new attitudes to the page", in: *Renaissance and Renewal in the Twelfth Century*, ed. R.L. BENSON and G. CONSTABLE with C.D. LANHAM (Oxford, 1982), pp. 191-219.

ROUSE, R.H., and M.A. ROUSE, "Concordances et index", in: *Mise en page et mise en texte du livre manuscript*, ed. H.-J. MARTIN and J. VEZIN with J. MONFRIN (Paris, 1990), pp. 219-228.

ROWLEY-JOLIVET, E., "The emergence of text-graphics conventions in a medical research journal: *The Lancet* 1823-2015", *ASp [Online]* 73 (2018), pp. 5-24 <https://doi.org/10.4000/ asp. 5107>.

ROWSELL, J., D. BLOOME, M.L. CASTANHEIRA, and C. LEUNG, "Introduction: Lost in our meditations about re-theorizing literacy practices across complex social and cultural contexts", in: *Re-Theorizing Literacy Practices: Complex Social and Cultural Contexts*, ed. D. BLOOME, M.L. CASTANHEIRA, C. LEUNG, and J. ROWSELL (New York, 2019), pp. 1-11.

RUOKKEINEN, S., A. LIIRA, M.-L. VARILA, O. NORBLAD, and M. PEIKOLA, "Developing a classification model for graphic devices in early printed books", *Studia Neophilologica* 96.1 (2024), pp. 69-93.

SAENGER, P., "Orality and visible language", in: *The Oxford Handbook of Latin Palaeography*, ed. F.T. COULSON and R.G. BABCOCK (Oxford, 2020), pp. 693-704.

SAIRIO, A., "Bluestocking letters and the influence of eighteenth-century grammars", in: *Studies in Late Modern English Correspondence: Methodology and Data*, ed. M. DOSSENA and I. TIEKEN-BOON VAN OSTADE (Bern, 2008), pp. 137-162.

SALMI, H., "'I write not to expert practitioners, but to learners': Perceptions of reader-friendliness in early modern printed books", in: *The Dynamics of Text and Framing Phenomena: Historical Approaches to Paratext and Metadiscourse in English*, ed. M. PEIKOLA and B. BÖS (Amsterdam, 2020), pp. 187-207.

SALMON, V., *Language and Society in Early Modern England: Selected Essays 1981-1994* (Amsterdam, 1996).

SAMUELS, M.L., "Some applications of Middle English dialectology", *English Studies* 44 (1963), pp. 81-94.

SANCHEZ-STOCKHAMMER, C., "Present-day English hyphenation: Historical origin, functions and pragmatics", in: *Punctuation in Context – Past and Present Perspectives*, ed. C. CLARIDGE and M. KYTÖ (Bern, 2020), pp. 47-65.

SANDLER, L.F., *Omne Bonum: A Fourteenth-Century Encyclopedia of Universal Knowledge*, 2 vols. (London, 1996).

SAUER, H., "Flexible and formulaic: Binomials and multinomials in the Late Middle English: The Wise Book of Philosophy and Astronomy", *Acta Philologica* 50 (2017), pp. 62-78.

SAWYER, D., *Reading English Verse in Manuscript: c.1350-c.1500* (Oxford, 2020).

SCASE, W., "'Looke this calender and then proced': Tables of contents in medieval English manuscripts", in: *The Dynamics of the Medieval Manuscript: Text Collections from a European Perspective*, ed. K. PRATT, B. BESAMUSCA, M. MEYER, and A. PUTTER (Göttingen, 2017), pp. 287-306.

SCASE, W., *Visible English: Graphic Culture, Scribal Practice, and Identity, c. 700-c. 1550* (Turnhout, 2022).

SCASE, W.. "John Benet, scribe and compiler, and Dublin, Trinity College, MS 516", in: *Scribal Cultures in Late Medieval England: Essays in Honour of Linne R. Mooney*, ed. M. CONNOLLY, H. JAMES-MADDOCKS, and † D. PEARSALL (Woodbridge, 2022), pp. 241-258.

SCHAEFER, U., *The Beginnings of Standardization: Language and Culture in Fourteenth-Century England* (Berlin, 2006).

SCHAEFER, U., "Middle English: Standardization", in: *English Historical Linguistics*, ed. A. BERGS and L.J. BRINTON, 2 vols. (Berlin, 2012), 1, pp. 519-533.

SCHIFFRIN, D., *Discourse Markers* (Cambridge, 1987).

SCHIPOR, D., *A Study of Multilingualism in the Late Medieval Material of the Hampshire Record Office*. PhD thesis, University of Stavanger (Stavanger, 2018).

SCHRIRE, R., "Shifting paradigms: Ideas, materiality and the changing shape of grammar in the Renaissance", *Journal of the Warburg and Courtauld Institutes* 84 (2021), pp. 1-31.

SCRIBNER, S., and M. COLE, *The Psychology of Literacy* (Cambridge, MA, 1981).

SEBBA, M., "Sociolinguistic approaches to writing systems research", *Writing Systems Research* 1 (2009), pp. 35-49.

SERAFINI, F., "Multimodal literacy: From theories to practices", *Language Arts* 92 (2015), pp. 412-423.

SHERMAN, W.H., *Used Books: Marking Readers in Renaissance England* (Philadelphia, PA, 2008).

SMITH, J., "A content analysis of figure captions in academic journals from four disciplines", *IEEE Transactions on Professional Communication* 63.4 (2020), pp. 341-360.

SMITH, J.J., *An Historical Study of English: Function, Form, and Change* (London, 1996).

SMITH, J.J., "Punctuating Mirk's Festial: A Scottish text and its implications", in: *Preaching the Word in Manuscript and Print in Late Medieval England*, ed. M.W. DRIVER and V. O'MARA (Turnhout, 2013), pp. 161-192.

SMITH, J.J., "From 'secreit' script to public print: Punctuation, news management, and the condemnation of the Earl of Bothwell", *Huntington Library Quarterly* 80.2 (2017), pp. 223-238.

SMITH, J.J., "The afterlives of Nicholas Love", *Studia Neophilologica* 89.sup1 (2017), pp. 59-74.

SMITH, J.J., "Textual form and textual function: Punctuation and the reception of early English texts", in: *Punctuation in Context – Past and Present Perspectives*, ed. C. CLARIDGE and M. KYTÖ (Bern, 2020), pp. 131-150.

SMITH, J.J., *Transforming Early English: The Reinvention of Early English and Older Scots* (Cambridge, 2020).

SMITH, M.M., *The Title Page, Its Early Development, 1460-1510* (London, 2000).

STEINER, B. *Die Ordnung Der Geschichte: Historische Tabellenwerke in Der Frühen Neuzeit* (Köln, 2008).

STEINER, E., *John Trevisa's Information Age: Knowledge and the Pursuit of Literature, c. 1400* (Oxford, 2021).

STENROOS, M., "Regional variation and supralocalization in Late Medieval English: Comparing administrative and literary texts", in: *Records of Real People. Linguistic Variation in Middle English Local Documents*, ed. M. STENROOS and K.V. THENGS (Amsterdam, 2020), pp. 95-128.

STENROOS, M., G. BERGSTRØM, and K.V. THENGS, "The categorization of Middle English documents. Interactions of function, form and language", in *Records of Real People. Linguistic Variation in Middle English Local Documents*, ed. M. STENROOS and K.V. THENGS (Amsterdam, 2020), pp. 37-67.

STENROOS, M., and K.V. THENGS, "Local documents as source material for the study of late medieval English", in: *Records of Real People. Linguistic Variation in Middle English Local Documents*, ed. M. STENROOS, and K.V. THENGS (Amsterdam, 2020), pp. 3-21.

SYLVESTER, L., "The role of multilingualism in the emergence of a technical register in the Middle English period", in: *The Multilingual Origins of Standard English,* ed. L. WRIGHT (Berlin, 2020), pp. 365-379.

TAAVITSAINEN, I., "Changing conventions of writing: The dynamics of genres, text types, and text traditions", *European Journal of English Studies* 5.2 (2001), pp. 139-150.

TAAVITSAINEN, I., and A.H. JUCKER, "Twenty years of historical pragmatics: Origins, developments and changing thought styles", *Journal of Historical Pragmatics* 16 (2015), pp. 1-24.

TAAVITSAINEN, I., and P. PAHTA, "Vernacularisation of medical writing in English: A corpus-based study of scholasticism", *Early Science and Medicine* 3.2 (1998), pp. 157-183.

TANNENBAUM, S.A., *The Handwriting of the Renaissance* (New York, 1930).

Taxonomies of Knowledge: Information and Order in Medieval Manuscripts, ed. E. STEINER (Philadelphia, PA, 2015).
TAYLOR, J., "The development of the *Polychronicon* continuation", *English Historical Review* 76.298 (1961), pp. 20-36.
TEBEAUX, E., *The Flowering of a Tradition: Technical Writing in England, 1641-1700* (Amityville, NY, 2014).
TEBEAUX, E., *The Flowering of a Tradition: Technical Writing in England, 1641-1700* (London, 2017 [2014]).
TEBEAUX, E., *The Emergence of a Tradition: Technical Writing in the English Renaissance, 1475-1640* (London, 2017 [1997]).
THAISEN, J., "Transparently hierarchical: Punctuation in the Townshend family recipe book", *International Journal of English Studies* 20.2 (2020), pp. 11-30.
THAISEN, J., review of *Records of Real People: Linguistic Variation in Middle English Local Documents*, ed. M. STENROOS and K.V. THENGS (Amsterdam, 2020), *English Language and Linguistics* 27.1 (2023), pp. 214-221.
THAISEN, J., and H. RUTKOWSKA, "Introduction", in: *Scribes, Printers, and the Accidentals of Their Texts*, ed. J. THAISEN and H. RUTKOWSKA (Frankfurt am Main, 2011), pp. 9-13.
THENGS, K.V., "Compactness of expression in Middle English legal documents", *Filologia Germanica – Germanic Philology* 7 (2015), pp. 163-181.
THOMPSON, J.J., "The compiler in action: Robert Thornton and the 'Thornton Romances' in Lincoln Cathedral MS 91", in: *Manuscripts and Readers in Fifteenth-Century England*, ed. D. PEARSALL (Woodbridge, 1983), pp. 113-124.
THOMPSON, J.J., *Robert Thornton and the London Thornton Manuscript* (Woodbridge, 1987).
TIEKEN-BOON VAN OSTADE, I., "Standardization of English spelling: The eighteenth-century printers' contribution", in: *Advances in English Historical Linguistics*, ed. J. FISIAK and M. KRYGIER (Berlin, 1998), pp. 457-470.
TIEKEN-BOON VAN OSTADE, I., "'Disrespectful and too Familiar'? Abbreviations as an index of politeness in 18th-century letters", in: *Syntax, Style and Grammatical Norms: English from 1500-2000*, ed. C. DALTON-PUFFER, D. KASTOVSKY, N. RITT, and H. SCHENDL (Bern, 2006), pp. 229-247.
TIEKEN-BOON VAN OSTADE, I., "Grammars, grammarians and grammar writing: An introduction", in: *Grammars, Grammarians and Grammar-Writing in Eighteenth-Century England*, ed. I. TIEKEN-BOON VAN OSTADE (Berlin, 2008), pp. 1-14.
TIEKEN-BOON VAN OSTADE, I., "Letters as a source for reconstructing social networks: The case of Robert Lowth", in: *Studies in Late Modern English Correspondence: Methodology and Data*, ed. M. DOSSENA and I. TIEKEN-BOON VAN OSTADE (Bern, 2008), pp. 51-76.
TIEKEN-BOON VAN OSTADE, I., "Communicative competence and the language of eighteenth-century letters", in: *The Language of Public and Private Communication in a Historical Perspective*, ed. N. BROWNLEES, G. DEL LUNGO, and J. DENTON (Newcastle upon Tyne, 2010), pp. 24-45.

TIEKEN-BOON VAN OSTADE, I., *The Bishop's Grammar. Robert Lowth and the Rise of Prescriptivism* (Oxford, 2011).
TIEKEN-BOON VAN OSTADE, I., "Late Modern English in a Dutch context", *English Language & Linguistics* 16.2 (2012), pp. 301-317.
TIEKEN-BOON VAN OSTADE, I., *In Search of Jane Austen. The Language of the Letters* (Oxford, 2014).
TIEKEN-BOON VAN OSTADE, I., review of *Jane Austen's Letters*, 4th edn, ed. D. LE FAYE (Oxford, 2011), *English Studies* 96.1 (2014), pp. 103-107.
TIEKEN-BOON VAN OSTADE, I., *Nóg meer brieven van Lowth?!* (Leiden, 2021).
TONRY, K., "Reading history in Caxton's *Polychronicon*", *Journal of English and Germanic Philology* 111 (2012), pp. 169-198.
Transmitting Knowledge: Words, Images and Instruments in Early Modern Europe, ed. S. KUSUKAWA and I. MACLEAN (Oxford, 2006).
TRAUGOTT, E., and G. TROUSDALE, *Constructionalization and Constructional Changes* (Oxford, 2013).
TSCHICHOLD, J., *Formenwandlungen der &-Zeichen* (Frankfurt am Main, 1953).
TWYMAN, M., "Articulating graphic language: A historical perspective", in *Toward a New Understanding of Literacy*, ed. M.E. WROLSTAD and D.F. FISHER (New York, 1986), pp. 188-251.
TWYMAN, M., *The British Library Guide to Printing: History and Techniques* (London, 1998).
TYRKKÖ, J., "'Halles Lanfranke' and its most excellent and learned expositive table", in: *Words in Dictionaries and History: Essays in Honour of R. W. McConchie*, ed. O. TIMOFEEVA and T. SÄILY (Amsterdam, 2011), pp. 17-39.
TYRKKÖ, J., "Notes on eighteenth-century dictionary grammars", *Transactions of the Philological Society* 111.2 (2013), pp. 179-201.
TYRKKÖ, J., "Printing houses as communities of practice: Orthography in early modern medical books", in: *Communities of Practice in the History of English*, ed. A.H. JUCKER and J. KOPACZYK (Amsterdam, 2013), pp. 151-176.
TYRKKÖ, J., "New methods of bringing image data into historical linguistics: A case study with medical writing 1500-1700", *Studia Neophilologica* 89.sup1 (2017), pp. 90-108.
TYRKKÖ, J., "Quantifying contrasts: A method of computational analysis of visual features on the early printed pages", in: *Verbal and Visual Communication in Early English Texts*, ed. M. PEIKOLA, A. MÄKILÄHDE, H. SALMI, M.-L. VARILA, and J. SKAFFARI (Turnhout, 2017), pp. 95-122.
TYRKKÖ, J., and I. TAAVITSAINEN, "The field of medical writing in fuzzy edges", in: *Early Modern English Medical Texts: Corpus Description and Studies*, ed. I. TAAVITSAINEN and P. PAHTA (Amsterdam, 2010), pp. 57-62.
VAN GOG, T., "The signaling (or cueing) principle in multimedia learning", in: *The Cambridge Handbook of Multimedia Learning*, 3rd edn, ed. R.E. MAYER and L. FIORELLA (Cambridge, 2021), pp. 221-230.

VARILA, M.-L., and M. PEIKOLA, "Promotional conventions on English title-pages up to 1550: Modifiers of time, scope, and quality", in: *Norms and Conventions in the History of English,* ed. B. BÖS and C. CLARIDGE (Amsterdam, 2019), pp. 73-97.

VARILA, M.-L., H. SALMI, A. MÄKILÄHDE, J. SKAFFARI, and M. PEIKOLA, "Disciplinary decoding: Towards understanding the language of visual and material features", in: *Verbal and Visual Communication in Early English Texts*, ed. M. PEIKOLA, A. MÄKILÄHDE, H. SALMI, M.-L. VARILA, and J. SKAFFARI (Turnhout, 2017), pp. 1-20.

Verbal and Visual Communication in Early English Texts, ed. M. PEIKOLA, A. MÄKILÄHDE, H. SALMI, M.-L. VARILA, and J. SKAFFARI (Turnhout, 2017).

The Visualization of Knowledge in Medieval and Early Modern Europe, ed. M. KUPFER, A.S. COHEN, and J.H. CHAIES (Turnhout, 2020).

VOIGTS, L.E., "The 'Sloane Group': Related scientific and medical manuscripts from the fifteenth century in the Sloane Collection", *The British Library Journal* 16.1 (1990), pp. 26-57.

VOIGTS, L.E., "The Golden Table of Pythagoras", in: *Popular and Practical Science of Medieval England*, ed. L.M. MATHESON (East Lansing, MI, 1994), pp. 123-139.

VOIGTS, L.E., and M.R. MCVAUGH, "A Latin technical phlebotomy and its Middle English translation", *Transactions of the American Philosophical Society: Held at Philadelphia for Promoting Useful Knowledge* 74.2 (1984), pp. 1-69.

VON CONTZEN, E., and J. SIMPSON, "Introduction: Enlistment as poetic stratagem", in: *Enlistment: Lists in Medieval and Early Modern Literature*, ed. E. VON CONTZEN and J. SIMPSON (Columbus, OH, 2022), pp. 1-13.

VORLAT, E., *The Development of English Grammatical Theory, 1586-1737: with Special Reference to the Theory of Parts of Speech* (Leuven, 1975).

VORLAT, E., "On the history of English teaching grammars", in: *Sprachtheorien der Neuzeit* III/2, ed. P. SCHMITTER (Tübingen, 2007), pp. 500-525.

VULIC, K.R., "Prayer and vernacular writing in late-medieval England", unpublished doctoral thesis (University of California, Berkeley, 2004)

WAKELIN, D., *Designing English: Early Literature on the Page* (Oxford, 2018).

WALDRON, R., "Trevisa's original prefaces on translation", in: *Medieval English Studies Presented to George Kane*, ed. E.D. KENNEDY, R. WALDRON, and J.S. WITTIG (Woodbridge, 1988), pp. 285-299.

WALDRON, R., "The manuscripts of Trevisa's translation of the *Polychronicon*: Towards a new edition", *Modern Language Quarterly* 51.3 (1990), pp. 281-317.

WALDRON, R., "Dialect aspects of manuscripts of Trevisa's translation of the Polychronicon", in: *Regionalism in Late Medieval Manuscripts and Texts*, ed. F. RIDDY (Woodbridge, 1991), pp. 67-88.

WALKER, S., *Typography and Language in Everyday Life: Prescriptions and Practices* (Harlow, 2001).

WALLER, R., "Graphic literacies for a digital age: The survival of layout", *The Information Society* 28 (2016), pp. 236-252.

WEAR, A., *Knowledge and Practice in English Medicine, 1550-1680* (Cambridge, 2000).
WEBSTER, N., *The American Spelling Book, Containing the Rudiments of the English Language, for the Use of Schools in the United States* (Middletown, CT, 1831).
WENZEL, S., "Lexical doublets (binomials) in sermons from late medieval England", *Neuphilologische Mitteilungen* 123.1 (2022), pp. 157-170.
WERNER, S., "Where material book culture meets digital humanities", *Journal of Digital Humanities* 1.3 (2012) <http://journalofdigitalhumanities.org/1-3/where-material-book-culture-meets-digital-humanities-by-sarah-werner/>.
WEVERS, M., and T. SMITS, "The visual digital turn: Using neural networks to study historical images", *Digital Scholarship in the Humanities* 35 (2020), pp. 194-207.
WHITLOCK, K., "John Playford's *The English Dancing Master* 1650/51 as cultural politics", *Folk Music Journal* 7.5 (1999), pp. 548-578.
WHYMAN, S.E., *The Pen and the People. English Letter Writers 1660-1800* (Oxford, 2009).
WILCOX, D.J., *The Measure of Times Past: Pre-Newtonian Chronologies and the Rhetoric of Relative Time* (Chicago, 1987).
WOOLF, D.R., "From hystories to the historical: Five transitions in thinking about the past, 1500-1700", *Huntington Library Quarterly* 68 (2005), pp. 33-70.
WORMALD, F., and P.M. GILES, *A Descriptive Catalogue of the Additional Illuminated Manuscripts in the Fitzwilliam Museum*, 2 vols. (Cambridge, 1982).
WRIGHT, L., "A critical look at previous accounts of the standardisation of English", in: *The Multilingual Origins of Standard English,* ed. L. WRIGHT (Berlin, 2020), pp. 17-38.
WRIGHT, P., "Tables in text: The subskills needed for reading formatted information", in: *The Reader and the Text*, ed. L.J. CHAPMAN (London, 1981), pp. 60-69.
ZEEMAN, E., "Punctuation in an early manuscript of Love's *Mirror*", *Review of English Studies* 7.25 (1956), pp. 11-18.

Index

abbreviation stops: 19, 128-130, 134-137, 139-144, 146-149; *see also* abbreviations; punctuation
abbreviations: 19, 30n, 39-40, 54n, 79-80, 84, 98, 119, 129, 134-141, 143, 164n, 185, 269-270, 288, 301; *see also* ampersands; contractions; superscript letters
accounts, *see*: churchwardens' a.; definitions of a.; list-like a.; table for a.
adjectives: 3, 197-198, 221-222, 288, 291, 299
administrative manuals: 190
adverbs: 221-222, 224, 288, 291, 303
affordances: 2, 14, 17, 160, 177
ageing scribes: 81
Aickin, Joseph: 286-291, 294-298, 300-306
alphabetical tables: 19, 155-157, 159, 169, 177, 179-180, 297
amateur scribes: 109, 124
ampersands: 19, 36-39, 118-119, 124-125, 128-130, 134, 136-137, 139-141, 143-144, 146-147, 308; *see also* abbreviations
anatomical treatises: 20, 228-230, 232-234, 238-240, 251-257
Anglicana: 70, 81
Anglo-Norman: 191, 199
annotations: 4, 16-18, 20, 66, 87, 89, 100-103, 110, 209, 224, 234, 253, 255
annotators: 17, 85, 87
anticipated readers: 174
Arabic: 6
arithmetic notation: 235
arithmetical tables: 244
astrological tables: 241, 245

astrological treatises: 243
audiences: 8, 20, 48, 106, 108, 156, 159, 167, 179-180, 186, 217, 224, 227; *see* anticipated a.: 16, 167, 175; a. of dance manuals: 260, 263-266, 268, 278-279; a. of grammars: 287-288, 305; a. of historiography: 204; a. of medical texts: 228, 231-232, 240, 243, 251; a. of *tabulae*: 156, 159-160, 167, 169-170, 174-177, 179-180; a. of the Vernon MS *Pater Noster* table: 186; *see also* children as a.; clerical a.; consumers of texts; enlarged a.; expectations of a.; expertise of a.; foreigners as a.; general a.; imagined a.; intended a.; Latinate a.; lay a.; level of graphic literacy of a.; local a.; needs of a.; popular a.; primary a.; prospective a.; readers; readership; special a.; target a.; uneducated a.; university-trained a.; vernacular a.; wide a.
authors: 12, 13, 20, 42-43, 67, 69, 106, 111, 128-129, 132, 145n, 148, 153, 201-203, 209n, 213, 217-220, 223, 229-232, 235, 244, 249-251, 260, 264, 266, 276, 286-287, 290, 298-300, 304, 306; *see also* writers
Berkeley, Thomas: 156, 174-176, 178, 180
bibliographic codes: 60
binomials: 20, 186, 191-199, 222
blackletter: 91, 283, 299
book history: 21, 234, 309
book or manuscript producers: 20, 159, 202-203, 207-208, 210, 216-217, 219, 224, 228; *see also* text producers
books: *see* b. of accounts; b. of grammar; b. of

maps; manuals; medical b.; practical b.; recipe b.; text b.; treatises; writing
books of accounts; 13, 18, 57-58, 63
books of grammar: 14, 21, 127, 135-136, 281-307
books of maps: 277
braces: 20, 28, 39, 217, 228, 235-236, 239-241, 243-245, 249-250, 252, 256, 289-293, 295, 299-306; *see also* tree diagrams
Bray, Thomas: 266, 275-277
Brightland, John: 135
Broughton, Hugh: 215-216, 219-220, 223-224
Bullein, William: 251, 253-254
Bullokar, William: 284, 291, 298, 305
Butler, Charles: 287, 298-300, 303-305
Byrthferth's *Enchiridion*: 6-7
canon tables: 188, 218n
capitalisation: 4, 19, 111, 118-120, 124, 142-143, 147, 164n
capitals: 79, 83, 92-95, 143, 147; *see also* initials
captions: 15-16, 218, 222-223, 224n, 230, 235, 245, 252-253; *see also* linguistic cues
Caroline minuscule: 27
Carpenter, Thomas: 136, 138, 147
Carter, John: 136, 138
Caxton, William: 209, 284
change, *see* linguistic c.
charts: 241-243, 249, 252, 256, 290
chess: 154n, 181n, 185-191, 199
children as audiences: 288
chronicles: 20, 153, 175, 203-204, 206, 209-210, 214, 218
chronological tables: 206-207, 213-223
chronological writing: 218
chronology: 20, 153, 157, 170, 175, 201-225; *see also* synchronisation; time, representations of
churchwardens' accounts: 13, 18, 47-64, 308
circulation: *see* c. of books or texts: 45, 65, 255, 275; c. of graphic devices: 6, 159, 229; c. of knowledge: 228; *see also* dissemination; transmission
Clarendon Press: 135, 148n
classifying functions: 256
clerical audiences: 167

colons: 111, 113, 120-123, 125, 128, 140, 146-147, 276, 294; *see also* punctuation
colour: 9, 11, 15, 18, 33, 60, 78-79, 82-83, 85, 91-95, 98, 109, 116, 188, 191, 199, 234; black: 102-103, 174, 188-189; black-and-white: 190; blue: 93-94, 161, 178-179, 188; gilded: 93; green: 94, 188; green-and-white: 190; red: 11, 28, 30, 35, 37, 83, 85-87, 92-94, 98-101, 103, 116, 161, 168, 178-179, 183-185, 188; white: 188-189; yellow: 94, 188
commas: 105, 111-114, 120-123, 294; *see also* inverted commas; punctuation
'common' tables (*tabulae communes*) in *Polychronicon* manuscripts: 19, 156-162, 164-165, 167-170, 176-180
communication: *see* computer-mediated c.; enhancement of c.; graphic features of c.; multimodal c.; professional c.; successful c.; textual c.; verbal c.; written c.
communicative context: 207
communicative functions: 5, 10-11
communities: *see* c. of practice: 31, 41-42, 125, 308; *see also*: language c.; textual c.; writing c.
competencies: 325; c. for reading graphic features and devices: 8-10, 16; technological: 12
Complete Letter Writer, The: 137-139
complexity: *see* c. of diagrams: 228, 241; c. of graphic devices: 15, 17, 304; c. of information systems: 252; c. of layout: 49; c. of tables: 215-217, 305; c. of text: 126; *see also*: linguistic c.
compositors: 135, 142; *see also* typesetters
computer-mediated communication: 308
conjunctions: 28, 112, 119, 140, 291, 303
constraints: *see* c. for organising written text: 34; c. of grammaticalisation: 32; c. of transmission: 14; *see also* material c.; medium-related c.; pragmatic c.; technological c.
construction of knowledge: 6, 9
consumers of texts: 10, 13; *see also* audiences, readers, readership
context: 9-11, 60-61, 110, 120, 124, 126, 140,

Index 345

232-233, 301, 307; c. of culture: 108n; c. of text production: 13; c. of translation: 196; *see also* communicative c.; discourse c.; family c.; historical c.; instructive c.; linguistic c.; manuscript c.; material c.; meditative c.; pedagogic(al) c.; situational c.; social c.; socio-cultural c.; university c.; vernacular c.
contractions: 129, 134, 136-141, 143, 147-148; *see also* abbreviations
conventionalisation: 33-34, 39-40; c. of discourse: 41; c. of features of written books: 27; c. of title pages: 42-45; c. of transcription: 50n; c. of writing practices: 18, 27; *see also* model for c.
conventionalising strategies: 25
conventions: *see* c. of communities of textual practice: 31; c. of layout or organisation on the page: 18, 27, 30, 33, 58, 62; c. of punctuation: 31, 125, 135; c. of or in writing (written): 18, 27, 33-34, 37, 40-41, 43-45; c. of tables: 180; c. *see also* editorial c.; directional c., in dance manuals; discourse organising c.; genre-specific c.; graphic(al) c.; information-bearing c.; *see also* norms
Cooper, Christopher: 285, 288, 298, 302-304
copying texts: 14, 42, 64-65, 67-70, 76, 78, 82-83, 87, 90-92, 139n, 142, 154, 159n, 178, 186, 208; *see also* fair copies
copyists; *see* scribes
cues: *see* graphic c.; linguistic c.; paratextual c.
Culpeper, Nicholas: 241, 244-245, 249
culture of literacy: 27
dance manuals: 20-21, 259-279
dance notation: 259, 262
dance treatises: 262-263
definition, scope of literacy: 11-12
definitions of accounts: 49-50
design: 3, 7, 12-14, 25, 30-31, 33, 36-37, 39-40, 63, 156, 180, 190-191, 198-199, 215, 220, 228, 260, 266, 276, 302; *see also* graphic d.; information d.; visual d.
diagrams: 5-8, 15, 17, 19-21, 76, 182-183, 185-187, 199, 216-217, 219, 224, 227-230, 235, 239-241, 243-246, 248-253, 255-256, 270, 286, 289-293, 295, 299-300, 303-304,
306, 308; *see also* tree d.
Digges, Leonard: 16-17
directional conventions, in dance manuals: 269
discourse: 16, 26, 31, 41, 60, 106, 218; *see* d. communities: 308; d. context: 106; d. markers: 59; d. organising conventions: 41; *see also* metadiscourse; pragmatic markers
dissemination: *see* d. of books and texts: 17-18, 34; d. of norms: 33; d. of punctuation marks: 112; d. of rhetorical moves: 108; *see also* circulation; transmission
dots: 35, 40-41, 270, 276; *see also* periods; punctuation; punctus
'double' tables in *Polychronicon* manuscripts: 159-160, 167, 169-170, 177, 180
Early Modern English: 7, 13-14, 19-20, 108, 110-111, 119, 124, 194, 201-202, 209, 228, 232, 284
editorial conventions: 233n
editors, historical: 12, 128-129, 137, 142-143
elite readers: 239, 264
EMEMT (*Early Modern English Medical Texts*): 20, 228, 232-233, 235-240, 243-246, 256
enhancement of communication: 60
enlarged audiences: 175
epistemic functions: 223
epistolary literacy: 148
epistolary writing: 129, 140; *see also* letter writing
Eusebius of Caesarea: 206, 215n
Exchequer tables: 190
expectations of audiences: 12, 170
expertise of audiences: 218
fair copies: 15, 129, 133, 138, 140, 142, 144, 146
family context: 148
fonts: 4, 17, 27, 245, 271, 283; *see also* black-letter; italic(s); roman; typefaces
footnotes: 35
foreign readers: 305
foreigners as audiences: 287
form-to-function mapping: 292
'formal' tables: 213n, 272
functionalism: 307
functionality: 27, 31, 33-34, 41, 159, 179, 255
functions: *see* f. of accounts: 49, 64; f. of braces: 256, 292; f. of diagrams: 217, 230,

253, 256; f. of images or illustrations: 229-230, 241, 248, 250, 252-253, 255; f. of index entry references: 154n; f. of graphic conventions, elements, features, forms or devices: 5-6, 17-18, 31, 34-35, 37, 40-41, 62, 217, 231, 250, 307; of information on the title page: 44; f. of Latin and English in the Vernon MS *Pater Noster* table: 192; f. of layout: 49, 63, 236; f. of lists in historiography: 211; f. of metacomments: 15; f. of punctuation or individual punctuation marks: 106-107, 112-114, 118, 122-125, 128-129, 134; f. of recipes: 79; f. of rules: 291-292; f. of tables: 170, 177, 217-218, 251; f. of the musical line: 272; f. of (written) language: 32-33, 37, 309; *see also* classifying f.; communicative f.; epistemic f.; indexical f.; instructing f.; grammatical f.; organisational or organising f.; pedagogic f.; pragmatic f.; rhetorical f.; sociocultural f.
Galen: 228, 241, 250
genealogical tables: 211n, 215
general audiences: 231
general readers: 243
genre: 7-8, 11, 13-14, 16-17, 27, 30, 33-34, 39-42, 44-45, 106-108, 203, 225, 233, 250, 256, 262, 266, 277, 279, 284, 308
genre-specific conventions: 39
geography: 153, 175, 201, 204
Gildon, Charles: 135
grammar books; *see* books, g.; writing, of grammars
Grammar of the English Tongue, The: 135
grammars: *see* writing of g.
grammatical functions: 32, 134
grammatical punctuation: 106-107, 134
grammaticalisation: 18, 27-28, 32-34, 36-37, 39
graphic cues: 4, 113n
graphic design: 1, 13
graphic devices: 5-9, 13, 15-17, 19-20, 202-203, 207-208, 218, 224, 227-228, 231-240, 243-246, 250-253, 255-257, 281-283, 289-293, 295, 298-307; *see also* braces; charts; diagrams; illustrations; images; maps; roundels; tables; tree diagrams

graphic elements: 16-17, 21, 30, 228, 231, 244, 250, 281, 283, 286, 289, 295, 301, 303-304, 306-307; *see also* visual elements
graphic events: 11-13, 15, 17
graphic features of communication: 3-8
graphic literacies or literacy skills: 6, 8-11, 17, 20-21, 66, 92, 153, 232-233, 283, 305-306
graphic literacy: 3, 8-13, 17, 20, 66, 92, 153, 232-233, 283, 305-306
graphic practices: 3, 10-20, 27, 47-48, 66, 82, 109, 153, 207, 209, 225, 233, 260, 279, 283, 292
graphic(al) arrangement or organisation: 28, 30, 289, 300, 305-306
graphic(al) conventions: 13, 14, 17-18, 30-33, 37, 39, 70
graphic(al) features of text and writing: 3-5, 8, 10-14, 17-18, 21, 26, 35, 45, 70, 148, 282-283, 288, 297, 300, 305, 307
graphicacy: 8, 205
graphical literacy: 8
Greek: 6, 112, 287
Grete Herball, The: 246, 248
guides: 8, 228, 233-234, 238-239, 250, 256
Guillemeau, Jacques: 245
hands: 11, 54, 57, 71, 83, 85-87, 101-102, 105, 119n, 132, 157, 158n, 160-161, 168, 178-179; *see also* scripts
handwriting: 3, 16, 106, 309; *see also* hands; palaeography; scripts
Haugen, Einar: 33, 39, 284n
headings: 18, 30-31, 33, 50, 54, 60, 62, 66, 78-81, 83, 95-97, 143, 156, 160-163, 167, 177, 182, 209-211, 215, 246, 252, 276, 292, 294, 305-306
Hebrew: 6, 65, 67
herbals: 20, 230, 246-248, 256
Higden, Ranulph: 153-156, 161, 178, 209
historical context: 12, 17
historical linguistics: 4, 21, 309
historical pragmatics: 4-5, 15n, 21, 308-309
historiography: 16, 201-203, 206, 209, 211
house style, printers' or publishers': 128, 142, 147-148
hyphenation: 19, 128-130, 134-137, 139-141, 143-147, 298, 308; *see also* punctuation

Index 347

illumination: 91, 182
illustrated tables: 296-297, 301, 305-306
illustrations: 27, 68, 76-78, 91, 230, 234-235, 238, 243-245, 247-249, 252-253, 255-256; *see also* medical i.
images: 5, 8, 12, 20, 48, 110, 203, 218, 228-232, 234-235, 238-241, 243-246, 248-257, 260, 268, 290, 296-297, 300, 306
imagined audiences: 176
implied readers: 13, 16
indexes: 27, 80, 89-90, 153-157, 159, 170n, 180, 217-218, 268, 299, 302; *see also* tables
indexical functions: 60
'informal' tables: 213n, 272
information design: 42, 228
information organisation: 19, 30, 124, 154n, 207
information visualisation: 1, 9, 283
information-bearing conventions: 31
initials: 60, 62, 78-79, 83, 85, 98, 133, 143, 165, 168, 178-179, 182; *see also* capitals
instructing functions: 79
instructional writing: 260-263
instructions: 15, 17, 79, 128, 148, 169, 203, 213, 219, 229-230, 244-245, 250-251, 259, 269, 270, 276, 281; *see also* instructional writing; manuals
instructive context: 8n
instruments: 15, 239, 245, 249, 252, 255-256
intended audiences: 13, 108, 207, 261, 263-264, 268
internalised knowledge: 261
inverted commas: 37, 41
italic(s): 87, 109, 142-143, 147, 245, 250n, 270, 276, 289, 291, 302
Jacopo da Cessola: 189
Jeu des esches de la dame moralisé: 189
knowledge: 192, 196-197, 229, 251, 262, 272; k. of musical notation: 272; *see also* construction of k.; internalised k.; medical k.; organisation of k.; recalling to memory of k.; synchronising of k.; transmission of k.; validation of k.; visualisation of k.
language communities: 14
language learning: 6, 128, 282-285, 287, 305-306
languages: *see* Anglo-Norman; Arabic; Early Modern English; Greek; Hebrew; Late Modern English; Latin; Middle English; Old English
Lanquet, Thomas: 210
Late Modern English: 127, 129-130, 134-135, 148
Latin: 6, 14, 18-19, 21, 30, 37, 39, 50, 54, 58, 60, 62-64, 65, 67, 69-70, 79-80, 83-85, 87, 89, 91, 136, 140-142, 153, 154n, 155-160, 164, 167, 169-180, 182, 190-195, 197, 199, 203, 206, 208, 216, 219-220, 224, 231, 241, 248, 251, 253, 282, 284-288, 291, 295-296, 298-299, 301-302, 304-305, 307
Latinate audiences: 19
lay audiences: 240, 251
lay readers: 231
layout: 3, 5, 9, 14, 16-18, 25, 30-31, 33, 41, 44-45, 48-50, 53-55, 57-58, 60-64, 84, 106, 154, 157, 161, 168, 177-178, 185, 208, 212, 215-216, 218, 222, 235-236, 245, 252, 270-272, 282, 289-291, 300-302, 309; *see also* mise-en-page
letter writing: 19, 129, 138; *see also* writing, epistolary
letter-writing manuals: 129, 135-139
letters (epistles): 15, 19, 49, 68, 127-149, 308; *see also* private l.
letters (graphs or l. of the alphabet): 30, 35, 39, 79, 91, 111, 119-120, 124, 128, 134-136, 149, 161, 164-165, 168-170, 172, 175, 177-179, 241, 244, 246, 249, 255, 270, 283, 286, 288, 291, 296, 299-301; *see also* thorn (þ)
level of graphic literacy of audiences: 20, 240
Lily, William: 284, 291, 300n, 304
linguistic change: 18, 25, 32, 44, 145
linguistic complexity: 248, 303
linguistic context: 6, 11, 14
linguistic cues: 15n, 79; *see also* captions
linguistics: 1, 4, 130, 136n, 145, 307, 308; *see also* historical l.
list-like accounts: 212, 224
lists: 6-7, 18, 20-21, 27, 49-51, 54, 57-58, 60, 62-64, 84, 87, 119, 135-138, 154, 157,

161n, 174, 176, 210-213, 215, 217, 224, 241, 243, 249-250, 252, 264-265, 277, 289-292, 295, 297-298, 300-302, 305-306
literacy: *see* levels of l.: 106; l. competencies: 16; l. events: 10, 12, 16, 17; l. practices: 10, 12-13, 156, 159, 180; l. skills 10, 306; *see also* culture of l.; definition, scope of l.; epistolary l.; graphic l.; graphical l.; modes of l.; multimodal l.; musical l.; patterns of l.; pragmatic l.; reading l.; visual l.
local audiences: 174-175
Lowth, Robert: 19, 127-135, 138-149, 285n
Lye, Thomas: 298, 300, 303-305
Málaga Corpus of Early Modern English Scientific Prose, The: 110, 124
male readers: 174
manuals: m. for book production: 128, 135, 137, 142, 144, 147-148; *see also* administrative m.; dance m.; letter-writing m.; medical m.
manuscript context: 48, 91
maps: 8, 277, 290
material constraints: 13
material context: 5, 309
mathematical tables: 249
meaning: *see* social m.
medical books: 13, 18, 20, 68, 78, 89, 105-126, 227-257
medical illustrations: 68, 76-78, 91, 227-257
medical knowledge: 231, 239
medical manuals: 20, 252
medical practice: 67-69, 84, 92, 124, 229-231, 239-241, 243, 245-246, 250, 252, 255, 257
medical treatises: 17-18, 20, 65-103, 108, 110, 228, 230, 232-234, 238-241, 243-245, 248, 251-256
medical writing: 18, 20, 66, 68, 78, 87, 91, 108, 110, 227-257; *see also* manuals, medical; plague texts; recipes; regimens; medical tracts
meditative context: 199
medium-related constraints: 17
metacommunication: 15-16, 20
metadiscourse: 30, 283, 306
metaphors: 186, 199, 201-202
metatext: 18, 66, 79-83, 91, 113, 253

Middle English: 13-14, 18-20, 26-27, 41, 45, 49, 52, 68, 70, 83, 110-111, 119, 153, 155, 158, 170, 177, 181-182, 186, 191-195, 197-198, 284
midwifery: 233, 238-240, 243, 245-246
mise-en-page: 4, 13, 18, 28, 65-66, 75-76, 78-82, 92, 124; *see also* layout
model for conventionalisation: 45
modes of literacy: 185
monastic readers: 108
Moralitas de scaccario: 188
multimodal communication: 2
multimodal literacy: 8
multimodality: 1-2, 5-6, 8-9, 13, 17, 207
musical literacy: 266, 272
musical notation: 21, 235, 260-261, 271-276, 278-279
needs of audiences: 107, 160, 169, 266
norms: 31-34, 42, 44-45, 124, 173, 262; *see also* conventions; prescription vs. practice
Northern Homily Cycle: 28-30, 181
notation: *see* arithmetic n.; dance n.; musical n.
nouns: 45, 136, 140, 156, 164-165, 168-169, 171-173, 176, 180, 191, 193, 195, 197-198, 220-223, 291, 295, 299-300, 303-304
Old English: 5-6, 39, 195, 197-198
organisation of knowledge: 204, 211
organisational or organising functions: 31-32, 39
orthography: 26, 48, 62, 110, 285, 288, 291, 299, 305-306; *see also* spelling
Oxford University Press: 148
palaeography: 1, 3, 61, 70, 136n, 309; *see also* handwriting
paper: 15, 49, 66, 82, 84, 91-92, 262
paragraph marks: 19, 28, 35, 39, 79, 83, 85, 92-95, 98-101, 103, 107, 111-112, 113n, 116, 124, 161, 168; *see also* punctuation
paraphs; *see* paragraph marks
paratext: 4, 16, 25, 30-31, 33, 42, 44-45, 48, 217, 218n, 231, 234, 236, 246, 268, 277, 294n, 305, 308
paratextual cues: 305
parchment: 49, 51-52, 62
Paré, Ambroise: 252
parentheses: 41, 270; *see also* punctuation

Index 349

Parkes, M.B.: 3-4, 61, 63-64, 107
parts of speech: 193, 288, 291, 295, 298-304, 306; *see also* adjectives; adverbs; conjunctions; nouns; prepositions; pronouns; verbs
Pater Noster table: 14, 181-200; *see also* tables
patterns of literacy: 109
pedagogic functions: 167-170, 180, 229-230, 282, 306
pedagogic(al) context: 8n, 170, 205
pedagogy: 14, 21, 228, 262, 283n, 305; *see also* pedagogic functions; teaching
periods: 40, 107, 111-113, 120-123, 125, 136; *see also* dots; punctuation; punctus
perioslashs: 107, 111, 113, 120-123, 125; *see also* punctuation
philology; 1, 4-5, 21, 48, 204, 207, 221, 309
plague texts: 17-18, 65-103, 233, 238-239, 243
Playford, Henry: 265, 267, 274
Playford, John: 20, 259-279
politeness: 138, 141, 147
political treatises: 265, 279
Polychronicon: 14, 19, 153-180, 209-210
popular audiences: 264-265
positional constraints: 139n
potential readers: 305
practical books: 219, 221, 239, 240, 260-262
Practical English Grammar, A: 136, 138
pragmatic constraints: 40
pragmatic functions: 18, 48-49, 59, 63-64, 129, 134, 146
pragmatic literacy: 63-64
pragmatic markers: 59-61, 63, 54
pragmatics: 2, 4-5, 18-19, 21, 25, 31, 34-35, 40, 47-49, 63-64, 105-106, 109, 124-126, 129-130, 134, 139n, 145-146, 307-309; *see also* historical pragmatics; pragmatic markers; pragmatics on the page; visual pragmatics
pragmatics on the page: 5, 25, 47-48, 60, 308
prefaces: 16, 43, 218-221, 230, 249, 277, 286-288, 291, 293, 295, 298, 305-306; *see also* prologues
prepositions: 136, 140, 176, 288, 291, 300-304
prescription vs. practice: 129, 148; *see also* norms

present-day readers: 283, 289
primary audiences: 11, 288
Printer's Grammar, The: 135, 137
printers: 11-12, 15, 114, 128-129, 137, 147, 210n, 233, 245, 253, 261, 290, 306
printers' devices or marks: 43, 236
printing: 21, 42-43, 66, 82, 84, 91, 128, 147, 202, 209, 233, 261, 279, 284, 292, 296, 298; *see also* typography
private letters: 131, 133, 137, 139
private writing: 128, 148
production of books or texts: 5n, 12-14, 31, 34, 42, 44-45, 64, 82, 131, 157n, 158, 196, 207, 233, 257; *see also* book or manuscript producers; text producers
professional communication: 218
professional scribes: 83, 124
prologues: 190, 203; *see also* prefaces
pronouns: 140, 176, 195, 288, 291, 293, 295, 299-304, 306
prospective audiences: 109
prospective readers: 106, 232
Prudentius: 189, 199
publishers: 42, 132-133, 137, 142-143, 147, 260-261, 265-267, 273, 279
punctuation: 3-4, 9, 13, 17-19, 27, 30-31, 33, 37, 39, 41, 105-114, 118-126, 134-135, 137, 142-143, 147, 211, 276, 287-288, 301; *see also* abbreviation stops; colons; commas; dots; grammatical p.; hyphenation; paragraph marks; parentheses; periods; perioslashs; punctus; rhetorical p.; semicolons; virgules
punctus: 39, 125; *see also* dots; periods; punctuation
Ralegh, Walter, Sir: 213, 215, 217-219
readability: 273, 278-279
reader guidance: 16, 134-135, 137
readers: 6, 8, 12-13, 15-18, 20, 37, 49, 60, 66-67, 80, 85, 87, 92, 100, 106, 108, 111, 116, 129n, 130, 134-135, 156-157, 159, 169, 177, 180, 185, 189-190, 202-203, 207, 211-213, 217-220, 223-224, 229-232, 239, 243-244, 248, 250-251, 253, 260, 262, 264, 268, 271-272, 276, 278-279, 284, 286, 288, 290-291, 298, 302, 305-

306; *see also* anticipated r.; audiences; consumers of texts; elite r.; foreign r.; general r.; implied r.; lay r.; male r.; monastic r.; potential r.; present-day r.; prospective r.; readership
readership: 69, 207, 229, 231, 239, 264, 288; *see also* audiences; consumers of texts; readers
reading: 9, 11-12, 27, 58, 63, 67, 107-108, 129, 154, 156, 182, 185-187, 190, 192, 203, 206, 211, 217, 220, 244, 251, 260-261, 276-277, 305; *see also* r. strategies; reception of books or texts
reading literacy: 9, 11, 12n
reading strategies: 260-261
recalling to memory of knowledge: 229
reception of books and texts: 5, 12-13, 109; *see also* reading
recipe books: 13, 18-19, 30, 66, 105-126, 233, 238-240, 246, 249, 256
recipes: 13, 18-20, 30, 66, 68, 76, 79-80, 84-87, 90, 92, 98-100, 105-126, 228, 233-235, 238-241, 243-249, 256
regimens: 228, 233-234, 238-239, 250-251, 256; *see also* guides
register: 18, 34-35, 39, 41, 108
representations of time 201-205
rhetoric: 13, 219; *see also* visual rhetoric
rhetorical functions: 134
rhetorical moves: 19, 108-109, 114, 119-121, 123-125
rhetorical punctuation: 41, 106-107, 112, 134
Richard FitzNeal: 190
roman: 91, 250n
roundels: 186, 190-192
rubrication: 17, 35, 60, 66-67, 82, 84-85, 91, 97, 155n, 209n, 210n
rubricators: 11, 18, 79, 83, 85, 87, 92-94, 113n, 191
rubrics: 18, 121, 153, 155n, 182
rules, as graphic elements: 15, 31, 42, 157, 161, 164, 178-179, 210-217, 224, 272, 289, 291-293, 295, 297, 299-302, 305; *see also* graphic elements
ruling; *see* rules
Scaliger, Joseph: 206n, 212n

Scholar's Spelling Assistant, The: 136, 138
science: 1, 6, 110, 192, 202, 204, 207, 218
scientific writing: 110
scribes: 11-13, 18, 31, 35, 50-52, 54, 57, 60-64, 69, 72-73, 79, 83, 85, 92, 103, 106-107, 111-112, 116, 118-119, 156, 158n, 159n, 160, 166, 169-170, 177-179, 181, 197; *see also* aging s.; amateur s.; professional s.
script-switching: 80, 82, 85, 87, 91, 95, 97, 100
scripts: 4-5, 9, 14n, 17, 48, 60, 66-67, 79, 82, 84, 91, 95-97, 109, 116, 118, 124, 178, 191; *see also* Anglicana; Caroline minuscule; hands; script-switching; Secretary
Secretary: 70, 82, 92
'semi-informal' tables: 272, 278
semicolons: 111, 114, 120-123, 125; *see also* punctuation
shorthand: 39
situational context: 11
slashes; *see* virgules
Smith, John: 135, 137
social context: 261, 263
social meaning: 5, 11, 14, 130
socio-cultural context: 307
socio-cultural functions: 5
space, use of: 9, 18-19, 63-64, 67, 79, 81-84, 91, 93-94, 116, 118-120, 124-125, 161, 178n, 179, 211-212, 271-274, 289-292
special audiences: 177
'special' tables (*tabulae speciales*) in *Polychronicon* manuscripts: 19, 154-156, 159-161, 163-180
speed in or of writing(s): 129, 136n, 138, 140
spelling: 38, 110, 128, 135-138, 142-143, 147, 156, 286, 288, 298-300, 302, 304-305; *see also* orthography
spelling books: 38, 136, 298
standardisation: 18, 26-28, 30, 33-35, 39, 41-42, 45, 107, 112, 259, 284
successful communication: 13
superscript characters or letters: 128, 131, 135-137, 139, 141-143, 146-149; *see also* abbreviations
supports or surfaces of writing: 11, 91, 154n

Index 351

surgery: 20, 73-74, 82-83, 108, 110, 228, 230, 233-234, 238-241, 248,251-256
synchronisation: 20, 206-207, 211, 217-218, 220-222, 224; *see also* chronology; representations of time
synchronising of knowledge: 207
table for accounts: 190
tables: 6-8, 14-17, 19-21, 43, 71, 74, 82, 89, 153-180, 202, 207-208, 210-224, 227-228, 232-233, 235-236, 239-241, 243-245, 249-252, 256, 259-261, 268-275; t. in dance manuals: 259-261, 268-275, 277-279; t. in grammars: 281-283, 286, 288-292, 294n, 295-307; t. in medical books: 239-241, 243-245, 249-252, 256; t. (*see also* 'common' t.; 'double' t.; 'special' t.) in *Polychronicon manuscripts*: 153-180; t. of contents: 89, 156, 157n, 236, 286, 302; *see also* alphabetical t.; arithmetical t.; astrological t.; canon t.; chronological t.; Exchequer t.; 'formal' t.; genealogical t.; illustrated t.; 'informal' t.; mathematical t.; *Pater Noster* table; 'semi-informal' t.; tabular form(at); tabularisation; tabulation
tabulae; *see* tables
tabular form(at): 20, 154, 156, 188, 198, 206, 210, 213, 215, 218, 222, 224, 236, 259-260, 268, 272, 274-277, 279, 289, 301-304; *see also* tables; tabularisation; tabulation
tabularisation: 202, 207
tabulation: 19, 154, 179-180
target audiences: 106, 125-126, 218, 233
teaching: 207, 230, 263, 283-284, 287-288, 296; *see also* pedagogic functions; pedagogy
technical writing: 260-261
technological constraints: 13, 207-208
technologies of transmission: 2
technology: 2, 10, 12-14, 17, 135, 202, 207-208, 217, 308
text books: 135, 228, 231, 238-240, 252, 256, 281, 296
text category: 16, 238-240
text producers: 10-16, 66, 201-202; *see also* book or manuscript producers

text type: 17-18, 34, 39, 48-49, 61, 63, 66, 79, 107-108, 112, 124-126
textual communication: 48
textual communities: 27, 31
textual criticism: 21
textual transmission; *see* transmission of texts
theological treatises: 186
thorn, y for: 135
time: *see* chronology; representation of t.; synchronisation
title pages: 16, 17n, 28, 42-45, 132, 141, 221-223, 236, 245n, 264, 267-268, 275-278, 286-288, 306
tracts: *see* treatises
translation(s): 14, 19, 64, 67n, 68-69, 76, 78, 83, 91, 155-156, 158-160, 173, 175-176, 180-181, 194-197, 206, 209-210, 215n, 224, 231, 237n, 241, 244-245, 248, 251-252, 255, 285, 296
translators: 12, 175, 202, 217, 221
transmission: *see* t. of graphic devices: 10; t. of information or knowledge: 25-26, 203, 207, 228; t. of language: 307-308; t. of punctuation marks: 114; t. of texts: 11, 14-15, 107, 159, 178; *see also* technologies of t.; circulation; dissemination
treatises: *see* astrological t.; dance t.; medical t.
tree diagrams: 20, 216-217, 224, 228, 245, 249, 293; *see also* braces
Trevisa, John: 19, 153, 155-156, 158-160, 170, 173-178, 180, 209n; *Dialogue between a Lord and a Clerk*: 156, 158n, 160, 175, 180; *Epistola to Sir Thomas Berkeley*: 156, 158n, 160, 175-176, 180; *Polychronicon*, Middle English translation of: 14, 19, 155-159, 170-180, 209-210, 277-279, 281-283, 286, 288-292, 294n, 295-308
Tschichold, Jan: 36-37
typefaces: 14n, 80, 91; *see also* fonts
typesetters: 128-129, 137, 164, 244, 304, 306; *see also* compositors
typesetting: 136
typography: 5, 9; *see also* printing
underlining: 79-80, 82, 85-87, 91-92, 98-103, 142, 147
uneducated audiences: 176

university context: 154, 207
university-trained audiences: 251
validation of knowledge: 223
verbal communication: 12
verbs: 37, 45, 140, 142, 193, 221-223, 288, 291-293, 295, 300-304, 306
vernacular: 6-7, 13, 108, 191, 201, 207, 219, 222, 231, 248, 284-285, 301, 307; *see also* v. audiences: 17, 19; v. context: 7, 13
vernacularisation: 231
Vernon MS, the: 19, 181-200
vices and virtues: 189-191, 196, 199
virgules: 35, 61-62, 107, 111-114, 120-123, 125, 134; *see also* punctuation
visual communication: 12
visual design: 20
visual elements: 31, 60, 109, 114, 116-118, 124, 135, 185, 224, 271; *see also* graphic elements
visual grammar: 2
visual highlighting: 9, 18, 28, 65-66, 75-76, 79-80, 85-87, 92, 95-97, 177
visual literacy: 8-9, 12
visual pragmatics: 2, 19, 25, 47-49, 64, 127, 129n, 145
visual proficiency: 12, 15
visual prosody: 2
visual rhetoric: 2, 7
visual vocabulary: 12, 15
visualisation of knowledge: 1
visuality: 3, 5, 201-202, 205; v. of writing: 3, 5; *see also* graphic(al) features of text and writing
Wallis, John: 285-286, 288, 298-299, 301-304
Warburton, William: 19, 127-134, 138-148
Webster, Noah: 38
Wharton, Jeremiah: 281, 283, 286-293, 295, 298-300, 302-304, 306
whitespace; *see* space, use of
wide audiences: 108, 260
word classes; *see* parts of speech
word pairs, *see* binomials
writers: 6, 8, 11-12, 19, 33, 105, 107, 124-126, 128-129, 132, 135-137, 143, 148, 260, 275, 285, 287; *see also* authors
writing literacy: 9-11, 12n
writing: *see* w. communities: 34; w. literacy: 9-10, 12n.; w. of grammar: 203-284, 301 (*see also* grammar books); w. of history 203-204, 207 (*see also* historiography); *see also* chronological w.; (written) conventions of or in w.; epistolary w.; instructional w.; letter w.; medical w.; private w.; scientific w.; speed in or of writing(s); supports or surfaces of w.; technical w.; visuality of w.
written communication: 1-3, 5; w. systems 3-4, 30-31, 45; *see also* books

Notes on Contributors

Javier CALLE-MARTÍN (jcalle@uma.es) is Professor of English Linguistics at the University of Málaga. He has published on the history of the English language and manuscript studies, in particular on early modern scientific manuscripts. He has recently developed an interest in the standardisation of English and the connection between usage and prescription in Late Modern English.

Alpo HONKAPOHJA (ahonkapo@tlu.ee) is a Lecturer at Tallinn University and a Docent at the University of Helsinki. He has published extensively on Middle English and Early Modern medical texts, with a particular focus on multilingualism and abbreviation practices.

Marjo KAARTINEN (marjo.kaartinen@utu.fi) is Rector of the University of Turku and Professor of Cultural History (on a leave of absence). She has published on the Early Reformation in England and on early modern cultural history in general.

Aino LIIRA (aeliir@utu.fi) has recently concluded her postdoctoral research stint in the Early Modern Graphic Literacies project at the Department of English, University of Turku. She has published on late medieval and early modern books, focusing on the materiality and visual aspects of texts as well as on paratextuality and related phenomena in both manuscript and print.

Colette MOORE (cvmoore@uw.edu) is Associate Professor of English at the University of Washington. Her research focuses on historical pragmatics and historical discourse organisation, and she is presently working on the history of standardisation in English.
Matti PEIKOLA (matpei@utu.fi) is Professor of English at the University of Turku, specialising on Middle and Early Modern English philology, textual scholarship, and book history. He has recently published on paratexts and multimodal communication in manuscript and print. He is currently PI for the project Early Modern Graphic Literacies, funded by the Research Council of Finland.

Jesús ROMERO-BARRANCO (jromer@uma.es) is Lecturer in English Linguistics at the Department of English, University of Málaga. He has published, among other things, on historical linguistics (language variation and change), and palaeography and codicology, particularly in Late Middle and Early Modern English.

Hanna SALMI (hanna.salmi@utu.fi) is a University Teacher at the University of Turku. She has published on visual pragmatics and paratextual communication in early English books; her current focus is on instructive texts.

Wendy SCASE (W.L.Scase@bham.ac.uk) is Emeritus Geoffrey Shepherd Professor of Medieval English Literature at the University of Birmingham. She has publications on medieval manuscript production and use; literary cultures of the medieval and early modern periods; and histories and pedagogies of literacy.

Janne SKAFFARI (janne.skaffari@utu.fi) is a University Lecturer at the Department of English, University of Turku, specialising in descriptive grammar, linguistics, and the history of English. He has published, in particular, on multilingual practices in English texts from the long twelfth century.

Jeremy SMITH (Jeremy.Smith@glasgow.ac.uk) is Professor Emeritus, University of Glasgow, and Honorary Professor, University of St Andrews. Recent publications include *Transforming Early English* (2020) and *The Victorian Reinvention of Medieval Liturgy* (with David Jasper, 2023). His current project is *Discourses of English Religion 1380-1850*, funded by the Leverhulme Trust.

Carla SUHR (carla.suhr@helsinki.fi) is a Senior University Lecturer at the University of Helsinki. Her research focuses on genre, discourse, and visual pragmatics in early modern English medical and news writing.

Kjetil V. THENGS (kjetil.v.thengs@uis.no) is Head of Department and Associate Professor in English language and linguistics at the Department of Cultural Studies and Languages, University of Stavanger, Norway. He has published, among other things, on linguistic variation and formulaicness in Middle English local documents, and is co-compiler of the Corpus of Middle English Local Documents (MELD).

Ingrid TIEKEN-BOON VAN OSTADE (I.M.Tieken@hum.leidenuniv.nl) is Emeritus Professor of English Sociohistorical Linguistics at the Leiden University Centre for Linguistics. She has published widely on the English standardisation process (codification and prescription) as well as on Late Modern English, most recently on Robert Lowth's grammar and the language of Jane Austen's letters.

Olga TIMOFEEVA (olga.timofeeva@es.uzh.ch) is Professor of English Historical Linguistics at the University of Zurich. She has published on Old English syntax, Old and Middle English lexis, language contact in the Middle Ages, historical sociopragmatics, and the evolution of the legal register in Early English. She is the author of *Non-Finite Constructions in Old English* (2010) and *Sociolinguistic Variation in Old English: Records of Communities and People* (2022).

Jukka TYRKKÖ (jukka.tyrkko@lnu.se) is Professor of English Linguistics at Linnaeus University, Sweden. His research interests extend from the Middle Ages to the present day, and he has published on a wide range of topics, including corpus linguistics, methodology, lexis and phraseology, the history of medical writing, multilingualism, historical lexicography, the language of politics, and the history of the book.

Mari-Liisa VARILA (mljvar@utu.fi) is Lecturer at the Department of English, University of Turku. She has previously published on medieval and early modern English book production, including scientific writing and paratextual communication.